NEW YORK REVIEW BOOKS

CLASSICS

MEMOIRS OF
LORENZO DA PONTE

LORENZO DA PONTE (1749–1838) was born Emanuele Conegliano, the son of a tanner in a Jewish ghetto near Venice. His father had the family baptized, changing their name to Da Ponte in honor of the local bishop, and enrolled his son in a seminary, where the young Da Ponte soon mastered Latin and the works of the great Italian poets. Da Ponte's long and exceptionally varied career led him across Europe and, eventually, to New York, where he died some years after opening the city's first opera house.

CHARLES ROSEN is a pianist and Professor Emeritus of Music and Social Thought at the University of Chicago. His books include *The Classical Style*, which won the National Book Award, *The Romantic Generation*, and *Romantic Poets, Critics, and Other Madmen*.

MEMOIRS

Lorenzo Da Ponte

■

Translated by
ELISABETH ABBOTT

Edited, Annotated, and with an
Introduction by
ARTHUR LIVINGSTON

Preface by
CHARLES ROSEN

THE NEW YORK REVIEW BOOKS

nyrb

THIS IS A NEW YORK REVIEW BOOK
PUBLISHED BY THE NEW YORK REVIEW OF BOOKS

MEMOIRS OF LORENZO DA PONTE

This edition published in 2000 in the United States of America by
The New York Review of Books
1755 Broadway
New York, NY 10019

1 3 5 7 9 10 8 6 4 2

Library of Congress Cataloging-in-Publication Data

Da Ponte, Lorenzo, 1749–1838.
    [Memorie. English]
    Memoirs of Lorenzo Da Ponte / translated by Elisabeth Abbott ; edited
and annotated by Arthur Livingston ; introduction by Charles Rosen.
        p.   cm.
    Includes index.
    ISBN 0-940322-35-8 (pbk.: alk. paper)
    1. Da Ponte, Lorenzo, 1749–1838. 2. Librettists—Biography. I. Title.
II. Livingston, Arthur, 1883–

ML423.D15 A3 2000
782.1'092—dc21   99-046014
[B]

ISBN 0-940322-35-8

Printed in the United States of America on acid-free paper.
May 2000
www.nybooks.com

CONTENTS

PREFACE

ALL AUTOBIOGRAPHERS LIE, by commission as well as omission. We do not read them for their accuracy but for their vivacity, and Lorenzo Da Ponte is among the most vivacious.

Memoirs rarely tell us what we want to know, or what we think we want to know, but the best of them inform us in unexpected ways. For example, it would be fascinating to know what it felt like to be a young converted Jew in Venice and how the conversion took place when Da Ponte was fourteen and what difference it made in life afterward. Da Ponte does not say a word about this, for he does not want to admit to his early background. He does not even tell us what his family name was, but only that he took the name of the Bishop of Ceneda, who had become his protector and his patron (but he does not mention that it was the bishop who baptized his family). Da Ponte expunged all this from his account and probably from his consciousness as well. His *Memoirs* are not an intimate exploration of his own identity and character but rather a picaresque adventure story. What we learn about his personality is revealed inadvertently: he had no intention of giving himself away, nor does he give psychological portraits with any depth of the various actors in his *Memoirs*.

The model for his book is, of course, the memoirs of his friend Casanova (although he is careful to distance himself prudently from Casanova's morals), and like Casanova he makes good use of the narrative effects of the adventure novels of the Spanish tradition. Unlike Casanova, he has no radical views of society, but he gives a wonderful image of the particular upper-class society that he had to deal with in his efforts to make his way in the world. European and American cultures come to life only as a setting and background scenery for his road to success or failure. The liveliness of his style is indeed infectious; in spite of being written over many years, which is reflected in the disorganized form, the *Memoirs* hold together as a picture of an ambitious author's world.

Da Ponte has come down to posterity above all as the greatest of Mozart's librettists, producing the texts of *The Marriage of Figaro, Don Giovanni,* and *Così fan tutte.* He does give an account of his work with Mozart, but here, too, he does not tell us what we would like to know. As we can easily perceive from Mozart's correspondence when he was writing the earlier operas *Idomeneo* and *The Abduction from the Seraglio,* the composer did not passively accept a text from his librettists: he always insisted on changes, sometimes to accommodate the singers, sometimes to realize his own dramatic ideals. It is unlikely that he made no demands upon Da Ponte, but we learn nothing of this from the *Memoirs*.

What we do get from Da Ponte, on the other hand, is an invaluable picture of how the operative world of intrigue and bureaucracy functions, and an account of the struggle to get operas past the administration or the court which supplied the money. He tells us, however, nothing of the production of *The*

Marriage of Figaro except for his success in getting permission for a ballet, but this is actually slightly misleading. The ballet is not an important spectacle in this work, but a short fandango that is an integral part of the action: it is danced by the singers, who have to observe each other, exchange a letter, and even sing a few notes. (It is a slow formal dance, generally performed much too fast today.)

Da Ponte's account of the dress rehearsal as a silent pantomime is extremely improbable: the music could not have been omitted even if there were no extra dancers since Figaro dances with Susanna. It is evident that the court was trying to cut down and economize on expenses. There was to be no important ballet comparable to the elaborate one that ended Mozart's *Idomeneo* for the court at Munich. However, Da Ponte is concerned to tell a story of his victory over the court bureaucracy, to make the affair another adventure in which he triumphs over the opposition. His story of the incident, while inaccurate in detail, certainly reflects the problems of dealing with an administration ruled by a court. His accounts of administrative rivalry and obstruction are important and infinitely entertaining.

Of his artistic ideals in opera, we learn very little. However, he gives the finest description of the idiosyncratic structure of the opera finale. It is interesting that he should single this out for discussion, as he created the most masterly forms of the finale in the history of opera. Nevertheless, before Da Ponte arrived on the Viennese scene, Mozart had already made a specific point of demanding effective finales from his librettist, and even had the libretto of *The Abduction from the Seraglio* rewritten in order to provide him with a satisfactory finale to the second act. I think it is possible that Da Ponte's discussion of this one point of operatic structure derives directly from his work with Mozart and was influenced by the composer's own formulation of operatic style.

After Vienna, Da Ponte left for Paris and then went to London. The traveling composer had always been important since the fifteenth century, when the Netherlands exported musicians to Italy and France. Up to the first half of the eighteenth century, however, musicians largely tried to find at least a semipermanent position in some important center. In the latter half of the eighteenth century the situation was becoming somewhat more fluid. Virtuosos traveled more and more frequently, composers and librettists went from one place to another for specific projects. It is clear that the world of music was changing from one that was ruled largely by local conditions to an international organization. With Haydn's trips to London and his work for the Count D'Ogny in Paris, and Mozart's travels to Munich and Prague, prestige now depended more and more on these individual voyages than on a salaried position. (It is interesting, however, that neither Beethoven nor Schubert traveled, except for Beethoven's displacement to Vienna from Bonn, but also that neither of them was dependent on a singular post in Vienna for his livelihood.)

For a dramatist who specialized in opera librettos, to travel and find work abroad was perhaps more difficult than for a musician, but Italian was to a certain extent an international language, and operas were written in Italian by German and French musicians to be produced in their own cities. The basic operatic language was Italian, and it dominated the international scene. Goldoni, however, went from Venice to Paris to write for the French theater in French, and by Da Ponte's time French was displacing every other tongue as the foundation of international communication.

The rest of Da Ponte's life must be seen as an attempt to restore the prestige of Italian culture and the Italian language wherever he went. It is interesting that he never discusses the French theater although his debt to it was very great (for example, his libretto for Mozart's *Così fan tutte* is heavily dependent on French eighteenth-century models). At one point, he seems even slightly embarrassed by the fact that Mozart, with whom he had made his greatest triumph and his international reputation, was Austrian rather than Italian. One feels he would have been happier if he could have become Rossini's librettist, and he certainly felt that he could do better than the poets chosen by Rossini.

He finally arrived in New York and became the unofficial ambassador of Italian culture in America. As with his treatment of Mozart, we do not learn about his own engagement with any specific part of the Italian tradition. He makes, of course, a perfunctory bow to the great classic names like Tasso and Dante, but his mention of the Italian classics remains impersonal. He does not confide in us about his literary ideals. What we do learn, and it is invaluable, is how one went about the attempt to bring Italian culture to early-nineteenth-century New York. What interests Da Ponte is how to form a library, and how to raise money and support from the local residents with some kind of authority, administrative as well as social. He spread Italian culture by teaching at Columbia, by running a boarding school, by making the Italian classics available.

Da Ponte naturally found in New York a combination of welcome and incomprehension. (In his attempt to establish the importance of Italian, he came up very soon against the rival pretensions of Spanish.) The latter part of his *Memoirs* remains one of the most entertaining and instructive on the problems of diffusing culture to the ignorant. He writes:

> In almost every city [of the United States] one finds the wines and grapes of Sicily, the oil, the olives, and the silk of Florence, the marble of Carrara, the gold chains of Venice, the cheese of Parma, the straw hats of Leghorn, the ropes of Rome and Padua, the rosolia of Trieste, the

sausages of Bologna, and even the macaroni of Naples
and the plaster figurettes of Lucca. Yet, to the shame
of our country, there is not, in the whole of America,
a bookstore kept by an Italian! All the books in this
city, aside from the volumes I introduced myself, have
either been brought casually by travelers, or been sold at
auction with other books on the death of some foreign
inhabitant.

Very little has changed in our day. It is still difficult to find
Italian literature in America (although Italian olive oil is present everywhere) and Da Ponte's experience remains exemplary
for all those working in the promotion of culture. Above all, he
is frank about his main interest, which was to make money
from culture: not many memorialists have written about this
as openly and as amusingly.

—CHARLES ROSEN

INTRODUCTION

ONE MORNING OF the year 1807, the wealthy, distinguished, and earnest-minded Clement Moore, future author of
"The Night Before Christmas," founder of the General Theological Seminary in New York, Trustee of Columbia College,
etc., etc., had an interesting encounter on Broadway. He had
dropped into Riley's bookstore to inspect the latest importa-
tions from England—to look, perhaps, for some new editions
of Pufendorff, some new translation of Beccaria, or the latest
treatises on Christian apologetics. And he had entered, as he
always did, into a literary discussion with Mr. Riley—was
there, or could there be, an American literature; was Milton, or
Tasso, or Dante, supreme; were Racine, Corneille, and Voltaire
really comparable to Shakespeare?

As the talk turned on Italian literature a stranger approached
and broke in on the conversation. He was a tall, well-built,
handsome person, impeccably groomed, his shoulders erect
and thrown back from the waist till he found it almost more
comfortable to support himself on a cane which he carried

preferably behind him. He was a man well past middle age, but still youthful and vigorous. He had no teeth, and the smile that played about his sunken jaws had a crafty but gentle cast. The man was evidently a gentleman. Courtly of manner, soft, with a trace of a defect in his speech, he spoke English fluently, if with a foreign accent, his every word betraying joviality and wit. There was something engaging about his address, at once insinuating and considerate.

Interested in all the literature touching Heaven, Hell, and sacred things, Clement Moore had aspired in days faraway to read Dante in the original. After that he might take a glance at the "Jerusalem" of Tasso. Here now was a fellow who knew Tasso by heart. Give him half a chance and he would start chewing his knuckles off to declaim the episode of Ugolino. Clement Moore followed the news from literary Europe. He had heard of Metastasio and Alfieri; and a sweet, kind-hearted poet himself, he longed some day to translate the more tuneful songs of the former. Had Mr. de Ponty—that was the name?—had Mr. de Ponty read Metastasio? Had he read Metastasio, indeed! Mr. Da Ponte had known Metastasio personally! Why, one evening in Vienna . . .

Having netted his lion, Clement Moore thought he would venture to put the chain and collar on. He would invite Mr. Da Ponte to dinner and introduce him to his father, the Bishop, to his cousin Nathaniel, to his sisters, to friends of the family. And it was surprise on surprise! Bishop Moore passed for knowing Hebrew. He had indeed studied it for years, and come to the point of following with some understanding the moot questions concerning the precise words that had issued from the very lips of God. But this man could not only read Hebrew; he could quote, and even make apothegms, in that sacred tongue. The Vulgate and the Roman ritual he had at his fingers' tips. Everyone had read six books of Virgil, and the more venturesome had gone on to nine or twelve. This person knew

Virgil, Horace, and other Latins, by heart. He could turn a perfect Latin distich *ex tempore*. With Homer, too, and others of the Greeks, his knowledge, while not so vast, was precise and alive.

Who was the man? Those Americans all looked wistfully across the sea to Europe, the storehouse of history, cultivation, literature, art. They all hoped some day to take that disgusting trip of a hundred days, between over and back, in a filthy packet, and for two or three thousand dollars, just for a glimpse of some palace of the Popes or the Medici, of a statue of Michelangelo, of the *Piombi* (underground!) in Venice, or Versailles, the Tuileries, Westminster. But this man had lived all that— Venice, Vienna, London, Prague; Dresden, Hamburg, Amsterdam; Emperors, Dukes, Countesses, opera singers, actresses; Paisiello, Martini—Mozart! The man who wrote the words for Mozart! A man who had heard an opera and was actually author of the words for two score librettos, knowing the ins and outs of immortal rhythms and melodies so that he could talk music with a precision that dazzled and an authority that brooked no argument!

Others came and looked Mr. Da Ponte over—the Livingstons, the Hamiltons, the Duers, the Ogilbies, the Onderdoncks. The ladies thought they might call on his wife. She too was a nice person—sweet, hard-working, stern with her children, intelligent—imagine a woman who could talk French, German, Italian, Spanish, Dutch, and discuss literature and music quite as learnedly, and even less disconcertingly, than her husband.

The Da Pontes were received. They, in fact, were the find of the social season of 1807 in New York. And the excitement of novelty past, there was something that endured in the years that followed. Mrs. Da Ponte's cuisine was a revelation —*spaghetti alla napolitana, cappelletti alla bolognese, bisi col riso alla veneziana, rosolio* from Trieste, brandies distilled with French exquisiteness by Mr. Da Ponte and by his father-in-law out in the Susquehanna country. There was a family, quite a family, as time went by: two beautiful daughters, the elder, Louisa, a quiet, earnest maiden of thirteen, when her family moved in from Elizabethtown—almost ready for a husband; and soon she found one, the son of a distinguished merchant on lower Broadway; the other, Frances—Fanny, as she came to be called and known—a tiny chit of a girl, an adorable blonde; two younger, but well-bred and well-mannered boys, Joseph and Lorenzo, both precocious, seeming both to inherit the charm and the genius of two such parents; and finally a sweet baby, Charles, born at Elizabethtown in 1806. There were others, in and about the family: sometimes Dr. John Grahl, a venerable German gentleman, who came on with his son's wife from Pennsylvania—Mrs. Da Ponte's father; and for some years, her vivacious sister, a French woman with an Italian husband, people well-to-do, these latter, fresh from England, with connections of note in London and making new ones wherever they went in America—Baltimore, Philadelphia, the western counties. The ladies were deft with their fingers and almost as interesting as the head of the family— gowns in French style, millinery of unheard-of delicacy and taste, artificial flowers and valentines that were a wonder and a delight. Mr. Da Ponte, himself, wore well. He was a curious person, to be sure. He would declaim you an ode and then ask you for a loan, or an endorsement on some note. He was always in trouble with Mackinleys, Dunhams, Tellers, and such rabble from the business section and from New Jersey. He liked to talk too much about his troubles and could be a positive bore, in this sense, when he chose. What a pity a man of his culture and refinement could not find a position truly congenial to his talent! What could be done for him and his family? Could one imagine a more precious heritage of learning than his, and his wife's, for the youth of growing

America? Why should he not teach Latin, Greek, Italian, the poetry he knew?

Unpleasant rumors came in from time to time, from London, from Italy, from Austria—banishments, immoralities, bankruptcies. But America was a free country and no questions asked! Didn't Joseph Priestley leave England in a barrel? Between the past in Europe and the future in America an Atlantic Ocean rolled. It took republican institutions to bring out the man in a man!

Such, more or less, was the vision which New York first had of Lorenzo Da Ponte, *olim* Emanuel Conegliano, ex-Jew of Ceneda, friend and comrade in adventure of Giacomo Casanova, librettist to Mozart, poet to His Imperial and Royal Majesty, Joseph of Hapsburg. This vision New York had of Da Ponte, and this vision, by and large, America has chosen to retain, in spite of the different picture that European scholarship would paint of him. Among the millions of immigrants that America has received from Europe, Lorenzo Da Ponte stands almost in a class by himself. We had religious believers cast off by the religious wars of Europe. We had patriots hurled upon our shores by political convulsions abroad. We had the hopeful and laborious poor of every nation attracted by the economic prospects of a new country. But in him we had an individual pressed forth by a chain of circumstances from the rotting core of the collapsing intellectual aristocracy of the Old *Régime*. Why so much astonishment that in Europe he should have had the defects and blemishes of that dying *Régime*? When, on the morning of June 4, in the year 1805, he passed the Custom House in Philadelphia, a new life began for him—the life of Lorenzo Da Ponte, the American; an American who lived an interesting and useful life in the country of his adoption, left abiding traces upon the trend of American culture, and imparted a high-minded conception of the spiritual life to his children and his children's children, whereby our country, both North and South, has profited not a little.

At the head of this American translation of Lorenzo Da Ponte's *Memoirs* I cannot refrain from pointing to that vision of Da Ponte, from emphasizing those facts, to offset and put in truer perspective that body of erudite scandal-mongering which has grown up in years past about his *Memoirs* and too strongly colored critical views of them.

What the *Memoirs* are, how they came to be written and published, what their value and accuracy, what the pressures, spiritual or external, that determined their content, are questions that cannot be answered in a word. The *Memoirs* are not a work of pure literature as the kindly Abbé Marchesan supposed thirty years ago; they are not altogether a personal apologetic as a brilliant Italian critic of Da Ponte, Fausto Nicolini, believed in 1918. The situation is more complicated. I venture to describe it as I see it myself.

In the month of September 1792, the Abbé Lorenzo Da Ponte, driving northward in a one-horsed barouche from Trieste on what was partly a flight, partly a wedding journey, and largely a tour of job-hunting, stopped off at Dux, near Prague, in Bohemia, to call on his old friend, Giacomo Casanova, introducing his wife as his mistress to retain such standing as he had with that master adventurer so fastidious as to sanctities. As the event proved, the device succeeded. It was not till some time later that Casanova learned that the Abbé Da Ponte had married, and, unable to believe his ears, set his friends in Italy and Austria to investigating to see whether such an enormity could really be true. However, at Dux, in Bohemia, Casanova, then an aged man, librarian to the Duke of Waldstein, was writing his famous *Memoirs*. Did he speak of them to Da Ponte, during the latter's visit of three days? The conjecture has a certain plausibility. Da Ponte, at any rate, with a way he had of seizing inspiration from On High in a flash, must have spoken to Casanova of his own *Memoirs*, and Casanova must have imparted the news to his friend Pietro Zaguri in Venice. Zaguri, in fact, replied (Zaguri to Casanova, Oct. 24, 1792), "I enjoyed the Ponte letter. It begins to verify your prophecies. If he truly writes his history, it will be interesting, if for nothing else, for the verification mentioned."[1]

As we examine the *Memoirs* of Lorenzo Da Ponte in their varied tone and content, the chance of this early inspiration and conception cannot be ignored. Later on when Da Ponte knew Casanova's autobiography in its printed form he judged it (*Mem.*, V, 420) as a work largely of the imagination, where "history" had been retouched in the direction of literary interest. So, originally, he must have conceived his own *Memoirs* as a record of *galant* adventures more or less founded on fact, but adapted to suit an eventual reader's taste. It is in the first three books that we find romantic episodes in the style of the "Gothic" novel—the adventure with a Duchess Matilda undiscoverable to historians; the story of the wealthy beggar who offers him his daughter in marriage; the remarkable fortunes of Girolamo Tiepolo, brother of Angela, first an aristocratic gambler in the *Ridotto*, then an idealistic beggar in the Venetian fish-market.

There is, accordingly, a literary motivation in the *Memoirs*.

But quite apart from any problem of literary history, Da Ponte lived on his memories the greater part of his life. That was the specifically Venetian element in a character that drew richly and deeply on the triple inheritance of Venice, Italy, and Judah. The Venetian is, to adopt a phrase of one of

---

1. Molmenti, *Carteggi casanoviani*, Palermo, Sandron, 1918, II, 209; "*La lettera Ponte mi fu cara. Ella vassi avverando le vostre profezie. Se scriverà vero la sua storia sarà interessante in questo solo rapporto della avverazione detta.*"

Casanova's mistresses, incurably *bavard par calomnie*. Somehow he takes the greatness of his city's history for granted, to sit there peacefully under the shelter of his Byzantine arches and gossip maliciously and spicily of the petty affairs of the world. Immune to the philosophical fancifulness of the Southerner, stranger also to the devious, treacherous intellectuality of the Tuscan, unmoved by the Lombard's panting eagerness to rise in the world through studious application, the Venetian likes to enjoy life talking of frivolous things, believing the worst of everybody and saying it, not, however, to hurt—just to amuse. This was Da Ponte at all times and places. In his youth, his facility at gossip, coupled with a solid classical training, and a ready gift for parlor literature, made him welcome among the powerful. A man of maturer years, in England and America, he seemed a miracle to quiet, stodgy-minded, virtuous men like the Englishman Thomas Mathias, or the American Clement Moore, let alone the young ladies and gentlemen he entertained in his Italian classes in New York. How Da Ponte could talk of himself! And how he could talk of others! How much he had lived, even if one could not always cry how well! Imagine his background in a village like Sunbury, Pennsylvania! Imagine it in Philadelphia! Imagine it in post-Revolutionary New York, or, for that matter, even in London! How often had he not been told that he ought to write his memoirs! And Da Ponte, ever concerned to use all his resources in the game of life, was well aware of this resource. We have memoirs of his in at least five different forms—not counting the most prolific of all forms, the oral reminiscence. In the days of his dotage this awareness amounts to a disease— then he keeps on remembering when, really, he has nothing to remember. Like a true Venetian, he dies gossiping.

There is also, therefore, a temperamental motivation in the *Memoirs*.

But there is something more fundamental than gossip in

Da Ponte. To call him, in his European phase, a Casanova is at once to slander and to overpraise him. He was not, even in Europe, a charlatan, a swindler, and a sharper, taking advantage of the stupidity of others for the excitement of using his wits: he was, rather, at the worst, a usurer and a speculator, handicapped by a large dose of native honesty and a tender heart. In Casanova there was a certain Satanic scorn of men, angels and gods, that impelled him to flaunt his cynicism in the face of his contemporaries and of posterity alike. Nothing was more precious to Da Ponte than the good opinion of men contemporary and unborn. Da Ponte's libertinage, too, reduces to the fact that he talked in print and out of print of a number of his love affairs—to the great relief of musical critics ever since who have found his indiscretions ready at hand to put a touch of sex appeal in their articles on Mozart. This element, at any rate, in Da Ponte's *Memoirs*, so far as it is not a speculation on Casanova's market, as he glimpsed the latter in 1792, is less a philosophy than uncontrollable *bavardise*. After all, what we know of Da Ponte's inner workings we know from Da Ponte himself; and since he was honest, less perhaps by intention than by practical bewilderment, his revelations are trustworthy. His attitude on all this side of life is most faithfully reflected—just so!—in his *Penitential Psalms*!

Da Ponte was not a Casanova. He was, let us say, a Julien Sorel. He was one of those men of humble origin, and a Jew to boot, who set out, with a deal of unquestioned talent, but with insurmountable defects of temperament, to climb the ladder of the Old *Régime*, of that Old *Régime* which was not reconciled, as yet, to climbers, which did like to be amused by clowns and bootlickers, but thought that tanners had better stay tanners and Jews, especially, Jews. Da Ponte's, therefore, were not so much adventures as misfortunes (of these his *Memoirs* are the record), and he had, not so much a philosophy of adventure, as a philosophy of career.

This subordination of the artist to the practical man reveals itself, as Professor Nicolini admirably stresses, in a curious way in the history of the *Memoirs*. They contain a fascinating picture of an artistic temperament; but they do not express any great artistic urge. They were written in various sections and at various times, and always on some practical pretext. It was as though the gossip and the litterateur in Da Ponte had always to kill several birds with one stone.

The *Memoirs* were first formally announced for publication in the year 1807. Da Ponte had just returned to New York from Elizabethtown, leaving a record of business failure and litigation behind him. A question, therefore, was being asked about the American metropolis in connection with this smooth, engaging, and withal suspicious foreigner: "Who was Da Ponte?" The question was being answered: Da Ponte was a professional insolvent; Da Ponte had failed in London previously, transferred his assets to his wife, followed her to America to escape imprisonment, and was now repeating the offense in a new field of operations! In those circumstances Da Ponte, already a practiced polemist, thought he was called upon to make answer himself: "fighting falsehood with truth, as my friend, Foscolo, once said." He could sell the *Memoirs*, meantime, realizing thus a literary plan he had long held, and satisfying the prayers of his admirers, friends, and pupils, who had often told him he should write the story of his life. Da Ponte must have considered the moment urgent. Not having the *Memoirs* ready, or perhaps unable to find a publisher, he hurried into print with a *Compendium* of the larger work, telling, in fact, who he was, and all he was, and explaining just how things had gone at Elizabethtown.

There are differences of tone, both subtle and broad, in the various portions of the *Memoirs* as they finally appeared. The first book may have been written while he was still in Europe. The other two must have been largely written in New York at this time, to be finished and polished later on at Sunbury, where, in spite of his troubled life, Da Ponte also found time to write the first draft of his *Catalogo ragionato* (a systematic dictionary of Italian writers). The question of completing them, however, was not to trouble him again for eleven years, nor the publication, for fifteen. The fourth book was torn from him in 1818, when he was living at Philadelphia, unemployed and still smarting under the disappointments of Sunbury. But once again in New York, and again under the patronage of Clement Moore, a new difficulty faced him: the competition of a group of Italian patriots in exile who were also making their living as teachers of Italian.

The theory of evolution is not necessary to explain all things in human life. The Italian "colony" in New York is one of them. It did not evolve. It was born full grown. The Italian colony in New York in 1820, small as it was, was the same Italian colony that has been there ever since, a colony fighting the battle of life in personal terms with personal weapons, a battle of gossip, slander, treachery, and blackmail. In such a battle Da Ponte inherited, one may say, from nature, the part of the defensive. The most conspicuous and distinguished man in the colony, he was also one of the most vulnerable. And the issue was straightway joined, on the terrain of character, and on the terrain of competence.

As for the former, one knows the allegations: Da Ponte was a renegade Jew; Da Ponte was a renegade priest; Da Ponte had been banished from Venice for his crimes. The story of Vienna and Joseph was a fabrication of his own. Then there was London! Among other things, an anonymous letter was sent to all of Da Ponte's private pupils, accusing him of twelve different crimes, among them murder.

As for the competence, Da Ponte could more justifiably be attacked. We know from the *Reminiscences* of Kelly that he talked with a lisp, having difficulty perhaps with his "s's."

He was furthermore a Venetian, doubtless speaking his Italian with a Venetian singsong, slighting his "l's" and his double consonants, turning his liquids into "j's," showing, in a word, all that the Italian purist might call defects at a time when language was a patriotic question in Italy. Not only, furthermore, had he been, as he sometimes pleads, absent from his native country more than a quarter of a century. He had learned his Italian out of books, and never wrote it, especially in verse, as forcefully as his native Venetian. He made errors in Italian —errors of grammar, errors of diction, errors that the proverbial schoolboy in Tuscany would never have made. There were a few of those schoolboys in New York, and they made fun of Da Ponte's language—points, as everybody knows, of the greatest importance in the eyes of that particular private clientele of aristocratic youths and damsels which must always have its authentic grammar and its authentic accent from an authentic teacher before it essays to speak a foreign language however badly.

To be sure, Da Ponte was not fighting this latter battle without weapons of his own. He was a famous author. If he did not know language he knew "style," and was master, specifically, of the "sublime style." He could turn a faultless Petrarchian ode *ex tempore*. He knew the idealistic jargon of Arcadia. He could dash off, even in English, a smoother pentameter than the very author of "The Night Before Christmas." He could quote from memory more sections of the poets, both Italian and Latin, than the Ferraris, the Casatis, the Aloisis, put together, had ever seen; and once they ventured any raid within his entrenchments, he was there to count their syllables, examine their rhymes, dissect their metaphors, enumerate their violations of good sense and the classic style.

Such the manifold provocation of the *Memoirs* in their first edition of 1823—to tell, in the face of competition and personal attack, who he was and what he had been, capitalize his past, expose his enemies, defend himself and therewith give evidence that he was not a mere poetaster of operatic librettos, but could write a book in good Italian, as interesting as Casanova's, as elegant as Boccaccio's. There was even a consideration of a humbler sort. Da Ponte's oral reminiscences were his stock in trade for his classes in Italian conversation. Once printed he could use them and sell them as a textbook, and offering his *Memoirs* to his students along with the great classics he would provide from his bookstore, he would figure before their eyes, by that material juxtaposition, as one of the great writers of Italy. Meantime, they would be positive publicity for his classes, his bookstore, and his other enterprises, and with no restrictions as to form or content enable him to force his claim (ill-founded—there had been, at least, Bellini and Mazzei), that he had been the first to introduce Italian to Americans.

Just what the *Memoirs* were to contain Da Ponte never decided. Had he managed to prepare them for the press in 1807, they would have ended with the third book, as, in fact, he printed them in the volume of 1823. But long before that time he had lived another volume in Sunbury, and part of another, at least, in New York. Satisfied with the first venture, he went on with the Fourth Part in 1826–7, piecing out the tiny pamphlet of sixty pages with a "History of Italian Literature in New York," not so much a treatise on frogs in Ireland, as on toads in Broome Street, and at any rate, pure publicity for his work as a language master. But even then he was not ready to put the period to what, in his dotage (he was then a man of seventy-seven) he was regarding as his steady occupation. The angers of 1823 had moreover mellowed. Some of the old enemies had died, to give place to new ones. His text had been criticized by friends and foes alike. He thought himself that improvements could be made in it. Hence the second edition of 1829, wherein the "History of Italian Literature" had grown to a Fifth Part, reaching to September 20, 1830, before the proofs were ready. These were the *Memoirs* proper, as we know them. But Da Ponte had announced the Third Part in the Second, the Fourth in the Third, the Fifth in the Fourth. So in 1830, now at the age of eighty-one, he announced the Sixth in the Fifth.

Was the Sixth ever written? We have to answer yes and no. The momentous event alluded to at the end of the Fifth Part was his operatic enterprise for importing the Montresor *troupe* for which he had begun negotiations in August of 1829, and which was to materialize during the theatrical season of 1832–3 in New York and Philadelphia. That adventure, truly remarkable in a man so aged, he was to recount in 1833 in two writings: "The History of the Montresor Company" and the "Story Incredible but True" (both in Italian). In the latter, also, he alludes mysteriously to stories he is about to tell, following out the same advance publicity for the Sixth Part which he had initiated in the Fifth Part and in the preface to his "Sonnets to Ann" (1832). These writings are all that we have of the Sixth Part, and critics who go hunting for the latter should note that they bear to the Fifth Part the same relation that the "History of Italian Literature" had borne to the Fourth. In spite of his indomitable spirit, Da Ponte lived at a slackened pace in his later eighties, and, as he observed, in a quiet place like New York nothing ever happened to anybody anyway! To have written his Sixth Part (and announced his Seventh!) Da Ponte would have had, as Nicolini wittily remarks, to survive his death and his funeral; and, what a glorious chapter they would have made for him! As a matter of fact they had to come from other hands, from Dr. Francis, Samuel Ward, Professor Tuckerman.

The *Memoirs* have had a varied fortune over the course of the years. They did not enjoy that success in Italy and Austria which Da Ponte hoped for them. Reviewed favorably in the

Antologia of Florence, they were successfully suppressed by the Austrian police for their disposition to argue with the Austrian Royal family. No publisher thereafter would touch them and they were shortly forgotten. "Discovered" in 1858 by the French poet Lamartine, and praised by him in 1860,[2] they had a French adaptation in that year by La Chavanne, which passed to Germany in the translation of Burckhardt the following year. Then again came a period of relative forgetfulness, broken in 1871 by Bernardi's adaptation of the *Memoirs* in Italian, and in 1874 by a novel called *Da Ponte and Mozart* written by Julius Grosse in Germany. During all this period Da Ponte had been chiefly remembered by music lovers, in virtue of his *Don Giovanni* and *Figaro* and his other connections with Mozart and Salieri. In the course of the following quarter century he was more extensively examined by erudites of Italy and Austria, particularly in view of a rising popularity of Venetian history; while the studies of the American, Krehbiel, made him better known in the United States in connection with the Mozart celebrations of 1889. The Da Ponte revival dates really from the second decade of the present century when the discovery of the papers at Dux put a new face on the *Memoirs* of Casanova and, therewith, on the *Memoirs* of Da Ponte.

If, by virtue of the fulsome praises of Grillparzer, Wagner, and Saint Saëns (see below, Marchesan, 317), not to mention less famous critics of musical things (Krehbiel, Giuriati), Da Ponte has always stood high among librettists, especially as the

---

2. *"Voici les Mémoires les plus originaux et les plus anecdotiques que l'Italie artiste ait jamais offerts à la curiosité publique. Les Mémoires de Benvenuto Cellini ne sont ni plus naïfs ni plus amusants. D'Aponte est dans ses mémoires aussi écrivain que Goldoni, son compatriote, aussi léger que le chevalier de Grammont, aussi aventureux que Gil Blas, aussi plaisant que Figaro, aussi malheureux que Gilbert."* (Preface to the Chavanne translation, Paris, 1860.)

librettist of Mozart, the same cannot be said of his standing among men by virtue of his connections with Casanova, the other float on his pontoon of immortality. That association, along with the singular support which such labels as "libertine," "rascal," "adventurer" always find in the malice of people once they can, with a semblance of justice, be tagged to a man, has of late made him suffer in his moral reputation more than he had gained by his positive achievement. Nor did he help himself much by his auto-apologies, since it is largely from his arguments for the defendant that the prosecutor-historian has drawn the indictment.

So far as the point bears on the character of Da Ponte, one must say that the indictments are there, and the defense is there, the latter now presented with justification and extenuation, now with the plea of guilty and the appeal for the mercy of God and of men. Lamartine's heart as a man was more discerning than his words as a critic: he locates Da Ponte's naïveness in the wrong place, I should say, but the naïveness is there, the honesty is there, even the naïveness of the man who is overshrewd, and the honesty of the Machiavellian in private life. There are, among others, two kinds of people in this world: those who are rascals by nature, and who adopt the cloak of virtue and conformity as a convenience and security in the battle of life; and those who are honest and peaceable by nature, but whom the battle of life constrains to compromises, hatreds, and cruelties. The former have little regard for the inner essence of virtue, but a keen perception of the code of virtue and a high esteem for its usefulness. The latter love virtue for its own sake and then stand bewildered before the demands of practical life. Da Ponte belonged, undoubtedly, in the second of these groups. He found himself ever in the strange predicament of being as honest at heart as he was shrewd and scheming of will. How one may solve this moral dilemma I do not know, unless we would share the bewilderment of the most keen of all observers of the complexities of the human soul and follow His counsel of judging not that we be not judged.

A tolerance which might seem virtuous in all people, but which certainly is obligatory upon the historian and the critic, whose task is to establish the facts, leaves the judgment to the varied emotional utilities of society in its changing moods in history! Whatever Da Ponte may have been, he was not a liar. Despite the efforts to shake the veracity of his *Memoirs*, they stand there as the engaging record of a soul's labored and painful passage through this world, and a substantially accurate account of what that soul experienced here. Substantially, not absolutely: the *Memoirs* contain lapses of memory, misapprehensions, confusions. They show literary reworkings of fact, enlargements and reductions for the sake of interest—Da Ponte told his story so many times orally, and always, we may be sure, in such different ways, that in the end he hardly knew just what the truth was. On the polemical side, he was fighting now for an advantage, now for his reputation, now for his livelihood. Combat is combat: it is not an ethical exercise, and only rascals of the first class mentioned above pretend it is, for the advantage there is in doing so. Presenting the argument for the defense in such cases, Da Ponte was under no obligations to present the argument, or collect the evidence, for the prosecution. As a historical document, therefore, the *Memoirs* of Lorenzo Da Ponte, like every other historical document the world has ever seen, needs control.

The present translation is based on the text of the *Memoirs* as constituted by Signor Gambarin for the Laterza edition (Bari, 1918). My annotations for parts I, II, and III of the *Memoirs*, the European portion, taking the lead from Nicolini's admirable summary of Da Ponte literature in Europe, are based on secondary sources almost altogether, my effort, however, being so far as was possible from secondary sources, to credit the various discoveries to the scholars who made them. The sources thus utilized are as follows: Jacopo Bernardi, *Memorie di L. da P.*, Firenze, Le Monnier, 1871 (quoted as Bern.); Marchesan, *Della vita e delle opere di L. Da P.*, Treviso, Turazza, 1900 (quoted as March.); Gambarin-Nicolini, *L. Da P., Memorie (Scrittori d'Italia)*, Bari, Laterza, 1918 (quoted as Nic.); Sheppard, *Memoirs of L. Da P.*, London, Routledge, 1929 (quoted as Sheppard).

The notes on the American section of the *Memoirs* are almost entirely new. In this department my principal predecessor was Krehbiel (quoted as Krehbiel) in his various articles in the New York *Tribune* (1888–1899), which had the merit of discovering the reminiscences of Kelly, of utilizing (rather hastily) certain directories of New York, and of solving the problem of Da Ponte's burial place. Theodore Koch unearthed Da Ponte's notes on Dante for his study on *Dante in America*, Boston, Ginn, 1896 (quoted as Koch). For a letter of Da Ponte to Dr. Jackson, I am indebted to Russo's *Lorenzo Da Ponte, Poet and Adventurer*, New York, Columbia University Press, 1922 (quoted as Russo).

—ARTHUR LIVINGSTON
SWAN'S ISLAND, MAINE

MEMOIRS OF
LORENZO
DA PONTE

PART ONE

SINCE I AM not writing the memoirs of a man illustrious by birth, by talents, by rank, wherein the slightest things are wont to be judged of greatest consequence because of the importance of the subject of which they treat, I shall speak but little of my family, my neighborhood, my early years, as of matters trivial enough in themselves or of scant moment to the reader. I shall speak rather of things, which, if not altogether great by their nature, and capable of interesting every country and every reader, are nevertheless so singular in their oddity as in some manner to instruct, or at least to entertain, without wearying.

I was born on the tenth day of March in the year 1749 in Ceneda, a small but not obscure city of the Venetian State.

When I was five years old, my mother died. Fathers, as a rule, give little heed to the early years of their children. My father completely neglected mine: up to my eleventh year reading and writing was the extent of my knowledge. Not until

5

then did it occur to my father to give me a little education—
education meant Latin in those days: and to my misfortune he
chose a poor teacher.

The latter was the son of a peasant, who, in exchanging
ox and plow for the schoolmaster's ferule, retained even in
the classroom the harsh and uncouth manners befitting his
birth. This fellow put Alvaro's grammar into my hands and
made a pretense of teaching me Latin. I studied for several
months—and learned nothing! A vivacious manner of speaking, a certain readiness at repartee, and above all, an insatiable
curiosity to know everything, had earned for me the reputation of being gifted with a memory and an ability above
the ordinary. My father was surprised, therefore, that I should
be profiting so little by the peasant's lessons and took it upon
himself to investigate the causes. It did not cost him much
effort to discover them. One day he chanced to enter our study-
room and placed himself, unobserved, behind my tutor's back.
Annoyed at a certain error I had made in reciting the lesson, the man clenched his right fist in boorish rage and with
the callused knuckles of his bumpkin's fingers began belaboring my forehead, like Steropes or Brontes beating Vulcan's
anvil—a way he had of daily stimulating my brain. I do not
know whether it was more shame or pain that drew one or
two silent tears from my eyes. My father saw them, seized the
tutor suddenly by the hair, dragged him out of the room, and
flung him down the stairs, followed by inkwell, pens, and the
Alvaro.

For more than three years there was no further talk of
Latin. My father believed, and perhaps it was true, that the
cause of my scant progress in the study of that language had
been my aversion for my teacher. The effect, however, of this
little episode was very serious for me. Up to my fourteenth
year I was left completely ignorant in all branches of letters,
and while people kept exclaiming: "Oh, how clever! How

talented!" I could inwardly feel only shame at being the least educated of all the young boys in Ceneda, who used to call me in jest the "clever dunce." I could not tell how deeply all this stung me, and how it made me long for instruction! Chancing one day to go up to our garret where my father was wont to throw his old papers, I came upon some books that constituted, I believe, the family library—among these the "Buovo d'Antona," the "Fuggilozio," the "Guerin Meschino," "Barlaam and Jehosaphat," "Cassandra," "Bertoldo," and a few stray volumes of Metastasio. I read them all with incredible avidity; but the author I read twice was the Poet Laureate of Austria whose verses aroused in my soul the very emotions of music itself.

Meantime my father, now a widower for ten years, took a second wife, giving us as stepmother a young girl not yet seventeen. He had passed his fortieth year. Stirred therefore on the one hand by the desire to embellish my mind with some enlightenment, and foreseeing, on the other, what the consequences of such an unbalanced marriage would be, I sought to obtain from the charity of others what I could not hope to gain from paternal solicitude.

The Bishop of Ceneda in those days was Monsignor Lorenzo Da Ponte,[1] a man of renowned piety and charitable religion, and eminently gifted with all the Christian virtues. He was,

---

1. Da P. assumed the name of Monsignor Lorenzo Da Ponte on Aug. 29, 1763, when his father, Geremia Conegliano, a Jewish tanner of Ceneda (part of the now famous Vittorio Veneto) accepted baptism for himself and his family at the hands of that prelate, in order to make a second marriage with a Christian lady, Orsola Patetta (Sept. 10, 1763). Geremia became Gasparo Da P., and his three sons, Emanuel, Baruch, and Anania, respectively Lorenzo, Girolamo, and Luigi. Lorenzo was to acquire three half-brothers and seven half-sisters from his father's second marriage. His own mother was a Jewess, Rachele ("Ghella") Pincherle. March., 1–3, 463–466, utilizing studies of von Löhner, Zopelli, Marson.

moreover, greatly devoted to my father and to all my family. I presented myself to him courageously, begging him to find places for me and for one of my brothers[2] in his seminary. The excellent prelate was pleased with my commendable forwardness, and perceiving in me as well as in this brother of mine a lively desire for instruction, united, to the best of appearances, with a ready talent and a happy memory, he not only joyfully granted my worthy aspiration, but, with rare kindness, supplied the money for the not inconsiderable expense of our tuition.

The progress we made in our studies fulfilled in a measure the expectations of our benefactor. In less than two years we learned to write Latin with some degree of elegance, which language was taught us with particular care by the very able professors of that learned seminary as the one most essential for aspirants to the priesthood, for whose benefit such institutions are chiefly established in Italy. The modern languages—Italian not excepted—were almost entirely neglected. My father, being deceived in the choice of my career, and allowing himself to be guided rather by his circumstances than by his parental duty, was thinking of turning me to the Altar; though that was utterly contrary to my vocation and my character. I was therefore trained after the manner of the priests, though inclined by taste and, as it were, made by nature for different pursuits; so that, by the time I was seventeen, while I was capable of composing in half a day a long oration and perhaps fifty not inelegant verses in Latin, I could not for the life of me write a letter of a few lines in my own language without making ten errors. The first to destroy such a prejudice and to introduce good taste among the pupils in that

---

2. Girolamo. The boys were at the Under-Seminary in Ceneda between 1763 and 1767. Nic., 267.

school—and therewith a predilection for the Tuscan tongue and a noble emulation—was the very learned Abbé Cagliari, a young scholar full of fire and poetic aptitude. Recently graduated from the colleges of Padua, from which Dante and Petrarch were no more excluded than were Virgil and Horace, this young man began to read and expound the prose and the poems of our Italian writers and to instill in a goodly number of the youths entrusted to his care a capacity for enjoying their beauties.

Two of the liveliest and most cultivated of the many talented wits of Ceneda, Girolamo Perucchini and Michele Colombo,[3] frequented his delightful classes. To emulation of these two young men more than to aught else do I owe the rapidity of my progress in poetry. I will here narrate a little anecdote which, though frivolous and of scant import in itself, will serve nevertheless to give an idea of the power that good example, fear of censure, and an honest desire to excel, exert upon youthful minds. Michele Colombo had completed his elementary studies before entering the seminary of Ceneda, and under the guidance of excellent instructors. He wrote in Latin well, and could turn an Italian verse that was full of delicacy and grace. Nor did he disdain at times to read them to me (whom he loved devotedly), in order to incite me, as he would say, to "make trial of my poetic vein!"

One day, in fact, I set myself to the task. Being in need of a small sum of money for the usual diversions of a boy, I thought to obtain it more easily from my father by asking for it in verse.

---

3. They were to remain lifelong friends of Da P. and were still in correspondence with him in the 1830s. Colombo became a writer and critic of some note, Perucchini, a lawyer, father to the composer Giambattista. Many of Da P.'s letters to Colombo were published by Bern., 147–196. The teacher referred to above was Giannandrea Cagliari. March., 184.

Here therefore is the first quatrain I scrawled, of the fourteen lines that I made bold to call

A SONNET

Mandatemi, vi prego, o padre mio,
Quindici soldi o venti, se potete,
E la cetera in man pigliar vogl' io,
Per le lodi cantar delle monete.

(Send me, I pray you, O father mine,
Fifteen *soldi*, or twenty, if you can,
And the zither I will take in hand
To sing the praises of pennies!)

Scarcely had I finished this last line, when I heard behind my back a loud guffaw, at which, turning my head, I perceived my friend Colombo, who showed that he had been reading over my shoulder by chanting my last verse in the drone of the blind beggars on the streets of Italy, and pretending to strum a lute with his fingers. I wept for shame and rage: and for more than three days I did not speak to Colombo, nor did I look him in the face. He, nevertheless, continued maliciously to sing my verses in blindman fashion and to strum his imaginary instrument. He was the first, after tormenting me thus for some time, to encourage me to new trials; and I promised him to make them. I thereupon set myself to reading and studying the good authors of our language and with such fervor that I no longer thought either of food or of sleep, to say nothing of those idlings and amusements by nature so dear to young men, and whereby so often the fruits of the most conspicuous talents are lost. Dante, Petrarch, Ariosto, and Tasso were my first masters: in less than six months I had learned by heart almost all of the "Inferno" by the first named, all the best sonnets and not a few of the *canzoni* of the second, and the most beautiful passages of the other two. After this training, and after having composed secretly, and burned, more than two thousand verses, I hoped I would be able to test my strength with my fellow students and to write verses not solely to be thrummed on the blindman's lute. At just that time the rector of our college chanced to be appointed to another distinguished post, so that he was obliged to leave us. Among the compositions presented by many of the pupils in his praise on that occasion, I also recited a sonnet of mine.[4] I print it below in these Memoirs, not because it seems to me worthy of being published, but that the progress I had made in only six months may be judged of and thus become an incentive to those who even a little late in life may turn, *natura favente*, to the pursuit of poetry.

Before this sonnet, I had never allowed anyone to see my Italian verses—with the exception of the blind beggar's quatrain. As a result no one would believe that these fourteen verses could be mine. Colombo alone pretended to think so, and took solemn oath never to write in Italian again: an oath which, later on, he broke for the sake of a charming and very beautiful girl of whom we were both enamored, and for whom we wrote things each in turn. This general reluctance to believe me the author of that first sonnet was a new kind of praise, which, without unduly flattering my pride, encouraged me to greater efforts and made me resolve thenceforward to devote myself entirely to Italian poetry. In less than two years I had not only translated into verse, *diurna et nocturna manu,*

---

4. *Quello spirto divin, che, con l'ardente, etc.* The following sonnet was composed on that same occasion by my friend Colombo. I publish it here, hoping to please him, by proving to him that sixty-five years have not been sufficient to wipe from my memory the verses of a friend so dear. *Quanto è possente amor! Padre avevamo, etc.* —L. Da P.

all the ancient poets, but read and reread all those Italians who circulate among the general as writers of real merit, with the sole exception of our seventeenth century authors, whom I did not dare to read until I felt that I had acquired the necessary insight to distinguish the good from the bad, and the seemingly beautiful from the truly beautiful. And I was not content with reading them: I must needs transfer into Latin the noblest passages of our authors, copying and recopying them again and again, criticizing them, expounding them, learning them by heart, trying my hand repeatedly at every style of meter and composition, striving to imitate the most beautiful thoughts, to use the most graceful phrases, to select the most elegant expressions employed by my usual standard-bearers, preferring always and above all others those of my idolized Petrarch, in whose every verse I seemed to find some new treasure at each rereading.

In this manner and as a result of this constant and indefatigable study, I succeeded, toward the beginning of the third year, in ranking with our foremost pupils and my verses not infrequently carried off the honors. I obtained much praise for a *canzone* which I wrote in competition with the most cultivated youths of Ceneda; but it did not make me overproud nor cause me seriously to believe that my poem was a beautiful one. I had, from the beginning of my studious career, the good fortune to understand that the praises I received sprang solely from a courteous intention to fortify my youthful powers and lead me in time to deserve them in truth. This preserved me from foolish pride and from a vain opinion of myself, shoals on which the studious frequently run aground through thinking they know everything, so that they often stop at a point where they ought to begin. Some poetic talent I had been endowed with by Nature, and my infinite passion for poetry, wedded to principles so sane, would perhaps have earned for me one day the rank and reputation of a good poet, had Fortune not inter-

12

fered continually with my worthy intentions and drawn me with tyrannical hand, and almost by main force, into the cruelest and most dangerous whirlpools of life, thus depriving me of that peace of mind, those resources, and those placid leisures, without which the human mind strives in vain to attain the topmost summits.

Enflamed as I was by a noble desire to embellish my mind with all the enlightenment and accoutrements requisite in a poet, I had acquired, by dint of savings and youthful economies, a modest collection of Latin books, which I was preparing to enrich with the best Italian authors. We had, in Ceneda, a bookseller who, though an ignorant and a stupid man, kept, as a pure whim, a shop of excellent books. The moment I found myself in possession of a few *lire*, off I hurried to pay him a visit and selected a number of books, for the most part Elzevirian editions, the value of which far exceeded the contents of my miserable purse. However, the bookseller had a son, a shoemaker by trade, and the good old man found an excellent makeshift to fit both his own needs and mine.

"Bring me," he said, "some of the stained leather or calfskin that your father makes and we will arrange matters."

I was delighted with the expedient: I ran home, stole secretly into the warehouse, chose three calfskins, made a very tight bundle of them, tucked them in between my cassock and my back, and started for the door, to go out. As my bad luck would have it, there on the threshold stood my stepmother gossiping with a few women of the neighborhood. Fearful lest she might remark the theft, I cut a little circle and went around by another door. But once on the street, I must needs pass in front of the group of women. I had taken only a few steps, when I heard one of them exclaim in a loud tone: "Oh! What a pity that boy should be so hunchbacked!" Such in fact the hidden bundle made me appear! As I hopped diagonally across the road, the bundle fell to the ground. The women burst out laughing. My stepmother ran to pick it up and I, without turning around or saying a word, hurried slinking on my way to the good bookseller. Relating my misfortune to him, I gave him a few *lire* on deposit and urged him fervently to keep the books for me, which he did. My stepmother did not fail to report the affair to my father, who came to the seminary the next day and had no end of things to say. I could devise no way to placate him, to say nothing of obtaining the money I needed in order to buy my books, though the sum could not have been greater than twelve dollars. The anecdote came to the ears of the excellent Bishop. He sent for me at once, bade me repeat the whole story, to which he listened *lacrymoso non sine risu*, and then gave me the money necessary for my purchase.

But the pleasure of such an acquisition was not of long duration for me. A terrible illness, which kept my family for more than six months in constant fear of losing me, various domestic difficulties that came to beset my father in those days, and above all, the death of Monsignor Da Ponte,[5] my protector, not only cut me off from the means of pursuing my studies, but reduced my father to extreme poverty; for he too had constantly derived patronage and succor from the kindness of that prelate.

In this manner between illnesses, tears, and idleness I lost more than a year; and in the end I was constrained to sell most of the books I had acquired, now in order to cover myself with a decent coat, and now in order to meet the daily needs of our household. The state of poverty, in which my family found itself at that time, caused me to renounce the hand of a noble and beautiful girl whom I tenderly loved,[6] and induced

---

5. July 7, 1768. March., xix.

6. A girl named Pierina Raccanelli. Bern., 186.

me to embrace a career wholly contrary to my temperament, my character, my principles, and my studies, thus opening the doors to a thousand dangers and strange vicissitudes of which the envy, hypocrisy, and malice of my enemies rendered me for more than twenty years a pitiable victim. Permit me, gentle reader, to cover with a veil of mystery this grievous moment in my life, thus sparing my pen a resentment that would arouse bootless remorse in a heart which, in spite of everything, I do revere, and which I shall never cease to revere.[7]

After this storm, which I weathered with courage and resignation, Monsignor Ziborghi, a venerable canon of that cathedral, who had inherited the deceased prelate's charitable inclinations toward us, managed to procure for me as well as for my two other brothers, the assistance of one of those noble foundations which in the happy days of ill-fated Venice crowned that Republic with such honor and glory. We were all three placed in the seminary of Portogruaro,[8] where a new field was opened to me for pursuing my interrupted studies with ease and decorum.

I devoted the first year to philosophy and mathematics, not, however, losing sight of my favorite muses. While our proctor[9] was laboriously explaining Euclid or some abstruse treatise of Galileo or Newton, I would be surreptitiously reading now Tasso's "Aminta," now Guarini's "Pastor Fido," which I had almost learned by heart. Toward the end of the first year I

---

7. Yet, under the Old *Régime* entering the clergy was the easiest way for a boy of Da P.'s station to climb into an intellectual life. He seems to have taken at least minor orders in Nov. 1770, and was ordained a celebrant priest on Holy Saturday (March 27), 1773. March., 20. Nic., 268.

8. Nov. 1769. Nic., 268. The brothers were Girolamo and Luigi. March., 12.

9. Dr. Modolini. See *Mem.*, V, p. 448.

publicly recited a poem in praise of Saint Louis. It was greatly
applauded, these three lines finding especial favor:

> Ma sel ritolse il ciel, quasi sua gloria
> Fosse manca e men bella
> Senza la luce di quell'aurea stella.

(But Heaven withdrew him, as though its glory were
deficient and less beautiful without the light of that
golden star.)

A "bravo" escaping the lips of a learned personage of noble
birth earned me straightway the Chair of Rhetoric which Monsignor Gabrielli, Bishop of Concordia, a man famous for his
learning and his character, and eminent for his piety, offered
me that very day.[10] At the time I had been thinking of perfecting myself in my knowledge of the Hebrew language, which I
had studied assiduously in my early years, and of applying myself at the same time to the study of the Greeks, since it was
my firm conviction that without those authors no one could
become a great poet.

For that reason I hesitated several days before making a
decision, allowing myself to be won over in the end, partly
by the suasions of our good rector, who was deeply devoted
to me, but even more by my father's situation, which I hoped
to ameliorate with the emoluments of my new position. I accepted therefore: and at an age in which I myself had need of
learning an infinitude of things, I set myself to the arduous
task of teaching others.

---

10. Da P. became instructor at Portogruaro in Nov. 1770, master of Italian language the following academic year, and, on April 14, 1771, vice-rector, or dean, of
the Seminary, at a salary of forty ducats a year. Nic., 268, following letters to
Colombo in Bern., 164–71.

I do not think, however, that that sort of interruption was the occasion either of delay or of detriment to my progress in letters. I was not yet twenty-two at the moment of my appointment. Entrusted to my care were thirty or more youths, full of enthusiasm, talent, and eagerness to excel, and up to that time, my fellow students. The Bishop was perpetually provoking and intensifying in my mind the strongest and most stinging prods of pride. The eyes of the town were all upon me. My reader may imagine how I trembled. I accordingly redoubled in diligence, meditation, and effort, in order to meet the duties of my office not without glory; and what my masters did not have time to teach me, I learned, as a scholarly rabbi once said, from my pupils: *Umitalmidai rabàdi miculàm.* Indeed from my pupils I learned more than from my masters.

The fortunate outcome of my honorable efforts excited in some individuals the iniquitous pangs of envy. Two or three teachers in that seminary became my untamable persecutors.[11] Pretending that I had not gone deeply into physics and mathematics, they sought to attack me on that side, shouting that I was nothing but a chatterbox, a rhymester without scholarship. I thereupon composed a number of poems, in Italian as well as Latin, on divers questions of physics, which were publicly recited toward the end of the year by boys from my group. The verses were generally liked, but above all, a dithyramb on odors—"*Qual felice avventura*, etc.,"—in which, people thought they could detect some sparkle of Redi's fire.

The mortification of my enemies was proportionate to the praises and caresses heaped upon me by the *literati* in that city, by the pupils in my school, and by the Bishop himself; all

---

11. Da P. began his battles in literary life by attacking these enemies and rivals in anonymous verses published at his own expense in Venice. Nic., 268, following Bern.

of which embittered the hatred of my rivals beyond all reason. I endured in patience for two years. Then I resigned.[12]

Unfortunately, I went to Venice. I was at the boiling point of youthful spirit. Eager and lively by temperament, and, as everyone said, attractive in person, I allowed myself, through the customs and examples about me, as well as by my own inclinations, to be swept away into a life of voluptuousness and amusement, forgetting or neglecting literature and my studies almost entirely.

I had conceived a very violent passion for one of the most beautiful, but at the same time, most capricious ladies of that metropolis.[13] She occupied all my time in the usual follies and frivolities of love and jealousy, in convivialities, carousals, and debaucheries: and with the exception of an occasional hour at night which I ordinarily devoted to some book or other, I do not think, in the three years' time that the affair lasted, that I learned a single thing I had not known before, or which was really worth knowing.

It was as though Providence at last decided to free me from the terrible danger that was hanging over me. Despite all the whims and jealousies of the lady in question, I had clung to the excellent habit of going of an evening to a certain café where the most cultivated and scholarly men of Venice were wont to foregather, and which was therefore called the "Café of the *Literati*."[14]

---

12. Aug. 1, 1772. He resigned in the autumn of 1773 (Nic., 268), but probably with some ecclesiastical post in Venice to depend on.

13. Angiola Tiepolo (identified by Von Löhner, see March., 20), a girl of a poorer branch of the aristocratic Tiepolo family. Her brother, who will figure again in the *Mem.* (Three, pp. 268–271) was named Girolamo (Sheppard, 44) and received public dole with the other *barnabotti* at St. Barnaba.

14. Gathering place of the Academy of the *Granelleschi*, comprising the two Gozzis, Carlo and Gasparo; Forcellini, brother of the famous Latin lexicographer; Crotta; and Dalle Laste; all enemies of Goldoni. March., 27.

One evening as I chanced to be there, half-masked, a gondolier entered, looked about the room, caught my eye, and beckoned to me to step outside; and on the street he motioned to me to follow him. He led me to the brink of a nearby canal and bade me enter a gondola that was moored just opposite the tavern. Believing that I would find my lady, who came at times to fetch me at that spot, I obeyed without further question and sat down beside her. The night was pitch black. A street lamp some distance off had so far lighted my path: but once inside the gondola, the boatman let fall the usual curtain over the opening, leaving us in total darkness. As the lady and I exchanged greetings both at the same time, we each discovered, from the sound of a voice that was strange, that the gondolier must have made a mistake. On sitting down I had taken her hand to kiss it, according to our Italian custom—a hand rather more plump than my lady's. She tried quickly to withdraw it, but I held on with gentle violence, assuring her in fervent words that she had nothing to fear. She replied in courteous tone, begging me nevertheless to go away. Noting that she was not a Venetian, as she spoke a purest Tuscan, I was seized with the greater curiosity to know who she was; and I employed all my eloquence that she should allow me to accompany her to her door. After many evasions she consented to accept some slight refreshment on the understanding that I should promise to leave the gondola then without further press of questions. The gondolier went to a nearby café for the dainties and returned, bringing a lantern. In the burst of light there was offered to my gaze a girl of marvelous beauty and evidently of noble family. She did not seem, and, in fact, was not yet, seventeen years old. Gowned in attractive taste, she had an exquisite charm of manner, and her every word bespoke wit and breeding. We sat both in silence for some time. It seeming to me, however, that she was looking upon me with sentiments not unlike those with which I was gazing at her, I took courage and told her all those things which on like occasions one says to a beautiful woman. Again I begged her to vouchsafe me permission to attend her to her dwelling, or at least to inform me with whom I had the good fortune to be conversing.

Perceiving that I was observing toward her all that delicacy and respect which her station demanded, and which as a rule suggests the character of a well-bred man, she seemed pleased at my insistence and spoke as follows:

"The curious circumstances in which I find myself forbid me to gratify your wishes. Who knows, however, but what they may change? In which case we may meet again—that much I promise you! Or, if you would have more, I may tell you frankly that I too desire such a happy outcome and shall use every means to bring it to pass."

I then told her who I was, and we designated that same spot, and that same hour, for our future meeting. A few moments later she was gone!

I do not know whether curiosity, or the hope that this adventure might liberate me from a too violent passion for a woman who, from the beginning of our intimacy, did not seem suited to my happiness, caused me to go regularly every evening to the café in question: but after a time my expectation began to wane. Meanwhile my passion for the other lady grew from day to day and, therewith, her tyrannical dominion over me. She had a brother who was ever a most despicable object in my eyes, and who was inclined to share in his sister's authority, making me his slave, his confidant, his treasurer. I resolved all of a sudden to leave Venice, hoping that absence might serve to cure me. Instead it increased my weakness and my desire. I had not the strength to resist. After a week of most tormenting struggle I returned to Venice and, to my misfortune, I accepted the offer the woman made me that I should go to live in her house! I did not fail, however, to return in the evening to my customary resort, where I heard, not without disappointment, that a gondolier had called there for me a few days before, and that the proprietor had told him I had left the city. It seemed improbable, therefore, that I should ever hear again of my fair Incognita.

But, some days later, as I was crossing the Piazza at San Marco, I felt a twitch at my coat sleeve, and heard myself called by name.

It was the young woman's boatman and he was exclaiming with greatest joy:

"I am glad you have come back. I will take the good news to my mistress. Farewell till this evening, sir!"

He was off, without waiting for a reply; and that night he appeared at the café, with the beautiful girl waiting nearby. As I entered the gondola she said:

"You see? I have come to keep my word!"

After the usual exchange of compliments, she ordered the gondolier to row us to her home, and, arrived there, led me into a beautiful room. She herself passed on into an adjoining alcove, from which she reappeared a few seconds later sumptuously but simply gowned, and addressed me as follows:

"It is but just that, before aught else, I should tell you who I am and of the strange reasons that have led me to Venice. I am a Neapolitan, and my name is Matilda, daughter of the Duke of M——a.[15]

"My father had only two children when my mother died. After remaining a widower for ten years he married the daughter of a grocer who gained a truly despotic dominion over him, and, taking advantage of his naturally weak character, rendered still weaker by his senile passion, she succeeded in chilling, if not extinguishing in him all fatherly affection for me as well as for my brother. It was at her bidding that my

---

15. Otherwise unidentified. Nicolini (269) believes her a pure invention on Da P.'s part. So also for the wealthy beggar in the following anecdote.

brother was sent to a military school in Vienna, where in less than six months he died: and I myself was not yet eleven when I was placed in a convent in Pisa, where I lived, against my will, for six years, without the comfort of seeing my father, or of having any news of him. The nuns of that convent tried by every means to induce me to embrace their vocation, which, however, I steadfastly refused to do. Then, all of a sudden, my stepmother arrived in Pisa, my father with her, though the cruel woman did not permit him to visit me. She came alone, and, feigning for me a mother's tenderness and love, she said:

" 'My daughter! I am told that you do not feel a calling to give yourself to God. We must therefore give you to the world. Your father has left your future happiness in my hands, knowing well that I could not love you more had you been my own daughter. He now offers you a husband; and I have already chosen for you a man who can insure the true happiness of your life. If you will promise to obey my wishes, which are those of your father also, you may prepare to leave these walls you do not love tomorrow. Otherwise . . . !'

"I hated the convent, the nuns, and my association with them. After six years of prison, I was yearning for liberty, above all that I might see and embrace the being to whom I owed my life. The moment I heard that 'Otherwise . . . !' I rose impulsively from the place where I was sitting, threw myself upon the neck of that woman whom I so little knew, crying, 'Anything, dear mother! I am ready to do anything that pleases you!'

"Whereupon she, too, embraced me and kissed me tenderly many times, and it was her pleasure that I leave the convent without delaying till the morrow.

"We went to an inn, where my father was awaiting us.

" 'Is this my daughter?' he cried aloud at sight of me.

" 'Your daughter, and an obedient daughter!' replied the perfidious woman.

"Then Nature asserted her rights! I need not tell you of his kisses and caresses, of his joy and mine.

"We left straightway for Naples, whither arrived, naught else was thought of but the preparations for my marriage. My stepmother had given me two rooms adjoining hers, wherein she kept jealous watch over me, not allowing me to see or to speak alone with anyone. I could not imagine what opinion to form of this strange seclusion. One day, as I sat pondering that very thought, my stepmother unexpectedly entered my room, drew me after her into her own, locked herself in with me, and drawing from a wardrobe a little casket filled with pearls and jewels said to me:

" 'This is your husband's first gift. The rest, which corresponds perfectly to his rank, you will find in your new home. Do not be ungrateful for my kindness, my friendship.'

"Saying which, she flung open the doors and I saw coming toward me an old man of horrible aspect, whom I judged to be more than sixty years of age, followed by an imposing suite of squires, lackeys, and pages, and by two ministers of the Church. Last of all, silent, and with lowered eyes, came my father.

" 'And here, Matilda,' cried the woman cheerily, 'here is your husband!' And turning to him, 'Here, O Prince, is the woman you now receive from my hands, and will shortly receive from the hands of the Church, as your consort!'

"At the very first I had lost all power of motion, let alone of speech. The monster, for his part, muttered a number of words which I did not grasp. But at last I came to my senses, and spirited, so to speak, by my disappointment, my disgust, my despair, I uttered a terrible cry, tore from my head the veils they had pinned upon me, along with a great part of my powdered hair, and forcing my way furiously between those present, I flung myself at my father's feet, crying between my sobs and my tears: 'Father, father, save me!'

23

"This was enough to throw that serpent into a towering fury! I could not describe the uproar she made. The guests vanished, and I was left alone with her and with my father, he with neither the courage, nor the strength, to defend me. At last she called two servants who dragged me away, half conscious, into a carriage—I had again lost the use of my senses.

"When I came to myself, I do not know how long thereafter, I found myself in a room which had all the appearance of a prison. In it there were only a bed, two chairs, and an old table. The windows were secured by heavy iron bars and placed so high in the walls that I could not reach them in any way. Torn by a thousand fears, I passed the remainder of the day in plaints and tears. Toward evening I heard a jingling of keys without, and the door opened. I saw a woman, horribly misshapen, enter my room carrying in her hand a little basket, which she placed on the table. After staring fixedly at me, she went out again without saying a word. I looked into the basket and found a bottle of water, two eggs, and some bread. But I was in no state to take any nourishment other than that of my tears, on which more than on aught else I fed over the fortnight my imprisonment lasted. I believe that despair would have killed me, had I not reflected that any misfortune was preferable to that of marrying a fetid corpse. Such indeed was the husband that was offered me.

"I was beginning to suspect that that prison was to be my tomb, when, on the night of the fifteenth day, at a late hour, after I had lain down to sleep, I heard my door open very softly, and saw a woman enter bearing a lighted lantern.

" 'Fear not, my child!' she whispered, reassuringly, 'I am your nurse!'

"And she flung her arms about my neck and, after bathing my face with her tears, exhorted me to put on my clothes at once and follow her. I knew that that woman loved me as dearly as her own soul. I did not hesitate to obey. She helped

24

me dress, and led me down the stairs. At the door of the house stood a chaise drawn by four horses, and with it a coachman and a young boy in traveling clothes, who was holding a man's cloak and hat in his hand. My nurse embraced me again, and in a voice broken by sobs she said:

" 'Here, my child and my mistress, lies your one road to freedom and safety. This is my son. He will accompany you to a place of security, and will be your most faithful servant, as I would be myself. For the present, I cannot tell you more: our time is precious. You must hear the rest from him!'

"She draped the cloak about me, put the hat on my head, and helped me into the calèche.

"We drove so rapidly that we reached Garigliano in a few hours. The next day we were in Rome and the third day in Florence. But we did not halt either by night or by day till we reached Padua, where I begged leave to rest. However, my companion was unwilling to stop more than a night.

"I had learned from him how my nurse had succeeded in eluding the vigilance of the guards that wicked woman had placed about me; how my stepmother had resolved to let me languish in that prison (an ancient family castle, situated three miles from Naples) till I consented to marry the monster she had chosen for me; and how she had been lured to that choice by a promise he had made to pay her an exorbitant sum in exchange for a fief that belonged to me by inheritance from my mother.

"I learned, moreover, the whole career of that revolting libertine, who, despite his many grandeurs, had not found a woman who did not refuse his hand, and this not solely because of the deformity of his body, but even more because of the deformity of his soul. I felt, therefore, as though I had been saved from a shipwreck, or from an earthquake, and I thanked Providence from the bottom of my heart. But neither I nor my companion knew which way to turn to assure my freedom and security. He had already given me a gold purse and a jewel case that had belonged to my mother and which my unhappy father had saved, I know not how, and given to my nurse for me, not only acquiescing in her plans, but imploring her to do what she did to liberate me. But such riches were calculated rather to betray than to hide my identity. To sojourn in Padua seemed to me dangerous, so we decided to go to Venice, where the custom of wearing masks was very common and it would be easier for me to stay in hiding.

"As a greater precaution I secured a man's coat, and took passage on the usual packet from Padua. There were only three passengers that day: two women of lowly appearance, and a gentleman who, from the titles the boatmen gave him, I perceived to be a nobleman. His manners were distinguished, his person pleasing. I feigned illness, talked very little, and kept my face covered in such a way that it could not be clearly seen. In spite of this, we had not been two hours together before he suspected my sex, and frankly told me so. My blushes, and the embarrassment I could not manage to conceal, increased his suspicions, and encouraged him to greater boldness. He had, however, the discretion to speak softly, that the two women who were present might not overhear what he said. Finding no way to defend myself, I begged him to hold his peace and promised him that, on my arrival in Venice, I would appease his curiosity, at least in part. Among other things he gave me to understand that he was of the noble Mocenigo family, one of the first in Venice. On our arrival in that city he would have it that he should attend me to an inn, where, persuaded by certain favorable appearances, and even more by the need I felt of a person of importance to rely on in the circumstances in which I found myself, I at once related to him a part, and a few days later, the rest, of my adventures. Within the week our relation had become a mixture of friendship and passion. I was not in love, but I was beginning to be. He had wit, vivacity, good manners. Thinking that I had fallen into good hands, I had no hesitation in allowing my companion to return to Gaeta where he had left a wife he loved dearly, and three children.

"Then I rented this little place and continued living here always in strictest retirement. However I was not without some anxieties. Mocenigo observed this and one day remarked:

" 'I see that you are not at your ease: you would be, I am sure, if you became my wife. I am ready to make you that whenever it may be your pleasure!'

"He had passed majority and was absolute master of himself. I asked for time to consider my answer, though his proposal was not unwelcome to me.

"One evening he called on me at an unusual hour, and asked me for a hundred sequins, which he was to return the following day. I did not hesitate to give them to him. At that time not the slightest suspicion had crossed my mind. He did not cease his visits, but for several days he did not mention the subject of the money. One morning he sent one of his servants with a note, and asked me for another hundred. I still had a number of Spanish doubloons, in addition to the casket of jewels, which I believe to be of no small value. Having no pressing need for the sum, I sent him the second hundred.

"I began, however, to suspect that the poor cavalier might have, in common with almost all Venetian noblemen, the vice of gambling. I frankly stated my thought to him and he confessed. I further gathered that he had sustained huge losses that Carnival season, which he was not finding it easy to cover. True, he promised me to give up gambling; but I soon perceived that his promises were those of all inveterate gamblers. His visits were no longer as frequent, nor as prolonged, as formerly in the first days. He would sit melancholy and pensive, and ever found ready excuses to evade going out with me, though he knew that I never left my house under any circumstances without him. To this conduct on his part I owe the pleasure of your acquaintance. He was to have been at the same café where you were, the evening of our first meeting. You are very like him in dress and figure, and were in addition in mask. That was why my boatman made the mistake, and brought you, in his stead, to my gondola.

"Intent on his gambling, Mocenigo continued to neglect me. I knew the resorts he frequented and went to see him. I then judged it prudent to server all relations with him. Whether he were enamored of some other woman, or whether he were so absorbed in his play that no room was left in his heart for another passion, it seemed that his love had not only cooled, but was almost dead. He readily acceded to my decision, and went to the country for a time. It was then that I sent for you; but on learning that you had left Venice, I almost gave up hope of seeing you again. Now here you are with me. You have heard my story and my present situation. If your heart is free (which at your age does not seem likely), if you have the courage to leave your native land, if the beautiful things you said to me the first time we met are true, I make gift to you of myself, and of all I possess—which I judge may be quite sufficient to permit us to live decorously in any part of the world. The question is only to find a country where my freedom will be secured. I would have no fears for my safety, so long as I should be with you."

However alluring so generous an offer may have appeared to me, I had not the courage to accept it without previous reflection. I asked her for three days only in which to decide, a surcease she seemed to accord not without some irritation and bad humor. It was as though the unhappy girl had an inward presentiment of the tragic fate that was hanging over her head. I remained with her two hours. Returning home, I fought a little battle of jealousy with my mistress, passing the remainder of the night in thought and meditation.

It was difficult to say which of the two women was the

more beautiful, though they were as different one from the other as could be imagined. The Venetian girl was *petite*, delicate, the picture of grace—a complexion white as snow, with two soft languorous eyes, and two charming dimples on cheeks that were like fresh blown roses, all the lines in her figure regular! She had no great education so far as mind was concerned: but she was blessed with such charm of manner, and with such vivacity of speech, that not only did she weave her way into one's heart, but fairly bewitched everyone.

The other was a tall girl, rather than not, with a majestic carriage that inspired awe. A brunette, with eyes and hair almost black, she could not boast very regular lines, yet so well did they harmonize as to form a whole marvelously beautiful and pleasing: and these beauties were animated by the charms of a cultivated mind, a purse of doubloons, and a casket of diamonds which she was not reluctant to show me!

I had therefore a furious struggle with myself. My heart was more inclined toward the Venetian girl—I had loved her longer than the other. But good sense was declaring itself for the Neapolitan—she too was supremely pleasing to me, and I judged I should be happier with her.

While I was still vacillating and undecided in my choice, a jealous outburst on the part of the Venetian caused me to decide for the other. Not three, but eight days, had passed since my return to the capital. I did not fail to go several times a day to visit Matilda, and I remained with her one evening somewhat later than usual.

"My dear Da Ponte," she said to me as I was leaving, "enough of this: either tomorrow we leave Venice or I go to a convent!" I swore I would satisfy her the next day—tell her, that is, what I thought of doing.

At home I found the devil let loose. Angela met me stiletto in hand, bent I really could not say whether on killing me or herself. I managed to disarm her, but the episode filled me

MEMOIRS

with horror. I broke the weapon and withdrew to my room.
She appeared there a moment later and peace was made. She,
thereupon, went off to bed; but I left the house again and went
to the Neapolitan's, resolved to depart with her, suggesting
Geneva or London as our refuge.

It had not yet struck two in the morning.

I pounded and kicked at the door several times before anyone came to open. At last an old woman, who lived with her as
maid, came down and told me, with much weeping, how, just
after I had left, a sergeant of the Inquisitors of State, accompanied by several guards, had routed the unhappy girl from bed,
seized all her trunks, and carried her off to a gondola.

My grief knew no bounds. The mystery in which that diabolical tribunal cloaked its barbarous and despotic sentences,
and the terror its awful judgments inspired generally in Venice,
caused me not only to despair of being able to aid her in any
way, but even of ever discovering what had become of her.

I could not help feeling that in some way I had contributed
to her misfortune with my unjustified hesitation, and the
thought sharpened my sorrow and remorse. I had to bow, however, to the right of the stronger and content myself with
shedding a few tears over the cruel fate of that delightful girl,
of whom for twelve continuous years I was unable to learn
anything. It was the Chevalier Foscarini,[16] ambassador of the
Republic at the Court of the Emperor of Germany who, on
hearing this little anecdote from my lips, told me, after many
reciprocal exclamations of astonishment, how Matilda had
been shut up in the Convent of the *Convertite* at the insistence of her persecutrix; how he, Foscarini, had known her intimately; and how, at length, he succeeded in getting her out of
the convent after six years imprisonment, and in sending her

16. Sebastiano Foscarini was Venetian ambassador at Vienna from 1781 to 1785.
Nic., 269, Mol., I, 23.

30

back to her father, who, on the death of his wife, had resumed his post as head of his family.

This rival gone I immediately returned to my first ties which for two whole years were stronger and more dangerous than ever. The lady I loved was continually agitated by a passion for gambling. Her brother, an insolent, overbearing, headstrong youth, was, to our fatal misfortune, even more vicious than she. I humored his failings now out of courtesy, and now for lack of better to do. In that way I too gradually became a gambler. No one of us three was rich, and soon we lost all our money. Then we began to borrow, now selling, now pawning, till we had stripped our wardrobes bare. Still flourishing in those days in Venice was the famous gambling house known commonly as the *Pubblico Ridotto*—or "Resort," where wealthy noblemen alone enjoyed the privilege of playing to unlimited stakes with their own money, and the poor, for a certain consideration, with the money of others (with the money, to be more exact, of numerous fat-pursed descendants of Abraham). Thither we three repaired every evening, and from thence every evening we returned home, cursing cards and the man who invented them. The establishment was open only during Carnival. The last day of that season had come, and we had no money, nor the means of procuring any. At the urge of vicious habit, and even more of that fallacious hope which ever animates the gambler, we pawned or sold such clothes as were left us, and scraped together ten sequins; then to the *Ridotto* we went and in a twinkling had lost them too. Our state of mind as we quitted that room can be imagined. We walked in sullen silence toward the place where we were accustomed to take a gondola every night. The gondolier knew me—I had treated him to handsome gratuities several times. Remarking our silence and bad temper, he divined what had happened and asked me whether I were in need of money. Taking the question as a jest, I replied, likewise jesting, that I needed fifty sequins. He looked at me, smiling, and without adding a word, rowed for a few moments, singing, then stopped at the ferry landing at the Prisons. There he left the gondola, but returned in a few minutes and placed fifty sequins in my hands, muttering between his teeth:

"Go, play your cards, and learn to know Venetian boatmen better!"

My astonishment knew no bounds. At sight of so much money, so overpowering temptation grew that it left me no time for certain reflections which, from a sense of delicacy, I would have made at any other time. We returned forthwith to the *Ridotto*. Entering the first room I picked up a card and approaching one of the banks laid half of the money I possessed on that card. I doubled my money. Then I went on to many other banks, playing for more than half an hour with such constant good luck that I shortly found myself laden with gold. I dragged my companion to the stairs, hurried down with her, ran to the gondola, and, having returned the gondolier's money and given him a fine present, bade him row us home.

I had hardly emptied my pockets and heaped all that money together on the table when we heard a knock at the door. It was my lady's brother! At sight of the money, he uttered a shriek of joy, swooped down upon it with Barnabot talons and took full possession, pocketing part of it without more ado and tying the remainder up in two handkerchiefs.

The following dialogue then passed between us:

"You won this money at cards?"

"Yes, Excellency!"

"Have you counted it?"

"No, Excellency!"

"Would you like to double it?"

"Yes, Excellency!"

"I am going to open bank at the *Ridotto*—don't worry about the outcome!"

"No, Excellency!"

This "no" was not altogether clear; so he added, gritting his teeth, which were of enormous size:

" 'Yes, Excellency! No, Excellency!'—Do you want to, or do you not?"

"Yes, Excellency! Yes, Excellency!"

Of what use could "no" of mine have been?

"Very well then: take my sister with you and follow me."

"Yes, Excellency!"

"Don't be late!"

"No, Excellency!"

This said, he was off down the stairs, and I followed after with his sister, scratching my head and cursing His Yes-Excellency, the Book of Gold, and the whole quarter of Saint Barnabas.

Arriving at the *Ridotto*, he spread all the money out on one of the tables and began to shuffle a pack of cards. Immediately a goodly number of gamblers came running up, among them not a few of the same who had lost to me a short time before. Aware of my connection with the fellow, they divined what had happened at a glance, and were straightway seized one and all with a mad lust to win back their gold. It was already past midnight, and all the other bankers had laid down their cards. The play therefore was desperate. During the first two cuts, Fortune was most favorable to the man. A pile of gold was rising before him. I was sitting to one side of him, and his sister on the other. We did not dare speak, but with eyes, hands, and feet, we signaled him to stop playing. To no purpose! He opened a third cut, but did not finish. Along toward the middle, all my gold had vanished! He laid down his cards with amazing coolness, looked at me, guffawed, shook his head; then taking his sister by the hand, bade me good night and departed.

My feelings need not be described. I made my way to the

"Chamber of Sighs" (a certain room, so called, at the *Ridotto*, whither lovers, or unlucky gamblers were wont to go to pass their time in conversation, moaning, or slumber). After some time I too fell asleep. I did not awake till broad daylight. All the company had departed save only a few who like myself had spent the night there.

A man in a mask who was seated beside me, on seeing me awake, asked me for two *soldi*. After ransacking my pockets in vain, I thrust my hand into the side pouch in my coat, and what was my surprise and joy to find in it a number of gold coins, which had been crammed deep under a handkerchief and covered. I was not aware of having them and had not pulled them out with the others on emptying my pockets on the arrival home of His Hangman-Excellency. I could hardly master my joyous confusion. Having no smaller coin, however, I offered my neighbor one of those sequins. He refused it at first, but then, looking at me fixedly, he said:

"I will take it, but with the proviso that you permit me to return it to you in my home."

Thus speaking, he drew a playing card and, on the back, noted the street and the number of his residence, assuring me, as he handed me the card, that I would not regret paying him a visit. At that time my head was full of the money I had saved, and fuller still of my mistress. I stuck the card carelessly into a pocket, and ran home at top speed.

The woman was at a window, waiting for me. She beckoned to me not to knock, came down immediately, opened the door, put out her head, and, without letting me utter a word, commanded: "Go to the café nearby, and do not come until I send for you." She locked the door and went back to her window. I did not know what to think of all this. I went to the café. After I had waited two hours, the servant appeared, motioned to me to step outside, and to follow him.

He led me to a narrow out-of-the-way street, at the end of

which my lady was awaiting me. We entered a gondola; whereupon she burst into a storm of sobs and tears. I could not imagine why, for all that.

"If you are mourning for the money we lost, console yourself," I told her.

"No, no," she interrupted. "I am weeping for my cruel fate. I am weeping for the wickedness of my brother. He forbids me absolutely to see you anymore, and much less will he let you live with us. The treacherous rogue thinks he can no longer bleed you to any great extent, having already got all you have. He is planning to bring into our house a rascal with money. What is worse, the man is your implacable enemy."

Supposing that all those tears were genuine, and solicitous to relieve her distress, I let fall a handful of clinking sequins into her lap. A little smile at once swept over her face and her joy increased as the money before her grew.

I told her the story of the two *soldi*: we counted, with a joy which may be imagined, one hundred and seven sequins; and after many reciprocal congratulations, we began devising ways to put them to the most profitable use with her brother—that metal alone had the virtue of bridling that unconscionable ass. It occurred to us to make him think that I had a secret for making gold; and this the sister succeeded admirably in doing. (The joke, however, came near to costing me my life, as we shall shortly see.)

His Excellency had already given orders to the servant to sell my bed—the one piece of furniture so far left me by his unrestrained greed—and to give him the money he would receive for it. The servant, however, was kindlier disposed toward me than toward him, and pawned it, instead, and gave him back six sequins. With these he had gone out to gamble. Knowing the house which he frequented I repaired thence with all speed and began to play at a table near him. He did not greet me when I entered. I placed several sequins on the table and pretended not to be aware of his presence. The sight of my money aroused his interest. He greeted me at once with sorrowful tenderness, shook my hand, and smiled. A few minutes later he asked me quietly for ten sequins: instead I gave him twenty, with which he had the good fortune to win fifty. He was beside himself with pleasure. He offered to return the twenty I lent him; but I urged him to keep them, as coins that brought him luck. The play at an end, we went out together and turned into the street that led to his house. He made a thousand apologies for the money he had lost the night before and asked a thousand questions about the money that had miraculously remained to me. I assured him that I cared nothing about my loss, and that, if he would be discreet and never press me on things I could not confide to him, I would always have a sequin or two at his disposal. He embraced me cordially, vowed that he would never dare ask me any secret; and, requesting me to wait a few moments in the shop of a certain bookseller where I often went, he hurried home, told his sister no end of fine things, ordered her to redeem the bed, and then returned to fetch me. Those coins had indeed a lucky charm. He played for several weeks, always winning; though what he gained in gambling, he squandered in short order on a hundred other vices of which His Excellency was a veritable storehouse. For some time, accordingly, I had neither quarrels nor disputes with him. All was peace in the family; and what is stranger still, both I and my lady gambled with prodigious luck, which somewhat increased, or at least did not diminish, our little treasury.

But I must not omit here a little story which, extraordinary as it may appear, is nevertheless just as true as all the others narrated in these Memoirs.

The first Sunday in Lent, in removing some papers from my clothes, I came upon the playing card which the man in the mask had given me at the *Ridotto*. As I had nothing in particular on my mind, curiosity impelled me to go to his house and see the end of that story. Arrived at the address noted, I judged that the exterior gave no great promise of any important adventure. I knocked several times before the door was opened. At last a rope was pulled, the door swung open, and I went up to the second floor. There I knocked on another door, which was opened in the same manner. As I entered the room within I heard a voice requesting me to be seated and to wait a few moments. Eventually there issued from a study at the side an old gentleman whom I thought I had seen before. He was dressed decently enough. His countenance, of aspect venerable, had an expression of exquisite gentleness, and the musical tone of his voice filled the heart with a sense of actual pleasure. He greeted me courteously, took me by the hand and led me from that room, in which there were only two chairs and an old table, to a little study lined with books on its four walls and decorated with notable attractiveness.

He showed me to a seat on a sofa where he too sat down; and still holding my hand in his, addressed me as follows:

"I thank you, my kind young man, for the favor you do me today in calling on me, and I hope that, if possible, your visit may prove a source of pleasure to both of us."

I was about to reply to his compliments, but he interrupted me, begging me to listen to him in silence and beginning again in this fashion:

"I am getting old, as you see. A few days since, I completed my seventy-eighth year. In the natural order of events, I have not much longer to live: but before quitting this world, I should like to put the finishing touches to a task which for many years has absorbed all my interest and concern. On you I have cast my eyes for the completion of the labors in question."

"On me?"

"Yes, on you: but do not interrupt me. If we except the burden of my years and my anxiety of heart as regards this desire

37

of mine, my situation is as fortunate as may be. Do not measure it by the two *soldi* I begged of you at the *Ridotto* and from the appearance of this house! I am rich. I am healthy in mind and in body. I have neither debts, nor regrets. And since I wish you to be fully informed before making your decision, I must tell you what I was, in days gone by, and what I am at present.

"I come from Leghorn. My father, a rich merchant of that city, died and left me, at the age of twenty-two, sole heir to the goodly fortune of fifty thousand *scudi*. From this far-sighted and benevolent father I had previously received an excellent education—I studied in the best boarding school in Florence. I thought of devoting myself, for an avocation, to medicine; but the necessity of carrying on my father's business, at least for a time, transferred me in spite of myself from school to counting house. In four years' time I perceived that I had entered on a most stormy sea. On the impulses of a kindly and compassionate heart I allowed myself to be drawn into lending, entrusting, or indeed giving my monies, to anyone who chose to take advantage of my inexperience; and at the end of the fifth year the inheritance left me by my father scarcely sufficed to pay the debts I had contracted through my imprudent course. I paid them one and all; but from that moment I conceived an insurmountable aversion to any sort of business, and if not to all men exactly, at least to any intercourse with them; for, in my days of duress, I failed to find in any one of them the meager comfort of pity, not to speak of gratitude.[17] So, secretly, I abandoned Leghorn, went to Bologna, and two months later to Venice. A few days after my arrival hither, I was attacked by a slow fever which, little by little devouring me, finally reduced me to the extreme of misery. Friendless, without clothes to cover me, without money, I saw myself constrained, in order

---

17. An excellent portrait of myself! —L. Da P.

to sustain a life which I firmly believed could not long endure me, to go out and beg alms.

"I was prosperous in this new profession. For three or four months continuous, I would return home each evening with ten, twenty, thirty, *lire* in my pocket—a sum twice, thrice greater than I needed for my living. In spite of that, I was minded several times to give up a manner of life which did not seem worthy of an honest soul; but fear of falling again into new troubles through my same goodness of heart, and, even more, uncertainty as to the occupation to which I should apply myself, held me to it for forty-seven unbroken years, in the long course of which I not only recovered my health, but improved my fiber through frugal living, constant watchfulness, and bodily exercise. Arrived at the age of fifty, the largess of my benefactors had so increased, that I found myself possessed of ten thousand ducats, not counting eight thousand more, which I expended on my frugal sustenance, on a collection of books not unrespectable, and in alms which I dispensed through my confessor to many poor more needy of succor than myself.

"I was tempted at that time to return to Leghorn, whither a certain affection for the ashes of my fathers attracted me; but I could not persuade myself to leave Venice, where I had found so much charity toward the poor; and much less a certain young lady I will speak of in due time.

"You must know that, shortly after my arrival in this city, I took modest lodgings in the house of a widow, with whom I lived over the term of twenty-two years. When I first met her, this woman had only one child—a little girl a few months old. She remained a virtuous woman in her lot of poverty, and that was enough to warm my heart toward her. But the baby girl, whom for several years I was wont to treat with the affectionate intimacy of a father, grew up imperceptibly before my eyes, and at her fourteenth year was not only a woman, but a prodigy of wit and beauty. Her mother gave her the usual female

39

upbringing, and I trained her, for my own diversion, in letters. She was twelve when I began. You cannot imagine the progress she made! At seventeen, she could write with some grace both in prose and in verse.

"I was not made of stone. I fell so passionately enamored of her that I could no longer live without her. There was a difference of almost thirty-five years in our ages: but this disparity did not suffice to moderate, let alone extinguish, my passion. One evening, being all alone with the mother, I told her in full my story, which she knew only in part, and asked her whether she would consent to give me her daughter as a wife.

" 'May God forbid,' she replied, 'that ever I should deny you anything in my power to bestow. May you be as happy with my Lisetta, sir, as she most certainly will be happy with you.'

"These few words said everything. She immediately called the girl who, being an obedient and well-behaved miss, replied calmly that she was disposed to do whatever should be pleasing to her loving mother; and a few days thereafter I married her.

"Whereupon, I rented this little house where for sixteen years I experienced all the bliss of which living man is capable in this world. After that space, a long and painful illness robbed me of my wife, who left me, as the comfort of my old age, only one little girl. This child is the work begun by me, the work which, before I die, I long to complete by assuring—as far as I can—her happiness. She deserves it. She is a good girl, not ignorant, and to my eyes beautiful—in such a matter my father's love may be deceiving me. Look at her, judge of it: I will then proceed."

With which words he left the room, almost immediately to return, leading by the hand his daughter who looked, in truth, an angel.

After the usual bows, made in silence, we resumed our seats: "And here, Annetta," the old man continued, "is the person of whom I spoke to you, and whom I offer you in marriage if he is satisfied with you."

The surprise of this adventure had all but completely robbed me of my powers of speech. Seeing that I made no reply he added:

"Come with me! I am going to loosen your restive tongue!"

And, thus speaking, he took me by the hand and led me into a third room; where, opening a great iron chest, he said:

"Now, I am going to show you what down to this moment *nec oculus vidit, nec manus tetigit.*"

There flashed before my eyes in divers boxes without tops countless gold pieces of various coinage, and among them one, the largest, in which was naught but sequins.

"Here," said he, "are five thousand sequins, that will be yours the day you marry my daughter. Then, on my death or before, if need arise, you shall have another four thousand, which is all that I possess: but I want you to promise always to remember the poor. I believe you are capable of that. I have been observing you for two years. Your person attracted me the moment I saw you. My good will and my esteem for you grew with the repeated acts of charity you showed toward me, there on the steps of the Ponte San Giorgio, where I have been sitting for some years now, and where you pass every day. The alms you gave me seemed to me a marvelous thing in view of your circumstances and caused me to believe your heart the image of that charity which for me is the sum of all the virtues and the soul of true religion."

Great had been my astonishment, but it grew by leaps when I discovered that my name, my studies, and my past experiences, were known to him, and even my adventures with the lady I loved, and her brother. One may well imagine how embarrassed I was to make answer. Aside from the amorous passion which was then in possession of me and prevented me from accepting an offer which could but appear, in every respect, advantageous, there was another and greater obstacle though I chose not to disclose it to him. However, his generous offer deserved a frank reply, even at the risk of hurting. I therefore answered:

"Sir, the weight of the treasure you offer me I feel in the living tissue of my heart: but it is not God's will that I should be the possessor of it. Since I can return your kindness in no other way, I shall at least reward it with a sincere confession which can not offend you. I must tell you straightforwardly that I am not in a position to marry."

The good old man sat silent a few moments, then he added this simple comment:

"I am sorry for your sake, my dear child."

I stayed with him and with his daughter the remainder of the day, both of them overwhelming me with courtesies and favors, and both manifesting in word and manner a spirit worthy of honoring rather *regum turres* than *pauperum tabernas*.

But I was so much enamored of the other lady that the sacrifice of this fortune for her sake seemed nothing at all to me. It was not long before I perceived the great mistake I had made in refusing the offer. I repented of it, but too late. A few months later that charming girl married a young Venetian lad, who went into commerce with his father in Vienna. I saw them both frequently and intimately later on during my sojourn in that capital.

I returned home somewhat late that evening to find my *amica* in the clutches of a thousand furies. In her accesses of jealousy she had a brutal temper. As I appeared at the door of her room, she did not speak, but flung a bottle of ink at me. With a natural gesture to shield my face I threw up my hand, but the fragments of glass that pierced it inflicted such wounds that for more than a month I was unable to make any use of it. Not content with this—though at sight of the blood that gushed out from my cuts she seemed both placated and sorrowful—the she-devil came to my room that night while I was sleeping, and with one snip of the scissors clipped off all the hair that curled down about my neck: an operation she performed so dexterously that I was not aware until the following morning that my Delilah had made of me a second Samson. Her purpose therein was to prevent me from stirring from the house, in which purpose—*Vedi se Amor m'avea tolto il cervello!*—I was so blind as to content her.

The complaisance cost me dear. A Venetian noblewoman had engaged me as tutor to her two young sons, paying me handsomely and treating me as a friend. The state I was in prevented me for some days from going to her house. Put out at that, she came to call on me personally, and shrewd and perspicacious as she was, saw the people I was living with, and a day later dismissed me.

The loss of this post was fatal to me in point both of reputation and of interest. The jealousy of that woman was passing all bounds. I could leave the house only at night and went always in her company, now to the theaters or public spectacles, now to dinners in society, spending a great deal and never earning anything. In this fashion our not excessive resources dwindled and Fortune had turned her back on us at cards. That brother of hers had also begun again to milk my purse and to disturb my peace of mind. One evening, having lost all his money, he strode into my room in menacing demeanor and demanded, *armata manu*, one hundred sequins. On my assuring him that I did not possess such a sum, he replied:

"Make it, then! I know very well, milord Lorenzo, that you know how to make gold: I demand therefore, and think I have a right to demand, that you give me the secret."

To tame the bear I was obliged to give him every penny I had, and to promise that within four or five days I would produce the hundred sequins. However I was beginning to open my eyes, and see the danger I was in of ruining my public reputation beyond repair. My wise and loving brother, to whom I was bound by chains, I know not whether more of friendship or of nature, frequently strove to rouse me from my lethargy; but I was too violently beset of my twin passions of cards and love: and however clear my perception of the evil impending, yet I had not the strength to free myself of them.

A strange occurrence at last effected what neither a brother's advice nor a thousand dangers and misadventures had been able to effect over three whole years.[18] A priest from Friuli,[19] who had been a schoolmate of mine in the seminary at Portogruaro and who frequented my rooms in all intimacy, came to see me one evening, as he was in the habit of doing whenever he needed a supper, or a dinner, as was very often the case. We passed several hours together in amiable conversation, and, supper finished, he departed. A few minutes later, desiring to go out myself, and the night being cold and rainy, I asked the servant for my cloak. I myself had put it as usual on a chair that stood near the stairs, and no one, except the priest, had been in the house that day.

But the cloak had disappeared! I could not suppose that he had stolen it; and at this juncture my brother arrived and began hunting with me in every nook and corner of the house. Our servant was shrewder than I, and had no great liking for the priest. He finally said, laughing:

"You want your cloak? I'll find your cloak!"

And thus speaking he went out of the house. In a few moments he was back, calling:

"Don't worry—your cloak is all right and in a very safe place. The Abbé pawned it for eighty *lire* at the shop next door."

The news astounded me. I would have sworn I was dream-

---

18. An exaggeration: it was at the most a year; resigning at Portogruaro in 1773. Da P. was at Treviso in 1774. Nic., 269.

19. Unidentified but for F——ri, below.

ing. My brother went out with the servant and got the cloak on paying the amount of the pledge. The dear boy brought it to me with tears in his eyes and said only this:

"See, dear Lorenzo, to what a pass our passions bring us!"

Pressing matters prevented him from remaining longer with me; and left to myself I began to consider the situation seriously.

"How can it be," I said to myself, "that the principles of religion, of education, of honor, are not enough to restrain a man possessed of passions, and to keep him, if not from licentious enjoyment, at least from acts that are branded with social infamy? A man enters my house under guise of hospitality and friendship. Yet he can be blind to the point of stealing a cloak from his comrade, benefactor, and friend! And what drives him to that? Cards and women!"

As those two words drifted across my mind I shook with fear from head to foot, and then and there made praiseworthy resolve to abandon cards, mistress, and—above all—that very, very dangerous metropolis. Losing not a second, I seized pen and wrote my brother these few lines:

> Girolamo:
>
> No more gambling, no more women, no more Venice! I would leave tonight if I had money. But I take oath not to stay here three days longer. Let us thank God and the poor thief! I will see you in the morning!

I sent the letter by the servant: but my brother, instead of waiting for the morrow, came at once to see me, and after an affectionate embrace, drew out his purse and gave me all the money he possessed. It was sufficient both for the moment's need and to put me in a position to depart from that city.

This was not the first nor the only act of brotherly affection which that angelic youth performed for me. His death, which

snatched him from me at the unripe age of thirty,[20] robbed me
of comrade, counselor, and friend—traits, as a rule, so rare and
so difficult to find in a brother. To such great merits he added a
splendid mind, a vast erudition, and an exquisite taste in all
forms of Italian letters, qualities which combined with a mature wisdom, an amazing modesty and rare urbanity of manner, earned for him the love and admiration of his fellows. I
have never ceased to mourn his irreparable loss. I shall never
mourn it enough. Forgive, courteous reader, this little digres-
sion, and lend your sympathy to this tribute of tears and of
gratitude that I so deservedly pay to the honored memory of a
brother so dear.

To go back to our priest! The dawn of the following
morning had not yet broken, when I received a letter in this
vein:

> Dear Friend:
>
> Last evening I committed an unworthy act. I stole
> your cloak and pawned it for eighty *lire*. The worst of it
> is, I then gambled and lost the money. I am in despair.
> I would send you my own, but it is old, frayed at the
> edges, too short for you, and not just what you need in
> this weather. [It was in fact a tattered affair in camelot,
> that seemed to have been designed as a scarecrow or a
> watchdog.] You, however, need a coat. What can I do? I
> will do anything you say.
>
> Yours devotedly, F——ri.

The letter made me laugh. I left the house at once, and

---

20. Girolamo, born in 1752, must have died some eight years later—about
1783. Of his writings an operatic libretto and a translation into Latin survive.
March., 465.

went to see him. But as I appeared in his room, he saw that I had my cloak on. He gasped in astonishment and, without saying a word, gave me a terrified glance, dashed out into the street, and began running like mad. I followed. He chanced to enter an alley that ended in a canal, and, there on the edge, was about to jump into the water—perhaps he never seriously intended to do so. In any case I overtook him and was in time to prevent the catastrophe. But instead of rebuking him, I calmly repeated what my brother had just been saying to me: "See to what a pass our passions bring us!"

This poor fellow was in the grip of these. My leniency touched him deeply. He could not refrain from tears, nor I from weeping with him. I embraced him, bade him be of good cheer, and promised him never to mention cloaks again, if he, for his part, would promise me to leave Venice. He did so. I gave him some money, and he went away. Not lacking in intelligence and energy, he applied himself earnestly to study and not many years later obtained a chair of letters in the seminary of C——a, and thereafter the curacy of a wealthy parish. There, in devout commemoration of that lucky cloak, as I was afterwards told, he clothed *aere proprio* every year, a certain number of the destitute.

The example of that unhappy youth strengthened me again in my salutary resolve to remove myself from that dangerous city. Happy me, had I had the courage to do the same on all other occasions in which my soul was rent by great passions, as I must surely have done, *si mens non læva fuisset*, had I always kept before my eyes the fortunate effects of that virtuous resolve. Neither the prayers, nor the tears, nor the threats, of that woman were able at that time to detain me.

I went to Ceneda; and ten days had not passed before Providence crowned, so to speak, my victory.

Two posts in letters chancing to be vacant at that moment in the seminary at Treviso, a noble and cultivated city of the

Venetian State, they were offered to me and my brother.[21] We both accepted with rejoicing. He renounced an important position as secretary in an illustrious Venetian family for the sole pleasure of being near me. It is not easy to describe my joy when I perceived that I was free from my chains of shame—for such mine were, in truth! She, who for three years continuous had held me bound and whom I continued to love madly, even at that distance, threw herself, a few days after my departure, into the arms of a new lover; nor did she shrink from jeopardizing my life at the hands of my wicked rival, in order to convince him by that act that she had ceased to love me.

The lady was in the habit of writing to me every day from Venice, omitting in her letters neither artifice nor phrases calculated, as she believed, to persuade me of her tenderness and constancy.

On New Year's day she wrote me as follows:

> Lorenzo:
>
> If you love my honor and my life, come to Venice at once. About ten o'clock in the evening you will find me at my cousin's.
>
> Your faithful love.

On reading this missive, I rushed without delay to the post, took a carriage, and went to Mestre. The excessive cold of that year had frozen the Lagunes and it was only at cost of much money and trouble that I succeeded in having a channel opened

---

21. October 1774, by Monsignor Paolo Francesco Giustiniani. A priest of Ceneda challenged the election on moral grounds. It was revoked. But Da P. managed to clear his traces, and became "master of humanities" at a salary of 217 *lire* a year, and Girolamo, master of "lower grammar" with 155 *lire* a year. March., 31.

for me between Mestre and Venice by four young and sturdy gondoliers. It was almost midnight when I landed on the *riva* of the palace where my Origille was. The palace portal was closed. As I raised my hand to the knocker, I felt another hand fall upon me, and, pulling violently at the cloak in which I was muffled, drag me by main force some steps away. At the same time I heard a hoarse voice whispering:

"*Sior paronsin, no andè là drento, per carità!*"

It was my old servant whom, on quitting Venice, I had left to that treacherous woman and whom I succeeded in recognizing in the light of the street lamps, or rather by the sound of his voice. Not leaving me time to answer, he continued dragging me with him until we reached the other end of the bridge, at the foot of which the palace indicated in my letter was situated. When at last he judged he was in a safe place, he said to me with shaking voice:

"I must tell you that your little lady has a new lover—a certain Dondorologi,[22] a Venetian gentleman too, but one of the most arrogant and dangerous bullies in Venice. Knowing that the *paronzina* had been in love with you, he pretended jealousy for some time; and though she swore she had ceased to love you, he refused to be persuaded unless she promised him to have you come by night to Venice. Then, when you came and entered her house, he would, to use the words he used, 'break your bones with a club!'"

Needless to describe my stupefaction on listening to such a tale. After struggling a little with that good servant and with the proper admonitions of prudence, my jealousy, anger, and spite drove me half mad with rage to the woman's house, determined to avenge myself *aut certæ occumbere morti*. That poor old man followed to lend what aid he could. But I was

---

22. Unidentified.

well enough supplied with courage and with weapons to defend myself, single-handed, from any assassin.

I knock. The door is opened from above, as someone pulls a cord attached to the bolt. Cautiously I climb a flight of stairs lighted by the feeble flicker of an old lantern. Entering the vestibule, I see that perfidious creature just issuing from her cousin's room. She was alone. Toward twelve o'clock that evening, as I afterwards learned from my servant, the new lover, who added gambling to his other vices, *impatiens moræ*, had grown bored with the long wait for me and gone out. But on catching sight of me again, that unworthy female uttered a cry of affected joy and ran forward to throw her arms about me. The indecent attire in which she appeared before me, and even more that fresh act of brazenness, redoubled my rage. I threw her off impetuously, uttering these prophetic words:

"May the hand of God destroy such a race of rascals!"

Then I ran down the stairs at breakneck speed, like a man escaping from a great danger, rushed to the nearest landing, took a gondola, returned to Mestre and thence to Treviso, and with the most steadfast will never to see or hear of that woman again. It was as if at that point a ray of light from Heaven had descended on my mind to illumine my reason and cure me entirely.

Thus my liberated soul began anew to wander among the sweet and delightful fields of the Muses. It had, to tell the truth, every opportunity and the most noble incitements: a beautiful and copious library which I had the leisure and authority to set in order and to enrich with all those books which, in my estimation, seemed desirable; a town (the town of Trento and Riccati—is that not enough?) abounding in gifted and discerning minds, who inspired others to holy and noble emulation; a selected number of young men full of vivacity and talent, and fired with love of renown; a bishop wise and magnanimous and devoted to his school; a brilliant society, friendly to letters and to *literati*; a climate which, with its cool pure air, its smiling landscape, seemed to prompt the fancy, and fill the poet with divine fire—all this formed for more than two years the truest happiness of my life.

I spent all my time between my dear brother and Giulio Trento, a scholar of endless reading, sound judgment, and exquisite taste, to whose kindly and penetrating criticism, no less than to his gay familiarity and to his well-earned reputation among the learned, I owe most of the success of my literary efforts at Treviso. The *Cechino*, a novelette in octaves, which I recited before an academy founded in that city at that time,[23] greatly increased my fame as a poet and the good opinion my Bishop and that region had of me. My reader will not be displeased to find it reprinted in these Memoirs.[24]

At the beginning of the scholastic year we were promoted, both my brother and I, to more responsible posts.[25] This unexpected promotion hurt the vanity of other teachers of that institution, who thought that they should have been preferred to us by virtue of imaginary rights. They were mistaken. Though not destitute of erudition and scholarship, they were utterly deficient in that genius and good taste which are the soul of letters and which, if not supplied by nature, are acquired with the greatest difficulty and rarely at that. And good taste in letters—I venture to say quite frankly—was for the first time represented in that seminary by my brother and by me. For forty years our methods have been followed, our rules adopted, our authors read, though the names of these were unknown to

23. By the historian, Rambaldo degli Azzoni—the Academy of the *Solleciti*, and a "colony" of Arcadia. March., 39.

24. In the appendix of the edition of 1830. The *Cechino*, a charming idyll in verse, remains among the best of Da P.'s poetry.

25. Da P. became "master of rhetoric" with 279 *lire* annually, Girolamo rising to the post Lorenzo had vacated, becoming also "master of the Gregorian Chant." March., 48–9.

professors of that institute when we came to Treviso. From that period date the great events and the strange vicissitudes of my life, and I was pushed from that point into a career quite different from the one to which by habits, circumstances, and past studies, I believed myself destined.

It was incumbent upon me as professor of Italian and Latin literature to have the pupils under my instruction recite on the last day of the scholastic year, compositions written by me on some scientific theme.[26] The one I chose that year was, to my misfortune, the following: whether mankind had attained happiness by uniting in a social system, or could be considered happier in a simple state of nature. The theme itself, and especially the manner in which I treated it, through the dense ignorance of my judges and the evil interpretations of my rivals, appeared—or at least was made to appear—scandalous, unwise, and contrary to the good order and peace of society. The heads of the educational *Riformatori* were especially turned, men who had more need of being reformed than morals and sense to reform with. It was they who brought the matter before the Senate which, for the first time, saw fit to usurp executive form and prerogative, and give to a poetic caprice—my exercise was nothing more or less than that—the semblance of an important public matter. The day for the debate was solemnly designated. My relatives and friends, especially the Messrs. Giustiniani, to whose illustrious family the Bishop of Treviso belonged, advised me to go to Venice to defend myself.

A few days after my arrival in that capital I had the fortune to make the acquaintance of Bernardo Memmo, one of the

---

26. Aug. 1, 1776. The sensation caused in Venice by this "commencement," followed by Da P.'s trial before the Senate and his expulsion from teaching, was even greater than he describes here. Monsignor Giustiniani was publicly censured, the censor Rovigo reprimanded, and a general investigation of "radicalism [i.e. democratic liberalism] in Venetian schools" ordered.

most prominent and learned citizens of that Republic. He listened to my story and promised to help me. He at once procured for me the support of Gasparo Gozzi, the outstanding literary man of those days who stood in good favor with the *Riformatori* of that year, and was their actual Counselor. At the suggestion of Memmo I sent him my ill-starred poems and addressed to him the well-known epistle—*Gozzi, se un cor gentil*, etc.

My writings made an excellent impression on the noble spirit of that great writer. He spoke warmly of them, though his words had no other effect than to supply fresh reasons for my chastisement.

"This young man," said Gozzi, "has ability: he ought to be encouraged."

"So much the worse," rejoined the *Riformatori*: "we must deprive him of the means of becoming dangerous."

This was their pretext for covering the hatred and hostility they felt toward the Giustiniani family, to which, as I have just said, the Bishop of Treviso belonged, and him they thought they could humiliate by humiliating me. Several years before, one of the Bishop's brothers had spoken effectively in the Senate against a professor at Padua, because of certain antipapal writings published by the latter; and they designed to get revenge by depriving me of the chair of letters in the seminary of Treviso, just as their protégé had lost his professorship at Padua. So in the unhappy days of that moribund Republic were ability and innocence oppressed, now for vengeance, now for mere caprice, the seductive and fallacious eloquence of the minority betraying the majority into erroneous judgment, so that, either loyal through baseness or compliant through ignorance, the latter became the tools and the mainsprings of despots.

Meanwhile the afternoon fixed for the senatorial debate arrived. Memmo and Zaguri, with a few others, who might have been able to defend me out of plain love of justice, either impressed by the statements and prestige of my adversaries, or else believing that the very nature of the charges against me would be sufficient to acquit me, did not deem it wise or necessary to speak. A very forceful orator, the Procurator Morosini,[27] attacked me, and at the same time, the two Public *Revisori*, whose function it was, *ex officio*, to prohibit or permit the publication of my theses. The ecclesiastical *Revisore* was a monk, whom Barbarigo, an indefatigable defender of the cowl, loved and favored *usque ad aras et ulterius*. Barbarigo undertook his defense, joining meantime with Morosini in denouncing me, and seeing, or thinking he saw, that sentiment was on his side, he read in stentorian tones a Latin elegy, which must have been but vaguely understood by those worthy Pantaloons, but which, declaimed energetically with a dressing of invective and sarcasm, served marvelously to arouse those ill-humored pigtails against me. "The American in Europe" was the title of the elegy: *Ergo ego semotæ tactus telluris amore*, etc.

After reading these Latin verses, of which the Most Serene Venetian Senate heard much, understood little, and knew nothing at all, the shrewd cripple read one of my *sermoni*, which, being in Italian, must have proved more intelligible to them: "Man, by Nature Free, becomes a Slave through Laws." Unimaginable the tumult that arose in the assembly at the reading of that poetic skit, composed by me for no other reason (as indeed were all the other compositions of that scholastic entertainment) than to supply practice for a certain number of my pupils in the art of declamation. I had, in fact, refuted it in the opposing thesis written on Cicero's well-known adage: *Servi legum facti sumus, ut liberi esse possemus*. That, however, my accuser did not take the trouble to read.

---

27. Francesco Lorenzo Morosini (1714–1793), Da P.'s "hunchback," became Procurator of Saint Mark in 1755. Pietro Barbarigo, the "cripple," was counsel to the Holy Office in Venice.

"Listen, Your Excellencies," cried the dishonest orator in a loud voice, "listen attentively to the scandalous principles of this young man, and then judge of what answer you must make."

And here he repeated several passages of that poem, among others the following, which was more emphatically disapproved and hissed than the others:

"Subject and slave through error of mortal men, once I feel the weight of chains whose jingle the sane man hears from afar, I fear no longer the fasces of consul or the threatening frown of censor. I embrace in one glance the king on his throne and the ragged beggar on the street to whom, at times, I toss a worthless coin that he may pay his crossing to the Ferryman of the Stygian swamp. The chatter of those Lords who proudly lift their gilded horns on high seems the light breath of a nascent zephyr; and while worshipful throngs pay them homage, I, self-possessed, lift calm eyes upon the clouds to follow some passing crane or, mayhap, some winged Hippogriff, or now lower them to gaze reflectively at the marble statues of Pasquino and Marforio."

The greater part of those poor wearers of the toga thought they saw in the "golden horns" I ridiculed, the little horn of the Doge's cap, and unable to endure the horrible profanation, voted against me with one general cry. The great verdict was then announced: the two *Revisori* were declared *uno ore* innocent, and I alone guilty and deserving of punishment. (Memmo came running to give me news of everything.)

However, a suitable punishment for my crime had not yet been voted—that responsibility was left to the Reformers themselves.[28] The importance attached to the affair by my

---

28. Inexact. The Senate itself voted Da P.'s expulsion from teaching and the disbarment was comprehensive. The fact that he taught privately later on was an item in the indictment of banishment. If he was called before the Reformers the sentence was also read to him publicly in Treviso by Zuanne Moro, *podestà* of that city. March., *loc. cit.*

adversaries, and the dazzling apparel given the prosecution of a public senatorial trial, led many people to think that the aristocratic majesty I had offended could be appeased only by the complete sacrifice of my liberty or of my life.

My brothers and my friends wished me to evade the thunderbolt by flight. But I laughed at them and at their fears. I could not believe that they would proceed with severe punishments after having beaten so many drums to make an effect. Venetian policy never barked when it intended to bite.

I was not mistaken. My punishment, if such it may be called, was as light as it was ridiculous. Summoned to appear, after several days, before a court of the Reformers, my sentence was read to me by the secretary. It was couched in the following terms:

"Your name?"

"Lorenzo Da Ponte."

"Where born?"

"Ceneda."

"Lorenzo Da Ponte of Ceneda: by order and decree of the Most Excellent Senate, you are enjoined never to exercise again in any school, college, seminary, or university of the Most Serene Venetian Domain the functions of professor, reader, preceptor, proctor, instructor, etc. etc. the which, under pain of the Sovereign displeasure. *Vade.*"

I bowed my head, pressed my hand and my handkerchief to my lips to keep from laughing, and went out.

On the stairs of the Ducal palace I met my brother and Memmo. A pallor of death was spread over their faces, but the smile that flashed on mine reassured them.

Memmo had been State Inquisitor many times and knew the laws and policies of his country thoroughly. He waxed ecstatic at my recital of the affair and from his lips dropped the words: *Parturient montes....* But then, laying a finger across his two lips, he embraced me and led me home. We passed the remainder of that day in carousals and feastings, at the expense of the Reformers and their *Vade*. Toward evening, we emerged and went to call on Zaguri, who was I do not know whether more pleased or surprised.

The same evening[29] Memmo offered me a dignified refuge in his house where I passed several months amid the delights of hospitality and philosophy. I was introduced at this time by my two benevolent patrons to the most cultivated and distinguished citizens of the Republic, by whom, through the notoriety of my adventures and even more perhaps because of the prestige of my sponsors, I was graciously received and made much of. I was not conscious of my recent misfortune. So far as literary recognition and financial prosperity were concerned, I had everything that could gratify an eager spirit. Memmo's purse was open to all my reasonable needs, which he was ever anticipating with a rare generosity. I was meeting no one but men illustrious in letters and in rank. The beauties of Venice vied in showering praises and favors upon me; they were all eager to see me, all eager to hear my verses; and they all blamed the hunchback, the cripple, the Reformers, the Senate, and their sentences.

It was in those days that, having had occasion to meet various extemporizers celebrated in Italy, among them the Abbé Lorenzi, Monsignor Stratico, and Altanesi,[30] I too tried my hand

---

29. Dec. 10, 1776. Bernardo Memmo, born in 1730, brother of the more famous Andrea Memmo, Goldoni's friend. He was still living in 1798. The Teresa, mentioned below, was a certain Teresa Zerbin, daughter of a workman in the Arsenal. The husband was Marco Ferro, whom she married in 1777. After his death she loaded all her family on Memmo's shoulders, and rewarded him with two more children. Nic., 271, following Aldo Ravà.

30. Bartolommeo Lorenzi (1732–1822); Bishop Giandomenico Stratico (1732–99); Gian Francesco Altanesi (?–1783). Nic., 271.

at improvising and my brother likewise. We both succeeded well enough to be listened to with some amusement. We became generally known as the "Extemporizers of Ceneda."

This facility, almost peculiar to Italians, for reciting or singing *ex tempore* in good verse on any subject whatever and in any meter, should be sufficient to show how poetical and in every way estimable our language must be judged, since, with its graces, its melodies, its richness of phrase, it offers instruments for saying *ex abrupto* things which are written with difficulty by versemakers of other languages even after long study and meditation: things not only charming and most deserving of being listened to and praised, but calculated to delight, surprise, and fire the minds of those who hear them; as people who have had the good fortune to hear the incomparable Gianni and Dal Mollo, or even the Corilla woman, la Bandettini,[31] and a few other celebrated *improvvisatrici*, well know. This new talent, which I developed so unexpectedly, immensely increased Memmo's good will toward me and, therewith, his desire to help me. But this affection of his all but caused my ruin.

This famous man, who, in family station, in knowledge, and in greatness of spirit, had not perhaps his equal in the Republic, kept in his house a young lady who, with no great distinction whether of beauty or mind, was mistress of all that shrewdness and artifice of which a wicked woman may dispose. She had gained a tyrannical ascendancy over Memmo's will, and made him vassal absolute of a blind passion. Vainly would one have striven to open his eyes.

For three or four months I was lucky enough not to displease this girl. However, Memmo was in the habit of spending many hours with me, reading or discussing. He was also going

---

31. Francesco Gianni (1760–1822); Corilla Olimpica (1727–1800); Dal Mollo (?–?); Teresa Bandettini (1743–1813). Nic., 271.

out more frequently than had formerly been his custom. Through me, in a word, he had more numerous demands on his time, which gave more freedom to the girl and greater leisure to amuse herself to her own liking. As my bad luck would have it, the girl fell in love with a young man whom, at first, Memmo was inclined to like. And he was planning, in fact, to make him her husband.

For reasons that need not be mentioned, Memmo soon began to dislike the young man, to such a degree that not only did he drive him from the house, but commanded the girl to have nothing further to do with him. But she loved the boy desperately, and submitted to this prohibition most unwillingly. After trying all avenues and all her usual artifices to move Memmo from his resolve, she induced me, by stress of tears, to use my influence on her behalf.

My efforts were not fruitless. That very day the lover appeared in the house, escorted thither by Memmo himself and by me. To the great rejoicing of the household a marriage was arranged, the terms settled, and the date fixed. After our supper, which was uncommonly gay, I went as usual to Memmo's rooms, which were on the second floor of the house, adjoining mine. We passed several hours in pleasant philosophical conversation. When the hour for retiring came, Memmo clasped me to his heart and bade me good night in these words:

"A peaceful sleep to you tonight, Da Ponte. This day you have wrought Teresa's happiness." (Such the name of that base woman.)

The door of my room was near the stairs: betaking myself thither on tiptoe in order not to disturb those who had retired, I became aware of whispering voices, a murmur of hushed words coming from the foot of the stairs. Halting to hear who was speaking, I recognized the voices of the two lovers. The deep silence pervading the house at that moment enabled me to hear their every word distinctly.

"Da Ponte," the man was saying, "has too much influence over the master. He is a danger to us in this house. See how he made him change his mind on a point on which you as well as your mother and all our friends found him inflexible."

"If you feel that way," replied the treacherous girl, "I will attend to getting him out of the house in short order."

I need not describe my impression on hearing these words. My bewilderment robbed me for some moments of power to speak or stir. At last I went on to my room half in a stupor, and quite beside myself. I could not decide what I had better do. I passed the remainder of the night in a tumult of conflicting thoughts. In the morning I entered Memmo's apartment, and elected to tell him calmly what I had heard that night.

"You dreamed that, my dear Da Ponte," that kindly gentleman replied coldly.

We spent some time together without further reference again to what had occurred. At last we were called to breakfast, and then Memmo began to see that the matter was not a dream. We went down to the first floor where the young girl lived with her family. She did not look at me, nor return my greeting; and she failed to offer chocolate to me, although she did serve the others. Memmo gave me his own cup and left the room.

I followed him. We went out of the house together. But neither he nor I made any allusion to the little episode. He was, however, very moody. We returned home for dinner, during which the girl conducted herself toward me exactly as she had in the morning. There were more guests than usual. Memmo fumed—and I more than he.

"Why don't you serve Da Ponte?" he said at last, aloud.

"He has two hands of his own and two of yours to serve him—he can have no particular need of mine."

Knowing that the blood was boiling in my veins like a Vesuvius, I could not trust my self-control. I rose from the table, went to my rooms, and, taking a few clothes with me, ran to the landing where a packet left every evening for Padua. There I embarked.[32]

I had only ten scudi when I left Venice. On paying the expenses of my journey, which I made partly by stage, I had only six left. My anguish of spirit may easily be imagined. At one blow, through the ingratitude of two treacherous ingrates, I had lost a benefactor, a protector, a friend, and—I will say so frankly—a master; and with him, many future hopes which the kindness of that true gentleman had aroused in me. I could furthermore foresee the miserable state of indigence into which I must very soon be plunged. I had a brother in Padua who was about to finish his studies in that university; but that good young man was more in need of receiving help than of giving it.

I hoped, to be sure, I would have a friend in the city to whom I could confide my misfortunes, and be certain of some assistance, but in that man too I was deceived. He was a priest from Dalmatia[33] whom I had met at Memmo's. Memmo was very fond of him. Through the patronage of a certain lady he had obtained a post as professor of canon law in the University of Padua. The man knew very little Latin and had left in Memmo's hands an oration which he was to deliver as an introduction to his course before the numerous students and his fellow professors at Padua. Memmo gave it to me to read and I, in all honesty, was obliged to tell him that I found it very badly written. Memmo was greatly distressed and told his candidate what I had said. The man, to his good fortune, was neither vain nor obstinate. He, too, believed that he wrote rather badly in a diction not pure enough. He had not read Cicero for thirty years, and he had forgotten Erasmus and

32. March or April 1777. Nic., 271.

33. Unidentified.

Cæsar, while playing the *cavalier servente* in Venice. For the rest, he felt that his oration, so far as material went, was a fine one. However, he would be obliged to leave for Padua three days later. Noting Memmo's interest in him, I offered to recast his discourse, rewriting it as to style, a task which I managed to perform within the sole space of twenty-four hours. He went to Padua, delivered his oration, and garnered praises and honors for it. One could hardly guess in what terms he thanked me, both orally and in letters, and how many promises and avowals of an eternal gratitude he made both to Memmo and to me.

I thought, therefore, of paying him a visit, and of asking him for some aid in my unhappy situation, telling him of my experience with that woman whom he knew perfectly well. I was in high spirits and went to his house; but as I knocked on the door I raised my eyes toward the windows as was natural to do, and saw hastily vanishing a head which I took to be that of the good priest.

After a slight delay, the door was opened by a servant who, to my request to see the professor, replied, not without embarrassment, that the *Signor Professore* was not at home.

Doubting that I had been mistaken, and to make sure of what I had seen, I withdrew a distance from the house and began stealthily to watch whether he would come out. I knew that it would soon be time for him to go to the university. In fact, it was not long before he appeared. I went up to him at once and said to him only these words:

"I thank you, *Signor Abate*, for giving me this opportunity of knowing you."

This said, I turned away; but, taking me violently by the hem of my coat, he murmured a thousand excuses, which, however, in my judgment more and more evidently revealed his ingratitude and his truly vile soul; wherefore, disengaging myself of him, I departed. I had written to Memmo the moment I arrived in Padua: and he had informed this man of everything, recommending me to him. But neither that gentleman's recommendations, nor the fresh memory of my services, operated on the stony Dalmatian in such guise as to render him human, let alone generous and grateful. It was his fear of seeing himself held up to scorn that induced him to make courteous offers which he doubtless hoped I would decline, and which in fact I dared to decline consistently. He remembered that he had left the original of his barbaric oration in my hands, and seeing me in a fury, trembled lest I publish it. I remarked his fear, sent him his manuscript the following day, and never saw him again. He wrote the story to Memmo in his own way, but could not refrain from confessing his fears in these words:

> Da Ponte made me a greater gift in restoring my manuscript to me than in recasting it. I would willingly have paid him fifty sequins to have it back again.

But, instead of avenging myself by publishing a document that would have dishonored him forever, I sent it back to him of my own accord, without even being asked for it, satisfied to punish with a generosity that confounded him, a baseness and an ingratitude without parallel. The manner, however, in which he had received me, forewarned me to keep my poverty hidden from all. I strove, on the contrary, to offer an appearance of prosperity and wealth, and, so far as in me lay, I did so.

Some days after my departure, Memmo was kind enough to send me the few clothes I had left in his house. I was therefore able to present myself in decent attire in the cafés and public resorts of that city, where every day I showed myself neat, and faultlessly groomed. I divided into fifty parts the fifty *lire* of that country (a guinea), intending that they should last me for fifty days, and hoping meanwhile that *dii meliora ferant*. I had

63

therefore one *lira*, that is twenty Venetian *soldi* a day to spend: eight *soldi* I paid for a bed, and five for a cup of coffee every morning; seven being left me for my daily sustenance. I had the fortitude to feed myself for forty-two days continuous on bread and certain blackish olives which, being rich of salt, increased my thirst for water. Thus did I hide, not only from others but from my brother, the harsh deprivations of my more than poetic parsimony.

The which came to a fortunate end through a strange little incident. A youth who had great opinion of himself as a player at draughts stuck up a manifesto in a coffee shop challenging all comers. I thought myself inferior to no one in that game, and decided, therefore, to risk a test. I had my offer imparted to him and he accepted, fixing the sum of money to be played for and the number of games. I had money to pay only for the first, had I lost. Since, however, I won, we continued playing and I won in short order the twelve matches agreed upon, ten of them for double stakes. He paid me twenty-two piastres on the spot, and admitted his inferiority.

Several youths of the university, who had watched the matches, and thinking perhaps of avenging their friend by winning back his money from me, suggested to me a game of *ombre*. According to customs in that town, it would have been discourteous to refuse. It behooved me therefore to accept, however much against my will. But I had the good luck to win even at that game; and before midnight had struck, I returned home, with a good supper to my credit and thirty-six piastres in my pocket. This unexpected reversal of fortunes seemed to me of happy omen for the future. I continued to play for a number of days, winning invariably. But this manner of life was not to my liking. It is true that I had occasion thercat to converse frequently with the most notable personages and with the most brilliant minds of that city, especially with the incomparable Cesarotti, to whom I had been endeared I know not whether more by Memmo's commendations or by some of my verse. But though I had found in Fortune's favor what the pity of man had denied me, nevertheless remembering my past experiences and desiring to follow more honorable paths, I resolved suddenly to depart from Padua and to return to Venice. Caterino Mazzolà,[34] a learned and graceful poet, the first perhaps to succeed in writing a good musical comedy and with whom I had formed ties of close friendship in Memmo's house, insisted on taking me back to that gentleman at once. Two things I had learned from him: the one, that the young rogue in question had been driven anew from the house a few days after my departure; and the other, that the perfidious female had slandered me to Memmo, persuading him that I had fallen enamored of her, and that only to cure me had she treated me in that fashion; whereupon Memmo had marvelously commended "her wisdom and virtue and lamented the weakness of his poor friend, Da Ponte." I could hear of such a villainous imputation only with rage and flamed at once with anxiety to undeceive him. I went most willingly, therefore, to pay him a visit.

I was received by him and by Teresa as well, not so much with courtesy, as with joy. That very day he offered me both board and lodging, which I refused to accept. I went frequently to visit him, however, and he came to my house. In a few days our intimacy was renewed, and more cordial than ever. The estimable Zaguri[35] welcomed me with like joy, chose me as his private secretary and as his companion in studies. Many blissful hours I passed with him. He was a gentleman

---

34. We shall meet Mazzolà again in Part Two.

35. Pietro Antonio Zaguri (1733–1805), a Venetian gentleman, who held a few public offices and wasted his patrimony, outstanding in the gay life in Venice between the '70s and the fall of the Republic. He introduced Casanova to Da P. Mol., II, v–ix.

distinguished by great and versatile learning, a good poet, a good orator, and a man of taste, fired with a love for good letters, more generous than rich, and friendly more to others than to himself. He it was who presented me to the famous Giorgio Pisani, who was the Gracchus of Venice in those days, and of whom I shall have more fulsome occasion to speak in my story. The latter saw fit to entrust to me the whole education of his children, a charge I willingly assumed. I therefore saw myself, at one blow, favored and protected by three most notable and powerful individuals, who vied with one another in offering me friendship and kindnesses. I composed few verses in those days, because the occupations of my double employment, and perhaps even more the pleasurable distractions of that city—too well suited to my years and to the inclinations of my temperament—left me little leisure for writing. Moreover I was frequently, at the insistence of my friends, exercising myself at improvisation which had then become the fashion. I must confess that I found such practice quite incompatible with written verse; and it must seem a surprising thing that among the many sublime geniuses who speak or sing most beautiful verses *ex tempore*, there should be very few who do not fall into the mediocre the moment they turn to writing.

Meanwhile I seized an opportunity to undeceive Memmo as to the things that unjust girl had caused him to believe of me. I had touched on the matter several times previously with much frankness; but, he being obstinate in his credulousness, we all but came to a fresh rupture. He asked me one day—and it was the first and the last time in his life—whether I knew with whom I was speaking. This was an expression that Venetian gentlemen had commonly on their lips. "Yes," I answered; and I added that "I should have been neither so free nor so frank, had I not known." He caught my meaning, threw his arms about me, and thanked me.

"In that case," I then continued, "you must allow me to convince you; and that I shall do, if you promise me not to say a word of it to your Teresa."

"Very well," he replied, "convince me, if you can. I will promise to say nothing."

I set myself, accordingly, to the task. The girl was ardently passionate; but, as usual with women of her kind, she would change the object of her interest with the greatest volubility. She soon consoled herself for her lost lover and cast eyes on a certain youth who was frequenting the house on familiar terms, and who, being without any gifts of fortune, seemed disposed to correct that deficiency by marrying a woman of wealth, paying little regard to other requisites. Becoming aware of this situation, I aimed to make friends with him, and he, seeing my intimacy with Memmo, met me more than half way.

Shortly he unbosomed himself to me and begged my assistance. I promised him everything, on condition that he obtain from Teresa a sincere confession of the calumnies she had laid against me, and so maneuver that she herself should impart the truth to the misled chevalier. This he easily obtained from her, since she knew she could do anything with impunity with a man already blind.

One day I chanced to enter that gentleman's room just as the girl was discussing the matter with him.

"Come," said he to me, laughing, "I have discovered the truth and I am glad of it, both for your sake and mine. For your sake, because now in my eyes you are worthier than ever of my friendship and esteem; for mine, because I feel that Teresa loves me so much that she could not in any way endure a rival in my heart, even though he were one of masculine sex. She thought, poor little girl, that I loved you more than her. Fear of that caused her to be unjust: we must forgive her." "No, no, *Teresa mia*," the good-hearted soul then added, all tenderness, "I do not love, I have not loved, and I shall never love, anyone

67

more than you." Saying which, he took her hand, kissed her on the forehead a hundred times, and shed a few tears; and she— *asciugavagli gli occhi col bel velo!*

This passion, this blindness, this fanaticism endured ineradicable in that excellent man and eminent philosopher to the day of his death. A few months later on, Teresa married her new suitor in Memmo's house: she became the mother of several children, in Memmo's house: she was left a widow and found consolation in Memmo's arms; and, just as before her marriage, so in her married life, her widowhood, her old age, she was sole and absolute mistress of his property,[36] his will, his heart, his every thought! What a lesson for our poor humanity!

But let us go back to my story!

At this juncture, accordingly, I was loved of women, esteemed of men, blandished by patrons. The future lay bright before me. For some time I lived in this manner in perfect tranquillity. Even my enemies seemed to have fallen asleep, or to be no longer concerning themselves with me. But the fair season was not long to endure. My evil star would have it that the uncorruptible honesty of Giorgio Pisani and his profound knowledge of the laws of Venice and of the Venetian constitution which he thought should be reestablished—I was assisting

---

36. This gentleman had placed some hundreds of silver coins in his own wardrobe and had counted them over himself in my presence and that of a certain Muti at the time he locked the drawer. A few days later he took out a few—twenty, if I remember correctly, and again locked the chest with a key. Three days had not passed when, on opening it for twenty more, he found at least a hundred missing. Muti was again present and so was I. He could not recover from his astonishment. "But they are gone!" said I. "No doubt of it!" said Memmo. The good-natured Muti, a gentleman and a philosopher and a friend of Memmo's, remarked: "I am not greatly surprised. There are many pairs of hands about the house!" "Silence, wagging tongue!" commanded Memmo. "I shall sooner say I took them myself, than these good people!" The father of those "good people" had been turnkey in a prison, the mother a scullion! —L. Da P.

him not a little with my work and my studies—should arouse first the jealousy and then the alarm of all those whose names were synonymous with greatness and power in Venice. These long plotted his ruin in vain. His formidable eloquence and above all his unimpeachable integrity had won for him such a following among the nobility that he outweighed, if not in wealth and offices, at least in numbers, the party of the powerful and the wealthy. These turned on me the first thunderbolts of their revenge.

People began to say that it was strange that a man of my character and principles, author of "American Elegies," ridiculer of pig-tailed aristocrats and of Ducal horns, should be daring, in contempt of the Senate and its decrees, to offer instruction—therewith instilling the dogmas of a dangerous doctrine—to the sons of a man who seemed to have been born for naught else than to oppose the party of the *grandi*, who, to the exclusion of the majority, wished to be sole rulers in the Republic. While this tacit and virtually hidden fire was being fanned to my damage, there suddenly became generally known, through the indiscretion of a few people, a sonnet which my devotion to Pisani, and even more my love for my country, had wrung from my pen on an occasion when, in an election for a most important office, one of the most servile henchmen of the so-called *grandi* had been preferred to him.

There, O lords of Venetia, you have the true reason for my banishment from my country! *Veritas odium parit!* What I said was not only true. It was prophetic!

> Se 'l fosse anco el Pisani un impostor,
> un prepotente, un ladro, un lecamone,
> se 'l stasse co le bestie buzarone.
> col Bafo in man per so legislator;
> se 'l gavesse anca lu, come ga el sior,
> cento bardasse al fianco e cento done,

> perdio tute ste cosse saria bone
> per volerlo in Venezia avogador, etc.

(If Pisani, too, were an impostor—Bully, thief, whore-
monger,—If he stood with the crowd of strumpeteers
—With Baffo in hand for his books of laws;—If he had,
as has Milord, a hundred tarts, a hundred sluts, then verily, who could help but have him as a Venetian *avo-
gador*? etc.)

This sonnet, being written in the Venetian dialect, could be
read by everybody, and in a few days it was the talk of cafés,
assemblies, and dinner tables—anyone who has ever encountered Venetian aristocracy may imagine the noise such a lampoon would arouse.

It was well enjoyed, and this intensified the rage and the
anger of those gentlemen. The ladies who liked Pisani and me
learned my lines by heart, despite the togas, the wigs, and the
aristocratic poses of their husbands, declaimed them for their
own amusement and, amid peals of laughter, repeated the pi-
quant passages to such as would feel their sting most sharply.

Unable, for the moment, to beat the horse, they found here
a pretext for belaboring the saddle. Accusations and accusers
were sought and easily found. One rascal who frequented a certain house where I went at times, volunteered to bring various
charges against me before the Magistracy of Blasphemy. He said
I had eaten ham on a Friday (he had eaten it with me!), and that
on a number of Sundays I had failed to go to Mass (he had not
been to Mass in his whole life). I learned of the two indictments
from the very person who presided over that tribunal, and who
was the first to advise me to leave Venice without delay.[37]

---

37. Da P. has made a grave omission here. Having been diplomatically warned by
the Chief Magistrate of the Court of Blasphemy, he must have known that the

"If these accusations are not sufficient," said that gentleman, who was a good friend of mine, "they will find others. They want you guilty, and guilty they will have you."

My friends and relatives then concluded that my liberty, and perhaps my life, were in danger. A nobleman, Giovanni da Lezze, in whose house my brother was living as secretary, and even more as friend, urged me to retire to one of his country places where he offered me a safe retreat until the storm should blow over.

But I could no longer enjoy a country so unjust both toward Pisani and toward me, so blind to its true interests and so near, in fact, to its collapse. I resolved to leave Venice forever. I went to call on my three patrons and on a few other friends, who listened to my decision and approved it with tears in their eyes. Then I abandoned my ungrateful country, and went to Gorizia.

---

principal item in his prosecution was the Bellaudi incident, of which he will give his version much later in the Mem. (III, 262) in recounting his second expulsion from Venice (this time at the hands of the Austrians). Da P. was deeply compromised, in appearances at least, in the life of the underworld in Venice.

PART TWO

GORIZIA IS A noble, ancient, and cultivated city of German Friuli, situated on the banks of the Lisonzo, a few miles—twelve, I should say—from Venetian Friuli.

I arrived there on the first day of September in the year 1777[1]—before attaining my twenty-ninth year, that is. Since I did not know anyone in that city and had brought no letters of introduction, I went straight to the first inn I found, carrying under my arm a bundle which comprised part of a suit, a few undergarments, a tiny Horace (which I carried with me thirty years, lost later in London, and recovered some time ago in Philadelphia), a Dante which I had scribbled with notes, and an old Petrarch.

So much baggage did not dismay the mistress of the inn. Scarcely had I entered, than she came toward me, gave me an expressive glance, which foretold what was to happen between

1. Da P. recollects his chronology somewhat confusedly here: he arrived in Gorizia in May or June 1779, and left there on New Year's Day, 1781. Nic., 274.

us, and led me to a good room. She was a young woman, very pretty, fresh, and vivacious beyond all belief. She was dressed in the German style: on her head a cap of gold lace; a Venetian necklace of fine-linked gold encircled at least thirty times a well-rounded throat (it was whiter than alabaster) and, descending in everwidening coils, reached a beautiful breast, which it partly and charmingly hid from view; a well-fitted bodice encased her plump figure with alluring elegance, and silk stockings, that ended in two rose-colored slippers, guided the willing eye to the exquisite shape of a tiny foot.

It was not yet six in the evening; but as I had taken nothing that day save a few sips of wine and a little bread, I decided to order supper. To my misfortune she spoke only German, or perhaps Croatian, and I did not understand a word of what she said to me, nor she of what I said to her. I began to make signs with my hands, pointing to my mouth and my teeth, a language which she took, it seemed, for an amorous declaration. I had an appetite that would have made little of granite. While I was struggling to make her understand that I would like to eat, a maid passed in front of the door of my room with a plate of fried chicken intended for another guest. I dashed upon her with the agility of a cat, seized a leg and second joint and had them down in a second, bones and all, I do believe. At last she understood what I wished, and in a jiffy I saw laid out before me a delicious meal, all the more sweetly and tastefully seasoned by the continued company of my comely hostess. Not being able to speak, we sought to communicate with glances and gestures. When the fruit was brought, she drew from her pocket a little knife with a silver blade, removed the peel of a pear, cut half of it for me, ate the other half herself, then handed the knife to me—and I did likewise.

She drank a small glass of wine with me, and taught me to say *Gesundheit*, and from the movement of the glass I understood that she would have me know that I should drink to her health as she had drunk to mine. Since I did not pronounce the word very well, she had me repeat it twice and thrice, each time filling the glass with cool new wine and emptying it.

I know not whether it were Bacchus or some other divinity that began to warm her blood somewhat; after two good hours of like conversation, a deep flush was coloring her cheeks, and in her eyes shone the fire of voluptuousness. She had become a beauty. She would rise from her seat, stretch herself, gaze at me, sigh, and then sit down again: all this, however, in the presence of two pretty maids, dressed as she was, who had served us all through the meal and our conversation. At last, one of them departed, and shortly the mistress beckoned to the other to withdraw, saying something meantime in German which I did not understand. A second later, the maid came back, left a book, and departed again. When we were alone, my hostess took a seat close to me, began hunting for words in the book, put slips of paper to mark them here and there, and then motioned to me to read. The book was a German-Italian dictionary; from the places indicated I pieced together three words: *Ich liebe Sie*; and I found that they meant "I love you." As the second half of the book was the Italian-German part, I began with the conjunction *and*, and made her reread the same phrase: *Und ich liebe Sie.*

The little scene then became charming indeed: we conversed for at least an hour and a half with the aid of the dictionary, each saying things that seemed destined to end rather seriously. Fortunately a number of carriages drew up at the door. The beautiful innkeeper was obliged to leave against her will and at last I remained alone.

I began to reflect on the strange episode. How is it possible, I said to myself, that in a country ruled by Maria Teresa, a princess so famous for the severity of her laws; in a country where nightly perquisitions are common; where a stranger the moment he arrives must swear in all solemnity, whence he comes, whither he goes, what he is doing; and where he is obliged to give in writing name, surname, birthplace, and so on; in a country in short where the priest, the monk, and the government spy have such unbounded influence—how is it possible, said I, that in the taverns there should be a liberty that can pass in a second into the most scandalous license? Contradiction in everything, even in Governments!

While I was immersed in these reflections, lo, my hostess, all gaiety, entered my room with the same two maids who had assisted at our supper, the latter bearing ices and sweets, of which I must perforce partake in her company; and one of the girls began to sing in voice not displeasing a German song beginning: *Ich liebe einen welschen Mann.* . . .

Calypso and Leucotheë, I thought, and I in the rôle of Telemachus! The song of the German nymph ended, she withdrew with the other maid, and once more I was left alone with the mistress. Telemachus had never more need of his Mentor. But courteous Morpheus was mine. I picked up the dictionary and pointed to the word "sleep." She was discretion itself. She rang the bell. One of the two maids entered, and the hostess, with exquisite tact, withdrew. The maid turned down my coverlet, showed me where the water for washing and for drinking was, and then halted with smiling face, at my side. I did not understand this ceremonial. I thought that she was expecting a tip, and offered a coin, which she refused disdainfully; whereupon, lifting my hand with much grace, she imprinted a kiss upon it, and withdrew.

This little comedy had lasted not less than five hours and entertained me beyond words. But I could not drive from my mind the priests, the monks, Maria Teresa, and all her penal codes: things which I had heard spoken of as one speaks of the Holy Inquisition of Spain.

At last I went to sleep. Arising in the morning later than was my custom, I found in the next room an excellent breakfast, and my hostess awaiting me. By this time I had learned all the principal compliments—"Good morning!" "How are you?" "Did you have a good night?" But no compliment interested that woman save *Ich liebe Sie*!

After breakfast she was obliged to leave me, and I returned to my room to find two or three women waiting for me with baskets filled with divers articles of merchandise which are sold in the taverns to strangers. In two hours I had no less than twenty visits of the sort. And this custom, too, seemed rather strange to me: in a land where morals were watched so rigorously, it was nevertheless very easy, under pretext of selling pins, needles, handkerchiefs, necklaces, ribbons, and similar furbelows, to sell things not to be found in baskets.

I spent ten or twelve days in the woman's tavern. We had daily conversations of four or five hours each, now with dictionary, now with grammar in hand, and almost always on subjects beginning and ending with *Ich liebe Sie*! By that time I found that I had amassed a certain vocabulary, but composed almost wholly of words and phrases of love. It was to be of great service to me in the course of my youthful flirtations in that city and elsewhere. And I also remarked another little matter to which I had given no great thought before, that my purse, namely, was all but empty; for, though I had been spending very little in that tavern, that very little had been sufficient to exhaust the more than very little I had brought with me to Gorizia. That good woman became aware of my approaching embarrassment, and with a generosity rare in persons of her profession, made offers of assistance that touched my heart. One evening, even, she tucked under my pillow a purse containing some gold coins, which I returned to her amid kisses and tears! But I never learned the trade of depleting the purses of women, however often they may have depleted mine. I therefore resolved to leave her tavern. We remained good friends, however, and I continued to cherish sentiments of sincere good will and esteem for her as long as she lived, which was only for the space of seven months, at the end of which time she died, at the age of twenty-two, of an inflammatory fever. Many tears I shed for this beautiful and amiable young woman who deserved to be a princess, rather than keeper of an inn. She was beyond doubt one of the best women I have known in the eighty years of my life. Perhaps had she not died . . . But Death—*fura i migliori e lascia star i rei!*

I therefore changed lodgings, and tried to regain with my lyre what I had spent in travel and in the twelve days I had passed, like Ruggiero and Rinaldo, with the two beautiful fairies of Ariosto and Tasso. The Peace of Teschen having been signed in those days[2] between the Empress and Frederick of Prussia, it occurred to me to write an ode on that subject, and to entitle it "The Joust of the Eagles" in allusion to the ancestral escutcheons of the two Sovereigns. I dedicated it to Count Guido Cobenzl, one of the first lords of Gorizia and of Germany and father of that Cobenzl who had negotiated that peace and finally brought it to pass.

I will quote some verses of my poem here to give an idea of a composition which was from that time the source of all my literary adventures in Germany:

Quell'augel, che a risse e a pugne, etc.

I carried the ode to Cobenzl, who received me gracefully and with the greatest courtesy read it in my presence, and seemed infinitely pleased with it. He had it printed at his expense and scattered many copies of it among the noble families of that city, which were then very numerous. (To form some conception of the rank, antiquity, and number of the illustrious per-

---

2. May 13, 1779. Guidobaldo Cobenzl (1715–1797); his son, Johann Philippe was later minister of foreign affairs and ambassador to France for the Emperor Francis I.

sonages that little town could boast, one must read a little work by Count R. Coronini, entitled the *"Fasti* of Gorizia."] Among such people I found many patrons by whom, after those first verses, I was well and honorably received. Not without a lively sense of gratitude can I recall the names of Strasoldo, Lanthieri, Cobenzl, Attems, Tuns, Coronini, Torriani; nor can I ever praise sufficiently the courtesy and the liberality of those illustrious gentlemen. All vied in bestowing favors and largesses upon me. They liked both me and my verses. Pity for my misadventures moved them to soften in a hundred ways the harshness of my lot, generally forestalling my needs, and doing so with such nobility and tact that my pride could in no way take offense. Happy those cities in which such inhabitants abound! Then poverty itself becomes a font of blessings for the man of breeding who is capable of experiencing the joys of gratitude.

The happiness I experienced in their kindnesses caused me often to bless my past misfortunes. I was living in a little room which I had rented in the house of a grocer. He was as poor as I was, so we got on very well. The modesty of my hovel, however, was no hindrance to the visits constantly paid me. All lovers of the Muses desired to make my acquaintance; some to admire, others, perhaps, to find something for which to criticize me.

A certain Colletti[3] who had once been a corporal, next had turned printer, and was then dreaming of being a poet, could not endure this praise of me without annoyance, and one day publicly asserted that I could not have been the author of the poem on the Peace, for, since that time, though some months had passed, I had not composed another line. The fellow must have been suffering from some poetic itch. Every day there appeared some new elucubration from his bootlessly prolific reed. How then could a poet who was a poet keep silent so long? Another

---

3. Giuseppe de Colletti (1744–1815), a man of some achievement as scholar, publisher, and cultural organizer.

printer in that city—Signor Valerio de' Valeri, who hated him cordially, and had heard him say that thing of me—procured an introduction to me for the sole purpose of retailing it to me, hoping thus to arouse me against the man and engage me in a poetic war which might end by humiliating his rival. At first I laughed and advised that good man to laugh with me also. But he was too hotly incensed against his competitor in typography to acquiesce in my counsel. He continued paying me frequent visits, always droning in my ear the same antiphony; though I could not persuade myself that such a person deserved my resentment.

This Valerio, hearing that I was dissatisfied with my landlord, who had the unpleasant habit of getting drunk, and what was worse, of beating his wife when in that condition—in his cups he was violently jealous of her though she was neither young nor beautiful—graciously offered me a room in his house, and I had not the courage to refuse it. There he treated me with such hospitality and friendship that I thought myself in duty bound to do anything in my power for him.

He desired verses only, and I had none to give him!

"When are we to give our lesson to that crazy dolt?" he asked one day.

Colletti, however, was not only a dolt and a lunatic. To an abysmal ignorance of true poetic taste and a deficiency in all the accoutrements requisite in a man of letters, he added a nauseating vanity and arrogance. He was, moreover, mendacious, fawning, envious, hypocritical, and covered with the veil of Pharisaical devotions extraordinary inclinations toward licentiousness. He missed no occasion to speak ill of me behind my back, while to my face he loaded me with most farfetched adulation. Unable one day longer to refrain from asking me why I did not try to cement my reputation in Gorizia with some "new product of my inspired genius," I replied smiling:

"I will tell you in verse."

And I went home.

Judging that I must be in vein from a tingling which that strange challenge had aroused in me, I shut myself up in my room and wrote *ex abrupto* a burlesque skit in octaves which I presented that very evening to my courteous host, informing him of the amusing scene I had had that morning with our common friend.

Indescribable the joy with which he received the gift and the delight he envinced on reading it. He was not a poet, but neither did he lack that perspicacity necessary for discerning the good from the bad. I had touched moreover certain chords that tickled his ear immeasurably. I did not name anyone in those lines; but Colletti, with other rhymsters of his ilk, could see themselves marvelously portrayed therein. I recall two stanzas that pricked such poor wretches more especially to the quick. They were as follows:

> Dicono che famosi or quinci or quindi
> fatti si son col plettro e colla tromba;
> che lor fama volò da' mori agl'indi,
> che non andranno interi entro la tomba.
> Van per le strade attillatucci e lindi
> per ascoltar se il nome lor rimbomba,
> e, se non parlan gli altri, parlan essi,
> ed al silenzio altrui fan de' processi.
>
> Mi vergogno però ch'in altra forma
> non vedano se stessi e il proprio fallo;
> mi vergogno che Febo o taccia o dorma
> e non gli accoppi il pegaseo cavallo.
> Oh, come è ver ch'orgoglio il ver trasforma
> e mostra spesso all'uom verde per giallo!
> Che lungo un palmo si vedrien gli orecchi,
> se guardasser un dì dentro i miei specchi.

(They say they have made themselves famous, now here, now there, with plectrum and trumpet, that their names are known to Hindu and Moor, that not all of them will descend into the tomb! Prettily cloaked they walk about the streets to catch some boom of their echoing names, and if others fail to talk, they talk themselves, and prosecute the reticence of others.

What shame, alas, that they see not themselves and their faults in other light! What shame that Phœbus should be either speechless or asleep, that he does not slaughter their Pegasean horse! How true it is that pride transforms truth and often shows a man green for yellow. For they would see their ears a fathom long, could they but mirror themselves in me!)

Valerio made haste to publish the little satire from his presses and in a moment it spread broadcast through the town; and my friends, as well as those of my publisher, found it most amusing and made great ado about it. Colletti boiled with rage, but dared not open his mouth, lest he betray his recognition of himself.

"Everyone tells me," he said one day, "that you were driving at me in that poem; but really I do not see the likeness."

The truth was he saw a likeness much closer than I really drew, and he did not fail of his revenge in time.

This trifle, may I add, made me more welcome in the city. Not a day passed that did not bring me some new evidence of generosity and of friendship. Count Coronini asked me to translate his aforementioned "*Fasti* of Gorizia" into Italian verse and paid me well for it.

Eight months I passed in this comfortable and tranquil estate. One thing only embittered in part its sweetness: the thought, to wit, of having been so ill-treated—and without cause whatever—by a land I loved, and to whose real welfare I had been devoting myself. Nor could I fail to note in myself a certain longing to return thither, that I might see my relatives and friends again, above all Zaguri, Memmo, and Pisani.

Just then,[4] a dear friend of mine, Caterino Mazzolà, passed through Gorizia, on his way to Dresden, whither he had been invited as poet to the opera. He came to see me and told me of the tremendous catastrophe of Pisani. After being made Procurator of St. Mark, one of the most exalted offices in the Republic, he was seized at nighttime in his own house by order of the State Inquisitors and confined in the fortress of Verona. Mourning the fate of my friend, I had also to abandon all hope of returning to Venice, and begged Mazzolà to find me, if possible, some post at the Court of Dresden. Mazzolà promised me to do so, and held out good hopes of success, relying much on the favor of Count Marcolini, then Prime Minister to that Elector, whose protection and esteem my friend enjoyed.

Meantime, there came to Gorizia a good company of actors; and my friends and patrons urged me to compose an opera and a tragedy for its use. Never having written for the theater, however, I dared not risk such a venture lest I lose with the buskin what I had gained with the lute. I was obliged, nevertheless, at the instance of a noble lady, my patroness,[5] to make a translation of a German tragedy which was performed for only two evenings, I know not whether through defects of the original or of mine. To atone in part for this failure, I handed the same company "The Count of Warwick," a French tragedy, adapted in part by my brother, and in part by me. This was much better liked.

Society at Gorizia continued its favor to me and I continued my verses which were invariably well received and remunerated. About that time a "colony" of Arcadia, known as the "*Colonia*

4. Sept.–Oct. 1780. Nic., 274. Pisani's arrest, June 1780; his release, 1797; his death, 1811. Mol., I, 53.

5. Madame Lanthieri, née Countess Wagensberg. Nic., 275.

Sonziaca" was organized in Gorizia, whereof Count Guido Cobenzl was president. I, too, was enrolled among his shepherds
under name of "Lesbonico Pegasio." Colletti was a good printer.
He was made secretary of the academy that he might record
and publish its minutes. This created and cemented a sort of
literary partnership between him and me, which he, with great
shrewdness, gradually succeeded in making me believe sincere. I began to deal with him on terms of friendship, if not of
critical esteem, and supposed he had quite forgotten the "ears
a fathom long," and what could be seen in "my mirror." I confided to him, among other things, that I might perchance be
leaving shortly for Dresden; that Mazzolà, whom he had seen
with me, had held out good hopes of that, and that, in short, I
considered the matter a foregone conclusion. He seemed surprised and feigned grief, though I could see that nothing would
have given him greater pleasure. For that matter, I had dropped
the same hint to other people. Some two months later, I received a letter from Dresden, ordering me to betake myself
forthwith to that city in order to fill a distinguished post at the
Court of the Elector. It was not written by Mazzolà, but his
name was signed to it. It was in his handwriting, which I knew
very well. I had no reason to fear treachery on the part of a
friend so loyal who was always more than eager to do me a
good turn. I read the letter to my friends, and having weighed
the advantages, resolved, on their advice, to go to Dresden.

In the course of those last days I was the object of a thousand new testimonials of affection from the ladies and gentlemen of that city. The day before my departure, Count Luigi
Torriani, in whose house I had been residing for some time, invited all his friends to a splendid banquet; after which, it being
gayer than usual, the guests began to play at cards, a thing
which was done once or twice a month in the society of the
city in each house by turns. All the money lost at play was deposited in an earthen jar with a slit large enough to receive the

coins, and was then disposed of, on a certain day fixed in advance, for the amusement of the circle. Chance willed that that should be the last evening of the year, and three motions had to be made to determine the fashion in which the money should be next employed: one by the master of the house, and the others by two ladies drawn by lot. Since our host had to speak last, it remained for the two ladies to be first: one of them suggested a sleigh ride to Gradisca; the other a masquerade on horseback. The good Count then rose, and, after recounting the cause of my departure, moved that the money gathered in the vase be offered me for the expenses of my journey from Gorizia to Dresden. The vote was to be by "yea's" and "nay's."

"Sleigh ride!" called the Count.

A general "nay"!

"Masquerade!"

A "nay" more general and more emphatic than the first!

"Da Ponte to Dresden!"

"Yea! Yea!"

The clamor filled the whole salon.

The Count's wife, rather an angel of goodness than mortal woman, was laying hold on the vase to break it, when other ladies of the company desired to contribute further pieces to it, and their example was followed by all with great glee. When Count Strasoldo, who dropped the last coin, flung the vase to the floor, all those present scrambled about on hands and knees gathering up the money to put it into a beautiful silk handkerchief, which the mistress of the house held in readiness. She was then requested to present me with the gift, herself, and she did so in these words:

> Signor Da Ponte, pray accept this offering from your friends in Gorizia. May you have as much happiness in the land to which you are going as there are riches in

this kerchief. Think of us sometimes, as we shall think
often of you!

I was expected to make some response, but I was so embarrassed, so overcome, by this rare demonstration of kindness, generosity, esteem, and unequivocal good will, that I
could not open my mouth. The Count intervened to thank
that very noble company in my behalf, my silence speaking
in words more eloquent than any I could have found. They understood it, in fact, and my delicacy of sentiment was all the
more appreciated.

All these favors had such an effect upon me that for that
whole night I did nothing but weep at the sole thought of
being about to depart from that city where I had been so well
received by all good people that at times I came even to esteem
myself! At breakfast Count Torriani divined the furious struggle that was going on within me and took me to see Count
Cobenzl again. After renewed consideration, that gentleman
thought I had best set out. He gave me last letters of commen-
dation to his son in Vienna, to the gentleman, that is, who had
concluded the Peace of Teschen with the King of Prussia.

In Vienna I was, in fact, graciously received by that gentleman: he alluded to the ode I had written for him; and on my
departure made me a present of a travel diary to the frontispiece of which he had affixed with a pin a bank note for one
hundred florins, appending below:

"Cobenzl to Da Ponte, for traveling expenses!"

When I arrived in Vienna, Maria Teresa, a princess greatly
beloved in that city, had just died[6] and I found nothing therefore save tears and mourning. I remained accordingly only
three days.

---

6. Five weeks earlier, Nov. 29, 1780.

Arriving at Dresden, I hastened directly to Mazzolà.[7] When he saw me entering his room, he exclaimed in the greatest astonishment:

"Well, well, Da Ponte at Dresden!"

My stupefaction at this welcome may well be imagined! He ran to me with opened arms, but I had strength hardly to open my mouth, to say nothing of responding to his endearments. Noting my silence, he cried:

"Can it be that you have been called to the theater at St. Petersburg?"

"I came to Dresden," I then ventured, "to see my friend Mazzolà, and to profit, if possible, by his friendship."

I made this reply mechanically, hardly aware of what I was saying.

"Fine!" he replied. "You may have arrived in the nick of time!"

He took me to a nearby tavern, where for many hours he remained with me exchanging generalities and never once alluding in the remotest degree to his letter. It was past midnight when he departed. I spent the remainder of the night in a turmoil of thoughts. I could not believe that Mazzolà had intended to trick me. But certain as I was that the signature of that letter was his, I could not help meandering among a thousand hypotheses, without being able to embrace any of them.

I went to see him in the morning, but I succeeded in discovering no more than on the preceding day. Finally I asked him whether he remembered the promise he made me at Gorizia. "I remember very well," he replied, "but so far no opening has presented itself. I wrote you that."

"You wrote me that?" I repeated, in amazement.

"I wrote you that, but assuring you that I would not go

---

7. Caterino Mazzolà (?–1806), a Venetian (Cadore), wrote some seven librettos as poet to the Elector of Saxony and at Vienna. Mol., I, 350–3.

back on my promise. And now it happens that Prince Antonio, brother to our Elector, is looking for a secretary. I had already decided to recommend you to the Prime Minister. I will do so at once and with all the greater pleasure, since you are here."

I spent the rest of the afternoon with him, doing my best to hide my real perplexity. When I reached my room, I took myself in hand and set about disentangling the whole imbroglio again.

"Mazzolà," I said to myself, "wrote me a letter from Dresden which I never received. I did receive another, written in an unknown hand, with the signature of Mazzolà. May not that signature have been forged? But who could do such a thing? Who? Colletti! I had unmasked him in my verses; so long as I stayed in Gorizia I was a constant thorn in his side. Suppose, through some accident or device, Mazzolà's real letter came into his hands! Might he not have imitated the signature and, enclosing a sheet of his own within the fold of the original that bore the seal of the Dresden post, have worked this terrible trick on me?"

I reexamined the letter in question attentively. I thought I could at first detect material differences in the signatures. There were two seals, not one; and the sheet containing the address was of a noticeably different quality of paper from that of the sheet enclosed. It bore, moreover—a highly suspicious fact —the watermark of a stationer in Gorizia! Colletti, furthermore, had favored my departure for Dresden and hastened it in various ways.

I came then and there to the conclusion that Colletti had played me that ugly trick, and down to the present day, I have had no occasion to change my mind.

Providence ordained, however, that it should not have the fatal consequences for me that the man had hoped. It would seem, on the contrary, that my good Fortune had made use of it to lead me into a situation in life wherein I should have found permanent happiness, had not the premature death of a man tardily appreciated and never sufficiently mourned, the Emperor Joseph, I mean, come to destroy, along with the hopes of the world, my own.

Mazzolà did not succeed in obtaining the post at Court for me. Nevertheless I did not depart from Saxony. He treated me with such hospitality, liberality, and friendship, that I had not the courage to go away. I kept clinging to a certain illusory hope that, in time, I must find an opportunity for obtaining some dignified situation. Meanwhile I kept spending almost all my days and most of my evenings with him. He was very busy composing, translating, adapting operas to the needs of that theater which was, at that time, provided with one of the best operatic companies in Europe. In order not to sit with my hands in my lap, I volunteered to assist him in these theatrical labors; and he accepted my help, in a measure. I, too, therefore, began translating, or composing, for his plays, now an aria, now a duet, and now and then even some scene entire which he would first outline for me. At that time I had lying about a work by Philippe Quinault, entitled, if I remember correctly, *Atis et Cybèle*.[8] I thought the part of Sangaride very interestingly and movingly handled, and suggested to him that I translate it for him. I must assume that my version pleased him mightily; for, after trying me with a number of other characterizations, he could not refrain one day from asking me why I did not turn to writing for the Italian opera.

"As you know," I replied, "musical drama is in such a degraded state in our country that a fellow would have to have courage indeed to embrace such a career."

Among all the dramatic poets, serious and burlesque, who

---

8. The *Atys and Cybele* was an opera of Lully, 1676. Nic., 276.

were writing for the Italian opera at that time there was in truth not one who deserved being read. Metastasio was at Vienna; Moretti and Coltellini at St. Petersburg; Caramondani at Berlin; and Migliavacca first, then afterwards Mazzolà, had been subsidized at the Court of Dresden. Among the hundred others left, not one knew how to write a passable drama worthy of being published or acted on a stage. For their Euripides, and Sophocles, Rome, Venice, Naples, Florence herself, and the other capitals of Italy had their Portias, and their Zinis, their Palombas, and their Bertatis, and other such theatrical cobblers, who never knew a principle of poetry, to say nothing of those numberless rules, laws, and tricks of the trade which are essential for constructing a good *melodrama*!

The which arose from the shameful niggardliness of our mercantile impresarios, who were never inclined to encourage our best men to devote themselves to that most difficult form of composition: who stood ready to pay a thousand and two thousand a week to some warbling Narses or some philharmonic Thaïs, but would not blush to offer fifteen or twenty dollars for a libretto which would cost a writer of talent as much as three months of sweated labor. A dramatic poet once told me, and almost boastfully, that he was getting good money from his impresario. For four musical comedies he had written in a year, a certain Zardon had paid him eighty dollars. This poet must have lived on dewdrops!

To the disgraceful decline of this wonderful art in Italy there also contributed the unsurpassable ignorance of almost all our *maestri*, who generally would set the most beautiful music to the indecent and trivial contraptions of a Neapolitan *lazzarone*, quite as readily, or perhaps more so, as they would to the sweetest ditties of Metastasio. Such in my day was the state of the opera in Italy. I cannot say what it may be now, though from the operas for which Rossini has written such beautiful music, I get a very bad impression.

However, Mazzolà's suggestion did not drop from my mind; indeed, it was there later on, as we shall see, to give me courage to try my luck in the operatic lists on one of the foremost stages in the world.

Meanwhile Mazzolà had been presenting me to his friends, chief among these Count Marcolini, prime minister and a great favorite to that Elector; and an estimable and learned ex-Jesuit[9] (who also enjoyed the affection and high regard of the Sovereign). I shortly contracted such a close and friendly relation with the latter as to feel no hesitation in telling him my story. He was much moved, and after carefully examining the letter I had received in Gorizia, and hearing the whole affair of Colletti and my verses, judged my suspicions well founded. He also praised the reserve I had shown with Mazzolà, whom he loved and respected greatly; because, said he, that kindly gentleman would have been heartbroken at such a thing, without being able to remedy it. With most distinguished qualities of heart and mind this cultivated ex-Jesuit coupled an exquisite taste for poetry. For Cotta, Lemene, and Bernardo Tasso he had a sort of holy veneration. He appeared to read my verses with pleasure too; but I was soon aware that Mazzolà did not care to have me write or broadcast verses of mine in Dresden; but preferred rather to have me pass as an extemporizer—that amusement was coming into fashion in Germany at that time. He had his reasons, and I was neither blind, unjust, nor ungrateful.

Having nevertheless discovered Father Huber's fondness for the beautiful psalms of Bernardo Tasso, I thought it could not displease Mazzolà if I composed a number of them as a compliment to our mutual friend, this being a form of poetry altogether distinct from the operatic. I wrote seven, accordingly, and read them to Mazzolà. He was the first to advise me to

---

9. Michael Jerome Huber (1748–1812) was a Jesuit, born an Innischen, Hofmeister to the Count Sauer zu Ankerstein. Sheppard, 99.

give a copy of them to Father Huber, or even to dedicate them to him. I did not fail to adopt this suggestion and Mazzolà delivered the script in person. Huber was quite pleased with my offering and handed my poems on to the Prime Minister and to the Elector. I was praised and rewarded by all three; and their presents, for the most part pecuniary, to tell the truth, came in the nick of time.

I reprint here five of these odes, this being their proper place; and I hope my reader may find in them some recompense for the boredom caused him by so many other verses I have published in this autobiography, the which I have given, not because I thought them worthy of praise, but because on them in great part depended some of the most important happenings of my life. This hope I nourish, I may say, in view of the favorable reception accorded my "Psalms" by numerous Italian *literati*, among whom I will proudly mention Ugo Foscolo, that rare phenomenon of learning and talent who dares vie with Alfieri and Monti in the tragic, and perchance surpasses them both in the lyric. He praised these psalms, *et erit mihi magnus Apollo.*

SALMO I
Miserere mei, Deus, quoniam infirmus sum.

> Signor, di fragil terra
> formasti il corpo mio,
> a cui fa sempre guerra
> crudo nemico e rio,
> che nutre il fier desio
> del pianto de' mortali;
> e danni a danni aggiunge e mali a mali.
>   Ahi! quante volte, ahi! quante
> il barbaro mi vinse,

e dietro il volgo errante
l'anima mia sospinse;
quante il mio core avvinse,
che non temea d'inganno,
onde servo io divenni, egli tiranno!

Or ei guida i miei passi
per vie fosche e distorte;
ove per tronchi e sassi
si giunge a strazio e a morte.
Ma tu con man più forte
spezza il funesto laccio,
e me ritogli ancor a l'empio braccio.

Veggo quant'io peccai,
quanto il tuo nume offesi:
però, Padre, tu sai
che a lungo pria contesi:
sai che a l'empio mi resi
per mia fralezza estrema,
non già perch'io non t'ami e te non tema.

Su queste labbia spesso
suonò il tuo nome santo,
in quel momento stesso
ch'io ti fuggia dal canto;
e sparsi amaro pianto
su quei stessi diletti,
onde peccâro i traviati affetti.

Ma se de'falli miei
scusa non è che basti,
salvami, perchè sei
quel Dio che mi creasti,
e l'empio invan contrasti
col tuo voler superno,
ch'osa sfidarti ancor fin da l'inferno.

(O Lord, didst make of fragile earth my flesh of cruel
Foe beset, his dread intent fixed on mortal tears alone,
bringing ill on ill and woe on woe. Alas, alas, how oft
hath the Relentless One o'ercome me, thrusting my
soul into frivolous quest of passing things! How oft
his chains have drawn about my unsuspecting heart,
whereby tyrant he, I slave, became. Now my step he
turneth into pathways dark and twisting, where stone and
bramble threaten pain and death. But Thou, the stronger,
dost free me of his deadly snare, and redeemest me
from his impious clasp. I know my sin, what hurt I have
wrought Thy Godhead. But Thou, O Lord, dost know
how long I fought, dost know that I yielded to the
Impious One through mortal frailty, not for lack of love
or fear of Thee. On these lips of mine oft hath Thy
Name resounded in that very hour when I was departing
from Thy law; and bitter tears I shed upon those very
joys my wayward senses sought. But if for my sins no
penitence avail, save me, O Lord, for Thou my creator
art. Let not the Impious One contemn Thy Will
Supreme in challenge which he utters from the depths
of Hell.)

SALMO II
Iustus es, Domine, et rectum iudicium tuum.

Non verso, eterno Dio, etc.

SALMO III
*Convertere, Domine, et eripe animam meam, salvum me
fac propter misericordiam tuam.*

Aprite, eterno Dio, le porte aprite, etc.

SALMO IV
Misericordias Domini in æternum cantabo.

Abbastanza, O Signore, etc.

SALMO V
Cœli enarrant gloriam Dei.

Stiamo, o genti, a veder la gloria nostra, etc.

The printing of these psalms earned me the acquaintance of divers persons, among these, of a cultivated and talented Italian painter,[10] who had two very beautiful daughters. My heart, being strongly inclined by nature to passions of love despite many cares and much serious thought, allowed itself little by little to be caught in the net and I fell madly enamored of both of them. They requited my affection in good faith, each believing herself the favorite; and though they were extremely jealous of each other, they were at the same time good sisters and fast friends. The mother, approaching her forties, was a beautiful woman, full of charm and wit. Virtuous and modest as she was, she nevertheless loved to have people tell her she was as beautiful as ever! And since this could be said to her without dishonest flattery, I took to the habit of saying it quite often—too often perhaps not to make her a little vain and, within the bounds of propriety, an adorer of mine.

I believe this partiality of hers for me was the cause of an indulgence which came nigh to making me and others unhappy. At that time I was not more than thirty years of age and, as people thought, of a prepossessing person, some little wit, a poetic and Italian soul, not unversed in matters of sentiment. I must protest, however, that I never abused my

---

10. Unidentified.

perquisites in this connection; and from the time I first began to love, which was at the age of eighteen, up to the forty-second year of my life when I took a companion for all the remainder of it, I never once said to a woman: "I love you," without knowing that I could love her hitherward of any breach of honor. Often my intentions, my glances, and even my urbanities of ordinary politeness, were taken for declarations of love; but my lips never sinned, nor, without the consent of heart and mind, did I ever seek out of vanity or caprice to inspire in any credulous or innocent breast a passion which must perforce terminate in tears and remorse. Needless to say I found no great obstacles in the tender hearts of those two young girls. And my affection for them was great, keen and (strange as it may appear) equal, for one and the other. I often asked myself: "Which one do you love best?" I was never able to answer. I was happy only when I was with them both. I think that if the law had permitted such a thing, I would have become betrothed to both at the same time.

With all this I had the fortitude to frequent their house for more than two months without saying to either of them one word of love. To tell the truth, I was flirting much more with their mother; and one day I said to her in the presence of a number of people, jestingly be it understood: "Signora, were you not a married woman, I should never dare come to this house." She began to laugh, but then she whispered softly in my ear:

"He who loves the daughter, must blandish the mother!"

Later we were left alone and she addressed me as follows:

"Da Ponte darling, listen and do not interrupt; you must put an end to this comedy. My two daughters are madly in love with you and if I am not mistaken, you also are in love with my two daughters. You must see that a wise mother can not let things go on like this. I am greatly chagrined that I should have allowed them to go as far as they have. I am very much afraid that, in any event, some of us must suffer—perhaps all of us. The young men who come to the house are already aware of what is going on. Those who have intentions at all serious toward my daughters are very jealous and have no hesitation in saying so. My dear Da Ponte, you must make up your mind. I do not insist on a reply on the spur of the moment. I give you until tomorrow—but not an hour more."

This said, she was off like a streak of lightning.

Whether these words were so many thrusts of a knife into my soul, anyone who has a heart may imagine. A few moments later I rose to leave, but there was the father, entering the room with the two girls, both with tearful faces and dressed in traveling garb!

"Goodbye, Signor Da Ponte," said he, "I am going to take a little journey with my daughters. Your very good health!"

The two girls did not dare lift their eyes. And they departed with their father.

Blow upon blow! The state of my mind at that moment could not be described. I went home, entered my room, but could devise neither a remedy, nor a consolation. What despair! In other circumstances a marriage might have put an end to all the difficulties; but for me, not even that solution was possible. Aside from the senseless folly of falling in love with two girls at the same time, which increased the difficulties of making a choice, every appearance warned me that I could not choose the one without doing mortal hurt to the other.

I was floundering in that dilemma when Mazzolà came to my room. My agitation was such that several seconds passed before I was aware that he had entered. He could therefore see me in my despair, and hear me weeping and crying repeatedly aloud: "Oh, Rosina! Oh, Camilla! Oh, Camilletta! Oh, Rosina! What will become of you, poor things? What will become of me?" Imagine my embarrassment when I found

Mazzolà looking on! I covered my face that he might not see my blushes; but he burst into a guffaw which filled me with rage, but at the same time brought me to my senses. He was already informed of my dual passion, which at times made him laugh, and at other times puzzled him beyond words. I now told him the whole story, and he could do nothing but laugh and cry: "So much the better, so much the better!"

When he saw me fairly normal again, he said:

"Here is a letter from your father. It was sent, by his order, in one of mine, that you should receive it more safely."

It was sealed with black wax—enough to tell me the whole story. Mazzolà, who already knew what the letter would contain, handed it to me at that moment to distract me with a sad piece of news from a situation that seemed to him infinitely sadder.

The remedy was timely indeed. With trembling hand I opened . . . My beloved Girolamo was dead![11] I had long known that he was desperately ill, and that the doctors had abandoned hope of his recovery. But the news was nonetheless a shock to me.

Among his other wonderful qualities, that adorable youth was in the habit of giving our old and almost helpless father, burdened with a very numerous family, the greater part of his fairly considerable emoluments. His death must therefore be fatal to those others—incapable of earning their own living, to say nothing of lending our parent aid. This thought increased my agitation out of all proportion. My despair was so intense, so utter, that it deprived me of the saving relief of tears. I sat silent for more than an hour, although my friend did everything in his power to induce me to speak. Finally, as a distraction—

---

11. Read "Luigi." Da P. will correct the error (*Mem.*, III, 257). Luigi Da P. (*olim* Anania Conegliano), born April 1, 1754, must have died early in 1782. He was the brother Da P. found studying medicine at Padua in 1777.

to use his word—from my double affliction, he said, after further consoling remarks:

"Take yourself in hand, Da Ponte! I am now going to read you something else, which will probably make you laugh!"

He began unfolding another letter which he had received that same evening, a letter from one Viola,[12] a friend of his in Venice. It read, in part, as follows:

> They are saying in Venice that Da Ponte has gone to Dresden to do you out of your post as poet at Court there. My dear fellow—be on your guard! Those Da Pontes are a dangerous lot, as you well know.

Of these three successive blows in a single day I could not really have said which seemed the most disastrous to me.

"I was not aware, my dear Mazzolà," I said quickly, "that you knew any such thing!"

Mazzolà did not catch my meaning. While he was reading me the letter, I had noted a certain cast in his eyes, from which I would have sworn that he believed what they were saying in Venice. I deemed, furthermore, that had he not believed, he would not have read me the letter at all, the reading itself furnishing a most convincing proof of a cruel, unjust, and irrational suspicion, unworthy both of him and of me.

I added only a forced smile, and relapsed into silence. But a thousand and one thoughts were seething in my head, as a rapid mental glance seemed to embrace everything and a vivid imagination displayed before my mind's eye a complete portrait of my situation at that moment. An imperious voice called out within me:

"You must leave Dresden!"

---

12. Unidentified.

I reached for my pen and a bit of paper, and wrote as follows:

> Most Reverend Father Huber:
> I am obliged to leave Dresden tomorrow. The diligence departs at ten. I shall call to bid you a last farewell just before nine.
>
> Your servant and friend,
> Lorenzo Da Ponte.

I sent the little note to Father Huber without delay: it was ten o'clock in the evening. Five minutes later Mazzolà himself went.

Before eight the next morning, I hurried to engage a seat in the diligence for Prague, and thence to Father Huber's. I related my story to that honest clergyman in detail, and he, after praising my resolve and shedding some tears with me, requested me to return to him, half an hour before the diligence should leave. I ran home and wrote the following note to the mother of the two young girls:

> Madam:
> At a quarter past ten I shall no longer be in Dresden. I can think of no better relief for the harm I have involuntarily done. I have loved, it is true; but this is the first time that my pen has written such words: my lips have never uttered them, nor will they. I hope that my heart and those two little angels of earth will follow its example. May God grant you and your family all possible prosperity.
>
> Your devoted servant,
> Lorenzo Da Ponte.

At thirty-five minutes after nine I was with Father Huber

again. I found that he had gathered into a little basket coffee, sugar, chocolate, various biscuits made especially for travelers, two boxes of sweetmeats, and several bottles of an exquisite liqueur. With his own hands he drew over my shoulders a fine fur coat, and on my head a traveling cap, and insisted beyond all denial that I take his very own muff. In the latter was a hidden pocket secured with silver buttons. He ordered me not to open it before I should arrive at the first post. (This injunction I obeyed. When I did open it, I found a tiny copy of the "Consolations" of Boethius, and another of the "Imitation" of Thomas à Kempis; and then a purse containing twelve gold pieces each of a hundred florins.) My surprise may be imagined. I wept from sheer emotion, and I can assure my reader that never have I experienced in joy or laughter the sweetness and peace that I experienced in those tears of gratitude. When I parted from him he clasped me tightly to his breast and said:

"Go, my dear Da Ponte! My heart tells me that all will be well!"

His face, as he spoke, seemed to brighten with a celestial light. And to tell the truth, for a number of years his words, rather than conventional good wishes, were a seer's predictions. If my happiness was not unbroken, it was because the mutations of fortune give no truce to mankind, ever. As I write these Memoirs, close to the sixtieth year of my life,[13] I am obliged to admit that I have not always been happy. But I cannot say either that I have always been unhappy. And I wish to add, to the honor of humanity, that if I have found in the world of Gallerins[14] and Ganelons, I have also found Hubers and Mathiases! Permit me, most generous friend, to couple with

---

13. At that age I began to write the story of my life. I have now reached eighty and with Metastasio I may say: "My story is not yet done!" —L. Da P.

14. For the first half of this jingle see below, 243. Ganelon, the betrayer of Roland.

the name of an angel on earth, your name which I have revered and almost worshipped!

At the stroke of ten, I bade Father Huber a last farewell and ran to Mazzolà's wrapped in furs as I was! I did not allow him to say a word. I threw myself on his neck, embraced him tenderly, and said these mere words:

"My dearest friend, thank you for everything. I am leaving Dresden, a moment hence, for Vienna. Please write that to your friends in Venice, among others, to that Viola of the frayed strings."

He stood dumbfounded—and sorrowful too, I do believe. Again I embraced him, and called a farewell not with dry eyes. I hurried to the post, but hardly sooner than Mazzolà himself. He took a piece of paper and wrote these following invaluable words to Salieri:

> My dear Salieri:
> My beloved Da Ponte will hand you these few lines. Do for him everything that you would do for me. His heart and his talents deserve everything. He is, moreover, *pars animæ dimidiumque meæ*
>
> Your Mazzolà.

Salieri was one of the outstanding composers of those days, an intimate friend of Mazzolà, and favorite of the Emperor, cultivated, well-read for a musician, and fond of men of letters. I did not fail to deliver Mazzolà's letter to him on my arrival in Vienna[15]; and in time it produced the most far-reaching results

---

15. Early in 1782. The first solid point of reference for chronology here is the death of Metastasio, April 12, 1782. The famous Antonio Salieri (1750–1825) had been at Vienna as Director at the Opera since 1766 (!) and composer to the Emperor since 1774. Sheppard, 108.

for me. It was the real beginning of the favor I attained with
Joseph II.

Knowing no German, nor speaking their language well, I
began by frequenting the society of Italians. One of these, a
most cultivated man, was a worshipper of Metastasio and himself a good extemporizer. He spoke to that poet of me one day
and gave him certain verses to read which I had composed and
dedicated, at his request, to an important German nobleman
with whom he was on familiar terms. The poet thereupon
expressed a desire to make my acquaintance. What my keenness to meet him may well be imagined! I was accordingly
presented, and he received me with that peculiar urbanity
and grace which was his alone, and which transpired from all
his writings. He at once alluded to the verses he had seen,
and deigned himself to read to the learned circle that was
wont to gather about him evenings at his house, the following
verses which constitute the beginning of that poem. I have
ever since remembered them and shall always do so, as a precious memento.

PHILEMON AND BAUCIS

> Era Bauci una ninfa, a cui non nacque
> altra pari in bellezza a'tempi suoi;
> e al pastor Filemon piacque ella tanto,
> quanto il bel pastorello a lei piacea.
> Tacque da pria sul timidetto labbro
> l'alterna fiamma, lungamente chiusa
> ne' semplicetti petti: alfine, un varco
> ritrovando negli occhi, ivi apparìo,
> quanto celata più, tanto più bella.
> Piacque a Imeneo . . . in aureo nodo
> distrinse i cor de'giovanetti amanti.
> Ma non estinse mai Connubio o Tempo

di lor foco una dramma: ogni momento
il più dolce parea de' loro amori:
Un concorde voler, un genio stesso
animava i lor cori; ed in costanza
sol variata di novelli affetti,
vivean gli avventurati amanti e sposi.
Passar gli anni così, così solcate
lor fronti fur dalla rugosa etade;
e l'ardor moderò, non già distrusse,
invecchiata amicizia. . . .

(A nymph was Baucis, whose like for beauty was born not in her time and to Philemon, the shepherd, was she as pleasing as that fair swain to her. The mutual flames lay silent long on timid lips, long were they nurtured deep in heartlets simple. But on finding egress through longing eyes, they gained in beauty what they had lost in voice. And Hymen rejoiced thereat and bound the hearts of these youthful lovers with knot of gold. Nor Time nor Wedlock could quench a flicker of their passionate fire. Each moment the sweetest seemed of their love. Concordant wills, one sole desire, stirred in their hearts; and in fidelity, varied only by new joys, the happy lovers lived as man and wife. The years went by. Their brows grew furrowed with the wrinkles of time. The friendship of old age cooled the burns, but extinguished not the substance, of their love. . . .)

At this point Metastasio stopped, and invited me to read the remainder of the poem.

Several courteous expressions of praise that fell from lips so venerable caused me to be favorably remarked in Vienna. But I did not have the good fortune again to see the great man, who retained in his extreme age all the freshness and vivacity of youth and all his pristine vigor as a fertile and hardy genius. A pupil at such feet I should have profited greatly, but he died just a few days after our meeting, of grief, according to reports I had from intimate friends of his; and the story may interest my reader, as something not known to the general touching a man renowned in all parts of the civilized universe.

Through weakness of heart, perhaps, Maria Teresa had all but ruined the imperial treasury by dint of granting pensions. Whereof I may give an example. The Edling family of Gorizia comprised seven persons, one of whom was Bishop of that city. This man had obtained from the most complaisant Empress pensions for father, mother, brothers and sisters, and all his servants; and being with his sovereign one day, and recounting to her certain religious devotions which pleased that Princess mightily, he was asked by her with great solicitousness whether there were anything she might do for him and his.

"Your Majesty," replied the holy prelate, "you have pensioned us all. There is no one left save my father's two horses, two good old beasts who have served him devotedly thirty-three years; and he will have to sell them, not having the means to support them, making no use of them."

Before leaving the room the holy Bishop had received a pension of three hundred florins yearly from the Queen "for the good beasts of your father."

Joseph II ordered, on the death of the Empress and his ascension to the throne, that all pensions of a certain class, hitherto granted by the Queen Mother, should be canceled, reserving the right himself to renew them to such as he should deem worthy.

On hearing of this decree, Metastasio experienced such pain of resentment in view of the slight he thought had been offered to his merits for long service, that, in a few days he ceased to live. The truth was that before the decree issued, the Emperor had written a very charming note to the Poet Cæsarean

exempting him from the general rule and with very affectionate praise reconfirming all his perquisites. But this medicine
reached the good old man too late to heal the mortal blow
which had been dealt his spirit.

Praises be, I shall never die of grief at losing any pensions!
Envy, Professional Jealousy, Trouble, and Ingratitude are the
four Divinities to whom I owe almost all my benefices. When
a man loses such pensions, he has no reason for dropping dead!
I continued for some time to live without employment.[16] The
greater part of the money I had brought from Dresden was
gone, and I could not forget the black olives and the *eau de
Brenta* on which for more than forty days I had fasted a second
Lent in Padua. I therefore began to think of economizing.

Instead of holding my lodgings in town, which were costing
me a fair price, I took a little room with a tailor's family in the
suburb of Vidden. To my good luck I made at that time the
acquaintance of a cultivated and well-educated youth, a great
lover of Italian letters, who, though not rich, was so generous
as to supply me, with noble readiness, with enough to keep me
from dire straits over many months.

Meantime I chanced to hear a rumor that Joseph II was considering reopening an Italian Opera in his capital; and remembering Mazzolà's suggestion, the thought flashed upon me that
I might become a poet of Cæsar. I had always nourished sentiments of affectionate veneration for that Sovereign, of whom I
had heard numberless traits of humaneness, greatness of heart
and thoughtfulness of others: sentiments which just then forti-
fied my courage and brightened my hopes.

I called on Salieri, to whom I had delivered Mazzolà's letter
on my arrival; and he not only encouraged me to apply for
the post, but volunteered to speak himself to the Director of

---

16. Over a year. Nic., 277. His young Italian benefactor remains unidentified.

Spectacles[17] and to the Sovereign personally, of whom he was particularly beloved.

Salieri managed the matter so deftly that I went to Cæsar for my first audience, not to ask a grace, but to give thanks for one. Before this occasion I had never spoken to any monarch. Everyone had told me that Joseph was the most humane and affable of princes. Yet I could not appear before him without the greatest awe and perturbation. But the cheery expression of his face, his suaveness of intonation, and above all the utter simplicity of his manner and his dress, nothing of which I had dreamed of in a king, not only restored my self-possession, but left me scarcely aware that I was standing before an Emperor. I had heard said that he often judged men by their faces: mine could not have displeased him, such the grace with which he received me and the benignness with which he accorded me that first audience.

Of great curiosity on all subjects, he put to me many questions relating to my country, my studies, the reasons that had brought me to Vienna. I replied to everything briefly and to the point, whereat he seemed to be favorably impressed. Finally he asked me how many plays I had written, to which I responded frankly:

"None, Sire."

"Fine! Fine!" he rejoined smiling. "We shall have a virgin Muse!"

It is easy to imagine in what state I departed from that audience—my heart aleap with a thousand enthralling sentiments of joy, reverence, admiration. That was, beyond any doubt, the sweetest and most delicious moment of my life, and my happiness soared on high when Salieri, after talking with the Emperor, reported that I had had the good luck to please him. This

17. Franz Xavier Wolf, Count von Rosenberg-Orsini (1725–1796; Sheppard, 116) of whom much, later on.

fact alone gave me strength to endure everything in my not un-
prolonged theatrical career at the Viennese Opera; and it was
of greater help to me than all the precepts and all the rules of
Aristotle—little read by me and studied less. It was the soul of
my inspiration, the guide of my pen, in most of the dramas
composed by me for his theater. It brought me out victorious
from a terrible conflict waged against me, from the day of my
appointment, by a band of implacable critics, pedants, novices,
poetasters, *literati*; and when these were tired, by one of the
most celebrated and talented poets of our age, who did me the
supreme honor not only of envying me, but of intriguing in a
thousand disgraceful ways for my post—all things which we
shall see in the course of my story.

A few days later the opera company gathered by that
Sovereign from all parts of Italy arrived at Vienna, and a truly
magnificent assemblage it was. I set myself forthwith to writing a libretto. I looked about for all those that had previously
been written and produced in that city to get an idea of that
kind of composition and to learn something, if that were possible. A certain Varese,[18] who chose, like so many others, to call
himself a poet, perhaps because he too had written an *opéra
bouffe* (not to say buffoon) sometime before, had a marvelous
collection of them—some three hundred librettos. I called on
him and begged him to lend me a few volumes. He laughed at
my request, and replied as follows:

"This collection, my dear sir, is worth a fortune. I am the
only person in the world who can boast of such a thing. You
have no idea how much trouble and how much money it has
cost me. Some day it will be compared to the famous necklace.

---

18. In his *Reminiscences*, the Irish singer Kelly describes this Italian poet as
a miser (Sheppard, 112), and imitated him on the stage, as he did also Da P.
(Krehbiel).

No, no! Do not imagine I would allow a single volume to get out of these rooms. They are jewels, sir, treasures! All I have in the world I would not exchange for one of them. I would lose an ear, all my teeth" (of these he had many, though an old man) "rather than lose a single one of them."

The best I could obtain was the privilege of reading a few in his presence, he with his eyes continually on my hands for fear, I suppose, that I might pocket one of them. I had the patience and the courage to skim ten or twenty of those jewels of his.

Poor Italy, what trash! No plots, no characters, no movement, no scening, no grace of language or style! Written to produce laughter, anyone would have judged that most were written to produce tears. There was not a line in those miserable botches that contained a flourish, an oddity, a graceful term, calculated in any sense to produce a laugh. So many agglomerations of insipidities, idiocies, tomfooleries! Such were the jewels of Signor Varese, such the burlesque operas of Italy! I guessed that it should not be a difficult matter to compose something better than that! In mine, one would find, at least here and there, some clever turn, some smart quip, some joke; the language would be neither barbarous nor uncouth; the songs would be read without annoyance! Finding an attractive subject, capable of supplying interesting character and fertile in incident, I would not be able, even if I tried, to compose things as wretched as those that I had read! I was to learn by experience, however, that much more than that is required to make a drama that will please and, above all, that will please when produced on a stage.

Since my first production was to be set to music by Salieri (who was, to tell the bare truth, a most cultivated and intelligent man), I proposed to him a number of plans, a number of subjects, leaving him to choose afterwards. Unfortunately he elected the one which perhaps was least susceptible of beauty and of theatrical treatment—"Rich for a Day."

I set courageously to work; but very soon I realized how much more difficult in any undertaking is the execution than the conception. The difficulties I met were beyond count. The theme did not provide me with the number of characters nor the variety of incidents required to fill out, without flagging of interest, a canvas designed to last two hours. My dialogue seemed to me dry, my songs labored, my sentiments trivial, the action languid, the scenes cold; I felt, in a word, as though I had never known how to write, or rhyme, or "color," that I had undertaken to wield the club of Hercules with the hand of an infant.

However, I wangled, well or ill, through most of the first act. Only the *finale* was lacking. This *finale*, which must remain intimately connected with the opera as a whole, is nevertheless a sort of little comedy or operette all by itself, and requires a new plot and an unusually high pitch of interest. The *finale*, chiefly, must glow with the genius of the conductor, the power of the voices, the grandest dramatic effects. Recitative is banned from the *finale*: everybody sings; and every form of singing must be available—the *adagio*, the *allegro*, the *andante*, the intimate, the harmonious and then—noise, noise, noise; for the *finale* almost always closes in an uproar which, in musical jargon, is called the *chiusa*, or rather the *stretta*, I know not whether because in it, the whole power of the drama is drawn or "pinched" together, or because it gives generally not one pinch but a hundred to the poor brain of the poet who must supply the words. The *finale* must, through a dogma of the theater, produce on the stage every singer of the cast, be there three hundred of them, and whether by ones, by twos, by threes or by sixes, tens or sixties; and they must have solos, duets, terzets, sextets, tenets, sixtyets; and if the plot of the drama does not permit, the poet must find a way to make it permit, in the face of reason, good sense, Aristotle, and all the powers of heaven or earth; and if then the *finale* happens to go badly, so much the worse for him!

After this picture, it will not be difficult to imagine the embarrassment in which I found myself in composing my first *finale*. Ten times I was on the point of burning what I had done, and going to beg leave to resign. At length, by dint of biting my nails, squinting my eyes, scratching my head, invoking the aid of Lucina and of all the saints and midwives of Pindus, I completed not only my first *finale*, but the whole opera. I locked it up then in my wardrobe and did not take it out for a good fortnight, that I might read it as a whole with unclouded mind.

I found it colder and worse than it had seemed at first. I was urged, however, to get it into Salieri's hands. He had already set several scenes to music, and was calling for the remainder every day. I went to him with my ears laid back, like a donkey ready for the lash, and put the libretto into his hands without saying a word. He read it over in my presence, and then said these words:

"It is well written, but we must see it on the stage. There are songs and scenes I like very much. On the other hand, I will need to have some little changes made here and there, more for the musical effect than for anything else."

I left him as cocky as a paladin, and since we willingly believe what most we desire, I began to hope that my book might not be as bad as I had judged at first. But what did the "little changes here and there" consist of?[19] Of shortening or lengthening most of the scenes; of introducing new duets, terzets, quartets; of changing meters half way through a song; of mixing in choruses to be sung by a German ballet; in deleting almost all the recitatives, and therewith all the plot, all the dramatic quality of the action, if any there were. When the drama went on the stage, I doubt whether there remained a hundred verses of my original.

---

19. To Da P.'s nervousness and excitement in this connection, Mozart refers in a letter to his father, May 7, 1783. Sheppard, 113, following Jahn.

The music was ready,[20] and the opera was shortly to be produced, when there arrived in Vienna the celebrated Abbé Casti, a poet of the greatest notoriety in Europe, especially for his risqué tales, which were as admirable for their poetry, as they were shocking and impious on the side of morals. On hearing of the deaths first of Maria Teresa (who did not care to have him at Vienna) and then of Metastasio, he thought he might perchance obtain the post of the deceased poet laureate, partly through just merit and partly through the patronage of very powerful friends he had, notably of the Count von Rosenberg, who though of extreme age greatly admired

> L'arpa profana del cantor lascivo
> che sentir gli facea ch'era ancor vivo.

At the same moment the celebrated Paisiello appeared in Vienna, a composer very dear to the Emperor, and particularly popular among the Viennese.

Casti judged, accordingly, that he could hardly fail, and, certain that, succeeding, his success was made, he set out to write an opera. "Rich for a Day" was therefore put to sleep, and there was no talk of anyone but Casti. Imagine the expectations of the singers, of Count von Rosenberg, of the not very chaste *Castiani*, in fact of the whole city, which was filled with the resonance of the *cognomen castissimum*!

Since it was part of my duty to provide for the printing of all operas produced in that theater, I was almost the first to

---

20. Just below, 116, Da P. will say that Salieri wrote the music after his return from Paris, where his *Danaidi* was presented, April 26, 1784. Giambattista Casti (1721–1803), one of the best-drawn portraits in Da P.'s *Mem.*, reached Vienna in April or May 1784; and Giovanni Paisiello (1741–1816), on May 6–7, with immortal laurels won in Russia. Nic., 277, following Molmenti. The "Theodorus" of Casti was presented Aug. 23, 1784; the *Ricco d'un giorno*, Dec. 6, 1784.

have "Theodorus" in hand—such the title of Casti's work. I could not wait to get home to see it. I hurried to a coffee shop, and read it twice from beginning to end. Certainly it was not deficient in purity of language, fineness of style, grace and music of verse, wit, elegance, a certain sparkling quality. The lyrics, moreover, were very beautiful; the ensembles delightful; the *finale* a lyrical masterpiece. And yet the drama itself was neither warm, nor interesting, nor amusing, nor theatrical. The action was languid; the characters insipid; the catastrophe implausible and in an almost tragic vein. The parts, in short, were admirable, but the whole monstrous. I was reminded of a jeweler who spoils the effect of many priceless stones by setting them badly and arranging them without order or symmetry. I could well console myself for the defects of "Rich for a Day," which I could see as clearly as I saw those of "Theodorus."

I realized then that it was not sufficient to be a great poet (Casti was that, beyond question) to write a good play; that no end of tricks had to be learned—the actors, for instance, had to be studied individually that their parts might fit; that one had to watch actual performances on the stage to note the mistakes of others and one's own, and then, after two or three thousand booings, find some way to correct them—these things, however necessary, being nevertheless very difficult to attain, there hindering now the pressure of time or money, now the niggardliness of the impresario, now the author's own vanity. At the moment, however, I did not dare impart my thought to anyone, being most certain that had I done so, they would have stoned me or thrust me as a lunatic into an insane asylum. Casti was more infallible in Vienna than the Pope in Rome. I therefore left it to Time, the judge of all things, to pass sentence.

It was not long before the opera was produced, and had an astonishing success. Could it have been otherwise? The singers were excellent without exception; the set was superb; the costuming magnificent; the music heavenly; and the signor poet, with a smile of approbation, took in the applause for the singers, for the decorator, for the tailors, for the conductor, as though it all belonged to him. But while *la Casti-Rosenbergica famiglia* was gloating proudly: "Oh, what a fine libretto! Oh, what a fine book!" the few impartial people (and the discerning Joseph at their head) were adding, "Oh what music! Oh what music!" At any rate the sensation made by the whole affair so frightened Salieri, that he no longer dared propose "Rich for a Day" to the directors for that season. He shortly left for Paris to do the music for "The Danaids" and, everything considered, I was glad of the postponement. It would give me time to reflect on things and study the stage. In fact, I discovered two things at one and the same moment: first the secret intrigues of my powerful rival against me; and second, that at last—as it seemed to me—I could write a libretto without the defects of my first.

Salieri returned from France and my opera had suddenly to be produced. The lead was given to Mme. Storace[21] who was then in her prime, and the delight of all Vienna. But she chanced to be ill that evening, and her part went to another lady who was as much fitted to replace her as a dove would be an eagle.

The fiasco was complete. But that was nothing. I had given the libretto to a certain Chiavarina to copy. Chiavarina was a young man of some talent, but extremely poor. I had tried to help him with a sort of paternal interest. He had made friends, however, with a certain Brunati who aspired, like numberless

---

21. Anna Storace (1766–1817) came to Vienna that year from the Italian circuit; her brother Stephen Storace (1763–1796), a composer, worked primarily in London. They had an English mother. See Sheppard, 118, 121. Brunati, Chiovini, Chiavarina are otherwise unidentified. Gaetano Costa, Casanova's valet who robbed him of the loot taken from the Marchioness d'Urfé, also participated in this attack on Da P. (see *Mem.*, III, 218). Nic., 278-9.

other pigmies of Parnassus, to the post of poet in that theater. Chiavarina gave him "Rich for a Day" to read, and Brunati had the inspiration to make a criticism of it and publish it the evening of the performance. He wrote the thing, accordingly, and thinking to please Casti, showed it to him, asking him to obtain permission to have it published in the theater. This Signor Casti obtained very easily. He corrected numerous errors in the admired rhapsody; straightened the legs of verses that had either too few or too many; added a line here and there and a few witticisms. Chiavarina, wrapped in a cloak which I had charitably bought for him a few days before in order to cover his nakedness, was the man who sold that noble lampoon about the theater, and to please the Abbé Casti and the latter's patron!

I desire that this story, however trivial, should not fade from the memory of my readers. They should begin from this moment to see what, unfailingly, my tendencies of heart were, what the gratitude with which my countrymen repaid me; what, in fine, the battle I had to fight over many and many a year. I could not say, indeed, that "Rich for a Day" would have had a much better success, if instead of a satire from the poetaster Brunati (we shall shortly see whether he was anything more) I had had a eulogy of it from Casti himself. The book was positively bad, and not much better the music. Salieri came back from Paris with his ears full of Gluck, of Lais, of Danaids—of a shrill screaming music. He was writing in an entirely French style, and the beautiful melodies and popular songs whereof he was once so fertile he had drowned in the Seine.

But as for the malice of my persecutors, I need hardly say that though many things contributed to the failure of our opera, they tried to make out that the fault was mine alone; and while generally in the case of musical comedies, words are counted, if at all, only as a frame to support the canvas of a beautiful picture, on this occasion my words were taken as important enough to determine the whole effect of the opera all by themselves. And it was not only partisans of Casti, my personal enemies, and rival aspirants to the post of poet at the Imperial Theater, who led the shouting against me. The singers themselves, and at their head, Salieri, said things that would make one shiver. They did not know, they said, how they had even been able to recite such wretched words; or how the *maestro* had ever managed to set them to music; and Salieri, for his part, a judicious man, moreover, and no dunce, solemnly swore he would lose his fingers rather than again set verse of mine to music.

And what did Signor Casti do? He waged his war in a manner of his own. He was the only one to unsheathe a sword in my defense. But his praises were a thousand times worse than the censure of the others: *pessimum inimicorum genus laudantes.* "Da Ponte," he would say, "does not know how to write an opera? What difference does that make? Can he not be a man of merit without knowing how to write a play? You can't deny that he has talent, good taste, and a really great competence." Casti was concerned only with having it believed that I could not write an opera. Praising my talent, my good taste, and my competence, he gained the right to be believed in the places where he chose not to praise.

A quite different style my other rivals took with me. Every day there appeared some criticism, some satire, some lampoon against me or my verses. A certain Nunziato Porta, a poet on the cut of Brunati, or worse, wrote a poem that ended with these two compliments so subtly turned:

> Asino tu nascesti, ed asino morrai,
> Per ora dissi poco, col tempo dirò assai.

(An ass you were born, an ass you will die;
This little for the moment,
Later I will tell much more.)

But such people I counted as they deserved. It is true that I, too, wrote on that occasion a few poems, of a rather pungent and satirical tone, but I did so rather as an amusement and a joke, than out of any feelings of anger or spite. Of all these I shall offer my readers (in the third volume of these my Memoirs) some octaves I sent to the nobleman, Pietro Zaguri, which began thus:

Ho presa dieci volte in man la penna. . . .

and perhaps certain sonnets in accented finals which I wrote against Chiovini, calling him "Chiappino" because of the astounding resemblance between his face and . . . ; which verses not being of the opera, the Abbé Casti did me the honor to praise, comparing them to a satire called the *Giuleide* written by himself.

Casti, therefore, was the only one I had to fear, by virtue of his unquestioned merit and even more of his shrewd artifices and his omnipotent protector. From them, however, the Emperor was defending me, and the more they exerted themselves to discredit me, the more outspoken was he in my favor, looking forward to a turning of the tables.

"This young man," he said one day to the Venetian Minister (Andrea Dolfin[22]) who was still standing by me, "has too much talent not to make Casti jealous. But I shall stick to him. Last evening, after the performance of 'Rich for a Day,' Count Rosenberg said to me: 'We shall need a new poet.' Casti was in the box. I suppose he was expecting me to say, 'Take Casti!'

---

22. Read "Sebastiano Foscarini," as Sheppard well suggests, 121.

Instead I replied: 'First I would like to see something else by Da Ponte.' "

The bad impression left by my first effort robbed me of the courage to go to him. But, one day, encountering me by chance on one of his morning walks, he stopped me, and remarked most graciously:

"You know, Da Ponte, your opera, after all, isn't half so bad as they would like to have us think? You must take courage, and give us another one!"[23]

Meantime Storace (brother of the diva) and Martini[24] arrived in Vienna, two young composers who hoped to place operas with the Italian theater. The former had on his side his sister, a *virtuosa* of merit, favorite of the Sovereign himself; and the second, the Spanish Ambassadress, with whom also the Emperor seemed to be on friendliest terms.

After various maneuvers and secret comings and goings on the part of the singers and the *castus Abbas*, a great coup was prepared. They thought they had found a way of forcing me out of my post regardless of the Sovereign will. It was suggested, therefore—and Casti was at the head of the conspiracy—to have a libretto made for Storace by that same Brunati who had written the lampoon against me; and as for Martini, whose ears were filled every day with the story of my first fiasco, they concluded that he would never risk his reputation with my verses and that I would never risk my verses with his music; and working in this double sense, they spoke ill to him of my poetry, and to me of his music.

"He is an excellent instrumentalist," they said, "but as for the vocal—Lord deliver us!"

23. That Da P. had had an opera produced also made an impression in unfriendly Venice, where Zaguri nominated him to an Academy. Nic., 279.

24. Vicente Martín y Solar (1754–1810). His friendship with Da P. was to last some years, to end in a break in London (see *Mem.*, III, 239).

My royal patron very soon cut this knot. He suggested to Martini through the same Ambassadress to ask me for the words for an opera and to me he himself said:

"Why don't you do an opera for that Spaniard? I think it would please!"

At just this juncture, my work was entirely interrupted by a strange and cruel adventure which deserves to have a place among the more unusual incidents of my life. A wretch of an Italian, neither handsome, nor amiable, nor young, nor rich, had fallen desperately enamored of a beautiful young lady, with whose family I was living. Not only did she not requite him, but she held him in such hatred and disgust as a young lady might have for the most deformed of men. But he pressing her one day to know the cause of this dislike of hers, she answered:

"First, because you are uglier than the devil; second, because I am in love with Da Ponte."

And to torment him the more, she launched into a panegyric of me, as though I were a veritable Adonis.

I had not spoken to the girl six times in all my life, nor had I ever had reason to suppose her attracted to me; because she knew well that I was enamored of another lady, dwelling in that same house. She spoke as she did, perhaps, to rid herself of this annoying individual, or to rebuke him for having presumed to tell her that he loved her. The consequence of her jest, at any rate, was disastrous to me. It deprived me of my teeth, at the age of thirty-four; it gave me a year of complete misery, and very nearly cost me my life.

Believing that I alone was the cause of his unhappiness, the man became bestially jealous, and conceived an implacable hatred of me and a lively desire to avenge himself. He chanced to encounter me one day in a coffee shop, and seeing me somewhat pensive, he asked me with feigned sympathy the motive thereof. Knowing on the one hand that he practiced surgery, and nothing, on the other, of his love affair and his jealous aversion to me, I had no reason not to tell him that I was feeling downcast because of the annoyance I should be under of having an excrescence on one of my gums lanced, a tumor caused by the extraction of a tooth, and which was daily growing larger.

"And who," said he, "advised you to have it cut?"

"Signor Brambilla," I replied (Brambilla was First Surgeon to the Emperor).

"Bad, bad!" he replied, "It could not be worse! Give me a sequin, and I will rid you of your trouble without any cutting." I gave him the money, and he departed, returning in a few minutes, to give me a little bottle containing a liqueur so powerful that in less than a week the excrescence was almost gone. He had ordered me to soak a bit of cloth in a small quantity of that liqueur, and then to apply it to the growth, taking care not to swallow any considerable amount of it. A maid who kept my wardrobe in order chanced to enter my room as I was performing this operation for the seventh time; and in a glance seeing me place the dampened cloth in my mouth, gave a scream: "Holy God, nitric!" And she snatched the bottle and the cloth from my hand, reexamined them, and again screamed: "Nitric! Nitric!"

She was accustomed to using that substance in washing my silk stockings and knew what it was.

My feelings may easily be imagined. She made me wash my mouth with water, then with vinegar and milk, and I know not how many other things; but the harm was already done. Within a week I had lost eight teeth, and from swallowing certain doses of that powerful poison I had lost so utterly my appetite for food, that over a whole year's time everybody thought it a miracle that I could live with the little nourishment I took. The extent of my fury I leave to those to judge who know what it means to be deprived of those mainsprings of digestion and of enjoyment of food and of health. I ran about the streets of Vienna like a madman for more than two weeks, in the meantime dropping eight more of my teeth from my gums, as though they were made of wax. The fellow learned of my anger, and sought safety in flight. Nor did I encounter him for more than eight years. Then being at Gorizia, with Mr. John Grahl and his daughter, whom I was courting at that time, and getting out of a stage on the Traunig, I saw at some distance a crowd of people running as if in curiosity to see something strange. I joined the press and saw a man, huge and fat, fallen face down on the ground, all grimy with his own blood, his whole face crushed in, and scattered about him on the stones, four large teeth which seemed to have just then fallen from his mouth. Several persons helped him to his feet, and then, with some difficulty, I recognized him as that same Doriguti (such the name of the villain) who eight years before had caused me to lose mine.

After these tribulations, seeing that there was no more help for my teeth, I sought to find one for my appetite (though, in truth, it was not until two years later that I had it back again) and then I resumed my studies and devoted myself wholly to Martini.

I selected the theme of the "Good Natured Grumpus" (*Il Burbero di buon cuore*) as the subject for our opera, and set to work. The moment my choice became known, Signor Casti, still stubborn in his twin design of obtaining the post of poet laureate and of persecuting me, whom he thought to be the sole obstacle to his progress, began saying aloud and in public that that was no subject for a musical comedy, and that it would not raise a laugh. He even made bold to say as much to Cæsar who repeated the thing to me in these words:

"Da Ponte, your friend Casti claims that the *Burbero* will not make a laugh."

"Your Majesty," I replied, "we shall have to endure that. I shall be satisfied if he weeps."

Joseph caught my twist of the meaning and added:

"I wish you luck!"

In fact the opera was put on the stage and was from beginning to end applauded. It was observed that many spectators, among others the Emperor, sometimes applauded the strictly recitative parts. He met me as he was leaving the theater, came up to me, and whispered:

"We have won!"

Three words that for me were worth a hundred volumes of praises!

The next morning I paid my call on the Count. He was sitting with his dear Abbé, gossiping. The grimness with which they both welcomed me filled me with alarm.

"What can I do for the *signor poeta*?"

"I have come to hear my sentence from the *signor Direttore*!"

"The *signor poeta* has already heard his sentence from our most kind-hearted public! How just a one, I am not in a position to say!"

And here protector and protégé smiled wanly, and courteously turned their backs on me.

I was not surprised at this insult, but resolved then and there to resign.

"These two enemies," I reflected, "are too powerful. The royal favor will not be sufficient to save me from their intrigues. It is better to resign than to be discharged."

In this intention I hurried to the palace. But I had scarcely crossed the threshold of the Prince's room when he exclaimed in great jubilation:

"Bravo, Da Ponte! I liked both the music and the words!"

"Your Sacred Majesty," I replied modestly, "Your Director seems not to be of that opinion!"

"It's not the Director, but Casti, speaking," Cæsar replied. "But it is your triumph. You have made him weep! Go back home now; take courage, and give us another opera with music by Martini. We must strike while the iron is hot!"

The Emperor used the very same terms to Rosenberg, who was stupid enough to repeat them to me later on.

But this was not enough to make those two shrewd courtiers lose hope of winning in the end, though Casti was somewhat embarrassed, and did not have the courage to speak ill in the open of an opera everybody was praising. He took a middle course. He praised, but adding so many "buts" that the compliment was itself a censure.

"But after all," he would say, "it's only a translation.[25] We must wait and see how something original might turn out. . . . It's unfortunate he knows so little language. *Taglia*, for example, does not mean 'stature' (in which meaning I had used that word). . . ."

I happened by chance to be standing behind him when he began in mocking tone to gargle this verse of mine, and rather through his nose than in his throat (he had lost his palate):

La taglia è come questa. . . .

I stepped around from behind his back till I faced him. Then imitating his nasal gargle, I chanted this verse of Berni's:

Gigante non fu mai di maggior taglia.

He looked at me, blushed, but had the honesty to say:

"By God, you are right!"

"Signor Abbé," I then resumed. "If you can find nothing but a few words to criticize in an opera, you are paying it a great compliment. I have never criticized the gallicisms in *Teodoro*."

---

25. Of Goldoni's *Bourru bienfaisant*.

I did not give him time to answer me, but took myself off. The singer laughed and the Abbé (as that singer, Stefano Mandini, told me afterwards) did not utter a syllable for more than ten minutes.

It can be seen from this that all is not gold that glitters. To Casti no one can deny an infinite merit as a poet. But he was not a scholarly or widely read man. He had an encyclopedia in which he hunted out things he did not know, when it suited him to make use of them. In his opera, *Trofonio*, alluding to the *Dialogues*, he wrote:

"Plato nel suo *Fedon*, nel suo *Timone*."

Fortunately I was supposed to attend to the printing of it and was the first therefore to read his play. I caught the error, and changed it to *Timeo*. When I gave him publisher's proofs for the final correction, and he reached that line, he hesitated a second at the word *Timeo*, and asked me who had changed *Timone to Timeo*.

"I did, *signor abate*," I replied.

He ran to consult his dictionary, saw his mistake, gave his forehead a resounding slap, blushed, thanked me, and insisted that I take his dictionary as a gift. (I cherished it for more than twenty-five years; then it was snatched from me by some rapacious hand.)

The success of my second effort, and especially the unmistakable favor shown me by the Emperor, created a new fire in me, redoubled my enthusiasm for the labors I had undertaken, and gave me courage not only to meet the attacks of my enemies, but to look upon all their maneuvers with disdain. Before long several composers had turned to me for librettos. But there were only two in Vienna deserving of my esteem: Martini, at the time the composer most favored by Joseph II, and Wolfgang Mozart, whom I had the opportunity of meeting in just those days at the house of Baron Vetzlar, his great admirer and friend. Though gifted with talents superior perhaps to those of any other composer in the world, past, present, or future, Mozart had, thanks to the intrigues of his rivals, never been able to exercise his divine genius in Vienna, and was living there unknown and obscure, like a priceless jewel buried in the bowels of the earth and hiding the refulgent excellence of its splendors. I can never remember without exultation and complacency that it was to my perseverance and firmness alone that Europe and the world in great part owe the exquisite vocal compositions of that admirable genius. The unfairness and envy of journalists, gazetteers, and, especially of biographers of Mozart, have never permitted them to concede such glory to an Italian; but all Vienna, all those who knew him and me in Germany, Bohemia, and Saxony, all his family and more than anyone else, Baron Vetzlar, under whose roof the first scintillation of that noble flame was allowed to glow, must bear me witness to the truth which I now reveal.

And you, kindly *signor barone*, of whose courteous remembrance I have, to my joy, had recent proofs; you who loved and esteemed that celestial soul so highly and who have your own share in his glories now only exalted by envy and by all our age confessed:—if ever these *Memoris* come into your hands (and I shall do my best to have them reach you) pray do me a justice which two partial Germans have so far failed to do: pray bring it to pass that the published writings of some author of authority may proclaim a truth which the malice of others has been hiding, that a ray of light may some day play upon the honored memory of your friend Da Ponte!

So then, after the success of the *Burbero*, I went to Mozart and recounted my experiences with Casti and Rosenberg on the one hand, and with the Sovereign on the other; and asked him whether he would care to set to music a drama I should write for him.

"I would do so most willingly," he replied at once. "But I am certain that I should never get permission."

127

"That," I added, "will be my affair."

I began, accordingly, to consider the choice of two subjects best suitable to two composers each of highest genius, but almost diametrically opposed to each other in the manner of their composing.

While I was engaged in this work, I received an order from the Directors of the theater to write a libretto for Gazzaniga, a composer of some merit, but of a style no longer in vogue. To be rid of this annoyance cheaply, I chose a French comedy,[26] called *L'Aveugle clairvoyant*, and dashed off a libretto from it in a few days' time. It had no success at all, whether as regards the words or the music. A passionette for a lady past fifty, which was disrupting that good man at the time, prevented his finishing his work on the date specified. I was obliged therefore to piece out the second act with bits he had written twenty years before; take various scenes from other operas, both his and by other masters, in fine, concoct a pudding, a scramble, which had neither rhyme nor reason, was produced three times, and then put to sleep.

This failure, however, did no great harm to my prestige; so I returned in all peace of mind to my search for subjects to be written for my two dear friends, Mozart and Martini.

As for the former, I could easily see that the sweep of his genius demanded a subject of great scope, something multiform, sublime. In conversation with me one day in this connection, he asked me whether I could easily make an opera from a comedy by Beaumarchais—*Le Mariage de Figaro*. I liked the suggestion very much, and promised him to write one. But there was a very great difficulty to overcome. A few days previous, the Emperor had forbidden the company at the

---

26. Giuseppe Gazzaniga (1743–1819?) already had a libretto—*Il finto cieco*, produced in 1770. The basic text was an Italian libretto by Pietro Trinchera, 1752. Da P.'s version was performed in 1786. Nic., 280.

German theater to perform that comedy, which was too li-
centiously written, he thought, for a self-respecting audience.
How then propose it to him for an opera? Baron Vetzlar offered,
with noble generosity, to pay me a handsome price for the
words, and then, should we fail of production in Vienna, to
have the opera presented in London, or in France. But I refused
this offer and proposed writing the words and the music
secretly and awaiting then a favorable opportunity to show
them to the Directors, or to the Emperor himself, for which
step I confidently volunteered to assume the responsibility.
Martini was the only one who learned of the beautiful secret from me, and he, with laudable high-mindedness, and because of his esteem for Mozart, agreed that I should delay
working for him until I should have finished the libretto for
Figaro.

I set to work, accordingly, and as fast as I wrote the words,
Mozart set them to music.[27] In six weeks everything was in order. Mozart's lucky star ordained that the Opera should fail of
scores at just that moment. Seizing that opportunity, I went,
without saying a word to a living person, to offer *Figaro* to the
Emperor.

"What?" he said. "Don't you know that Mozart, though a
wonder at instrumental music, has written only one opera, and
nothing remarkable at that?"

"Yes, Sire," I replied quietly, "but without Your Majesty's
clemency I would have written but one drama in Vienna!"

"That may be true," he answered, "but this *Mariage de
Figaro*—I have just forbidden the German troupe to use it!"

"Yes, Sire," I rejoined, "but I was writing an opera, and
not a comedy. I had to omit many scenes and to cut others
quite considerably. I have omitted or cut anything that might

---

27. Mozart was at work before Nov. 1785, when his father speaks of *Figaro* in a
letter. Sheppard, 130.

offend good taste or public decency at a performance over which the Sovereign Majesty might preside. The music, I may add, as far as I may judge of it, seems to me marvelously beautiful."

"Good! If that be the case, I will rely on your good taste as to the music and on your wisdom as to the morality. Send the score to the copyist."

I ran straight to Mozart, but I had not yet finished imparting the good news when a page of the Emperor's came and handed him a note, wherein he was commanded to present himself at once at the Palace, bringing his score. He obeyed the royal order, allowed the Emperor to hear various selections, which pleased him immensely, or, to tell the truth without exaggeration, astounded him. Joseph had an exquisite taste in music, as indeed he had in all the arts. The great success this opera had throughout the civilized world was soon to show that he had not been mistaken in his judgment.

This news was not to the liking of other composers in Vienna: it did not please Rosenberg, who did not like that style of music; much less did it please Casti, who, after my *Burbero*, no longer dared insist that: "Da Ponte could not write a play," and was beginning to feel that it was not impossible that I might at last have written one that would succeed as noisily as "Theodorus."

The Count, meanwhile, after failing in all his surreptitious maneuvers, ventured into the open with his request that the post of poet laureate be given to his new Petronius. And since the manner of his doing so was rather odd, I imagine it will amuse the reader to hear the story.

The Emperor had offered the ladies of Vienna a most delightful *fiesta* in the palace at Schoenbrunn, and in the little theater there, the Director of Spectacles had ordered presented a little German comedy and an Italian opera, the words of the latter, written at his suggestion, by Casti. It was entitled *Le*

Parole dopo la Musica.—"The Words after the Music."[28] Rest assured that it was a thoroughgoing botch, witless, incoherent, empty. It is sufficient to know that no one, except the Count, dared say a word in praise of it. But the better to assure the success of their intrigue, they had the notion of writing a pretty satire on the then incumbent Poet of the Imperial Opera, and one may well imagine that Signor Casti was not as flattering with me as Apelles was with Antigonos. But apart from my clothes and the way I dressed my hair, the caricature was more the portrait of Casti than of me. Among other things he alluded to my love affairs with women of the stage, and the amusing part of that was that of both the two ladies who sang in that skit he himself was the patron and the cavalier.

The day after the *fiesta*, the Count, as Grand Chamberlain to Joseph II, had orders of that Sovereign, at the latter's levée, to note on a bit of paper the names of the singers and actors, and to append to each name, in the measure of service rendered, a certain sum in sequins that would reflect the royal gratitude. While the Emperor was dressing, the Count made the list, and, as soon as it was finished, he presented it to him. Cæsar glanced at it, smiled, and, taking pen in hand, added a zero to the Count's various figures, so that a ten became a hundred, fifteen a hundred and fifty, and so on in succession. Then handing back the list he remarked:

"It was not Count von Rosenberg who gave the *fiesta*. It was an Emperor."

Numberless the acts of similar generosity that honored the life, and will always honor the memory, of that good prince, despite all those who through envy, hypocrisy, or ignorance, dared in his life and have dared since his death, to speak and

---

28. The title was sarcastic, Casti resenting the command to make words for music already written. March., 211. Kelly speaks of caricaturing Da P. (*Rem.*, I, 235–6) as a *trovata* of his own. Krehbiel.

write against his achievements, his policies, and above all his character. Not only was he a generous and kind-hearted man, but he accompanied his beneficences with such tact and graciousness, that he redoubled the joy and the wonder of those he favored. And certain of my readers' approval in so doing, I shall turn aside, for a second, from the story of Casti and his Mæcenas to recount two acts of this adorable prince, which, though in themselves most beautiful and worthy of the highest praise, nevertheless must have remained unknown to his biographers and eulogists because, to my knowledge, no one has ever written of them.

The wife of the tailor with whom I had taken lodgings was a pretty woman, young, accommodating, and amusing beyond all belief. Numerous persons frequented her house, among others a very rich widow, who, though safely arrived at her sixtieth birthday, was much more inclined toward another marriage than toward preparing for the world beyond. The lady had four sons, all of them burdened with copious offspring; but though children of a rich father, they were nevertheless obliged to earn their bread with the sweat of their brows, because the father had left more than two-thirds of his estate to his wife, and she was more devoted to herself than to her children, and to her own pleasure than to that of others.

To the house there likewise frequently came a young jeweler, attractive of person, gentle of manners, and as gay and lovable of temperament as person ever was. The widow of the twelve *lustra* surveyed him twice or thrice, and judging him a tender and tasteful morsel for her teeth, or more exactly for her toothless gums, felt her mouth water for him beyond all words, and imagined she could mend with her riches the damage the years had done her in the wrinkles in her face, and all the other defects of a nature past maturity. (For the rest, she was far from repulsive. For a man of her age she would have been an excellent match.)

132

So she broached the matter to Lisette (such the name of the tailor's wife), who made fun of her at first. But when she vowed that if Lisette should make the jeweler her husband, she would endow him with her whole fortune, and give to her, Lisette, a fine gold watch worth a hundred dollars, Lisette opened wide her eyes and began to take the subject seriously. One day, pretending to speak in jest, she told the whole story to the young jeweler, who without a moment's hesitation said: "Go and get your watch; then if she will make her property over to me, I will be her husband."

He spoke so evidently in earnest that the tailor's wife, without delay, hurried to Madame Agnes (so the widow was named) and imparted the good news, which the widow received, as may be imagined, with unbounded joy.

The future bride and groom met that same afternoon; agreed on the terms of the marriage contract, and signed it both in the presence of witnesses. After giving the watch to their go-between, and a hundred florins to cover the expenses of the nuptial banquet, which was to be celebrated in Lisette's house, the amorous widow, *impatiens moræ*, set the day following for the ceremony in church; and thence returning to Lisette's, forgetful of children, of grandchildren, and of herself, she delivered over to her sweet fiancé, in the presence of many witnesses, a little trunk which she had brought with her. Then she gave him the keys, and he opened it publicly, and found therein, what with gold, gems, watches and bank bonds, the fat capital of from sixty to seventy thousand dollars of which her deceased husband had left her mistress absolute.

All the wedding day was spent in boisterous merrymaking: refreshments in abundance, music, nuptial songs; a sumptuous banquet, dancing, supper; whereafter the old lady, who had stoked the fires of Cupid with the fuel of Bacchus, insisted upon dancing with her dear little husband; and the dance finished, which, I will be believed, made the bystanders hold their sides of laughter, the company took leave.

It was already past midnight and after not many minutes she asked her husband whether it were not time to be going to bed.

"Madam," he replied, "it is your place to go first."

Imagining that he said this out of proper regard "for her modesty and virginal decorum," she asked permission of the tailor, of Lisette, and of me, to imprint a first chaste kiss upon the lips of the handsome youth, and stepping up to him—"*la bocca gli baciò tutta tremante.*" However, from the way he returned her embrace, she might easily have seen that that first caress would be his last.

Whereupon, she went to her room. The jeweler sat with us for some time. Shortly, from upstairs came a whimpering call: "Cecco, it's time to go to bed."

A brief silence! Then the same exhortation, repeated in louder tone; to which the jeweler replied:

"Yes, Madam, in a little while!"

But then he called Lisette, whispered a few words to her, and left the house.

A few seconds later, the same voice, but in a more anxious and yearning tone:

"But Cecco, it's time to go to bed."

This time the tailor's wife answered from the foot of the stairs, and gave to understand that "Cecco" had been obliged to go out on some important matter and that he would return in the morning. The poor old woman refused to believe it. I could not say that she came downstairs: she flung herself downstairs.

No, she said, it could not be. We were joking—of that she was very certain. And she went hunting through all the rooms, under the beds, in the closets, behind the window-curtains, in every nook and corner of the house. Whereupon seeing that it was no jest, but the truth, she threw herself upon the sofa in despair, filled the house with her moans and cries, until, weary of weeping, screaming, writhing, wriggling, of doing everything, in short, that one would do with not one but a hundred devils in one, she fell asleep on the sofa—after an hour of tragicomedy —where we left her peacefully to snore till nine in the morning.

At that very hour, the young jeweler received in his house the woman's four children, whom he had invited thither by letter two hours previous. He bade them be seated; then, re-marking the frowns on their long faces, he addressed them as follows:

"Gentlemen, your poor mother, incapable in her old age of controlling the impetuous urge of her senses, lured whether by love or by irruptive sensuality, proposed marriage to me, offer-ing me as recompense for such complaisance the entire fortune which your father, perhaps unwisely, left in her hands. You are within your rights in supposing that love of riches may have influenced me to accept an offer so base and, at the same time, so ridiculous; but so supposing, my friends, you would be mis-taken. I have sufficient to live on with the fruit of my toil, and for the superfluous I do not care; but reflecting that this lady would have a husband at all costs, I hastened to bind her with the chains of matrimony, fearing lest refusal on my part oblige her to seek another who, mayhap, might be less just and more selfish than I. It was therefore out of consideration for you, of whose needs and rights I am aware, that I have sacrificed my liberty: it was to give you, from the hands of a foster father, that of which your natural parent intended to rob you."

Thus speaking he opened the trunk which he had set on a table, drew forth everything that it contained, and said:

"And here are the riches that belong to you, and which I, with real joy, restore to you. Divide them among you like good brothers, and God grant that they may serve to make you happy." They sat silent, dumbfounded, dazed for a time:

wherefore he, continuing, informed them that he had retained a capital of six thousand florins, the interest of which would serve for the maintenance of their mother, and which, after her death, he intended to restore to them, or to their children.

I could not describe the scene that followed among those five people—their tears and sobs of joy, their protests, their expressions of gratitude, their embraces, their blessings. I will say only that all four flung themselves at the feet of the magnanimous youth, whom they called father, friend, angel, guardian, protecting god: and not till after an hour of caresses and transports of joy did they separate to take their leave. The good jeweler wished to have me and the tailor as witnesses of this act of his, worthy of a Socrates, or an Aristides. I do not believe that I have seen or read of, in all my life, a scene which surprised and touched me more. He then begged us to go home, where we no sooner arrived than we were treated to the end of the drama. He sat down and wrote a letter to Madame Agnes, giving her a pathetic account of what had taken place. Enclosed in the letter were seventy-five florins which were to serve her for three months, and he assured her solemnly that she would never see him again.

The lady all but died on reading the letter. However, on the advice of friends, her four sons, their wives, and her grandchildren, all came to see her, and by dint of caresses, offers, tears, prayers, so comforted her that after everyone had embraced everyone else over and over again, she agreed to go and live with one of them.

I was not long in relating the whole story to the Emperor, who cried, with an exclamation of joy:

"God be praised! If there are wicked people in my Vienna, there are also some good men!"

And he straightway sent for the jeweler, praised him for such a noble act, and granted him a pension of four hundred florins a year for the duration of his life.

I have thought many times of turning this episode into a musical comedy; but the songstress willing to play the part of the old widow is not yet born, and I doubt whether she ever will be.

The second act which I am about to relate was not, in my opinion, less noble, nor any less interesting, since it combines with a supreme generosity, a supreme clemency.

A German poet, who was very dear to the Emperor for his many talents and had received from him unmistakable marks of generous favor, carried away by an inspiration other than poetical which he somehow could not bridle, published an ode which began: "Can a King be kind?" And the remainder of the poem corresponded perfectly with the beginning. The moment it appeared in print, some busybody took it to the Sovereign, giving it all those embroiderings and trimmings which are usually added on such occasions. Joseph read it, and was so displeased with the ingratitude of the poet that he banished him from Vienna and confined him at Temesvar.

Some days later the Emperor chanced to ask me whether I had read the ode and what I thought of it. I replied that I had read it and that I found it a very beautiful one.

"Beautiful?" he repeated.

"Yes, Your Majesty!" I replied. "It would have been an easy matter for you to prove that a king can be kind."

"How? How?"

"By pardoning him!"

"You are right!" he cried, with great vivacity, and rushing to a table, wrote a note to the Prefect of Police—Count Saur, at the time, if I am not mistaken—ordering him to recall the poet from exile and to tell him that the Emperor forgave him. He then sent two hundred sequins to the poet for the expenses of his journey, but refused ever to see the man again.

Let us go back to Rosenberg. He had not yet had time to recover from the mortification and surprise occasioned him by that *zero*. The Emperor, who had turned away, reapproached to ask why Casti's name did not appear on the list.

"Casti," repeated the Count, "and I with him, hope that Your Majesty will deign to honor him with the priceless title of poet laureate."

"My dear Count," replied Cæsar, "as for myself, I cannot use a poet; as for the Opera, we have Da Ponte."

I had this beautiful little anecdote that very day from Maestro Salieri, who had it from the Sovereign. A few days later the Emperor repeated it to me himself. The repulse, meantime, served only to increase their hatred of me. Neither Mozart nor I was without well-founded fears that we might have to suffer fresh annoyances from these two good friends of ours.

They could not do much, but they did what they could.

There was a certain Bussani,[29] who had a post as inspector of costumes and stage properties, and was jack-at-all-trades save at that of an honest man. Having heard that I had woven a ballet into my *Figaro*, he ran forth-with to the Count and in tone of amazed disapprobation cried:

"Excellency, the *signor poeta* has put a ballet in his opera!"

The Count sent for me at once, and frowning darkly, launched into this dialogue, a fine counterpart of the one I had with his Barnabotic Excellency:

"So, the *signor poeta* has used a ballet in *Figaro*!"

"Yes, Excellency."

"The *signor poeta* does not know that the Emperor has forbidden dancing in his theater?"

"No, Excellency."

"In that case, *signor poeta*, I will tell you so now."

"Yes, Excellency."

"And I will tell you further, *signor poeta*, that you must

---

29. Unidentified, save as husband of Dorotea Bussani, of the Vienna Company. Nic., 325.

take it out!" (His *signor poeta* had a significant tone of its own which gave the phrase the meaning of "Signor Jackass" or something of the sort. But my "Yes, Excellency" and "No, Excellency," had their innuendo too.)

"No, Excellency."

"Have you the libretto with you?"

"Yes, Excellency."

"Where is the scene with the dance?"

"Here it is, Excellency."

"This is the way we do."

Saying which he took two sheets of my manuscript, laid them carefully on the fire, and returned the libretto to me:

"You see, *signor poeta*, that I can do anything!"

And he honored me with a second *Vade*.

I hurried to Mozart. On hearing such a story from me, he was desperate—he suggested going to the Count, giving Bussani a beating, appealing to Cæsar, withdrawing the score. It was a task for me to calm him. But at length I begged him to allow me just two days' time, and to leave everything to me.

The dress rehearsal of the opera was to be held that day. I went in person to invite the Sovereign, and he promised to attend at the hour set. And in fact he came, and with him half the aristocracy of Vienna. The Abbé Casti likewise was in the royal party.

The first act went off amid general applause, but at the end of it there comes a pantomimic scene between the Count and Susanna, during which the orchestra plays and the dance takes place. But the way His Excellency Can-All had adapted the scene, all one could see was the Count and Susanna gesticulating and there being no music, it all looked like a puppet show.

"What's all this?" exclaimed the Emperor to Casti, who was sitting behind him.

"You must ask the poet that!" replied the Abbé, with a significant smile.

His Majesty, therefore, sent for me; but instead of replying to the question put to me, I handed him my manuscript, in which I had restored the scene. The Sovereign glanced through it, and asked why the dancers had not appeared. My silence gave him to understand there was some intrigue behind it all. He turned to the Count, asked him to explain; and he, spluttering, said that the ballet had been left out because the opera had no dancers.

"But can't they be procured at some other theater?" asked His Majesty.

Rosenberg answered that they could.

"Very well, let Da Ponte have as many as he needs."

In less than half an hour twenty-four dancers, what with supers, had come in. By the end of the second act the scene which had been suppressed was in shape to be tried; and the Emperor cried:

"Oh, now it's all right!"

This new manifestation of royal kindness redoubled the hatred of my powerful persecutor and whipped his thirst for vengeance to a frenzy. I had just previously requested that certain monies which by right of contract were due me should be paid from the theatrical budget. The man found one pretext or another to defraud me of it, and having many reasons for preferring not to speak of such a matter to my Royal Patron, I thought I might obtain by diplomacy what I had failed to get by right. Casti was the mainspring that moved the whole works in that weak being. I thought therefore of addressing an epistle in verse to that poet, not only voicing my request and my claims, but containing also a fulsome eulogy of his merit. By virtue of the latter, Casti found my poem a most beautiful one, praised it, and recited it to his friends and to the Count, and I obtained the payments I had requested without further opposition. *Laudes, crede mihi, placant hominesque Deosque.*

I reprint these verses at this point, since beautiful or otherwise, they were at least fortunate.

EPISTLE TO THE ABBÉ CASTI

Gentil Casti, ho stabilito, . . .

Meantime Mozart's opera was shown on the stage[30]; and in spite of the doubts, reserves, and headshakings of the other maestros and of their partisans, in spite of the Count, of Casti and of a hundred devils, it was a success with the public while the Sovereign and other real connoisseurs judged it a thing sublime not to say divine. The libretto, too, was reputed beautiful; and my *commentator castus* was the first to point out its beauties. But what were the beauties he found? To be sure it was only a translation from Beaumarchais; but it had some fine verses, yes sir, and some splendid songs. There were, for example, two most charming lines:

> Non più andrai, farfallone amoroso,
> Notte e giorno d'intorno girando. . . .

In a word the merit of my libretto consisted, according to him, in a pretty line here and there, or at the most in a few happy arias. Though the truth was that he began to give up hope of securing my post from Joseph, and let it be noised about, for effect of course, that he was thinking of going abroad with a wealthy gentleman to travel. The Count, however, trembling lest he lose this *eccitator di voluttà languente*, ordered him to make another libretto for Salieri, who was keen

---

30. May 1, 1786. Casti's *Trofonio*, however, was written and produced the season previous, Oct. 12, 1785. Sheppard, following Jahn, 141. Joseph had received the "Tartar Poem" as early as 1784. Sheppard, 143.

to eclipse Mozart's success with something magnificent of his own. So Casti wrote the *Grotta di Trofonio*. In this opera the second act, as regards the poetry, entirely destroyed the effect of the first, of which it was nothing but a repetition. In my opinion, nevertheless, it was a much better piece of work than the "Theodorus." But though the music was divine, and the sponsors of that poet set all the bells to ringing and beat their drums and blew their trumpets to advertise their own praises, not for all that, nor for all the miracles of the wizard Trofonio, could they dislodge the Emperor from his obstinate attitude. There was only one more thing to try: and they tried even that; but it was the very thing that finished Casti with the Emperor, who liked his verses very much, but liked the man not at all.

Casti had just completed his "Genghis Khan," a "Tartar Poem" (in my judgment, of merit very inferior to his "Tales" and the "Talking Animals"). He had a beautiful copy made of it and presented it with his own hands to the Emperor. Now it should be known that that Sovereign loved and idolized Saint Catherine. On the Saint's day which honors the name of that celebrated Princess, Joseph lighted a picture of her which he kept in his bedchamber with a galaxy of flaming candles, and celebrated the anniversary with various acts of joyous worship, according, among other things, every pardon that was asked of him. When now he found that Casti's poem was little but a satire of that Saint, he summoned him to his box at the Opera, made him a present of six hundred sequins, and said:

"These will serve for the expenses of your journey abroad."

A neat manner indeed of giving the *congé*! Casti understood the jargon and left Vienna a few days later.

His almost sudden departure roused my spirits greatly, restored my courage, and removed all the obstacles which he was putting in my way, to the disturbance of my peace of mind and to the harm of my dramatic reputation—things he could

well do as a man deservedly celebrated, protected by very influential patrons, and generally liked and sought after in
Vienna. His friends thought that I alone stood as a barrier to
his advancement. They were mistaken. The real reasons why
Joseph always refused to give him the position and the title
held by Metastasio—a poet so refined, so pure, and (let us
boldly say so) so saintly both in his character and in his art—
were his pornographic "Tales," his shameless love of gambling, of women, and of other forms of dissoluteness, and
perhaps even more than any of these, his bitter, vengeful disposition, and his ingratitude for benefits received.

His Majesty said to me one day:

"Have you read the sonnet the famous Parini writes against
your good friend Casti?"

"No, Sire," I replied.

"Here it is!" And he handed me, smiling, a page torn from
his memoranda. "I know you will enjoy it. In fact, I advise you
to make a copy of it."

The sonnet is published in the third volume of Parini's
works, the Milan edition. I quote it here as corroboration of
what I have been saying:

> Un prete brutto, vecchio e puzzolente,
> dal mal moderno tutto quanto guasto,
> e che, per bizzarria dell' accidente,
> dal nome del casato è detto casto;
> che scrive dei racconti, in cui si sente
> dell' infame Aretin tutto l'impasto,
> ed un poema sporca e impertinente
> contra la donna dell' impero vasto;
> che, sebbene senz'ugola è rimaso,
> attorno va, recitator molesto,
> oscenamente parlando col naso,
> che dagli occhi, dal volto, e fin dal gesto,

> spira l'empia lussuria ond' egli è invaso,
> qual satiro procace e disonesto:
> sì, questo mostro, questo,
> è la delizia de' terrestri numi!
> Oh che razza di tempi e di costumi!

(An ugly priest, old, loathsome, decaying with the new-fashioned disease, who, by freak of chance, has inherited from his family the name of "chaste," writes tales in which one may savor all the filth of Aretin, and a foul insulting poem deriding the saint of the Great Empire. Though he has lost his palate, he goes about, a tiring nuisance, reciting his obscenities through his nose. From his eyes, his face, his movements, oozes the impious lust that fills his frame—a virulent and dishonorable Satyr. And yet, this monster and no other is the darling of the Great of the Earth. In such times, under such morality, we live!)

When he saw that I had finished reading, he gave me a piece of paper that I might copy it.

"The autograph," he added, "we'll give to Count Rosenberg, who was bent on presenting me with that flower of virtue in place of Metastasio."

His ironical "flower of virtue" reminded me of a sonnet I had written for Casti's "Words after the Music," in which I, too, had used that phrase; and by virtue of that parallel, I ventured now to recite it to His Majesty, first recounting the occasion of it.

> Casti ier sera un'operetta fe'
> (—Divina!—dice il conte), ove pensò
> satiretta gentil scriver di me;
> ma il pennel traditore il corbellò.

144

> Tutto quel ch'ei pingea, pingea di sè,
> d'amor, di gioco (il resto io nol dirò);
> e, quando in man al nostro sir lo diè,
> lui riconobbe il nostro sir, me no.
> Quindi il conte proporgli indarno ardì
> in loco mio quel fiore di virtù,
> che il nostro sir gli rispondea così:
> —Casti è un poeta che vale un Perù
> ond'io gli do'l buon anno ed il buon dì;
> ma, se Casti pur vuoi, piglialo tu.

(Casti last evening gave a little skit (Divine, the Count calls it) wherein he thought to make pretty satire of me, but treacherous pen betrayed him. All that he drew of me, drew he of himself—women, cards, and—but this I will not say. And when he gave it to our lord to read, him saw our lord, me not. And when the Count made bold in vain to propose this flower of virtue in my place, our lord responded thus: "Casti, the poet, is worth a whole Peru, whence I would say, 'Merry Christmas,' 'Happy New Year,' and all the rest. But if you will have Casti, take him yourself!")

"Bravo, I like it! Give me a copy of it, and I'll have the Count read it along with Parini's."

"The Count, Sire?"

"The Count, yes—of course I shall not tell him that you wrote it."

I gave him the sonnet, and he to me, fifteen sovereigns, which he drew from his pocket without counting them.

But enough of Casti, for the moment: I shall have occasion to speak of him again on his return to Vienna.

Done with my persecutor, who had been the oracle speaking through others' mouths, it occurred to me to play a fine trick on my Zoiluses whom I was eager to treat with a lesson. Martini was already complaining at my excessive delay in giving him my words; and the moment I had finished *Figaro*, the brother of Storace, who had learned better to appreciate the talents of his first poet, obtained the Emperor's permission to have a libretto[31] written by me; whereupon, to satisfy him and be rid of the matter at small cost, I took a subject from a comedy of Shakespeare. As it could not seem possible that I should be writing two plays at the same time, I judged the moment opportune for putting my design into execution.

I went to Martini and made him promise that no living soul should know that I was to write a book for him. The good Spaniard served me splendidly, and to give color to the thing, pretended to be grumbling at my delay, and gave everyone to understand that a poet in Venice, who had written another libretto for him, had sent on a new book for which he was then writing the music. Meantime, as a favor to both him and the Spanish Ambassadress, his patroness, I had thought of choosing a Spanish subject, the which was mightily pleasing to Martini and to the Emperor himself, for I had confided my secret to him, he altogether approving. After reading a few Spanish plays to become a little acquainted with the theatrical temperament of that country, I was much attracted by a comedy of Calderon,[32] called *La Luna della Sierra*; and taking over its historical background and a certain atmosphere, I made my canvas with plenty of room to show off all the notable singers in our company to the best conceivable advantage.

The subject of the comedy was simplicity itself. The Infante of Spain falls in love with a beautiful mountain girl—a *serrana*. But she, enamored of her *serrano*, and the picture of

---

31. *Gli equivoci* (Nic., 281), which Kelly (*Rem.*, I, 235) lauds precisely for its fidelity to Shakespeare's *Comedy of Errors*.

32. Not by Calderon—by Guevara. Nic., 281, following Farinelli.

virtue, resists all advances of the Prince, both before and after her marriage. There I had my title: *Una cosa rara*, "A Rare Combination—Beauty and Virtue," supporting that script with the famous verse of the Satirist: *rara est concordia formæ atque pudicitiæ.*

I set to work, and I must confess that never have I, in all my life, written verses with such celerity, or with such delight. Whether it were my sense of tender partiality toward a composer who had shed the first rays of encouragement and theatrical renown upon me; or a desire to be done in one fell blow with my unjust persecutors; or indeed, after all, the nature of Calderon's plot, in itself so poetical and so amusing, I had the libretto finished in thirty days, and the good maestro was done with the music at the same time. As I have said, I ventured in that libretto to bring together all the leading singers of our company. The Italian Tigelli,[33] as ever nervous and troublesome, started the usual campaign against the composer, before they had seen a note of their parts. Me they could not reach, not knowing that I had written the words; and for once in my life *sic me servavit Apollo.*

The moment the parts were distributed, pandemonium broke loose. This one had too much recitative, the other not enough; for one the aria was too low pitched, for the other too high; these did not get into any concerts, others had too many; this one was sacrificed to the leading lady, another to the first, second, third, and fourth comedian. A general conflagration! It was said, however (and this to strike a double blow at Martini and at me, for they did not know I was author of the book) that the poetry was very beautiful, the characters interesting, the subject entirely original: that the play, in a word, was a masterpiece, but the music weak and trivial.

---

33. An allusion to Horace's Tigellius. Sheppard, 145.

"Read that book, Signor Da Ponte," said a certain singer to me in all earnestness one day, "and see how a comic opera is written!"

My inner gloating may be imagined.

But in the end, the volcano burst. Almost everybody sent his or her part back to the copyist, with the commission to tell Martini that that sort of music was not for them and that they did not choose to sing it. The drum beater of the conspiracy was the first comedian,[34] who particularly detested the Spanish composer as the target of too many tender glances from his unfaithful Dulcinea.

The news of this theatrical rebellion reached the ear of Cæsar, at length. He straightway sent for Martini and me, and asked for our side of the story. I ventured to assure him that neither had the singers ever been presented in a spectacle to greater advantage than they were in mine, nor had Vienna ever heard before this a music so charming, so appealing, so original, and so popular. He asked me for the libretto, which I, fortunately, had brought with me. Opening at random he came upon the first *finale*. It ended with these verses:

> Ma quel ch'è fatto è fatto
> E non si può cangiar.
>
> (But what is done is done,
> And can not now be changed.)

"Nothing could be more *à propos*," cried Joseph, smiling. He seized his pencil quickly and wrote on a bit of paper the following note:

---

34. I suggest Bussani, who did the part of Bartolo in *Figaro*. The Dulcinea, in that case, would be Dorotea Bussani.

My dear Count:

Tell my singers that I have considered their complaints about Martini's opera. I am terribly sorry but—
"What is done is done, And can not now be changed."

Joseph.

He sent in to Count Rosenberg immediately and the Count at rehearsal that same day had it read to the singers. The reading of the royal script frightened those crazy heads, but did not lessen their disgust. They took back their parts, never ceasing however to twitter about in groups, criticizing and cursing the Spaniard and his music.

Came the evening of the first performance.[35] The theater was crowded with an audience for the most part hostile and disposed to hiss. But, from the rising of the curtain, everyone praised such grace, such sweetness, such melody in the music, and therewith such novelty and interest in the words, that the audience was caught up in an ecstasy of pleasure. On an attentive silence never before lent to any Italian opera there followed a frenzy of applause, cries of delight, howls of enthusiasm. The claque of the cabal fell to pieces on the spot and there was an accord of handclapping and lively acclamation.

At the end of the first act the ladies in the boxes began inquiring who the poet was. These had heard my competence so roundly damned by Casti and his admirers that it did not occur to them that I might be the author; though the style of the *Cosa rara* was not different from that of the *Burbero*, the *Figaro*, or any of my other dramas; yet in all Vienna Kelly was the only one (though not a very cultivated or lettered man)

---

35. Nov. 17, 1786. Michael Kelly, b. 1762, author of popular songs, manager of King's Theater, London, 1793, wrote his *Rem.* in 1826. Kelly sang in the *première* of the *Cosa rara*. Sheppard, 147.

to recognize such resemblances. He had said to me one day, previously:

"I'll wager that you wrote that libretto, Da Ponte!"

I begged him not to excite the suspicions of the others; and he kept silent. The better to color my jest, I had not put my name in many of the books which are usually sold at the Opera for the convenience of the audience. I had, however, confided the secret to Lerchenheim, secretary of the royal cabinet and a very particular friend of mine. Moving about among the belles in the *parterre* (in Vienna frequented by ladies as well as gentlemen), and hearing what they were saying, he informed them that the poet was a Venetian at that moment present in Vienna, and that he would come before the curtain at the end of the performance.

"He," they exclaimed, "he is the poet we ought to have for our Opera. We shall ask the Emperor for him, if that be necessary."

"It will not be," replied my friend. "He has already been engaged by the Sovereign."

The charming ladies voiced their marvelous joy thereat, and the second act began.

It was as much of a success as the first (perhaps even more so). One of the duets especially appeared to electrify with a sort of heavenly beauty. Joseph was the first with voice and hands to call the encore, thus abrogating a rule he had made himself a few days before, that none of the so-called "concerted" passages should be repeated.

The performance over, Lerchenheim presented me to the ladies who had been demanding the new poet for their theater, and named me as the author of that libretto. I know not whether my amusement, or their embarrassment and surprise, were the greater. They asking me why I had concealed my name so studiously, Count Lerchenheim answered graciously:

"To make the cabal blush."

I then called on my comrades at the Opera, and presented each with a libretto in which my name was printed in capital letters. Words would be inadequate to describe their humiliation. They did not dare look me in the face, or say a word. I imagine they regretted having been born with tongues, having praised my words so highly before knowing that I was the author. They had done that with the idea of debasing me in my own eyes. Instead they had made my triumph more luminous.

I was invited that same evening to sup at a singer's whither frequently came the author of the famous lampoon—*Asino tu nascesti. . . .*

He came that evening also and on entering the room said:

"Who the devil wrote that pretty book?"

"One born an ass, my dear Signor Porta," I replied coldly (that was the name of my satirist), offering him a copy of the libretto that bore my name on the frontispiece. Needless to describe how he felt.

But all these amusing things were nothing compared to the real joy I experienced through the happy fortunes of this opera. The Germans, naturally so kind and hospitable, had hitherto taken little notice of me, thanks to the ridicule of my enemies and the praises, seasoned with "buts," lavished on me by Casti. They now sought to make ample amends for the wrong done me, by their courtesies, blandishments, and gracious welcome. The ladies in particular, who could see nothing but the *Cosa rara* and dress only in the styles of the *Cosa rara*, believed that Martini and I were in truth two "rare things" ourselves. We might have had more amorous adventures than had all the knights of the Round Table in twenty years. We were the lions of the hour to the exclusion of all others. That opera had worked the miracle of revealing graces, beauties, rarities that had not been detected in us before, and that were not to be found in other men. Sugary love letters, presents accompanied by enigmatic verses, invitations to drives, banquets, dinners, jaunts in the country, fishing parties, and all the rest! The Spaniard was much amused at all this and profited of it in every way. As for myself, I laughed, made certain sound reflections on human nature, and turned my mind to writing some other *Cosa rara* if that should be possible; all the more since Cæsar, after giving me conspicuous signs of his favor, advised me without delay to write another opera for "that excellent Spaniard;" and even Count Rosenberg (perhaps because Casti was not about) became more tractable toward me. Meeting me some days later on the street, he stopped me, gave me his hand, and said with an air of heartiness that seemed sincere:

"Bravo, Signor Da Ponte, you have surpassed our expectations!"

I bowed; but then I answered, frankly:

"Excellency, that was not difficult!"

I determined without loss of time, to think up some attractive subject, but of a different kind, on which I could write another book for Martini; but too many composers were now asking for books, either directly, or indirectly, through important noblemen of the capital, for me to be at liberty to choose the composer I liked best. Quite against my preferences, I saw myself obliged to write two librettos, for *maestri* I neither liked nor esteemed, the failure of which I deemed absolutely certain. One of these was Reghini,[36] in whose behalf I was pressed and implored by Salieri. The latter had decided to foreswear his oath, and was eager to do the music for something I should write. Salieri I judged it only fair to please in the matter of Reghini, mindful of his good offices in securing my appointment to the post as poet. I therefore wrote a comic op-

---

36. Vincenzo Righini (1756–1812), a composer living at Bologna, who went to the Berlin opera in 1795. The *Demogorgone* or "Philosopher Punished" was however repeated. Nic., 280. Francesco Piticchio's *Bertoldo* opened on June 22, 1787, and had eight performances. Piticchio had worked at Brunswick and Dresden.

eretta which I called *Il Filosofo Punito*. A better title would have been: "The Composer and the Poet Punished Each in Turn." The thing failed, as it could only do. Friends of Reghini laid the blame on my words: I laid it on the music and on the poor opinion I had of the composer. This drove every spark of poetical inspiration from my head. The argument was not then settled and never will be.

The other composer was Piticchio, a man of very modest intelligence and of no musical talent whatever. He had begun work on an opera with the famous Brunati, the same who had, *suadente Casto*, written the lampoon on "Rich for a Day." But the Emperor had shortly before seen another opera by Brunati, with the music of a German composer; and it struck him as the silliest thing he had ever seen produced on the Italian stage. He commanded, therefore, that no further "brunacies" should be presented at Vienna.

Piticchio was music teacher to the sisters of a Lady of Honor at Court and these in turn were close friends of Doctor Brusati,[37] a friend of mine and my physician. Doctor Brusati asked me to do him a favor, further exacting in advance my solemn pledge to do it whatever it should be. When I had given the promise, he asked me to write an opera for Piticchio.

"It will fail!" I warned.

"Never mind," he answered, "Piticchio has treated you shabbily. He should never have condescended to take words from such a fool—and your enemy to boot, when he could have obtained them from you. Everybody thinks you will try to get even by refusing him a libretto. I said that I knew you too well to believe that; that I knew that was not your way of doing; and I pledged my word that you would write an opera for him."

Demisi auriculas ut iniquæ mentis asellus, and said:

---

37. Unidentified.

"Come to my room!"

Among various plots I offered him, he chose the *Bertoldo*: it went to the devil, the only thing it could do. Aside from a difficulty I had in writing verses for composers who were asses, I had the still greater one of putting new words to music already written for the trash of Brunati. I could see its fate far in advance. Two or three days later I met the Emperor.

"Da Ponte," said he, "write for Mozart, Martini, Salieri; but drop these *potacchi, petecchi, pitocchi, peticchi*—what the devil was his name? Casti had better sense than you. When he wrote a book it was for a Paisiello or a Salieri."

So these two operas also were put to sleep along with "Rich for a Day" and the *Finto cieco*. *Figaro* and the *Cosa rara* were revived instead. I thought however that it was time to refresh my poetical vein, which had seemed to me utterly dried out when I was writing for Reghini and Piticchio. The opportunity was offered me by *maestri* Martini, Mozart, and Salieri who came all three at the same time to ask me for books. I loved and esteemed all three of them, and hoped to find in each compensation for past failures and some increment to my glory in opera. I wondered whether it might not be possible to satisfy them all, and write three operas at one spurt. Salieri was not asking me for an original theme. While in Paris he had written the music for *Tarar*,[38] and wished now to see it Italian in manner as regards both words and music. What he wanted, therefore, was a free adaptation. Mozart and Martini were leaving everything to me.

For Mozart I chose the *Don Giovanni*, a subject that pleased him mightily; and for Martini the *Arbore di Diana*. For him I wanted an attractive theme, adaptable to those sweet melodies of his, which one feels deep in the spirit, but which few know how to imitate.

38. Paris *première*, June 8, 1787. Nic., 283.

The three subjects fixed on, I went to the Emperor, laid my idea before him, and explained that my intention was to write the three operas contemporaneously.

"You will not succeed," he replied.

"Perhaps not," said I, "but I am going to try. I shall write evenings for Mozart, imagining I am reading the *Inferno;* mornings I shall work for Martini and pretend I am studying Petrarch; my afternoons will be for Salieri. He is my Tasso!"

He found my parallels very apt.

I returned home and went to work. I sat down at my table and did not leave it for twelve hours continuous—a bottle of Tokay to my right, a box of Seville to my left, in the middle an inkwell. A beautiful girl of sixteen—I should have preferred to love her only as a daughter, but alas . . . ! —was living in the house with her mother, who took care of the family, and came to my room at the sound of the bell. To tell the truth the bell rang rather frequently, especially at moments when I felt my inspiration waning. She would bring me now a little cake, now a cup of coffee, now nothing but her pretty face, a face always gay, always smiling, just the thing to inspire poetical emotion and witty thoughts. I worked twelve hours a day every day, with a few interruptions, for two months on end; and through all that time she sat in an adjoining room, now with a book in hand, now with needle or embroidery, but ever ready to come to my aid at the first touch of the bell. Sometimes she would sit at my side without stirring, without opening her lips, or batting an eyelash, gazing at me fixedly, or blandly smiling, or now it would be a sigh, or a menace of tears. In a word, this girl was my Calliope for those three operas, as she was afterwards for all the verse I wrote during the next six years. At first I permitted such visits very often; later I had to make them less frequent, in order not to lose too much time in amorous nonsense, of which she was perfect mistress. The first day, between the Tokay, the snuff, the coffee, the bell, and my young muse, I wrote the two first scenes of *Don Giovanni*, two more for the *Arbore di Diana*, and more than half of the first act of *Tarar*, a title I changed to *Assur*. I presented those scenes to the three composers the next morning. They could scarcely be brought to believe that what they were reading with their own eyes was possible. In sixty-three days the first two operas were entirely finished and about two-thirds of the last. The "Tree of Diana" was the first to be produced.[39] It had a most happy reception, equal at least to that of the *Cosa rara*. Of this opera I may recount a few things which my reader will perhaps hear with some interest.

Herr von Lerchenheim, of whom I made mention some time back, was the greatest admirer and friend of Martini. Two or three days before I delivered anything to the maestro, he came to me in the latter's company, and half jesting, half in irritation, said:

"When will our Martini be getting something to work with?"

"Day after tomorrow," I replied.

"So you have chosen the subject?"

"Of course!"

"What are you calling it?"

"The *Arbore di Diana*."

"You have sketched it out?"

"To the last scene!"

By good luck the call for supper came; and I begged my two friends to dine with me, assuring them that after dinner I would show them the canvas which they were so eager to see. They accepted.

I had not only not made any sketch, but in saying that the play was "The Tree of Diana," I had not the slightest idea of what that tree was to be. I feigned that certain things required

---

39. Oct. 1, 1787. Nic., 282.

my attention in another room and gave the order to be called in a few minutes. I left my two friends with my pretty muse and with my brother, who was living with me, went into a neighboring room, and in less than half an hour imagined and wrote out the whole plan of the opera, which, aside from some merit of novelty, had the timeliness of fitting admirably with certain policies of my august patron and sovereign.

The latter had at just that time issued a decree, holy indeed, abolishing the barbarous institution of monasticism in the states of his inheritance. What I thought of was this: that Diana, fabled goddess of chastity, had a tree in her garden which produced fruits of extraordinary size on its branches. If the nymphs of that goddess were chaste in deed and in thought, as they passed under the tree, the apples began to glow and shine and from them, and from all the surrounding branches, there issued murmurs and sounds that harmonized in a melody of heavenly sweetness. But if any one of them had sinned against the sanctity of that virtue, the fruits became blacker than coal, dropped upon her head, or on her back and disfigured her face, bruised her body or broke her limbs, the punishment being proportionate to her crime.

Love, however, could not endure a law so outrageous to his divinity; so he enters the garden of Diana in feminine disguise, enamors the gardener of the goddess, teaches him how he may seduce her nymphs one after the other, and, not content with this, introduces the beautiful Endymion therewithin, of whom Diana herself finally falls enamored. The priest of Diana discovers from the sacrifices that crime is stalking within the virginal precincts, and with the sacerdotal authority vested in him by the goddess, orders that all the nymphs and Diana herself submit themselves to the trial of the tree. The goddess sees that she will be discovered, has the miraculous tree cut down, and Love, appearing in a radiant cloud, ordains that the Garden of Diana be thenceforward the Realm of Love.

157

This play, in my opinion, was the best of all the operas I ever composed, both as regards the conception and as regards the verse: it was voluptuous without overstepping into the lascivious; and it interested, as a hundred repetitions of it testify, from beginning to end.

The Count von Rosenberg asked me where I had found all those pretty things; and I answered:

"On the backsides of my enemies!"

The Emperor, later on, catching the political allusion in my book and delighting in it, sent a hundred sequins to my house. Only the first performance of this opera had been given, when I was obliged to leave for Prague for the opening of Mozart's *Don Giovanni*[40] on the occasion of the arrival of the Princess of Tuscany in that city. I spent eight days there training the actors who were to create it; but before it appeared on the stage, I had to hurry back to Vienna, because of the fiery letter I received from Salieri, wherein he informed me, truly or not, that *Assur* had to be ready at once for the nuptials of Prince Francis, and that the Emperor had ordered him to call me home.

In returning to Vienna, I traveled day and night; but finding myself very tired at the midway I asked permission to go to bed for a couple of hours. I lay down, and, when the horses were ready, they came to call me. I leapt from the bed, half asleep, ran down the stairs, entered my carriage, and departed. Some distance along the road we reached a toll-gate and I was asked for a small sum to pay the toll. I searched in my pocket and what was my surprise to find not a cent in my purse, where I had placed fifty sequins that morning—money which Gardassoni, the Director at Prague, had paid me for that opera. I thought I might have lost them on the bed where I had lain down in my clothes. I returned at once to the inn; there was not a pfennig to be found. The innkeeper and his wife, polite,

---

40. Oct. 29, 1787. Nic., 283. The princess had left, however, Oct. 15. Sheppard, 156.

well-bred people, called all the servants, hunted, searched, threatened; but no one would confess having touched that bed. . . . However, a little girl of five or more who had seen one of the servants remake the bed for another guest piped up:

"Mamma, mamma, Catherine made the bed over when the gentleman went away."

The innkeeper's wife, thereupon, made "Catherine" undress, and found my fifty sequins in her corsage. I had lost two hours' time in the business, but happy to have found my money, I begged those good people to forgive their maid.

I went on without stopping, save to change horses, and I arrived the following day in Vienna. I sent for Salieri, and went to work. In two days *Assur* was ready. It appeared in due time[41] and such was its success that I was long in doubt as to which of the three operas was the most perfect, whether in the music or in the words.

I had not seen the *première* of *Don Giovanni* at Prague, but Mozart wrote me at once of its marvelous reception, and Gardassoni, for his part, these words:

"Long live Da Ponte! Long live Mozart! All impresarios, all *virtuosi* should bless their names. So long as they live we shall never know what theatrical poverty means!"

The Emperor sent for me, and overloading me with gracious felicitations, presented me with another hundred sequins, and told me that he was longing to see *Don Giovanni*. Mozart returned, and since Joseph was shortly to depart for the field,[42] hurried the score to the copyist, to take out the parts. The opera went on the stage and . . . need I recall it? . . . *Don Giovanni* did not please! Everyone, except Mozart, thought that there was something missing. Additions were made; some of the

---

41. Jan. 8, 1788. Nic., 283.

42. Joseph left for the field, Feb. 28, 1788; *Don Giovanni* did not have its Viennese *première* till May 7. Sheppard, 157.

arias were changed; it was offered for a second performance. *Don Giovanni* did not please! And what did the Emperor say? He said:

"That opera is divine; I should even venture that it is more beautiful than *Figaro*. But such music is not meat for the teeth of my Viennese!"

I reported the remark to Mozart, who replied quietly:

"Give them time to chew on it!"

He was not mistaken. On his advice I strove to procure frequent repetitions of the opera; at each performance the applause increased, and little by little even Vienna of the dull teeth came to enjoy its savor and appreciate its beauties, and placed *Don Giovanni* among the most beautiful operas that have ever been produced on any stage.

It was at this epoch, if I mistake not, that Madame Coltellini,[43] famous as an actress, but weak in voice, came for the second time to Vienna. She was the favorite of Casti, and therefore of the Count von Rosenberg, and not disliked by the Emperor himself. Having, or imagining herself to have, the ill will of Maestro Salieri, one of the most important directors of that Opera, whom she thought of as her persecutor, Coltellini wrote a letter so sharp and so fiery to the Emperor that there came his precise order to dismiss the whole company of the Italians. Thorwart, vice-director of the theater and mortal foe to the Italians, came in great glee to rehearsal, and read a letter written from the field to the Count Director, which bade him peremptorily to say to each one of us that at the end of that season His Majesty intended to close his Italian Opera.

This news saddened the whole city, not to mention the singers, and some hundred other persons at least—what with

---

43. Celeste Coltellini (1764–1817). Her first engagement at Vienna had been in 1785. Nic., 283. The vice-director was Johann Baptista Thorwart (1737–1813). Sheppard, 158.

musicians, stage lighters, supers, vedettes, costumers, painters, stage hands, and so on, who derived support for themselves and their families from that establishment. Into my head came the ambitious thought of making the Emperor change his mind, or at least of finding some means to retain the singers without depending on Court. I called on all those ladies who were especially devoted to our theater, and having drawn up a very simple plan, which would save at least a third of the expense without dispensing with any favorite voice, I proposed making up subscriptions to an opera fund of a hundred thousand florins which would be deposited in the royal bank without requirement of interest. I showed clearly that with this fund, plus the evening admissions, there should remain a balance of twenty-five thousand florins after paying all expenses.

Baron Gondar, a very wealthy gentleman much respected in Vienna, was to receive the subscriptions and serve as manager of the theater. I would be assistant director.

In less than a week, I had in hand subscriptions amounting to a hundred thousand florins.

Meantime the Emperor returned to Vienna, and I hurried to him without delay. The moment he saw me, he led me to his private cabinet, and asked me how the Opera was going.

"Sire, the Opera could not go worse."

"What's that? Why?"

"Because we are all in despair at having to leave our adored patron this September." And as I spoke the words tears gathered in my eyes.

This he noticed; and with a kindness not to be described in words, he exclaimed:

"No, you will not lose him!"

"But if the Opera ceases to exist, how many people, how many families, will perish?"

"But I can not think of spending such immense sums to amuse myself and other people. I have such urgent need at present for purposes much more important! Do you realize that the Italian Opera has been costing me more than eighty thousand florins a year? I can not take money from some individuals to give it to others. And then . . . and then . . . there's that dear Coltellini woman. . . ."

While he was thus speaking, I cautiously drew a large sheet of royal paper folded several times, in such a way that he would see it and ask me what it was. He did, in fact, inquire; and I replied that it was a brief memorial.

"Brief?"

"Very brief."

"On a sheet of royal paper?"

He unfolded the document with a rather long face; but on all that spread of white, there were but two verses, by Casti:

> Proposizioni ognuno far le può;
> Il punto sta nell' accettarle o no.
>
> (Proposals various anyone can make!
> The point resides in finding one to take.)

He could not restrain a laugh, and asked me what proposal I had to make him.

"Sire," I replied, "I ask only for the use of your theater, and I promise to give Your Majesty and Vienna the same Company and the same performances as now, three times a week."

"You? You are so rich then?"

"No, Sire! But here is what I have been doing since the sad news of our dismissal came."

Thereupon I drew from my pocket two other sheets. One of them contained the signatures of a number of gentlemen and ladies, each of whom promised to pay five hundred florin for a box on the first, second, or third balcony; or, in London style, a certain sum of money for so many tickets of admission. The other was an exact computation of the earnings and expenses, drawn from books of the Opera itself.

He glanced at them both.

"Well," he said finally, "go to Rosenberg and tell him that I give you the use of the theater."

Rosenberg received me with great jubilation; but Thorwart came in, and he, on this or that pretext, spoiled the business.

"Excellency, we have neither an adequate stage set, nor an adequate wardrobe. There would always be quarreling between Italian singers and German actors. Scenes cannot be shifted every day without the greatest confusion. Excellency, it can not be!"

The Count then chimed in, himself:

"It can not be, it can not be!"

Leaving his office, I ran to the royal palace, found Cæsar alone, and without waiting for him to speak, breathless and panting as I was, I began:

"Sire, Thorwart says and the Count von Rosenberg, echoing, repeats, that it can not be! . . ."

"Let me see your plan!" said he.

I handed it to him, and he wrote at the foot of it:

My dear Count:

Tell Thorwart that it can be. I will lease the theater again on my own account, according to this plan of Da Ponte, whose salary you will kindly double.

Joseph.

Back I went to the Count's office. He received me with greatest joy, and could not refrain from crying:

"Bravo, bravo! Hurrah for our Da Ponte!"

Shortly the news had spread through the whole city and I had some eighty people at my house coming to thank me and assure me of their gratitude, esteem, and friendship. But oh! how different are the words on the lips from the feelings in the heart! Or at least, how soon do men forget the benefits they have received, the promises they have made, the gratitude they owe their benefactors, on whom they so often turn the weapons of envy and hatred, thinking in that way to shake off the burden, so humiliating to ingrates, of their obligation! Who would believe that the very ones who profited most by this happy maneuver of mine, and who at first seemed most to sense and duly appreciate its merit, were those who afterwards worked hardest for my ruin, and who were not content until they had seen me completely discredited at Vienna? Not far distant is the moment now for seeing how

> Di buon seme mal frutto
> Colsi; e qual merito ha chi ingrato serve.

I must briefly develop this operatic conspiracy here. Though not of great interest in itself, I do not think I could properly omit it from these Memoirs, as it was something that produced a complete change in all the rest of my life. It is pertinent at this point to inform my reader that, though I have always in general been most susceptible to amorous passions, I nevertheless made it a very solemn rule of my life never to flirt with actresses, and for more than seven years I had the strength to resist every temptation, and observe my rule rigorously. But at last, to my misfortune, there came a singer,[44] who

---

44. Adriana Gabrielli-Del Bene, known as "la Ferrarese." The Ferrarese's German rival was Laura Caterina Cavalieri. Nic., 284.; Sheppard, 162–163. The Italian must have been Signora Bussani (*Mem.*, 185). The *Pastor Fido* was produced Feb. 11, 1789, the *Cifra* on Dec. 11; the *Scuola degli amanti*, better known as *Così fan tutte*, Jan. 26, 1790. The *Pasticcio* seems to have been produced already in 1789 as the "Musical Bee."

without having great pretensions to beauty, delighted me first of all for her voice; and thereafter, she showing great propensity toward me, I ended by falling in love with her.

She had in truth great merit. Her voice was delicious, her method new, and marvelously affecting. She had no striking grace of figure. She was not the best actress conceivable. But with two most beautiful eyes, with very charming lips, few the performances in which she did not prove infinitely pleasing. Her usefulness to the Opera increased my regard and my attentions to her, especially after I had become the primary cause of her continuance in that city. But the lady had an impulsive, violent disposition, rather calculated to irritate the malevolent than to win and retain friendships. Let alone the envy of other singers, she had angered two especially, the one a German woman, pushed perhaps a little too far by the good Salieri, the other an Italian *diva* who, though a ridiculous person of little merit, had by dint of facial contortions, clown's tricks, and perhaps by means more theatrical still, built up a great following among cooks, barbers, lackeys, butlers, and hostlers, and in consequence was thought a gem.

All this however did not rob my friend of her real merit, and therefore I supported her and defended her against all intrigues; and, as long as Joseph lived, vain were their efforts against her as well as against me. For her I wrote the *Pastor Fido* and the *Cifra* with music by Salieri, two operas that marked no epoch in the annals of his glory, though they had great beauty here and there; and then the "School for Lovers" with music of Mozart, an opera that holds third place among the three sisters born of that most celebrated father of harmony.

But it was not those three operas that aroused her enemies and mine. It was rather a Lenten production in a new vein, called *Il Pasticcio*—"Pot Luck"—and performed for the benefit of the singers; wherein I combined favorite selections from all the operas produced in past years on that stage, changing the greater part of the scenes every evening and heightening effects by unexpected combinations here and there. The text was a sort of running, but lively and witty, banter at the expense of our audience, our directors, the singers, the poets, the conductors, and finally of me, myself; and it met with such favor that it was repeated on ten evenings with growing success. The patrons of the Opera were eminently satisfied. The daily receipts doubled, and the Emperor himself paid a hundred sequins each evening for his box, and two hundred on the evening advertised for me.

However, I had made up that *pastiche* without the aid of composers, and selected from among the singers those who had some claims, by virtue of their services, on the munificence of the public and of the Sovereign. All the others who found themselves overlooked were furious, both against the lady in question, for whom I had created that entertainment, and against me. The one who felt greatest resentment was the good Maestro Salieri, a man whom I loved and esteemed both out of gratitude and by inclination, with whom I passed many learnedly stimulating hours, and who for six years continuous, from the production of the *Burbero* to that of the *Cifra*, had been, more than a friend, a brother to me. His too great affection for Madame Cavalieri (I will venture her name), a lady who had talent enough to have no need of storming the heights by intrigue; and mine, equally excessive, for the Ferraresi (I will name her too), was the unfortunate cause of our breaking the bonds of a friendship, which should have been of our whole lives, and which was cooled in me for some time, but which with distance and the passing years came to life again warmer than ever, bringing me to detest her who was the cause of our estrangement, and to ask pardon after thirty-three years for my own great fault, of God and of my dear friend—if he be still living, which it would be sweet to me to know.[45]

45. I learned, after printing these lines, that Salieri had died.. —L. Da P.

It was in these days, toward the year 1790, that is, that my august lord and patron died. The desire of this excellent Prince had been to place on the throne of Austria his nephew, Francis, the present Emperor, whom he had reared in accord with his own principles. Thus he hoped to give the last touches to labors he had begun. To this Leopold objected. His was the right of succession, and he insisted on ascending the throne himself. Joseph, nevertheless, died resignedly and in peace; and to the physician who had the laudable courage of announcing his imminent death to him, he made gifts worthy of such an Emperor.

The true story of that great event is as follows. I was in the antechamber of my dying master, with a few individuals who were there to perform the last rites for him in tears. The best physicians in the city were attending him, and however certain they all were that his dissolution was inevitable, no one had had the daring or, to speak more properly, the strength, to tell him so. Becoming aware of their irresolution, the Emperor summoned Doctor Quirini to his bedside and begging him, almost commanding him, to tell the truth, persuaded that noble physician to announce to him, in tears, the impossibility of his recovery. This took place on the day of the funeral of the Princess of Würtemberg, first wife to the now incumbent ruler, Francis. The obsequies ended with great pomp, Joseph placidly inquired how everything had gone. Then he ordered that the usual catafalque and the other paraphernalia for a royal burial be left intact, observing quietly:

"All that will be ready for me."

At the same time he ordered one of his first officials to send his richest carriage and two fine horses to the courageous doctor who had obeyed him. The next day

al ciel volò quell' anima beata.

Shortly afterwards, Leopold arrived in Vienna. For his advent to the throne I composed an ode, wherein, with tears for the death of Joseph, I sang the virtues of Leopold. Sincere my sorrow, equally sincere my praise of this Sovereign, whom a thousand fatal eventualities were later on to render unfavoring toward me. The things I am about to narrate will probably appear incredible, but they are well known in Vienna (for Vienna especially I write of them). They occurred toward the end of the past century, under the eyes of thousands and thousands who are still alive, who will read, I trust, these Memoirs, and whom I solemnly challenge to deny the things I write whether in the slightest circumstance of fact, or in the coloring in which I depict them.

At the beginning of Leopold's reign everything seemed to be moving favorably for me. The new Emperor, absorbed in most important affairs, had no time to devote to the frivolities and intrigues of our opera house. Then the King of Naples came,[46] with his daughters (destined as wives to the two Royal Princes), and there was no thought save of public merry-making. Prince Auesperg and the Marquis del Gallo took the lead in the feastings to the visitors. Among other diversions arranged in their honor, the Emperor desired that, on a certain day set apart for it, there be a *cantata* appropriate to the circumstances, and charged me with the choice of the composer, of the place where it should be produced, and of the quality and number of the singers, with full powers to order the costumes and the decorations. In his magnificent palace, in addition to a beauti-

---

46. Early in September, 1790. The Weigl mentioned was Joseph Weigl (1766–1846). The *Tempio di Flora* was presented Jan. 17, 1791. "Prince Auesperg" was Prince Adam Auersperg. Nic., 324. The cantata Da P. wrote for Marzio Mastrilli, Marquis, and later Duke, of Gallo (1753–1830), was *I voti della nazione napolitana*. The librettist who failed was the Abbé Gian Vincenzo Serafini, a friend also of Casanova's. Nic., 285.

ful little theater in which a comedy was to be performed, there was, in a great garden, a superb rotunda, with a statue of Flora in the midst and the remainder entirely empty.

I had only three days' time at my disposal. I chose the then young Weigl to write the music. I took him home with me in the evening, wrote the first aria of my cantata, which I entitled the "Temple of Flora," and, while he worked on the music for that, put all my mind to the remainder. The verses of the first aria were as follows:

> Di gemme e di stelle
> S'avessi abbondanza,
> Corona di quelle
> A te vorrei far.
> Ma il fato non diemmi
> Che impero de' fiori;
> Son questi i tesori,
> Che a te posso dar.

> (Had I abundance of jewels and stars,
> Of them would I make a crown for thee.
> But Destiny gave me the realm of flowers—
> These the treasures I offer thee.)

When I read these lines to that composer, it was as if a celestial fire swept through him and he had the music ready in no time, music of a truly marvelous harmony and exquisiteness. His enthusiasm inspired me, and between evening and morning the cantata was entirely finished.

Three days later it was sung with most surprising effect. The idea was so novel that it may seem worthwhile describing it more at length.

The rotunda accommodated about three hundred persons, aside from a small space reserved for the actors. I removed the statue of Flora and on her pedestal I put a singer, who stood there absolutely motionless so that the spectators took her to be the same marble goddess. A sort of curtain, draped behind the statue, hid from view an exceptionally large band of wind instruments. The rotunda was in total darkness. The royal company with its suite was to enter at my signal—their aisle barely lighted by one lantern. At this first entrance, all was still silent and dark. But suddenly the place was flooded with a bright light from hundreds of little lamps affixed to the cornices of the temple, and the hidden orchestra, playing to a gradual crescendo, filled the rotunda with a heavenly melody. In the light the spectators now unexpectedly found themselves seated on thrones of flowers. After the first aria and a recitative by Flora, diverse little Loves came dancing from behind the scenes, sent by Venus and Cupid, to offer roses and myrtles to the affianced couples. But as they were about to present their gifts, Minerva appeared, protesting the offering of such flowers, asserting rather that the olives of Minerva and the laurels of Apollo were better suited to the betrothed, and princes of like station. While this contention was at its height, Flora suddenly descended from her pedestal, and lifting the garland from her head, knelt before the Queen, mother to the young couple, and singing a soft music, presented it to her; whereupon the Queen, kissing her on the forehead, returned the gift to the profferer not however as a goddess, but as a singer.

This cantata was marvelously effective. Prince Auesperg was so pleased with it, that the next day he made rich presents to all the singers. To me he sent a beautiful stag with the horns covered with gold leaf, a box of the same metal, and a purse with fifty sequins.

Not so went the affair of the Italian Marquis. He entrusted the cantata to Piticchio, a countryman of his, and this Piticchio asked a certain Abbé Serafini (perhaps Serafini asked him) to write the words. This priest imagined that since he was sec-

retary to the Embassy of Lucca, he was secretary likewise to
the Muses. The truth was, he was about as much of a poet as I
a field marshal: and after having counted off on his fingers
these fourteen syllables—

> Da quel fatal istante
> Che ti perdei nell'onde,
>
> (From that fatal moment
> When I lost thee in the waves . . .)

he lost, along with poor Ferdinand, his inspiration and his lyre.
He tried to make believe he had the fever, and planted the
maestro, like a cabbage, for nigh on two weeks, without giving
him a single line more. It was just three days to the *fiesta*, and
they not knowing which way to turn, recourse was again had
to me. The Marquis del Gallo drove anxiously with his six-in-
hand to my house, got off a ministerial exordium, and did me
the honor to "implore" me to help him.

I have never liked jousting with the powerful. I replied that
I should be most happy to serve him. He departed exultant,
sent Piticchio to me, and in a day and a half I turned out a new
cantata for old music, which was a success as regarded both
words and music. The latter may have been the work of some
other maestro. If it was Piticchio's, it was the one good thing
he ever did in his life.

The Marquis seemed highly satisfied, and two days later
chose to give me some sign of his munificence. He sent me a
letter two pages long, in which he enclosed a bank note for
fifty florins (five guineas!), which I immediately presented to
the messenger.

The Marquis took offense at that. This Signor Gallo was very
popular at Court. He was young, handsome, well built, and of
an unusually lively wit. But generosity is not always combined

with such excellences. He dissimulated, nevertheless, and came to call on me again. His visit did not disconcert me, and before he could say a word, I began as follows:

"*Signor marchese*, the honor you have done me and the happy outcome of my zeal repaid each other mutually. In sending me fifty florins, you mortally wounded my pride, which was expecting nothing but a 'Bravo, Da Ponte'; and that, issuing from lips as influential as yours, would have been of more value to me than all the money in the world. I gave the florins, therefore, to one of your footmen, who would not recognize the value of such words, but who could appreciate your gold."

"Signor Da Ponte," he replied, "I am extremely mortified. Pray tell me, at least, if there is anything in the world I can do for you."

I had thought of speaking to him of Leopold. I was already aware that that Sovereign disliked me. But I gathered from a glint in that courtier's eyes that he was not sincere, so I thought it much wiser not to kowtow to him. I replied that really I could not think of a thing I needed. He sat silent for a few seconds, then drawing a watch from his pocket, he said:

"At least, be so kind as to accept this watch, as a memento of my gratitude."

It was worth not much more than the fifty florins, but I did not dare refuse it—I presented it a few hours later to my verse-inspiring muse.

The effect of this temerity was fatal in the extreme for me. The Marquis del Gallo became from that moment my relentless enemy, as Leopold himself was to inform me some time later.

Let us now return to the Ferraresi. That *virtuosa*, so deadly to me, with all her defects of personality and character, unquestionably rendered, as I have already said, indispensable services to that Opera. This augmented the number of her enemies, whether through the rivalry that comes of nature to that sort of people, or through the influences wielded by other singers.

Partly through love, partly as a matter of justice, but especially for the good of our Opera, which I loved almost as a thing of my own, I defended her with drawn sword. She had been engaged for two years and a half. That time was near expiring. Another singer had already been engaged, a woman, furthermore, distinguished by the favor of the Sovereign as well as of the Queen. In the face of all that, I made bold to propose renewing my friend's contract for just a period of six months. To whom did I make the proposal? To Rosenberg, and that too under seal of secrecy, adducing very strong reasons therefore, which he seemed to approve. However, ignoring the pledge he had given me, he talked of the matter to everyone and to those principally who detested the Ferraresi. They wrote to the lady favored at Court with all the fringes that envy, ill will, and self-interest are wont to supply, and she wrote fiery letters to her patrons, and to the Empress herself, who, in turn, read them, in the presence of others, to her consort, already not well disposed toward me.

"To the devil," Leopold cried, "with this disturber of the peace!"

I had no knowledge of this secret conspiracy for a long time. I noticed simply that the number of my enemies was increasing in proportion to my zeal for the Ferraresi, who, to add fuel to the conflagration, was gaining in popularity every day on the stage.

The effects may well be imagined. Every day some new informer came forth, some new accusation. My infinite patience was wearing out. One day[47] I started in despair for the Palace to

<hr />

47. Jan. 24, 1791 (*Mem.*, 182). Rosenberg's successor (March 4, 1791) was Count Johann Wenzel Ugart (1748–1796). Sheppard, 170. Da P.'s dismissal took place during that week, that is before March 12, 1791, date of Leopold's departure for Italy. Nic., 286. He was engaged at the time on the libretto for *Davide*. In saying that Mozart had been pensioned by the Crown of Austria Da P. is in error. To Da P.'s suggestion that Mozart accompany him to London, we have Mozart's written reply (Russo, 74–5), that he was thinking only of the "Magic Flute" and, thereafter, of death.

ask for justice; but unluckily I encountered the Vice-director of Spectacles. This man hated me secretly because I knew that he was cheating the Opera management and I was imprudent enough on one occasion to tell him so. Remarking my excitement, he asked me where I was going. My anger led me to overstep caution. I opened my heart to him: I told him I was going to the Emperor to ask him to put me in prison, where I intended to stay until he gave me justice.

The man tried in every possible way to stop me; he flattered me and implored me, told me that within a few days the Director would be changed, that the new incumbent, as he well knew, adored me and had the highest regard for my talent; that I should not anger him by going to the Sovereign; that the latter was being influenced by Salieri, but that the Count knew, and so on, and so on.

I let myself be cajoled, and refrained from making my appeal. Two days had not passed before I could see my mistake. I tried to see the new director and was not received. Meantime the tumult and the gossip were growing: the idle, the malicious, my false friends, pretended to be warning me out of compassion. They did so really to torment me. One day I was told that Rosenberg was trying to have me put in prison, because Bussani had told him that a certain opera was not ready through fault of mine. I all but lost my mind. Despairing of obtaining a private audience with Caesar, I wrote him a letter, but I did not know how to get it to him. A certain Lattanzio, a critic on the *Vox populi*, offered to place it in the Emperor's own hands. Circumstances forced me to accept the offer, though I knew that my messenger was a forger of bank notes who had escaped from the felon's prison in Rome, though he made pretense of being one of the foremost favorites of the Monarch.

The man inserted my letter in one of his manuscripts and handed it to his editor with this note:

"Here is a letter that merits the disapprobation of a wise King. It is said to have been written by Da Ponte."

I had presented him with a gold box and a gold medallion for volunteering to deliver my letter to the Emperor. I think I paid my executioner a very good wage for my stripes.

Two days later, he ordered me to publish the letter, and assured me that in a short time he would have the very finest news to give me. The news in fact could not have been better! I saw the man only once after that and that was to hear from his lips these words:

"The Emperor has ordered me to have nothing more to do with you!"

I smiled, and suggested that he lay that little story between two of his counterfeit bank notes or stick it to the doors of the jail in Rome.

In due time the fellow was punished for his crimes, and by Leopold himself.

Things were at this pass when my friend Martini wrote me from St. Petersburg that a poet was needed there for that Opera: and that the *Cosa rara* and the *Arbore di Diana* having greatly pleased, both at the theater in town and at Catherine's Hermitage, I could not fail of appointment there. I did not meditate a moment. I went and handed in my resignation. The Director however was not in Vienna at that time. I accordingly saw Thorwart, who discussed the matter with Leopold, and sent me word the following day that His Majesty would not permit me to leave until my contract had expired—it had still almost six months to run.

Not thirty days had passed, however, before the same Thorwart came to me and announced, as it were *pro tribunali*, that His Majesty the Emperor had no further need of my services, and that I would be free to depart. I replied that if His Majesty were willing to pay me for an opera that I was just then writing on order of the Directors, for all the librettos that remained to be sold, and, in addition, my salary for the five months still lacking to the fulfillment of my contract, I would leave immediately, though convinced now that it would be too late to go to St. Petersburg.

"His Majesty," he replied, "will willingly grant what you demand. Kindly make out your bill."

I did so without delay and had everything that I asked, it amounting to the sum of eight or nine hundred florins.

I had already written to Martini that they had refused to excuse me and that therefore I would not be able to go to St. Petersburg for many months. Suspecting that they had probably written to Italy already for another poet, I had talked with Mozart and strove to persuade him to go with me to London. But a short time previous he had received a life pension from the Emperor Joseph in recognition of his divine operas; and he was then setting to music a German opera, "The Magic Flute," from which he was hoping for new glories. He asked for six months' time to make up his mind, and I, meanwhile, fell victim to circumstances that forced me almost willy-nilly along wholly different paths.

Despite all my salaries for eleven years of service, the huge profit I had made in the sale of librettos, and all the gifts I had received on various occasions from Joseph and others, I had not, in view of my excessive liberality, saved more than a few hundred dollars, perhaps six hundred, over that long period. Nevertheless I thought that much should suffice me for a decorous livelihood until Providence should offer me some new employment.

I therefore continued living in all respects as before, and after not many days found myself in such peace of spirit, that it occurred to me to go and see my *Assur*, which was to be given with new singers. When I appeared at the door of the theater, I observed that the ticket-taker showed some embarrassment. In the old days I had been accustomed to enjoy free admission to all the theaters in Vienna. I had nevertheless provided myself with a ticket, and handed it to him without saying a word. He refused it politely, called me aside, and said to me with tears in his eyes:

"Dear Signor Da Ponte, you must forgive me; but I can not let you enter the theater."

"Who gave you that order?" I asked.

"Thorwart," said he.

Prince Adam Auesperg, who was at the entrance, overheard our conversation, took me by the hand, and led me to his box. I told him my story. He seemed surprised and grieved, and offered to speak to the Emperor that he should hear my case. I had begun to enjoy my peace, and begged him, as well as numberless other gentlemen and ladies who made me the same offer, to let the matter drop without taking a hand in it.

I could not be leaving Vienna with greater glory. In eleven years of service I had written fifteen operas, nine of which were the only ones to be produced hundreds and hundreds of times with ever increasing applause in that opera house, which, but for my devotion and shrewdness, would already have been closed. In the very year in which I was dismissed, those nine operas were the only ones to be performed in that theater, and were generally sought after and loved. During the same period two serious cantatas had been the delight of the city; and my ode on the death of Joseph II had been republished in Venice, in the *Anno Poetico*, at Treviso (with notes by the celebrated Giulio Trento) and in many other cities of Italy. My departure from Vienna was not therefore going to cause my name to perish! All these glories of mine, however, increased rather than assuaged the hatred of my enemies, and caused them to redouble their efforts to make me as unhappy as possible. In human misfortunes one most usually finds the consolation of compassion from others. But my persecutors were not generous lions to *parcere subjectis:* they were malign foxes and rapacious wolves, *non missuri cutem nisi pleni cruoris.*

The moment my dismissal was noised abroad, the exultance and the vindictiveness of those traitors (they were Italians one and all) no longer knew any restraint. What they did not say, what they did not do, to torment me! The Emperor had been just! That was the way to treat such rascals! My conduct had deserved all that and worse—mistresses, intrigues, partialities. . . .

All such talk, however, was very vague and the city was so full of a thousand conflicting rumors that it really could not be said what the real reason for my dismissal was. Meantime Leopold left the capital and departed for Italy. I was eager to be far away from a place where only objects of disgust and loathing were offered to my eyes. The need of putting various matters in order obliged me, however, to stay on for some time. Yet my presence there seemed dangerous. The new Director, at the instigation of several of my enemies, sent me a written order to leave the city. To induce him to take that illegal action they had persuaded him that at the opening of the new season I would seek partisans against the new *virtuose*. One of these women was base enough to tell him that she would not dare show herself in public so long as Da Ponte remained in Vienna. An excellent antidote for her fear was devised. I was ordered to leave Vienna on the very day the Opera was to reopen.

The effect of this blow on my feelings may well be imagined. I saw my reputation ruined forever by this kind of banishment. But what could be done against *force majeure*? I departed, retiring to a little mountain village two miles distant from the capital.[48]

What was my torment when I found myself in that solitude! The first day was one of the most terrible of my whole

48. Villages of Brühl and Moedling, late in April 1791. He was to stay there till the middle of June. He was back in Vienna on June 24th, and reached Trieste early in July. Nic., 286–7.

life. Sacrificed to hatred, envy, the profit of scoundrels! Driven from a city wherein I had dwelt eleven years on the honorable earnings of my talent! Abandoned by friends, toward whom I had practiced the most pointed and frequent beneficence! Slandered, cursed, humiliated by idlers, hypocrites, triumphant foes; excluded, even, from a theater which would not have been in existence save for me! I was many times on the sheer brink of taking my life by my own hand. My consciousness of innocence, instead of consoling me, intensified my despair. I might well protest my innocence—but how prove it to a judge who had condemned me without a hearing; and who, to crown my misfortune, was then far from his domains?

I spent three days and three nights in tears and despondency. At the end of that time, just two persons, to whom I had revealed the place of my retirement before my departure, came to see me. These advised me to wait where I was till the Emperor should return. They thought I should justify myself, take legal action against my accusers, defend my reputation, especially since I no longer cared about the place I had lost. I let myself be persuaded. I set down this story in brief and with the greatest clearness, offering incontrovertible documents in proof. Through the mediation of a personage of unquestionable integrity who came secretly out of compassion to call on me, I managed to get it to the Sovereign in Italy. The place of my refuge and what I was doing became known in the city, I know not how. My slanderers trembled. It was important for them to forestall the thunderbolt. There was only one way to do that— not to give me time to speak to Leopold, who was known to be already about to return. Two commissioners were sent unexpectedly to my house, dragged me out of bed, took me, without a word of explanation, to Vienna, and after leaving me two hours in suspense as to whether I were to be taken to prison or to the scaffold, they ordered me *pro tribunali*, and in the name of *Colui che tutto puote* to be gone within the space of twenty-four hours from the capital and all adjacent or neighboring towns. I was accustomed by now to hard blows. That prevented me from feeling the full violence of this one. I quietly asked from whom the order came. One of them replied dryly:

"From the one who gives orders here."

I asked permission to speak to the chief of that station. They made it no small grace that I should be allowed to do so. He proved to be Count Saur, one of the wisest, most just, and estimable citizens of his country. I can not remember his name without tears of gratitude and veneration coming to my eyes. I ran to his office and gave him an exact account of everything. He told me that he was only the executor of orders of others; that he was in ignorance as to the nature of my fault; that at Police Headquarters, of which he was chief, no accusation had ever at any time been laid against me; but that I did have powerful enemies at the Opera who had painted me in black colors at Court, and particularly to the Empress. I assured him of my innocence; I told him that I knew that I had never done anything against the laws, or against the duty of a responsible citizen. He seemed to believe me. Truth, in fact, has its features, easily recognized by an upright soul. I begged him to obtain for me a respite of a week which I should devote to clearing myself. He secured it from Francis I, at the time, co-regent.

During that week, I investigated, sought advice, and wrote out all statements that I considered pertinent to the circumstances. I offered testimony from unimpeachable witnesses to prove the honorableness of my civil deportment. Not knowing the precise slanders on which the atrocious procedures against me had been based, I enumerated all the crimes that can deserve punishments of human justice, even choosing to adopt the severest interpretations of the laws, and then proved that I was innocent. As pledge of my truthfulness, I was there to offer the hostage of my liberty and my life.

It was all to no purpose. Francis was executor, and nothing

more, of the will of his father. Having read and pondered my statements, he could do nothing but sympathize with me and advise me to go posthaste to Trieste, where Leopold would probably be found within a few days. There I could make my own defense and implore justice.

I embraced the counsel of that excellent prince forthwith. Arriving in Trieste, I presented myself to Count Brigido, governor of that city. He had heard the whole story of my adventures. However it may have been recounted to him, he did not disdain to welcome me with affable courtesy. He heard the narrative over again from my point of view, believed my account true, and with rare kindness offered me protection, assistance, friendship. And at no time did he fail in fulfilling any of these magnanimous offers. My soul has ever been mindful of kind deeds and of noble actions. It can not repress the expansion of its gratitude at the remembrance of the generosity and fairmindedness of this exalted man, whom I can never praise enough. Pray accept here, Count Brigido, without shudder of deprecation, this grateful testimonial of a man who acknowledges owing the preservation of his life and the rehabilitation of his honor to your beneficent hand. Without the support of your prestige and of your favor either I should not be alive, or would be in dishonor. A sublimity of virtue was required to offer me that support: you knew that I was under the Sovereign's displeasure, and in spite of that you dared vouch for me and you saved me. The circumstances and the place in which I find myself can leave neither in others nor in you any suspicion of adulation on my part; everything I write here is a tribute I owe to my conscience and to the greatness of your spirit. I can not repay you except in words and in propitious good wishes.[49]

---

49. It is probable that by the time these Memoirs are published, this blessed man will not be alive. But my gratitude is alive and will live forever in my writings. —L. Da P.

Only a few days had passed before Leopold arrived in Trieste. I ran at once to the governor, and he sought to obtain an audience for me, but in vain. This refusal plunged me into the depths of despair. Three days and three nights I passed in continuous mortal paroxysms. I was at the point of seizing some moment of the royal processions or of Leopold's appearances in public to present myself to him and demand justice. I thought of taking with me my seventy-year-old father with my seven sisters and my three brothers, who for many years had been blessing Providence in the fruit of my labors, and who were sacrificed in my sacrifice in like fashion. That plan I could not carry out: my father's family were a day and a half distant.

I was still considering the matter when suddenly I heard voices calling at the door of my room:

"Da Ponte! The Emperor wishes to see you."

I thought I was dreaming.

It was not a dream! Prince Lichtenstein had come at Caesar's command to summon me! I rushed to the royal hostelry almost out of my mind. A crowd of people were awaiting audience; but the moment I arrived the usher bade me enter the Sovereign's chamber. He stood looking out of the window with his back turned toward the door. Though my excitement of spirit had been somewhat calmed by my surprise at the summons, I was nevertheless full enough of impatience and eagerness to begin speaking myself. That posture on his part embarrassed me. Finding him in just that attitude I waited until he should turn around before beginning to speak. He turned around, but with a sentence already formed on his lips. That detail gave quite a different turn to our whole dialogue. I shall transcribe it here word for word, in the essentials: there will not be the slightest alteration. We spoke in a tone to be heard distinctly throughout the antechamber. It was in fact heard and repeated everywhere, but not everywhere faithfully. Here is the truth:

"Might one know the reason why Signor Da Ponte never chose to call on the Emperor Leopold at Vienna?"

"Because Your Majesty refused to receive me."

"I sent word to you that you were free to see me whenever you chose."

"I was told that Your Majesty had no time for me."

"Yes, when you asked me for a private audience."

"My innocence had the right to hope for one from Your Majesty."

"If you had been innocent you would have found means of letting me know as much. You know where I live."

"Had Your Majesty used Your Majesty's customary clemency with me as well, Your Majesty would have called me before condemning me. Your Majesty is not ignorant of the fact that a man fallen under Sovereign displeasure is never admitted to royal audience by ministers, who believe they are gaining merit with their lord in denying to the unfortunate access to the Throne. I am the proof of that."

"How is that?"

"On the twenty-fourth day of January, I ran like a madman through the streets of Vienna resolved to throw myself at Your Majesty's feet to appeal for pity. I met a secretary of the Royal Cabinet, and I begged him weeping to tell me how it might be done. He pointed to the place where Stefani[50] could be found and suggested that I have myself presented to the Sovereign by him. On the steps of the royal palace was Johann Thorwart, Assistant Director at the Opera. He saw from my expression my inner torment of spirit; he stopped me, studied me, and prevented me by main force from making my appeal. Your Majesty has witnesses to that in Your Majesty's own house."

---

50. This Stefani is mentioned in the letters of Casti as a man of importance at Court through the influence of his wife who was mistress to a great favorite of the Emperor, Professor Schloisznigg. Nic., 289.

"Thorwart! But he was the one who told me that you refused to come and see me, in order to be able to complain that I would not listen to you, that I was a tyrant. How could he prevent you?"

"He told me that Your Majesty was too much annoyed with me; that it was certain Your Majesty would not receive me, that I was running the risk of a rebuff; that the new Director would see justice done me, because he knew me, esteemed me, and was fond of me."

"Splendid! But it was just the Director himself who begged me to dismiss you, asserting that he could have no peace with you, either at the Opera or at home."

"That proves the honesty of my slanderers."

"But they are all your enemies! Directors, ministers, composers, singers—everybody, in short, denounced you to me!"

"That should prove my innocence."

"Perhaps! But why do they hate you so much?"

"The ex-Director, Rosenberg, being desirous of placing another poet in the royal service, easily allowed Thorwart to influence him. . . ."

"Oh, Rosenberg knows mighty little about managing an Opera. For his poets, besides, I have no use whatever: I have found one to my own taste in Venice."

"Ugart—"

"Ugart is a bag of straw. He does everything he is told to do; and the last man who speaks to him is always right. . . . Why is Thorwart your enemy?"

"Because I knew, and I told him I knew, certain dishonest doings of his."

"What? When was that?"

"When, through plain devotion to duty, I suggested that we light the theater at less expense; when I told him how he could provide silks of all colors and veils of the best quality, with a profit of eighty percent; when I tried to explain to him a new method of taking tickets at the door, which protected the box office from monopolies of various kinds, the existence of which I led him to understand that I suspected."

"And why did he refuse? What did he say?"

"That things had been that way for a long time, and that they couldn't be changed. On the contrary, he advised me not to breathe a word of all this to anyone, if I cared to remain in Vienna."

"The rascal! Now I understand why he gave such a bad report of you to me. Oh, at Vienna—at Vienna! Well, what then?"

"As for Salieri—"

"Oh, never mind Salieri, I know all about him. I know all his intrigues, and I know the intrigues of the Cavalieri woman. Salieri is an insufferable egoist. He wants successes in my theater only for his own operas and his own women. He is not only your enemy. He is an enemy of all composers, all singers, all Italians; and above all, my enemy, because he knows that I know him. I don't want either him or his German woman in my theater anymore. Then there's Bussani! Bussani is a regular rascal. But he will learn to know me. I have found a certain Madame Gaspari in Venice. She will chase the grasshoppers out of the head of that insolent rope-jumper he has for a wife, even though her vulgar jokes, her clown's tricks, her raucous screams off key, have won her quite a claque among the barbers, cooks, and messenger boys of my sweet Vienna. I have warned Gaspari not to give any leading rôle to that woman. If that does not work, we'll find other ways. . . . I am Director and Impresario of my Opera from now on; and my Count Bag-of-Straw will have nothing to say. I am going to give the orders and we'll see whether things go any better. . . . However, from all you have been telling me—and it seems very natural to me—I understand that you are not the man they wanted me to believe you were."

"I am not, praise God! Sire, I am not."

"I believe you, I believe you! But what's this book, something on the style of Madame Lamotte's against the Queen of France, which you are writing against me?"

"Oh, what a lie! Against Your Majesty?"[51]

"Ugart, Thorwart, Lattanzio, all told me so."

"Your Majesty can see the weapons my enemies made use of to create the impression that I was a dangerous man, and that it was better to rid the world of me. I have been living in retirement at the Brill and at Moedling. There I was visited several times by a few honest persons whose names I shall place in Your Majesty's hands. They have read all my writings. Deign to question them and if Your Majesty finds it is not true—"

"Oh, if what they told me is not true, I will fix them as they deserve; particularly that rascal of a Lattanzio, who passes himself off as my adviser, secretary, and confidant, and has tricked no end of people in Vienna with his lies and impostures. He even filched a gold box and a medallion from you for getting a statement to me. . . . Oh, if you knew how well he served you! But I will serve him even better, don't worry!"

"That will not prevent me from remaining the victim."

"Yes, it will! Yes, it will! Where are you thinking of going now?"

"Sire, to Vienna!"

"To Vienna, so soon? That cannot be! The bad impressions of you there are still too fresh. It will be my care to give the lie to them. . . . Then, later on . . ."

"Sire, I have not the time to wait for 'later ons.' I have a

---

51. This satire was read by Zaguri, who discussed it, on June 11, 1791, with Casanova, finding the verses bad and the substance "San-Servolic"—San Servolo being the lunatic asylum in Venice. Nic., 286, following Molmenti. To Lattanzio Da P. had given the versified appeal beginning "*Leopoldo sei re—giustizia imploro.*"

father seventy years old, seven unmarried sisters, three brothers who need me."

"I know that you help your family, I know that you are educating two brothers, that you are a charitable person; I like that . . . Why not have your sisters come to Vienna? Have they any talent? They might be of use at the Opera. . . ."

"Sire, my sisters would die if they had to leave their old father even for three days. They have no talent, nor any beauty other than virtue. If Your Majesty wishes to make twelve persons happy at one blow, have me alone return to Vienna: I will labor for them all, as I have labored for eleven years past! Every time I shall lend aid to that honorable family, twelve mouths will raise benedictions and thanks to the justice of Your Majesty. If I do not deserve to be Poet of the Imperial Opera, appoint me to some other post, send me to serve the lowliest of Your Majesty's servants, but this without delay, and above all, in Vienna."

"My theater may need two poets: I know that you are a good writer in the tragic as well; but for the moment I cannot."

"Your Majesty must, for the triumph of justice, for the honor of the Throne, for the solace of my humiliated honesty. I kneel at the feet of Your Majesty, whence I shall not rise until my prayer is heard. Pray let Your Majesty be moved by these tears of mine, which are tears of innocence. Yes, O Sire, I can say that, I can swear that: they are tears of innocence—unless it be a crime to be a man and to have the passions of a man."

"That no; yet they told me—"

"And for a 'they told me,' the wise, the understanding Leopold cuts off a bread which he did not give? For a 'they told me,' Your Majesty banishes me from a city which honored me for eleven years, which saw me practice over all that time the true religion of mankind—charity toward family, toward friends, even toward enemies—which ought to give the rights of citizenship, or at least of public protection?"

"Rise!"

"For a 'they told me,' Your Majesty stains my name with the eternal infamy of double banishment, puts me on a footing with the worst scoundrels in the world, denies me the refuge of a few square feet of land in all the Imperial States, makes me the talk of idlers, the jest of hypocrites, the butt of traitors?"

"Rise!"

"Sire, I must not, I cannot! Give me the strength to rise, by granting my prayer. Your Majesty must not leave me under the horrors of a sentence which my enemies enticed from Your Majesty's mistaken justice; which is not authorized by any law save the law of force. That is not in the code of Leopold!"

"Rise! I command you to rise! A Sovereign is at liberty to do what he chooses in his own house. He does not have to account for his decisions to anyone!"

"I prostrate myself, O Sire, more profoundly to implore pardon of Your Majesty's clemency. I swore at all costs to tell Your Majesty the truth. Such an intention can not displease the magnanimous Leopold! A sovereign can do only what is just."

"He will still be free to keep whomever he wishes in his service and dismiss the person he does not like."

"That I should not dare doubt. But dismissal is punishment enough for a man who has the misfortune not to please a sovereign. It is punishment enough, without dishonoring him with two exiles, and without imputing to him, as a well-grounded presumption, every possible crime."

"I have accused you of nothing."

"Would to Heaven that Your Majesty had accused me of something before condemning me. Then it would have been said: 'The Emperor has punished him for a crime!' Now they say; for a thousand crimes. The priests, because I was a scandal; the singers at the Opera, because of my intrigues and partialities; the half-wits, because of the bad teachings of my librettos; the slanderers, because of satires written against the

Sovereign; the idlers, the ill-informed, the gossipers in the cafés, because of anything which the moment, the caprice, their own advantage, the pleasure of destroying, suggest to them. With the result that there is no one in Vienna who has not invented, or credited to me, a different crime and who has not justified the severity of Your Majesty's punishments at the expense of my reputation."

He stood thoughtful for a moment, took two or three turns up and down the room in silence, then turning suddenly upon me as I still knelt there, and his face brightening, he said: "Rise!" and he held out his hand to help me, "I believe you have been persecuted, and I promise you compensation. Is that enough?"

"Yes, Sire, it is enough for me that my name should merit the remembrance of a Monarch occupied in cares of so much greater weight and that Your Majesty deigns to believe that the vehemence, perhaps excessive, that I have shown today, arises from naught else than from an uprightness wrongfully slandered by my unjust enemies."

"I believe you and forget everything! Where are you thinking of stopping?"

"I shall be here, O Sire, in Trieste."

"Yes, stay here, and let me hear from you once in a while. Now listen: in today's post from Vienna, they write me that things at the Opera could not be going worse, that there is nothing but harassings and intrigues against my singers. That's why I sent for you. I wish you would suggest some means for getting rid of such things."

"Your Majesty can now see whether Da Ponte was the cause of the trouble, or the very people who wished Your Majesty to believe that he was."

"Oh, that I do see, I do see."

"First of all, O Sire, one must attack the causes."

"Yes, the causes—what are they, the principal ones?" Then

189

he sat down, took pen in hand, and made ready to write. I repeated to him the things I had already suggested to the management, and he noted them down with great care, approving from time to time things which I dictated to him but which I do not rehearse in these Memoirs, since they would hardly interest my readers, nor throw any light on the story of my life. He took notes on my remarks for an hour's time, then talked of other things *che bello ora è tacere, siccome era il parlar colà dov' era*, assured me again that he would remember me, and reminded me to let him hear from me. Finally he asked if I were in need of money. I was not far from being in that need, but I was proud enough, and silly enough, to tell him that I needed nothing.

I left his chamber in the certain hope of witnessing the triumph of my innocence in a very short time. But we shall soon see the fatal consequences that assurance had for me. Meantime, it exercised the keenest fascination upon my mind. I began acting at once on promise of it, striving to drive from my thoughts any consideration which would forcibly have led me to some other picture of that prince. He was no longer an unjust man in my eyes. He had been deceived! What a pity he had such wicked counselors to inform him, and that a crew of fawning adulators should obey him only to betray him!

With this illusion in possession of me, I allowed some weeks to pass, doing and saying nothing. That was sufficient to exhaust the purse of a poet, who has never been either very saving or very rich. The Emperor's promises caused me to continue the support I had undertaken of my two brothers and of a sweetheart of ten years who had followed me in my misfortunes to Trieste.

My purse empty, I began to despoil my wardrobe. That too was exhausted in a few months. I turned to old friends. Where were they? And how did they receive me? Deaf, insensible, inexorable, they all turned their backs on me, either not answering my laments, or heaping abuse upon me for my unwise conduct. It availed me not to recall past favors, to appeal with words of friendship, to cry: "Succor me, for I am dying of hunger!"

There was an Italian whom I had kept, both him and his children, in my house for many months, assisting them in their time of calamity with the tenderness of a father. Through a quirk of fortune the man had become very rich. He was then a banker, living in Naples. I believed he would not deny me the loan of a hundred dollars, and I ventured to ask him for it. Here is my letter:

> My dearest Piatti:
>
> I need a hundred dollars. If you could lend them to me, I will make restitution within two or three months. I think that I need tell you no more to obtain this little favor from you.
>
> Your friend, L. Da P.

Here is his reply:

> My dearest Da Ponte:
>
> To lend money is almost always to lose the money and the friend. I do not care to lose either. Good luck to you!
>
> Yours, D. Piatti.

This good soul died young, and not in his bed.[52] If those who are like him should all end as he did, there would be fewer ingrates in the world.

---

52. Domenico Piatti, born in Trieste in 1743, was hanged with his son Antonio, at Naples, Aug. 20, 1799, in the cause of Italian independence. Nic., 288.

This man's rebuff made me lose hope of finding grace with others. I sought simply to hide my pitiable circumstances as carefully as I could from people in that town, in order not to give my enemies a chance to laugh.

The Governor of the city might have been willing to alleviate my distress, but I dared not reveal my trouble to him through a certain reserve for which later on he had the kindness to reprove me. My despondency was extreme. A most honorable and generous countryman of mine who was almost alone in not avoiding intercourse with a man generally regarded with contempt, was observant enough to detect it and to lend me some consolation with offers and aid. But he was not rich, nor I without sense of proprieties; everything I took from his mouth was an incredible burden on my spirit. Aside from that I was not alone; and many times at the very moment when I would sit at the table of my charitable Philemon partaking of a nourishment essential to life, my heart would be weeping for the three hungry mouths to which that day I had not been able to administer a crumb of bread. Such the horrible picture of the state in which I lived for more than three months.

Meantime there came to Trieste the usual company for the Opera of that season. The manager of the troupe, a well balanced and discerning, if not a generous, man, asked me to assist him in the production of the *Ape musicale*, an opera which I had written without a composer for the theater at Vienna. The performance was enough of a success for him willingly to pay me a certain sum fixed by him which, though moderate, was of the greatest relief to me in my then circumstances.

The opera troupe was followed by a company of actors. The few friends I had in the city—among them I will proudly name the Governor, Baron Pittoni,[53] Count Soardi and my country-

---

53. Baron Pier Antonio Pittoni was police inspector at Trieste, and a friend of many of Da P.'s friends, including Casanova and Zaguri. Mol., I, 226. Russo, 78, shows

man Lucchesi—urged me almost by force to have some play I might have written performed. I had received from my brother, some time before his death, the two first acts of a tragedy which had never been polished or completed. I revised it, wrote the ending, and made a present of it to that company. It was performed with success and the first to make glowing praises of it was Colletti. His shameless double-facedness aroused in me a resentment which I had hitherto smothered *pro bono pacis*. I did not judge it time, as yet, to touch off the mine, all the more since my heart, partly through the hopes I nourished in the promises of the Emperor, partly through the praises lavished on me for that opera of mine and this new tragedy, was beginning not only to grow tranquil again, but to acquire new energy and new life. The first proof that I had of this was a very serious relapse into the ties of love, from which, just before that, I had freed myself with an ease and perfection that surprised me.

Bear with me, courteous reader, while I relate this one more story of my loves. I believe that it will be the last of which I can permit myself to speak. But this one happens to be of too much importance in my life for me to overpass it in silence.

When I left Vienna for Trieste, the lady of whom I was enamored departed for Venice. My intention at that time was to have an interview with Leopold, defend and prove my innocence, and then to go on to Venice also.[54] But in spite of all the

---

that the play produced at Trieste in the autumn of 1791 was a *Messenzio* begun with his brother Luigi (not the "Duke of Warwick" [Nic., 289], on which he worked with his brother Girolamo). The *Ape* was the old *Pasticcio*.

54. Da P. made at least two attempts in this year (1791) to obtain revocation of his banishment at Venice; one in April, presented by his brother, Agostino, a "political broker," so to speak; another later in the summer or autumn. Both were refused. Nic., 286, 289.

proofs I had given of true friendship, in spite of terrible sacrifices I had made for her, in spite, in a word, of a thousand promises, a thousand protestations, of love and of gratitude, a vain yearning for a wealth longed for but never attained filled her natively romantic head with a thousand dreams of vanity and grandeur; and partly through weakness of character, partly through the seductions of a contemptible individual not worthy of mention here, she forgot not only every sentiment of affection and gratitude, but exerted herself unworthily to have withheld from me the sweet pleasure of returning to my country. However, this act of feminine iniquity was shortly turned by my good sense to my own saving. In less than a month I found myself free of an ignominious passion which for three years had continuously held me unhappy slave to that woman. After that I did not think it a possible thing for me to fall in love again. I was mistaken. My heart was not, and is not perhaps, able to exist without love; and regardless of the many tricks and betrayals women have worked to my damage in the course of my life, I truly cannot remember having passed six months in the whole course of it, without loving someone and loving—I choose to make boast—with a perfect love.

I happened, accordingly, at just this time, to be introduced to a young English girl,[55] daughter of a rich merchant,[56] who

---

55. Ann Celestine Grahl, a converted Jewess (Anglican), born in London early in the year 1769, a date I deduce from her death certificates in New York, Dec. 12, 1831 (Board of Health and Trinity Parish), and from a letter of Da P.'s to Dr. Francis, July 1831, which give her age as 62. Ann Grahl was the only one in that family of English birth. John Grahl was born in Dresden. Ann says that her mother, Antoinette, was a French lady. Louisa Grahl Niccolini passed in Sunbury as a French woman (traditions of the Hall and Colt families); while Sunbury oral tradition (reduced to writing about 1840) had Peter Grahl born in the French West Indies!

56. The Grahls, father and son, were expert chemists, a proficiency they turned for the most part to trade (drugs, spices, liquors, medicines); but also to distilling. In

had arrived shortly before in Trieste. She was talked of by everyone as most beautiful of person, combining with attractive manners all the graces of a cultivated mind. But as she kept her face covered with a black veil, which prevented my sight of her, I could think of nothing else than to know whether the fact corresponded to her fame. So I approached her a little more attentively; and with a certain assurance which an intrinsic intimacy established by me previously with her family allowed me, I said, as though in jest:

"Mademoiselle, the way in which you wear your veil is not in fashion."

Not catching my thought, she answered:

"How should it be worn to be in style?"

"This way, signorina."

And taking her veil by the edge, I raised it and draped it over her head. It seemed that my jest was not to her liking, and she left the room a few minutes after. But I had found her beautiful in truth, and regretted therefore infinitely having displeased her by that gaiety. For some days I had no further occasion to see her. Though the sister-in-law of the young demoiselle, who had great friendship for me,[57] assured me that the pout would soon pass, I did not even dare let it enter my head that she might be feeling any beginning of an attachment to me; and that not only because I was not less than twenty years her senior, but because I was poor, and she the daughter of a rich father, with numbers of suitors who were aspiring to her hand, all of them rich and very much younger than I.

She was living at the time with an English lady whose great friend she was, and came sometimes to her father's house to

---

addition they were usurers, and speculators in bad debts, notes, discounts, judgments, chattels, mortgages, real estate, the elder Grahl, especially, navigating in those turbid waters with a certain shrewdness and coming out on the winning end.

57. Elizabeth Grahl, wife of Peter Grahl.

pay visits to her people. Being a frequent caller at that house, I asked the father and brother one day whether they would consent to give the girl to an Italian merchant then living in Vienna, and who, before I left that city, had manifested to me a desire to marry an English girl. I informed them of the age, character, and estate of the young man. They discussed it with the young lady and, by common consent, I wrote and had a favorable reply. Portraits were exchanged and in a fortnight both parties seemed satisfied. But the girl had forgotten the business of the black veil, and was now on cordial terms with me, teaching me French while I taught her Italian. Both she and I were beginning to feel an indescribable something in our conversations which inclined them to last somewhat longer than they usually do between friends and language students, a something which worked upon us both with much effect and ended in a reciprocal enamoring between the promised bride and the go-between no longer young. However she spoke no word of love to me, nor I to her. But what lips did not say, affectionate glances, significant sighs, halting words, and above all the need we felt of always being together and always at each other's sides said eloquently enough.

I had already written to my friend in Vienna that the family consented readily, that his picture pleased, and that his coming to Trieste to settle the details, was eagerly awaited. His reply did not reach me for several days, days all of mortal agony for me. I was standing one evening at her side, when her brother entered and handed me a letter. I recognized the writing and with trembling hand and even more trembling heart opened it and read aloud. Here were the exact words:

> Dear friend:
>
> If the girl looks like her picture, she is very beautiful. Reports from all of my friends as to her breeding, character, and training could not be more favorable. But they

tell me that her father is quite wealthy. I have a plenty myself, but as a precaution in the interests of possible children, I should like to know what dowry he would settle on her on my marrying her.

I had scarcely pronounced these words, than the father snatched the paper from my hand, tore it into a hundred tiny shreds, cast them furiously into the fire, and then exclaimed angrily:

"Ah! Ah! So Signor Galliano" (Galliano was the merchant's name) "is after my money and not my daughter!"

He stood silent and thoughtful a few moments; took three or four steps about the room; and then turned toward me:

"Friend Da Ponte," he said, "do you want her?"

"Whom?" I replied, laughing.

"My daughter!" he answered. I continued laughing.

"And you, Nancy, what do you say? Will you have him?"

She lowered her eyes, smiled, raised them, looked at me with amorous bashfulness; and her father, thinking to see in my laughter and in her silence what was in fact in both our hearts, took my hand and hers, joined them very tightly together, and said to me:

"Nancy is yours!"

Then to her:

"Da Ponte is yours."

The mother, the brother, and the sister-in-law applauded this extemporized scene, but my joy and, I believe hers, was such and so great at that moment that neither she nor I was able to say another word for all the remainder of that evening. I left the house in a state not easily to be depicted. My entire wealth at that time consisted of five dollars. I had no present employment, nor much hope of finding any; and the destruction of the letter by the girl's father because of Galliano's request, gave me no illusions as to any fortune from him. But I loved her. She loved me. And that was enough to make me dare everything on that occasion and encourage me to leap all obstacles.

Six months had passed, meantime, since the day of the great dialogue. I judged that Augustus had had time enough to decipher things and cancel or contradict bad impressions. I ventured to recall my name to him through M—— S——,[58] who was still enjoying the Cæsarean favor; but my mediator replied that it was still too soon, that *Sua Majestas haberet inde multas molestias, quas tu scire non potes.*

I renewed pressures, depicted my situation, wrote letters, and had a word said for me by the Venetian ambassador who seemed still to be showing me patronage. The replies were invariably inconclusive, uncertain, vague, but they never omitted the "Don't worry, the Emperor will recall you," the *nondum venit hora tua*, or other things of like tenor that continued to keep me in a fatal hope and that brought me in the end to the verge of imminent desperation. Lucky for me that my "shrewd friend" freed me from it!

And who was this friend? The Abbé Casti! I owe my rescue to his acuteness. He had passed through Trieste two months previous, whence he pushed on to Vienna, and I had sought the pleasure of frequent conversation with a man whose lips rarely parted except to utter some delightful and pleasing remark. My veneration for true merit had caused me to forget all the past, and I believed that my vicissitudes must have induced him, too, to forget certain literary aversions. I therefore opened my heart to him, and asked him for advice with the greatest truthfulness.

"Seek a crumb of bread in Russia, England, or France!" that eminent tactician kept saying to me dryly.

---

58. Nicolini identifies tentatively as the same Stefani mentioned above, 183. Casti, however, had returned to Vienna before Da P.'s dismissal. Nic., 289.

"But the Emperor has promised to recall me."

"The Emperor will not keep his word."

"But his secretary wrote me to wait."

"His secretary is an ass."

"But my honor, my enemies!"

"Russia, England, or France! There you will get revenge on your enemies, and find again without trouble markets overstocked with honor!"

I could easily guess whence the stubbornness of this advice arose; though I could not attribute such weakness to my good Casti. He himself was kind enough to enlighten me:

"You know," he told me one day, "I was Court poet to Leopold when he was Archduke of Tuscany. I met him in Italy recently, and suggested that, since he had advanced in station, I had hopes of promotion, too. He answered that my request was very reasonable, and that I could consider myself as good as poet laureate, the moment I arrived in Vienna."

Casti then did me the honor to ask me to read four "tragic farces" for music, which he had designed to offer Leopold for his Opera. But that convinced me! "Casti," I said to myself, "does not want me at Vienna!" I could not bring myself to imagine that he could be honoring me by regarding me as a rival. I well knew that Casti had too sublime a conception of his own merit to let such nonsense even enter his head; but, whatever the reason, I concluded that he preferred to have no obstacles either great or small in the way of hopes that he still believed I had frustrated on another occasion.

What therefore should I do? The Emperor continued silent. Regardless of what my friends wrote, my hopes were invariably disappointed. My money was again giving out. Add to this the private interest of a Casti, whose powerful eloquence and shrewd maneuvering I knew of experience, having already found it most embarrassing to me in days gone by while Joseph was still alive. After much thinking, mourning, cursing, I resolved to adopt the counsel of the great poet. The first country that then came to my mind was Paris. I had a letter from Joseph to the Queen of France which I thought should be sufficient to help me find some position congenial to my studies.[59]

I wrote, accordingly, to Casti and begged him to say, or have someone say, to the Emperor that, seeing that circumstances had changed, I was limiting my expectation to asking some assistance in order that I might leave Trieste for Paris, where I intended to take refuge abandoning such hopes as his words had aroused in me. I was not mistaken in my conjecture. Casti spoke of the matter to Count Saur and the latter to the Sovereign. He continued silent. I could think of nothing else to do. Despair, at that point, tore the following letter from my pen:

Sire:

The cries of my despair should by now have reached the August Throne. I know not what effect they may have produced. No one has taken the trouble to inform me. I renew them therefore to Your Majesty myself, unable longer to endure the excess of a crushing misery, and constrained to implore from Your justice some decisive command that will take me from my hopes or from my error. I can not fear not being hearkened to: my supplication bearing with it the support of promises by a King, the deserts of a patient reasonableness, and the truthful picture of a man who finds himself at the extremes of indigence through his worshipful trust in Your Majesty's word.

---

59. He gave it to me at the time he dismissed the Italian company, with the words: "Antoinette likes your *Cosa rara* very much." —L. Da P.

I allowed three weeks to go by. Then seeing no response whether from the Emperor or from his ministers, and at the suggestion of the governor, I desperately resolved, *indocilis pauperiem pati*, to go to Vienna myself. But lacking the money to make the journey, I modestly disclosed my plan and my circumstances to the Bishop[60] of the place, a man of the greatest prestige through the fame of his sanctity and his learning. He did not care to have me in Trieste. An atrocious foe to the memory of the anti-Jesuit Joseph, who had loved and patronized me; disapproving the life and works of a free-living poet not always soaked in holy water, I concluded that he would do everything to be free of me, paying my fare to Saturn and beyond, to say nothing of to Vienna. He, in fact, listened to me with holy and charitable patience and was, or seemed to be, deeply touched by my peroration; but since, he said, I had had the misfortune to displease the Emperor, his master and mine, all he could do for me was to commend me to God in his devout prayers. Such fruit indeed do the devotion and the charity of certain sterile sprouts of the sanctuary often bear!

Departing from the Bishop, I determined to go to the Governor and declare my resolution and my circumstances to him. He had no reputation as a holy man, and was censured and hated of many. He listened to my story sympathetically, judged my decision a good one, and, without being asked, entered his study, and returning thence in a moment, placed twenty-five sequins in my hand with these words:

"Here are twenty-five sequins. That much will cover the expenses of your journey. Pray accept them, my dear Da Ponte, and rest assured that I give them to you most eagerly. When will you be leaving?"

"Tomorrow," I replied.

---

60. Sigismund Anton, Count von Hochenwart, formerly tutor to Leopold's children, later Bishop at Vienna. Nic., 290.

"Very well, call here again before you go, and I will give you a letter for the Sovereign."

I called, as he bade; but he had thought it over and concluded that it would be better to write to the Emperor before I should start, and await his reply. He wrote in fact. When after ten days, no reply had come, I departed, on his advice, for the capital.

Arriving at the gates of the latter, I found that Leopold had died that same morning![61]

The news stunned me; but after some reflection, I repeated with Casti in "Theodorus": *Sia che si vuol: noi non starem mai peggio.*

It is true that I could have demanded justice of Leopold and could ask only grace of his son. But the former did not have my name on his good list; the latter seemed to like me and believe me innocent. I therefore entered the city in good spirits, and took it into my head to go directly to Casti.

He seemed surprised at that, but listened to everything, approved of my course, and promised me his assistance. And in fact be it said to the glory of truth, that there was nothing he did not do to my advantage on that occasion, and whatever his motives may have been, I was nonetheless obliged to him, nor did I profess to him then, nor do I profess to him now that he is dead, a gratitude any less sincere. He was my persecutor: feeling as a man has a right to feel, but also through my plain duty as historian, I have had to paint him as such in my Memoirs. He was also my benefactor; and being such, it is my duty to confess it, and to profess for him the obligation that he deserves. It will appear in the course of these Memoirs, whether at the proper times I was able to remember that duty. The Abbé Casti advised me to go to Count Saur, who was his par-

---

61. March 1, 1792. Mme. Ferrarese went to Vienna at the same time, but refused to see Da P. Nic., 290.

ticular friend and whose kindness, integrity, and good disposition toward me, he could vouch for. The Count, furthermore, was a most powerful person through his post as chief of police. Casti insisted on accompanying me and became my defender, apologist, and most zealous eulogist. He succeeded in arousing the Count's enthusiasm to such an extent that he promised either to obtain a private audience from the new ruler for me, or to have my claims granted without reserve. And so it was. Francis could give audiences to no one on account of his father's death. But he sent me a hundred sovereigns through Count Saur, according an ample permission therewith to remain in Vienna at my own discretion, and to publish notice of the recognition of my innocence in the newspapers of all the Austrian States.

The effect of this blow on my enemies need not be described. I lingered three weeks in that city. More than a hundred Italians came to visit me, but I received very few of them. On the faces of these I could clearly see consternation, envy, displeasure, and, above all, a devouring curiosity to know just how such a metamorphosis had occurred. I amused myself hugely at their expense, telling one thing to one, and another to another, and to no one the truth.

The new poet at the Opera[62] was above all anxious to know whether I intended to leave Vienna, or settle permanently again. I knew his writings but not him. He had written an infinite number of operas and by dint of practice had learned something of the art of producing theatrical effects. But to his misfortune he was not born a poet and did not know Italian. In consequence his works were better adapted to the stage than to reading. The whim came into my head to meet

62. Giovanni Bertati (1735–1805). Da P. had used the libretto B. wrote for Gazzaniga's *Don Giovanni* virtually scene by scene in composing his own libretto for Mozart. March., 229–319. Gamerra replaced Bertati in 1794. Nic., 291.

him. I called on him in high spirits. When I arrived at his quarters, he was talking to one of the singers, at the door of his
room. I halted in front of him. He asked me my name. I told
him I had had the honor of being his predecessor and that my
name was Da Ponte. He seemed struck by a lightning bolt.
Embarrassed, confused, he asked me in what way he could be
of service to me, but never budging from the door. When I
told him that I had something to communicate to him, he
felt obliged to show me into the room, which he did, though
with some reluctance. He offered me a chair in the middle
of the room. I took one, quite without intention, near the
table where I judged by appearances that he usually wrote.
Seeing me seated, he took the desk chair, and began dexterously to set in order piles of papers and books that littered
the table. I was, however, quick enough to see what the books
in great part were: a tome of French comedies, a dictionary,
a rhymer, and Corticelli's grammar—these at the poet's right;
those to his left, I was not able to see. I then thought I
understood why he did not care to have me enter. He
asked me again what he could do for me and I, having no
excuse ready, said that I had called for the pleasure of meeting
a man of so much merit and to beg him to give me a copy
of my works, which at my departure from Vienna I had forgotten to take with me. He told me contemptuously that he
had nothing to do with my books, but that they were on
sale, on behalf of the management, at the box office. I spent
another ten minutes with him. Then having discovered that
in every respect the signor poet Bertati was nothing more
nor less than a bag of wind, I took my leave and went, in fact,
to the box office. I found, with as much surprise as satisfaction, that the librettos of nine of my operas had all been
sold; that they had been produced continuously for a year
with the same success; and that when a new opera was not
popular, which occurred very often, recourse was immediately

had to one of mine, particularly to those of Mozart, Martini, and Salieri. Enemies of mine in Vienna, if ye have not all yet taken your plunge to the depths of Malebolge, deny, if ye dare, this statement that I have made! I went back to find Casti and talked to him of the visit I had made to Bertati, of the apparatus on his table, of the manner in which he received me. But after listening for a moment or two, he made only this comment:

"He is just a poor donkey. He is writing an opera for Cimarosa. He does not deserve that honor—I'll write you how it turns out."

I parted from Casti as one parts from a friend; and in time I gave him proofs of being one, as we shall see in the proper place. Then I took leave of my good friends in Vienna and returned to Trieste. Since I had resolved to leave immediately for Paris, I seized that occasion to give a little poetical chastisement to my good friend Colletti, whose nauseating adulation and hypocrisy had doubled my anger and disgust. He had in just these days infected the city with a volume of verses, all of the same caliber. I accordingly wrote a burlesque ode, gave it to a friend to read to friends of his, but he, instead, published it in the press. I will repeat the first two lines for the benefit of my reader, and that Colletti may know that I was the author of the little lampoon which began:

> Mio caro Colletti
> non far più sonetti.

I know that all the people in Trieste were amused, and I know that Signor Colletti was not amused. But neither was I amused that first evening I spent at Dresden!

I was on the point of leaving the city, when a letter from Casti came. In it, among other things, he gave me news of Bertati's opera. These were his words:

Last evening came the *première* of *Il matrimonio segreto*. The music is marvelously beautiful, but the words fell very far below expectations, and everyone is dissatisfied, particularly the singers. They are all saying: "Da Ponte will not let this arrogant numbskull go unpunished." I am sending you the libretto, so that you may see and learn how to write pretty verses!

This was my reply:

Dear Sir:

I thank you for the libretto sent to me by you, but I will not follow your advice. You have good enough nails to pull your own chestnuts out of the fire. Bertati's verses are what they might have been expected to be. Let Vienna swallow them. As to the singers, I beg you to say to them: *Victrix provincia—plora!*

This was the first and last opera which the poet Bertati presented to the company at Vienna. It was not long 'ere he departed for Italy, to give place to Gamerra.

I departed for Paris, but not alone. If anyone cares to know with whom I went, he must read the third part of these Memoirs.

PART THREE

S O H E R E I am, courteous reader, in a calèche drawn by
a single horse, in charge of a boy of fifteen or sixteen, and, as
I said—not alone! And would you know who was with me?
My beautiful, fresh, and adorable bride, who after the ceremonies and formalities social, was handed over to me by her
parents, on the twelfth day of August in the year 1792,[1] about
two o'clock in the afternoon. In that equipage, in that company, and with a capital of six to seven hundred florins, at the
age of forty-two years and five months, but with the courage,
or, to be more exact, with the temerity, of a young blade of
twenty, I ventured to launch forth on the high emprise of

---

1. In recounting the marriage of the Duchess Matilde (*Mem.*, I, 23) Da P. distinguished between two ceremonies: the gift at the hands of the parents, and that
from the ministers of the Church. Of his own marriage he mentions only the former, and on two occasions—the betrothal scene with John Grahl, and now, here, a
"handing over" by the parents with ceremonies and formalities social. That some
rite was performed, and a very solemn one, is obvious the moment we consider
the circumstances, and Da P.'s conduct immediately following. It was a rite

reaching Paris from Trieste. My bride's father, it is true, had inquired after the state of my purse just before our departure; but
I could still hear ringing in my ears: "Ah! Ah! Signor Galliano
is after my money, not my daughter," and I could still see bits
of ash from that merchant's letter flitting through the air. I
replied promptly that my purse was in excellent health, that

---

solemn enough to satisfy all parties concerned, including a mother opposed to the
marriage, a father evidently anxious to "settle" his daughter, a groom eager to find
refuge from the tornadoes of life in some cellar well papered with bank notes. It
was a step so serious that in taking it, Da P. knew he was turning his back forever
upon the Latin world; so serious that he first concealed it from Casanova, then
gradually broke the news to him under pledge of absolute secrecy, worrying meantime, lest, for example, "young Wimmer's tutor knew" (Mol., I, 297) what people
in Venice were saying, what people in Vienna were *doing*; a step so serious that
Casanova himself advised Da P. "to flee Rome and all Italy forever," "a voluntary
banishment" Da P. pretended not to understand—"*se pur tu non svelasti il gran
secreto*" (italics his, Mol., I, 310). This is not the atmosphere of an ordinary intrigue: an *abate* with a mistress had nothing to fear in that society; an *abate* with
a wife was in a much more difficult situation. What rite, then? Leave that question to John Grahl, who understood navigation in troubled waters, and who knew
that when one cannot do what one should, one does what one can: five sequins
and a Protestant clergyman (as I should guess, Ann, and perhaps the other ladies—
the mother may not have been a Jewess—being Anglicans); or five sequins and a
rabbi—*inter nos judæos*, and in strict privacy, as is also possible. It was a rite so
queer that Trieste, in awakening to it, not knowing what to call it, called it
Jewish. Fourteen months later Zaguri wrote to Casanova (who knew more, by
then, than Zaguri did): "A propos of Ponte, do you know that that Nancy is an
English Jewess, whom he married at Trieste, to the unspeakable astonishment of a
man I know, one Savordello, who could not imagine what it was all about, for he
saw her married to a regularly ordained priest in a synagogue with a Jewish rite?
I'll bet you did not know that. Ponte probably kept it quiet. Savordello may have
been stuffing me; but how believe that, since he said it quite casually, speaking of
Ponte and his affair with the Ferrarese." (Mol., II, 246). Nicolini (292) says that
Zaguri did not believe Savordello. It is true that Zaguri here raises the doubt; but
only to dismiss it; and he wrote later (March 19, 1794): "How the devil did Ponte
manage to pass himself off as a Jew in Trieste, where he has (*sic*) been living for a
long time?"

I considered I should be more than satisfied with winning his daughter, making no pretensions to a penny of his money. But I was delighted nevertheless when her mother, an excellent woman and the real gem of the family, afterwards presented her Nancy with a little purse of gold coins to the value perhaps of a hundred florins. This sum, though trivial in itself, came in very handy at a certain moment later on, as we shall see.

That evening we reached Leibach, where we stopped for the night, and where Amor and Hymen taught me to dry the tears of a tender girl who was leaving parents and friends, perhaps forever, to be mine. We resumed our journey the next morning, and proceeded for a number of days without untoward incident. But in crossing the mountain of Lichtmessberg at twilight one evening, my wife fancied that in the distance she could see two men armed with guns. We had dismounted from the carriage to give the horse a rest while descending that steep crest. I had thrown one of my arms around my wife's waist and with the other hand was holding an umbrella to protect us from a fine drizzle that was then falling. Frightened by the lateness of the hour, the loneliness of the spot, and by what she had seen, my wife imagined that the two men were robbers, and without due care drew forth the purse her mother had given her, and stuffed it between my vest and my shirt, thinking perhaps that she was putting it between my shirt and my body. We went on down the road. The two persons drew near, greeted us courteously, and passed on. What we had taken for guns were nothing more than two long sticks with iron tips made for the convenience of mountain climbers; the "thieves," two farmers, very aged both, on their way home from work—and we laughed not a little at our fears.

But a few minutes later we arrived at the Abbey of Saint Edmund, situated at the foot of the mountain. There we ceased our laughing, and for a reason. When my wife asked me for the purse, I perceived that it was gone! We immediately went back up the mountain with lanterns and lighted torches, and for more than an hour searched every inch of the road. Our efforts vain, we returned distressed and disconsolate to the inn. In the morning we went to see the abbot at the monastery and he at once had our loss announced to the full congregation of his church. This, too, was vain. Nevertheless the good priest assured me that if any of his parishioners had found the purse, I could be quite certain of hearing from him—such the confidence he had in the uprightness of his people. He therefore wished me to leave him my addresses in the principal cities through which I was intending to pass on my journey before arriving in Paris; whereupon we left the monastery and started out again on the road.

We halted at Prague for several days, in the hope, which proved vain, of receiving news from the Father Abbot. Meanwhile I had an opportunity to attend performances of the three operas I had written for Mozart. It is not easy to convey an adequate conception of the enthusiasm of the Bohemians for that music. The pieces which were admired least of all in other countries were regarded by those people as things divine: and, more wonderful still, the great beauties which other nations discovered in the music of that rare genius only after many, many performances, were perfectly appreciated by the Bohemians on the very first evening.

I had been intending thence to go on to Dresden; but remembering that Giacomo Casanova owed me several hundred florins, and was living only a short distance from Prague, I ventured to pay him a visit in hopes of obtaining all or part of the money due me. I went and was well received; but soon observing that his purse was leaner than mine, I could not put him to the mortification of asking him for something he would have been unable to give; so after a visit of three or four days, I decided to go on to Dresden. As bad luck would have it, he asked permission to accompany me as far as Toeplitz, a city some ten or twelve miles distant from the estates of Count Waldstein, whose librarian and friend Casanova was. That compelled me to take another horse and another driver, and the new horse ran away and threw us out. We were obliged to stop for half a day to get our carriage repaired; but notwithstanding all the work done on it, when we reached Toeplitz I found that we could not continue our journey in it without danger of our lives. I therefore sold for sixty dollars a carriage and a horse that had cost me more than a hundred, and Casanova, who acted as broker in the sale, in counting out the money kept two sequins for himself.

"These," he said, "will get me back home; and since I can never return either these, or the others for which I am in your debt, I will give you three pieces of advice which will be worth much more than all the treasures of this world: first, my dear Da Ponte, if you would make your fortune, do not go to Paris—go to London; second, when you get to London, never set foot inside the *Caffé degl' Italiani*; and third, never sign your name!"

Happy me, had I religiously followed his advice! Almost all the ills and losses I suffered in that city (we shall shortly see why I preferred London to Paris) came from my having frequented the *Caffé degl' Italiani*, and from having signed my name imprudently and without understanding the consequences.

My wife had been dazed by the vivacity, the eloquence, the inexhaustible vein, and all the many ways, of that extraordinary old man. When we left him she desired the whole story of his life from me; and I entertained her pleasantly for many hours, recounting to her what I knew of it. It may not displease my reader to hear a part of the story; that portion, namely, which in one respect or another had some connection with me, or of which I myself was an eyewitness.

Giacomo Casanova was born in Venice. There, after numerous ups and downs of fortune, he was lodged in the *Piombi*

by order of the Inquisitors of State, and this because a certain
lady[2] complained to a member of that tribunal, who happened
to be her "serving cavalier," that Casanova had been reading
Voltaire and Rousseau with her children. After eight or nine
years of confinement he escaped from those prisons by an astonishing device, and the story of that flight, which he wrote
under title of "The New Trenck," is generally read with as
much wonderment as delight. He came to know many cities of
Europe, among others, Paris. Among the countless adventures
that befell him on his travels, I choose to select one which,
while greatly amusing my readers, will give, at the same time,
an accurate idea of the character of the man.

Highly tempered of passions, and with an infinitude of
vices, he required for the indulgence of the ones and the others, a great deal of money, as may well be believed; and when
he was hard pressed therefore, there was nothing he would
stop at to obtain it. Finding himself, on one occasion, reduced
to a penniless condition, he chanced to be introduced to a
very wealthy lady who, though nearly sixty, had a mad passion
for handsome men. Perceiving this weakness, Casanova began
to woo her with the greatest care, and pretended to be enamored of her. In her own relentlessly honest mirror the good old
woman could see only too clearly the wrinkles in her forehead
and the silver in her hair. She placed little credence in his
declarations of love. So one day, secretly, and with an air of
great mystery, he told her that he was skilled in the magic arts,
and that he not only saw her as she had been in her palmy

2. Maria Teresa Zorzi Dolfin, beloved of Antonio Condulmèr. However Casanova's
persecutrix was Bernardo Memmo's mother. Nic., 292. Casanova was in prison
not eight or nine years but sixteen months. Sheppard, 205. The French lady, mentioned at length below, was the Marchioness d'Urfé; the courtesan, one Corticelli;
the valet, Gaetano (not Gioacchino) Costa. Casanova puts his encounter with
Costa in Venice. Da P. met Casanova the second time in Vienna, probably in 1783,
while C. was secretary to the Venetian legation. Nic., 292–3.

days, but that it would be a very simple matter for him to bring everyone, including the lady herself with her own eyes, to seeing her as she had been at the age of sixteen or eighteen. To this tale she listened with amazed delight. Casanova, therefore, without losing a moment's time, set out to illustrate by actual demonstration the marvels of such a splendid art. To which the credulous woman consenting, he went straightway to a rather pretty courtesan of his acquaintance, dressed her up in his own fashion, instructed her as to everything that she must do and promised her a rich reward, if the business should turn out as planned.

Having dismissed all her servants from her rooms, the old woman went to a secret chamber to await her young Atlas; he arrived a few moments later with an old woman, who looked, on close scrutiny, to be not less than seventy years of age. Casanova drew from his pocket a little phial, and, mumbling a rigmarole of words, gave his old woman to drink of the contents—it was none other than red wine, but, according to Casanova, it was a miraculous liqueur from a certain font of his, whence was to proceed the great miracle. He made his accomplice stretch out on a sofa, covered her with a black cloth, and after various incantations, ordered his old woman to rise. She had already rid herself of her rags, her dyes, and her other disguises, and soon leapt forth with youthful sprightliness into the middle of the room, now appearing what in fact she was, a most attractive girl of sixteen or seventeen.

What the amazement of the old lady, is easier to imagine than describe. She threw her arms about the girl, pressed her to her bosom and kissed her hundreds and hundreds of times, and after asking her various questions, to which the sagacious maiden replied with much shrewdness, dismissed her.

Casanova pretended to accompany the girl, but returning shortly, found his old lady roiling in transports of joy, wonderment, and amorous expectation. She rushed upon him more

215

in guise of Bacchante than of woman, and dragging him to her wardrobe nearby, opened the latter, showed him a great quantity of gold and precious jewels, and vowed that all those riches, and in addition, her hand and heart, should be his, if he should work on her that same wondrous miracle of rejuvenation. Casanova had already arranged things for his own purposes and volunteered, accordingly, to work the desired metamorphosis at once. To which the silly female lending herself joyfully, she swallowed the miraculous liqueur to the last drop, stretched herself out on the same sofa where the young girl had been, and her beloved magician began his incantation. But the sweets and powders mingled in the wine were none other than a fair dose of laudanum. In a short time it did not fail of its accustomed effects. When he heard her snoring aloud, Casanova went to the wardrobe, made perfect sack of its contents, extinguished all the lights, and, laden with gold and gems, departed.

Gioacchino Costa was waiting at the door of the mansion on horseback, ready for the flight. Costa was a young man who had been living for many years with Casanova as valet, companion, and friend. Reposing in him a confidence he did not deserve, Casanova handed the treasure over to him and bade him go to a certain tavern some miles distant from Paris and wait for him there. It is said that even thieves have certain codes and certain moments of honor among themselves, to which they dare not play false. This same man, who had not scrupled to steal all that wealth from a deluded old lady, did not think it an honorable thing to leave Paris without rewarding the prostitute who had helped him work his trick. He went to pay her fifty *louis*, and to tell her, in transports of joy that were soon to finish in despair, the happy outcome of his jest. Since those fifty *louis* were all he had kept of the stolen money, he was left without a cent, certain as he was of shortly joining Gioacchino Costa at the inn appointed. But arrived thither, and finding no trace of him either there or in any other neighboring tavern, he cursed the old woman, the girl, Gioachino, and finally himself, since he had been smart enough to trick another with the greatest shrewdness, but at the same time enough of an idiot to let himself be cheated by a wretched lackey.

The state he was in may easily be imagined. It was then that the desire came to him to return to Venice. He wrote the "Anti-Amelot," a work full of spirit if not of scholarship, and was shortly recalled to his country which he had valiantly defended against that atrabilious publicist. It was about that time, in the year 1777, that I had occasion to meet him and gain a certain intimacy with him, in the house, now of Zaguri, now of Memmo, who both loved all that was good in him and forgave the bad. They taught me to do likewise; and thorough examination made of the man, I could not say, even now, on which side the balance tipped. A short time before I left Venice a difference of opinion as to some fatuous point of Latin prosody estranged him from me—that eccentric man would never be left in the wrong!

I departed from Venice and for more than three years I neither saw him nor heard mention of his name again. Finally, one night, I lay dreaming in bed, and I dreamed that I met him on the *Graben*, a street in Vienna where I was then living. It seemed to me that he gazed at me attentively, and then ran toward me with happy face to embrace me; and it seemed to me further that my friend Salieri was with me at that encounter. In the morning, on awakening, I told my dream to my brother —it had been such a curious one.

In those days Salieri was spending his mornings with me. He came that morning at the usual hour, and I went out with him for our walk in a public garden. But there on the *Graben*, I remarked an old man some distance off, who stood looking at me fixedly. His aspect seemed familiar. All of a sudden I saw him start, leap forward from where he was standing, and run joyfully toward me, calling:

"Da Ponte! My dear Da Ponte! What a surprise and what a joy to see you!"

These were the very words that he had said to me in my dream. He who believes in dreams is mad; and he who does not—what is he?

Casanova stayed a number of years in Vienna, where neither I nor others ever knew what he did or how he lived. But I met him frequently. He found both my house and my purse open to him on every occasion; and though I liked neither his principles nor his conduct, I loved him dearly and held his advice and his precepts in high esteem. To tell the truth they were of gold, and though I have profited little by them, I truly might have profited very much.

But to return to the Paris affair and to Costa! I was walking one day with Casanova on the *Graben*, when suddenly I saw him knit his brows, give a little yelp, grit his teeth, twist and wriggle his body, raise his hands to heaven; and then he leapt furiously forward to throw himself upon a man whom he seemed to know, shouting in a loud voice:

"Assassin, I have you!"

As a crowd of people quickly gathered at that cry and that strange aggression, I held off, in some unwillingness to join in such a brawl. Finally, however, I took courage, seized Casanova by the hand and almost by main force dragged him off. It was then that he told me, with the expression and gestures of a man beside himself, the story of the old lady, and explained that the man in question was that same Gioacchino Costa, by whom he had been betrayed. I knew Gioacchino Costa. Though his vices and evil practices had reduced him to menial service and he was at that very time valet to a Viennese nobleman, he too, for good or for ill, was a poet, was, in fact, one of those who had honored me with their satires at the time when the Emperor Joseph chose me as poet to his opera. Gioacchino, meantime, had entered a coffee shop, and while I was walking

up and down with Casanova, listening to his story, he dashed
off the following verses and sent them to Casanova by a boy:

> Casanova, non far strepito;
> Tu rubasti, e anch'io rubai;
> Tu maestro, ed io discepolo,
> L'arte tua bene imparai;
> Desti pan, ti do focaccia;
> Sarà meglio che tu taccia.

> (Casanova, make no noise—
> You a thief, and I a robber,
> You the master, the pupil I,
> You taught me like a master.
> You gave me bread, I give you biscuit—
> It will be much better not to risk it.)

The verses had a good effect. After a brief silence, Casanova
began to laugh, and then whispered softly in my ear:

"The rogue is right."

He entered the coffee shop, and signed to Costa to come
out. They began walking up and down as tranquilly as though
nothing had happened, and separated shaking hands many
times with every appearance of serenity and amicableness.

Casanova came back to me with a cameo ring on his little
finger, which, by a strange coincidence, figured Mercury, protecting god of thieves. That was its principal value. It was the
very all that was left of that rich booty, but it framed perfectly
with the characters of the two reconciled friends.

I shall shortly have further occasion to speak of this very
rare mixture of good and of evil. For the moment let us go back
to our journey.

Arriving at Dresden I had the sweet pleasure of embracing
Mazzolà again, and Father Huber; but not even there did I have

news of the purse lost on that fatal hillside. I stayed on, however, ten days, and this so depleted my little treasury that I decided to send my young *automedon* back to Trieste—now that my horse and carriage was gone he was of no more use to me. But the simpleton was so much enamored of a pair of leather breeches I had promised to give him on arriving in Paris and which I was then wearing myself, that in order to obtain them at the stated time, he persisted, in spite of all offers I made, in a determination to go on with us. I therefore took three places, instead of two, in the diligence to Cassel, and this added expense struck another blow at my pocket already depleted by a half.[3]

At Spires, however, I stumbled accidentally on a very lucky reinforcement without which I might perhaps have found myself in mortal embarrassment. A nobleman, whose name I hardly think it appropriate to mention, was desperately enamored of a beautiful damsel by whom he was not requited. The girl's father, however, loved the young man as cordially as the daughter despised him, and had suggested certain travels with both of them, hoping that time, habitual contacts, and withal the gentle qualities of the young man would finally inspire some sentiment of esteem, and perhaps of love, in the heart of the young girl. But it was all in vain. At dinner time on the day of my arrival in that city, the girl, knowing that her suitor had indeed all the virtues of a well-educated gentleman, but was not a poet, said half jestingly in answer to his pleading:

"Write me a pretty sonnet, and I'll promise to love you."

She believed that this was asking the impossible of him. The father was present at the little scene and said:

---

3. The Da P.'s had also had their baggage robbed at Oberleutendorf, as Da P. informs Casanova in one of the many letters (pub. by Mol., I, 260–316) which cover this northward trip, the first residence in London, and that in Belgium and Holland.

"Courage, my dear Count: try your hand at it once—and I hope that Love will work a miracle."

A few hours later, I arrived at their inn. Happening to be standing at the door there, the young Count saw me, recognized me, ran toward me with outstreched arms, and left me scarcely time to help my bride dismount from the carriage before drawing me aside with him into a room on the ground floor, where he began excitedly:

"A god has sent you here today to comfort me!"

He then told me the whole story and insisted that I write a sonnet for him. I knew the maiden very well. She was, in truth, an amazing combination of beauty, grace, and all those ornaments which make a young lady lovable. I set myself to work forthwith, and in less than half an hour handed him the following sonnet:

Facciam—disser gli dèi—facciam un opra, etc.

I declaimed the poem to him in grandiloquent style, and at each verse he seemed transported. He copied it in his best handwriting and, after a thousand thanks, begged me not to let his lady see me, that she might not suspect my handiwork. He then presented me with a splendid watch with chain and seals of gold which I sold at Rotterdam for two hundred florins (for me they were two hundred angels of paradise), and promised to inform me of results at Brussels, whither I believed I should be passing on my way to Paris. (In fact, they both wrote, and I learned that they were happy.)

I was however not more than a few miles beyond Spires when, the stage having stopped at a tavern to allow our horses to rest, I learned the distressing news of the imprisonment of the Queen of France and of the arrival of the French army at Mayence. After a brief consideration and remembering Casanova's advice, which happened to accord with a desire of my bride, I made sudden resolve to go to London instead of to Paris, and took accordingly the road for Holland.

On my journey between Spires and London, nothing of note happened to me, if one except the imminent risk in which I found myself on one occasion of seeing myself robbed of my bride. Arriving at a certain tavern (I do not remember just how far from Spires) a few hours before sundown, we stopped for several minutes to give the horses their fodder. In the room where we sat waiting, we found two individuals of most disquieting aspect who were idling at a table, gulping down huge goblets of wine one after another. Their eyes happened to fall on us, and believing perhaps that neither my wife nor I understood German, they began speaking to each other in that language. Though I did not catch everything they said we pieced together between us enough to make out that their design was to follow me on horseback and kidnap my daughter—such the difference in our ages made my wife appear. I then began to speak German with her, and gave them to understand that I was her husband. I asked the innkeeper, furthermore, for a few bullets for my pistol; and he seeming, as he was in fact, an honest man, I told him what I had heard, and he went to them and frankly told them that they should have a care of what they were saying for he had very ready means of punishing them.

"Sir," he then added, "I am the judge of this little village. Continue your journey tranquilly and it will be my care that these fine fellows stay to sup with me this evening."

With this assurance I departed tranquilly. What became of the two rogues I never heard.

So I arrived safely in London[4]: but my whole possessions at that time consisted of six *louis*, a watch with a gold chain, and a ring that I afterwards sold for six guineas. A sister of my wife

---

4. In Dresden on Sept. 26, 1792, Da P. must have reached London early in October. Mol., I, 267–72.

was living in London with her husband; but they were neither rich, nor generous.[5] We lodged with them for a few days, whereafter we took a little room of our own and in a very short time I saw the bottom of my purse.

Poet at the Italian opera in London at that period was a certain Badini: and prime mover of the policies of William Taylor,[6]

---

5. Louisa Grahl and her husband, Charles Niccolini, of whom more, hereafter.

6. Da P. abbreviates and confuses somewhat. His letters to Casanova (Mol., I, 273 ff.) are more exact. Michael Kelly and Stefano Storace were in charge when Da P. first arrived (Da P. did not hear of Teller [Taylor] till he was in Holland, Oct. 1793. It was for Kelly, not for Taylor, that he began negotiations for the importation of Martín from Russia). In Oct. 1792, the post of poet at the London Opera was vacant through the death of Antonioli. Da P. was a candidate, but himself proposed (he says) Carlo Francesco Badini, an Italian poet and musical critic already resident in London for twenty-five years. This was "to avoid unpleasantness." But when Badini was appointed (Dec. 1792), Da. P. announced a critical periodical, the *Bilancia Teatrale*, to intimidate the London management in his own favor, as he baldly explains to Casanova. In March he came out with a volume of verse—a *tributo del cuore* to Louis XVI. Of this Badini took advantage to entitle his rejoinder (to the *Bilancia*) as *Il tributo della coglionatura*, which Da P. had seen, and was already answering in April, with "twelve sonnets and a canzone," though Badini did not publish till May 2. In January 1793, he had already made arrangements with Mara (Gertrude Elizabeth Schmoeling-Mara, 1749–1833) for the reduction to libretto form of the *Mesenzio* (Russo, 78) which he had begun with his brother Luigi, finished and produced in Trieste (1791), and was to publish much later in New York (1834), receiving for it not thirty guineas but twenty-five *louis*. Meantime he was playing Casanova's patron, the Duke of Waldstein, then in London, for money (unsuccessfully—4 guineas!) and for an appointment at Dux; and the composer, Pietro dal Pozzo (his "Pozzi"), the Marquis of Salisbury, and Italian diplomats, for work at the Opera. Casanova meantime was suggesting that he turn language master, a proposal which Da P. deprecated, but nevertheless accepted, hiring a room and organizing a class which he thought would net him 15 guineas a month. Then Casanova suggested that he try promoting an Opera at Brussels, a suggestion which Da P. adopted on July 10. The residence in Belgium, where Ann joined him, Da P. does not mention in the *Mem*. In a word—the confusion in the narrative of the *Mem*. is straightened out if the paragraphs on Taylor and Federici are transferred to a point following Da P.'s return to London in the autumn of 1793.

proprietor thereof, one Vincenzo Federici. The former of these, to other distinguished qualities added that of surpassing Aretin in satire and destructive gossip, and kept a noose around Taylor's neck by virtue of his pen—he had learned English well and was employed as critic on a number of newspapers, whose opinions are accepted as good in London, perhaps to a greater extent than in any other country. The success of Taylor's operas, singers, dancers, and composers, depended in great part on Badini's paragraphs.

Federici was a veritable emporium of iniquities. It was enough for a man to have merit, or merely the reputation for having a little, to be hated and persecuted by him. Though Taylor knew this, he was nevertheless compelled to make use of him, because Federici had found various ways and devices for procuring him money and had no scruples about acting as his Mercury among the Amphitryons of the theater. Of Federici I shall have more to say presently.

With these two rascals at the head of the London Opera, I had not even a remote chance of ever obtaining the post there. My candle burned to the green as it was, I found signs of humaneness or friendship only in Signor Pozzi, a charming composer, and a man courteous, generous, and charitably disposed, though not rich. On various occasions he offered me his purse and introduced me to his friends, among others to the celebrated Mara, who begged me to write an opera for her and gave me thirty guineas when I delivered it, along with a thousand thanks and appreciative courtesies, which for not ignoble souls are worth much more than any amount of money. Finding myself in possession of such a sum, a very considerable one in the circumstances, and seeing that no favorable wind was blowing for me on the banks of the Thames, I left a part of the money with my wife, and decided with the remainder to go to Holland. There, I had heard, the French troupe was closing, and I thought it might be possible to establish an Italian Opera. I was not mistaken. I had not been two weeks in Holland, when I had the most beautiful prospects of a happy outcome. I found two enthusiastic supporters. One was the banker Hope, a very influential gentleman of those provinces; the other General Butzeler, who, aside from having two daughters deeply devoted to music, had a particular esteem for my Nancy, who had lived for many months with his family in Holland, and whose story I had told him by merest accident. Flanked by these two patrons, I offered my plan, and it met with great favor. I asked a guarantee of two hundred thousand florins for two Operas, one at Amsterdam, the other at the Hague. The Stadtholder at the Hague was the first to subscribe and to the amount of forty thousand for the Hague alone, where I planned to give two performances a week. This good beginning encouraged all the others, and I bade fair to have a greater number of subscribers than I really needed.

I accordingly wrote to my wife to come and join me, but she replied that she had not a penny left of the money I had given her. Even the twenty guineas I had brought with me were very near their end; and I really do not know what would have become of her and of me but for a visible intervention of Providence. One day I was telling my story to an honest Italian of my acquaintance. He would have very much liked to help me but he had not the means of doing so. Just then the servant of the house where I was living entered and handed me a letter; I recognized the handwriting. It was from my wife. I opened, with an anxiety that anyone may imagine; and with a surprise not less great than my indescribable joy I read as follows:

> Dear Lorenzo:
>
> I am sending you eighty florins, and am keeping twenty to come and join you. This money I received yesterday from your friend from Prague, who got it from

the good Abbot at Saint Edmund's. A certain peasant, Chersenbaum by name, found the purse on the Licht-messberg a day after our departure. He carried it faith-fully to that good priest, who presented him with two sequins; but not having received many of your letters, he did not know till recently that instead of going to Paris, we had gone to London. You see? You need never despair of Providence. Before a week is over, I shall be with you, and then I will tell you the rest.

Your Nancy.

And in fact she came; but our joy was of short duration. I had written my letters for the best singers and composers of Italy and everything was nearing conclusion,[7] to the rejoicing of all lovers of music and the Opera, when there unexpectedly came the terrible news of the total defeat of the English below Dunkirk, and thoughts of amusements and of festivities gave way to sorrow, lamentations, and prayers. In not many days I found myself in the most deplorable condition on earth: no friends, no property of value, no recourse in view!

The eighty florins did not last long in the hands of a man who to this day has never learned economy; and to cap the climax of our misfortune, it was very difficult to receive letters from anyone, on account of the excessive cold that had blocked

7. The failure at Brussels and at the Hague was due, more than to anything else, to the unwillingness of Italian singers to take Da P. seriously as an impresario. Rovedini, Ferrari, and Madame Storace first consented and then refused. The Ferrarese did not answer. Da P. turned in desperation to Gardassoni at Prague to procure singers; but that gentleman naturally had troubles of his own. Houchard's victory at Handschoote, Sept. 8–9, 1793, was the *coup de grâce*. The invitation to the London Opera came on Oct. 30, 1793. Da P. did not like to give up the good prospects at The Hague. He was still there, Nov. 17, though preparing to leave for London on the 19th. —A. L. following Da P.–Casanova, Mol., I, 290–312.

navigation from London, whence only I could still hope to receive some succor.

In that emergency I resolved to write to Casanova, and, the better to move him, I wrote him in verse, drawing him a pathetic picture of my state and asking him for some money. But he paid no attention to me, and replied wittily in excellent prose, beginning his letter thus:

"When Cicero wrote to his friends, he never mentioned business!"

I then began to give sack to my little trunk of clothes and linen, but that, too, was soon empty. I had taken a room in the house of a kindly-souled German where, with forced parsimony, we lived for more than a week, my wife and I: our breakfast was bread, and bread our dinner. Sometimes not even bread, but tears, made our supper! But the tears were not my helpmeet's! She endured everything with angelic patience, did her best to laugh and jest, obliged me to play at draughts with her, and for huge stakes, the loser to pay in caresses and kisses. These artifices of her tenderness, which in other circumstances would have been the delight of my life, now only increased my affliction and despair.

One evening, after we had had our usual supper of draughts, kisses, and tears, the German landlord, who rented me the room, entered in tears and said:

"My dear Signor Da Ponte, I know that you are not to blame for your present misfortunes, and I take you for an honest man. But that does not feed my family. You have not been able to pay the rent for your first week. Much less will you be able to pay for your second, which began today. Never mind the past: but for the future my poverty would not permit me to overlook such things. Will you therefore please to find other lodgings, and may God bless and assist you, as well as me."

Saying which he departed; but at just that moment entered a certain Cera, who had for many days been our consoling friend, though, being himself in dire poverty, he could do nothing for us except in words. He asked me how things were going, and I told him what had taken place just before he came in.

"Never mind," he commented with great joy, "I have had a beautiful dream, and I hope for the best."

Remembering my dream of Casanova, I begged him to tell me what he had dreamed. He did so, as follows:

"It seemed to me that I could see you and this charming lady in a very thick woods; and that an ugly beast was prowling about you and her, showing you enough of fangs and claws to give good cause for fear. You two tried to evade it as far as you could; but the beast came nearer and nearer and was opening its jaws to seize you; when lo, suddenly that gloomy forest was flooded with light, and from a lofty mountain afar off came a shaft of fire that struck the beast on the flank and stretched it dead at your feet, to be swallowed up an instant later by the earth."

"Dreams for dreams," I replied, "your dream could not be more satisfactory. May it please Heaven that it be rather a vision than a dream! But this poor girl, meanwhile, for all of her condition" (she was very close to being a mother) "has had nothing but bread to eat today, and this evening not even...."

He did not wait to let me finish, but rushed from the room, calling:

"I am going out! I'll be back in a moment."

He was gone so long that I had about given up hope of seeing him again when suddenly I heard the door of the room crash open and saw the good Cera entering with a handkerchief in his hand. This he set joyously on the table and cried:

"This for a good beginning!"

Whereupon he dug out of it bread, butter, eggs, cheese, and some smoked herring, and without losing a moment ran into the kitchen, procured pot and a grill, and was back, running like a deer, to our room. There whistling and singing he set himself to preparing the meal. While cooking his viands, he explained that he had suddenly remembered having lent a small sum of money to a friend some time before. He went to his house, found him, was paid, and with the money had done the shopping which we could see and which he believed would certainly be sufficient for that evening. When everything was cooked, he laid out on the table, for lack of a tablecloth, the paper in which the butter, the cheese, the sugar, the herring had been wrapped; drew from his pocket a little bottle of gin; put three chairs in their proper places; made us sit down, and finally sat down himself.

The joviality and pleasure that shone in his face could do nothing less than arouse like feelings in our own spirits. We ate gaily, found everything exquisite, and judging by the time that we spent at that meal it would have seemed that we had entirely forgotten our horrible predicament. The dinner finished, he mixed some water and sugar in his gin, made me drink a small glass of it, and as he sipped of another, toasted vivaciously:

"To my dreams, that they may come true!"

He departed a few moments thereafter.

We made no further reference to our misfortunes that evening, but went to bed, falling asleep very soon and sleeping peacefully. At the break of dawn I awoke with a strange tranquillity in my soul, a certain joy the source of which, no matter how I studied the matter, could I explain. What I could understand was that I had to leave that house that morning, and my high spirits began to wane, especially when, on answering a quiet knock at our door, I saw the landlord enter, holding out a piece of paper, without speaking. Supposing it to be his bill, and that that early morning presentation was a hint for our immediate departure, I sadly extended my hand to take it in. But he then drew back:

"Here is a letter for you, sir," he said, "but I cannot let you have it, until you give me a shilling. The postman is at the door, and must be paid."

From my pocket I drew my kerchief, the only thing still left me, and begged him to takc it and pay the shilling for me. The old man, deeply moved, waved the handkerchief aside, handed me the letter, and went out.

I looked quickly at the superscription. There was my name, and next to it, three words: "With twenty guineas."

Only people who have found themselves in circumstances like those in which I was can imagine the emotions that swept my soul as I read those words. I showed the letter to my Nancy, pointing to the address, and she cried, exultant:

"It is my sister, writing!"

Then she fell silent for more than five minutes, she, too, all but overcome as I was, by that new and unexpected act of Providence.

At length I opened the letter, and read:

> Dear Da Ponte:
>
> Badini's doings have obliged the manager at the Opera to dismiss him from that theater. Being in need of a poet, and having heard you spoken of, he sent for me and commissioned me to write to you and offer you the position. Since Badini had wormed sixty guineas out of him in advance on his salary, he wishes that you should be satisfied to pay them, deducting them from the two hundred which he offers you. I believe that you will do that, because it is not the money so much that ought to interest you, as the good opportunity to become known in London. On that basis, I ventured to assure him that you would come. He gave me twenty guineas for the expenses of your journey. Come, and come quickly! Your friends, among them, Ferrari, Rovedino, Kelly, and Storace, are waiting for you anxiously: and I am dying to have my Nancy with me again.

On reading that sheet of paper, I could not restrain my tears, which compensated me, in generous double, for those that I had been shedding for so many days and nights in Holland, since the Battle of Dunkirk. I leapt from my bed, went down on my knees beside it, and lifting my hands and my eyes to Heaven, repeated with every sense of religious gratitude four lines I had written for Atar, in my *Assur*:

> Dio protettor de' miseri,
> tu non defraudi mai
> quelli che in te confidano,
> che speran solo in te.

> (God, protector of the wretched,
> Thou never defraudest
> Those who place their trust in Thee,
> Who put their hope only in Thee.)

An hour had not passed when Cera came in. I could not decide where to begin, to give him the glad news. Finally I thought the simplest thing would be to hand him the letter to read, and I did so. The superscription alone, which contained that very lucky "with . . ." was enough to drag from his lungs a prolonged cry of delight which was heard, I do believe, from pole to pole. Then when he read on into what the sheet contained, his rejoicing, and his voicings thereof, were so excessive that I was in very truth alarmed. He sang, danced about the room, jumped into the air, embraced now me, now my wife, and then, after all those manifestations of festive contentment, burst into tears like a child.

At length he restored the letter to me, and said:

"My dear friends, as you see, my dream came true. The thick woods—that's Holland; the London Opera, the lofty mountain afar off; the manager of that Opera, the bowman who shoots the shaft; your poverty, the ugly beast that was menacing you; the Providence of God, the light that came to your succor!"

Verily, there are not many such friends in the world!

Not having anything to detain me in Holland, I departed for London two or three days after receiving that letter. I did not fail, the moment I arrived, to pay my call on the impresario; but, from the reception he gave me, I could see that he had no great friendship for the Muses. He was writing at a table when his friend Federici introduced me into his room, his back turned toward the door, and his face to the window.

"Here is Signor Da Ponte," said Federici.

The manager continued his writing without looking around.

"Mr. Taylor, here is the poet!" Federici repeated then in louder halftone.

The manager turned, bowed his head slightly, and went back to his writing. I stayed perhaps five minutes in the room; then Signor Federici, "passing a finger up from chin to nose," in sign of respectful silence, beckoned me to withdraw.

This was not, to tell the truth, a beginning of good augury for a man who had for ten years been poet to Joseph II of Austria, a Prince who was the true model of affability, kindness, and courtesy. I refrained nevertheless from forming any opinions until I should make a second call, which I judged would have to be soon.

As a matter of fact it was more than three months before I saw Taylor or he me. That was at the performance of Gazzaniga's *Don Giovanni*,[8] an opera suggested by Federici and given to the public on his advice, in bestial preference to the

---

8. March 1794. William Taylor, a restless, picturesque, truly Dapontean figure, started life as a clerk with Snow & Co., bankers. He successfully financed a purchase of the King's Theater, Haymarket, and eventually became sole owner of it. Sheppard, 14. Vincenzo Federici (1764–1827) came to London from Livorno in 1790 and was a composer of some merit. Between 1808 and 1824 he was professor

Don Giovanni of Mozart, brought to London and proposed by me. Taylor then saw himself in danger of finding his Opera dismantled and himself ruined forever; so he was pleased to send for me and ask my opinion on various points touching the enterprise, especially giving me strict orders to call Martini, who was then engaged at the Opera in St. Petersburg, to London.

The coming of that excellent composer all but cost me my post, however. The opera season was almost half over when two famous rivals came to London: the Banti woman, at that time one of the most celebrated singers in Europe in serious parts, and *la* Morichelli, equally celebrated in comedy. They were neither of them any longer young, and never had they been enumerable among the great beauties: but the one was much sought after and exorbitantly paid for the splendors of a glorious voice, the single gift she had received from Nature: the other, for her acting—she gave a performance that was true, noble, carefully worked, and full of expression and grace. They had therefore both become idols of the public but the terrors of composers, poets, singers, and impresarios. One of them alone was enough to make any theater where she was engaged tremble at her name. I leave my good reader to imagine, therefore, what the situation at the Italian Opera in London must have been at a time when both these stage heroines were engaged contemporaneously.

Which of them was the more dangerous and the more to be feared, is a question not easy to decide. Equal in their vices, their passions, their iniquities, their wickedness of heart, they were women of totally different, even contrary, dispositions, proceeding along different routes to the fulfillment of their designs. The Morichelli woman had plenty of talent and a

---

at the Conservatory in Milan. Nic., 299. Anna Bosello Morichelli (?–?) came to London from Spain in Company with Brigida Giorgi Bandi (1756–1806) in April 1794. Sheppard, 221.

notable cultivation of mind. An old fox, she covered her purposes deep under a veil of mystery and finest cunning. She took
her measures always at long range, trusted no one, never lost
her temper, and though fiercely practicing voluptuous in-
dulgences, nevertheless always managed to play the part of a
modest and retiring virgin of fifteen. The bitterer the gall she
harbored in her soul, the suaver and the more honeyed shone
the smile on her face. Of the temper of her dominant passion it
is hardly necessary to speak. She was an actress. Her principal
divinities were those of all her kind, but in an excessive degree: Pride, Envy, Money.

Banti, on the contrary, was an ignorant, stupid, insolent
woman. Accustomed from early girlhood to singing in cafés and
about the streets, she brought to the Opera, whither her voice
only had elevated her, all the habits, manners, and customs of
a brazen-faced Corisca. Free of speech, still freer of action, ad-
dicted to carousals, dissolute amusements, and to the bottle,
she showed herself in the face of everybody for what she was,
knowing no measure, no restraints; and when any one of her
passions was stirred by difficulties or opposition, she became
an asp, a fury, a demon of Hell, capable of upsetting an empire,
let alone a theater.

The moment they arrived in London, they joined battle for
the possession of the manager's heart. On him I do not think it
possible for anyone in the world to pass a just and accurate
judgment. Much less than for any one else is that possible for
me. Dragged by chance into his orbit from the dangerous pass
in which I found myself in Holland, I had, and have always
preserved, toward him all those feelings which gratitude, pity,
and friendship are wont to inspire in gentle and well-bred
spirits. To what extent I carried such sentiments, how finally
I destroyed myself and my family in trying to help or save
him, and how, in the end, he, like everybody else, paid me
with ingratitude, we shall shortly see. Those same sentiments

inclined me never to examine too severely nor study too closely his defects and his weaknesses, which I sought to defend or excuse, as a father would do with a child; and when they chanced to harm me, either I was silent, or exacted no other revenge than plaints. Without pretending, therefore, to draw an adequate picture of the man, I will tell simply what I think I know on the authority of others, or what I think I saw with my own eyes, of the character of William Taylor.

He was, or at least arrived in London, very poor, about the time the Italian Opera House was destroyed by fire. Inspired to become proprietor of a new theater, he made his plan, presented it to the leading gentlemen of that metropolis, and selling them a certain number of boxes for a certain number of years, he found himself in a position to have a theater built with the products of those sales. Then in a few years, after paying a balance still due to his predecessor, selling other boxes and a hundred seats ("silver tickets," they were called) for terms of years or for single seasons, he became absolute owner of that ample edifice, and, as was commonly said, without debts or encumbrances. How, and because of whom, William Taylor came to end his aged days in a prison, we shall see in the course of my story in London.

This singular man was a perfect mixture of two contrary natures. Left to himself he was humane, noble, generous. Influenced by others, he assumed, complete, the characters of those who led him, particularly of the woman he loved and of her favorites, who, forthwith, became his own. My readers may judge what such a man became the moment he fell into the power of a Banti! Not many days had passed when Federici, who had contributed much with his good offices and with services of various sorts to the victory of that woman, gave me an order, in the name of the manager, to write two operas: one a comedy, to be set to music by Martini, who had been called to London by me; and the other, in serious vein, by Francesco

235

Bianchi,[9] who had been brought on by the *donna seria*. Perceiving the dangerous enterprise on which I was embarking, I studied all possible means for keeping both women friendly to me; but what hope of success in that?

"The Lord help you," said Banti to me one day, "if Morichelli gets a better reception in Martini's opera than I do in mine!" Morichelli was not saying anything. But her leers, her halted phrases, a few pouts of admiration, and a sly way she had of alluding frequently to two operas of mine which she had sung with marvelous success at Vienna, gave me to understand clearly enough what was churning in her mind. At length I set myself, all of a tremble, to my double task. I chose the subjects, wrote my sketches, and presented them to the two maestros.

They both approved my choice, and that comforted me somewhat. In less than three weeks I had the *Capricciosa corretta* ready for Martini, who, living in my house, not only gave me inspiration to write with his ever smiling face and his pleasing reminiscences of things past; but, little by little, as I wrote the words, he would be setting them to music. And I gave Bianchi all the first act of *Merope*, which he approved and praised without any reserve whatever. Everybody supposed that the *opéra bouffe* was to be the first produced; but Banti, hearing the praises that were being lavished both on Martini's music and on my words, raised four devils with Taylor, who in turn raised forty devils with me. He ordered me to have the serious opera ready the following day; and he threatened to "poke" me ("poke" from "poker" I am told), when I smiled at such a command, telling me he was not paying me good money to sit scratching my head. Had the butler not brought in a bottle of Oporto just then, which made him forget the scrimmage, I really do not know how the business would have

---

9. Francesco Bianchi (1752–1810) had been a composer in Paris and was later a conductor in Milan. He died a suicide. Sheppard, 223.

ended. He began to drink; Banti followed suit; and while they sat there muttering things in English, which at that time I understood very little, I went to the door, rushed home, locked myself in my room, and in twenty-four hours finished the second act and sent it to Signor Bianchi.

This second act too he liked, but he did not write the music for it till a long time afterwards. He suggested to Banti, instead, another opera which he had written in Italy; and the woman had the shamelessness to tell the manager that it was a new creation and to insist that it be called and believed such, even by people who had seen it in Venice many, many years before. Then, suddenly, it was announced with great pomp in all the newspapers and on all the bulletins that "Madame Banti would give a second proof of her rare talents in 'Acis and Galatea,' an opera written especially for her in London by the celebrated composer, Francesco Bianchi."

Unfortunately for me, I happened to own the libretto of "Acis and Galatea" which had been printed in Venice; and I was imprudent enough to say as much to Federici. He told the singer, she the composer, the composer the manager, trying to make him believe that it was all an imposture which I had cooked up. Taylor came to my office, his face redder than a rooster's comb, and demanded to see the libretto; but as he had no red-hot poker in hand to "poke" me, I begged him to have a chair, and handed him a bottle of port instead of the book requested. Then when he seemed a little calmed, I picked up the libretto in question and laid it on my fire, promising him not only to hold my tongue, but to make speedy reparation for my ill deed. Taylor was not always blind. He saw then, as one sees a ray of light in total darkness, that Banti, as well as Federici, had fooled him, and some months later he told Bianchi so in my presence. But when he tried to broach the subject to Banti, she laid her hand over his mouth, and obliged him to swallow the pill in silence.

It was my task, meantime, to print the libretto. I sent the opera to the printer announcing it as new and with the same paragraph which had been published in the newspapers. But all those precautions were of little avail. Dress rehearsal came on: partisans and flatterers all cried: "Beautiful! Sublime! Divine!" But when the opera went on the stage,[10] though the room was packed with hands paid to applaud, and though Banti, before the performance, ate a hundred roasted chestnuts and emptied a full bottle, not a single piece of music pleased, and, despite all efforts made, it was not performed more than twice thereafter.

Recourse was quickly had to Martini for the *opéra bouffe*[11]: and despite partisanship and cliques, despite a claque of two hundred or more persons sent to the theater to hiss, despite, in the end, a satire they caused to be written and published (by whom? By Badini, who told me afterwards himself that he was paid by the manager to write it!) the opera was a success; and, despite them all, Martini, Da Ponte, and what was more im-portant, Morichelli, triumphed spectacularly!

After the good success of this first opera, Martini and I were hastily commissioned to write another—the *Isola del pia cere*,[12] to wit, the first act of which was a marvelous success, both for the composer and for me.

This was not the case with the second act. Martini was not

10. *Acis and Galatea* came March 21, 1795, having been first given in Venice in 1792. Sheppard, 226; Nic., 300.

11. The *Capricciosa corretta* was a reworking of a libretto called *Gli spôsi in con-trasto* produced in Russia in 1788. Its première in London took place on Jan. 27, 1795, with the title "The School for Husbands" (Sheppard, 224). The spirited but obscene attack of Badini was called the "School of Horns" (Lisbon, *i.e.* London, 1795). To it Da Ponte replied with "Pleasant Notes on a Base Libel," etc.—both ap-parently unknown to Nicolini and Sheppard, though first mentioned by Krehbiel, and thereafter by Russo. The *Scuola delle corna* alludes to the earlier sonnets hanging fire since 1792.

12. *Première*, May 26, 1795. Sheppard, 227.

very hard to please in the matter of women. He took a fancy to
a servant girl, young, but neither pretty nor interesting, while,
at the same time, he was courting and feigning passion for the
prima donna buffa, who might in truth have been his mother,
not to say his grandmother. This latter and rather mature Lalage
discovering Martini's already advanced and every day more
complicated intrigue with the not cruel servant girl, made bitter complaint thereof to him; and my good little Spaniard, being hard pressed for an excuse, whispered in his matron's ear
that it was to cover up a little misstep of mine that he had declared himself the lover of that girl. The matron did not keep
the secret. In a short time it spread from one mouth to another
and at length reached me. I decided to mention the matter to
Martini; but the moment I opened my mouth—"What's this,
Signor Martini . . . ?"—he divined what was coming, treated
the matter as a joke and sent twenty-five guineas to the girl,
the glimmer of which so flailed the appetite of a certain old
codger, that he married her. Martini, nevertheless, left my
house, and went to live with Morichelli; and our long, sweet,
and much envied friendship grew cold.

The second act of the "Isle of Pleasure" was written entirely on an Isle of Ice. As I worked on it I felt as though I were
writing for Reghini, rather than for Martini, the composer of
the *Cosa rara*. Certain ridiculous pretensions of the *prima
donna* contributed to my lack of inspiration. She had sung
Nina pazza per amore with great effect in Paris, and insisted
that, by hook or crook, the second act of my opera should have
a mad scene, which fitted about as appropriately there as Pilate
in the Lord's Prayer. The whole spectacle failed, accordingly,
on that account, nor were a number of pretty duets and several
beautiful songs, enjoyed as much for the music as for the
words, enough to save it. One of these, I think, deserves to be
read: I venture, therefore, to insert it in these Memoirs:

Gira, gira intorno il guardo;
mira il ciel, la terra, il mare:
armonia tutto ti pare
ciò ch'è in terra, in cielo, in mar.
Quelle stelle tanto belle
stanno in dolce amico accordo;
quegli augei, se non sei sordo
non fann'altro che cantar.
Il variar delle stagioni
son concerti belli e buoni:
canzonette son que'fiori,
minuetti que'colori,
quell'aurette, quelle fronde,
e quegli arbori e quell'onde
son rondò della natura;
e il sol batte la misura
coll'eterno suo rotar.
E noi tutti che mai siamo?
Piffaretti, clarinetti,
tamburini, violini,
e fagotti e chitarrini,
che, concordi negli accordi
delle parti componenti,
vivi e armonici strumenti
tra i gran timpani del mondo
non facciamo che suonar.

(Turn, O turn your gaze around, look at heaven and earth
and sea. One great harmony it all appears—all in sea and
earth and heaven. Those shining stars are in sweet and
amiable accord; the birds, if ears you have, do nothing
but sing. The changing seasons—what else are they but
concerts? Songs are those flowers, minuets those colors;
those breezes, those rustling leaves, those murmuring

trees and lapping waves are *rondeaux* of Nature, the sun beating time in his everlasting turns. And what are we— you and I? Clarionets and tambourines, violins and piffarets, bassoons and guitars, which, harmonizing in the blending of their parts are blaring harmonious instruments which do nothing but resound among the great tympanons of the world.)

To these words, the mellifluous Martini set a most trivial music, and a music hardly more exalted to other parts of the opera.

In the two first years, therefore, of my poetship in London, I wrote three operas, two comic, and one serious, the last, as I said, the *Merope*,[13] which was no better liked than the *Isola del piacere* of the Spaniard. With him gone, and Morichelli gone, came a lady, to replace the latter, who was not of sufficient importance to arouse the jealousy of the Empress of Many Tongues—Banti had been called "Semiramis" after her first great success in an opera of that name by Bianchi.[14] This gave us hope of a truce between our *prime donne* and of some tranquillity at the Opera.

But unluckily this was not to be. There was living in London at that time a certain Le Texier, a man of some little prestige in theatrical affairs, which he had acquired through an unusual ability at reciting entire French comedies all by himself in a sort of little theater which he had built. This he did with much grace and effect, changing his voice, his tones, his emphasis, and sometimes even his costumes. It was never known whether Taylor went to him to obtain money or whether Le Texier made the advances *sub conditione*; the fact was, I

13. *Première*, June 10, 1797. Sheppard, 225.

14. London *première*, April 26, 1794. Sheppard, 228.

suddenly began hearing it about that Le Texier would be a director of the Opera. Taylor from that time on had two commanders in his army, both ambitious, and both pretending to give orders even to him. For some time they waged secret war upon each other, not daring to fight it out in public. The woman knew that her rival had a patron in Mercury, God of Gold; the man that his female enemy had the beautiful Cyprine to protect her.

During the period of this ostensible truce, Le Texier thought of a scheme for making a great impression both on the public mind and on the manager and the singers; and since it was essential to interest his rival, he went to her one day and with a figuration of speech worthy of a Tullius, he said:

"Signora Banti, I am going to show you the sort of man Le Texier is. . . .

Saying which, he drew from under his cloak the score of *Zémyre et Azor*, with music by Grétry, an admirable thing considering the epoch in which it was written and more than admirable for an ear trained on the Seine.

"There," he exclaimed, "you have an opera really to show *la* Banti off! Never mind your Semiramides, your Galateas, your Meropes! Here's something that will name your triumph through the centuries to come. By virtue of it, Brigida Banti will live in the philharmonic world as long as the names of Grétry and France endure."

All this and more he said to her. She was by no means the person who invented gunpowder. She fell into the trap and began to scream about at the top of her voice: "Semira, Semira, Semira!"

But the opera was in French. How translate it? And who should do it?

The shrewd Federici was present, and from the first moment had cast envious glances on the profits to proceed from the sale of the librettos. He called Milady Brigida aside, whis-

242

pered a few words in her ear, and she, as happy as could be, snatched the score from Le Texier's hands and cried, laughing, "I! . . . I! . . . I'll attend to having the words translated!"

Le Texier having gone, she came to an agreement with Taylor and Federici; and Giovanni Gallerini, a wretch most worthy of his name,[15] was designated as Taylor's messenger boy to the two famous poets, Bonajuti and Baldinotti (I shall speak of these, at the proper time), to offer them twenty guineas for the translation of *Semira e Azor*, on the understanding that they yield the copyright to Madame Brigida and her favorites. At the end of a fortnight the music was copied, the decorations sketched, the costumes prepared, but milords the poets had not brought in even their first scene. Gallerini goes to them; Federici goes to them; they go to Banti; Mr. Taylor asks an explanation; Le Texier fumes and storms. But the muses of these two cobblers of the theater lay fast asleep, like the idols of Baal amid all the screaming of those poor priests; and for all of their squirming and swearing, their biting their nails and racking their brains, they did not succeed in translating a single scene of that opera!

They were the two poets least adapted to such a task. Bonajuti often made pretense of writing for the Opera, but his verses were harder than his head, which could have butted to advantage with a goat's. Baldinotti was an *improvvisatore* by profession, and sometimes said very witty things; but as for his written verses, the Lord deliver us! To this be it added that to translate an opera from one language into another something more than knowledge of versification is essential. The lines must be written in such a way that the accents of the poetry correspond to those of the music. Few the people who can do that well. A musical ear and long experience are unusually necessary. Both these things were lacking in those men; and

15. Suggesting *galera*, "penitentiary." See above, 103, note 14.

after three weeks' time they sent the score to the director on his asking for it, with this humiliating confession:

"We can not do it."

Quid agendum? I had had the self-control not to peep once on this whole matter. It was taken for granted, accordingly, that all the secret manœuvring was unknown to me. The director came to see me with Federici.

"Here, Signor Da Ponte," he said, "is a chance to let your fine talent shine."

Whereupon he handed me the score, and told me what it was all about. This brazen simulation turned my stomach. On the spur of the moment I did not know what to answer. I was on the point of saying: "With such swine an honest man can have nothing to do." But there was my duty as a husband, my duty as a father, and a little, too, perhaps, my personal pride. They came to the rescue in a few seconds.

"Sir," I replied, "I am not obliged, by my contract, to translate operas except for new music, but if the management is willing to pay me fifty guineas, I will translate this one."

"Who will get the profits on the libretto?" asked the sly Federici.

"Whoever you please!" I answered.

"When will you give us the opera translated?"

"In a week."

Federici exchanged a few words with Le Texier. They both agreed and left me the score on departing.

I set myself to the task at once, and did the whole translation in forty-eight hours. Then I went to see a friend who knew music well, tried out the words, and with very slight changes had it perfectly fitted to the notes of the composer. On the third day I sent the score to Le Texier, reporting that the poetry was translated, but warning him that my resolve was not to deliver the words till I had the fifty guineas in hand. He came to my room in a show of heat, but I held my ground. He was too pressed to give the opera, from which he thought his greatest glory was to come. He took me to his house, counted out the fifty guineas, and had the honesty to say—we were speaking in Italian:

"Signor Da Ponte, you deserve those fifty guineas, and they the *ba*..."

He did not finish the word, but I supplied, laughing: "*basto!*... (load for a donkey) or *bastone* (cane)?"

The opera came on *cum omnibus fustibus et lanternis* and to employ a technical phrase of the stage, made a *fiascone!*[16] Federici had to pay the fifty guineas to Le Texier, having promised him that sum for the profits on the libretto—the sales did not cover the expenses of the printing! Gallerini lost the five or six guineas he had advanced to "flat-purse" Baldinotti: Banti stopped shouting Semira, and went back to Semiramis. Taylor warmly urged returning to the *Capricciosa corretta*, because friends of music (and of the truth) kept telling him that that was a very beautiful opera. I laughed at everything, and gloated, fingering my fifty guineas over and over again—they seemed to me the prettiest and shiniest ones I had ever seen in all the length of my life.

Mr. Taylor, meanwhile, whether because of the happy outcome of my first opera, or for some other reason unknown to me and which I never succeeded in deciphering, seemed very desirous of becoming more intimate with me. He began to come frequently to my house, take long walks with me, ask my advice on various matters, theatrical or pecuniary, and seemed to be greatly pleased, as well by my remarks, as by my computations. I being in his company one day, along with *la* Banti, and he heated with wine rather than not, he asked me in tone of jest whether I thought I could find some money for him.

---

16. July 23, 1796. It seems, however, to have been a success. Sheppard, 231.

"How?" I asked.

Whereupon he drew from his pocket a number of notes endorsed by Federici and accepted by him. I took one for three hundred pounds sterling and without any great reflection said that I would try and that I hoped to succeed.

"If you can do that," said Banti, "your fortune is made!"

Once outside his door I asked myself: "However could I have undertaken such a thing? How can I raise money—I a poet by trade, and at a very moderate salary, and scarcely knowing what an acceptance, an endorsement, or a note, is?" I know not whether it was a spirit good or evil that reminded me of my first days in London when I had been obliged to pawn a diamond ring. I had entered a little shop, with a sign over the door: *Money:* and found a very smooth young man who lent me six guineas on a ring worth twelve at least!

I hurried to that little shop on this occasion, found the same young man, and handed him my paper. He told me that if I chose to buy a ring or a watch from him, he would give me the remainder in cash. He then presented a number of articles, and I chose a repeater, valued by him at twenty-two guineas, and worth perhaps fifteen. For the rest he gave me an order on the Bank of London. As I reached out my hand to take it, he offered me instead a pen, and bade me sign my name, under that of Federici, on the note I had brought him. I had no idea of the significance or the consequences of such a signature. I supposed it was simply a ceremony, or a receipt; but the moment I saw my name on that scrap of paper, one of the three admonitions given me by Casanova flashed through my mind—never to write my name on a note in England. I trembled all over like a leaf. It was as though a fatal presentiment were telling me at that instant: "You are lost!"

Nevertheless, I went back to Taylor's, and showed him Parker's check (Parker was the name of the money-lender) and the watch he had given me. Taylor had raised money on other notes through Federici and Gallerini, and with such rascals was accustomed to losing seventy, eighty, and even a hundred percent. He was agreeably surprised at the promptness with which I had served him and at the moderateness of his loss.

"*Bravo, poeta!*" cried Banti, in transports of joy. And—"Just what I needed!" she added in fresh joy, gracefully pocketing the watch which Taylor was on the point of presenting to me. The gossip sheet narrates that this repeater miraculously found its way into the pocket of Signor Ferlendis,[17] a great player on the cornet (Milady Brigida's favorite instrument). She, however, for the moment, saw fit to embrace me and give me a kiss, exclaiming again:

"Your fortune is made!"

In fact, the day following the impresario came to my room, bringing me a new contract, wherein he increased my salary by a hundred pounds sterling, and conferred on me divers other favors which over a certain space of time were most advantageous to me and mine. These favors and these advantages, coupled with the first feelings I had conceived in favor of Taylor when he called me from Holland, aroused and sustained in my mind such benevolence toward him, such affection for him, that not immense losses, not perils, not his own rebuffs, had the power ever to change, or diminish them. I continued to see him frequently, and he me. Since he was now in the habit of confiding his affairs to me, he told me one day that he needed three or four thousand pounds sterling, and had no doubt, from what he had seen me bring in, that he would be able to get them through me. I undertook to accommodate him, and in my evil hour, be it said, I succeeded. But shortly the note we had given to Parker fell due. There was no money to liquidate that obligation. I was therefore obliged to have recourse to

17. Giuseppe Ferlendis (1755–1804?) of Bergamo, in London since 1790, a cornetist of international fame. Nic., 301.

another usurer, and then to a third, a fourth, a fifth, now to pay
a debt, now to satisfy the needs, caprices and appetites of that
insatiable female wolf of the Opera. In less than a year the
money I had raised was approaching the sum of six thousand
five hundred guineas!

I was therefore the treasurer, spender, agent, paymaster,
teller—and favorite, of Taylor. Did they have to go to the country while the theater was closed? "Da Ponte will find the
money!" "There is no wine in the cellar!" *la* Banti would cry.
"Da Ponte will get some on credit from the store!" Mr. Taylor
must have shoes, shirts, handkerchiefs, what not? "Just speak
to Da Ponte!" The ushers at the Opera, the players, the dancers,
the singers—were they asking for their salaries? "Tell them to
go to Da Ponte!"

This intimacy of mine with Taylor, this seeing that I did
everything for him without, however, neglecting my duties as
poet, was the occasion for everybody's coming to me to obtain
the things they desired. And with the greatest alacrity I lent
myself to the service of my compatriots—a thing that made
me inwardly content, despite all the risks and losses I could
now foresee. For little by little I had learned to know what it
meant to write my name on scraps of paper in London! I often
had occasion to render a service to Taylor, in rendering one to
my wrongly so-called friends. He was on the point of dismiss-
ing from his opera, Bianchi, Viganoni,[18] and Weitzel (the latter
a great instrumentalist, brother to Madame Billington). That
was at a time when he was short of money and my own
sources had been sopped dry. Considering that those three gentlemen were all most useful to the Opera, I suggested to them
to lend me some money for the manager, assuring them that I

---

18. Giuseppe Viganoni (1754–1823), a famous tenor, had sung in *Theodorus* at
Vienna in Da P.'s time. Charles Weichsell, a famous violinist. Elizabeth Weichsell
Billington (1765–1818). Nic., 300–1.

would take care to have them paid—which I did; and all three were reengaged for terms of years! I shall have other things to say, in proper places, in this same connection, begging my reader urgently to forgive me for the annoyance that the recital of such frivolous things must give him. But all my life has been nothing but a series of kindnesses and favors by me rendered to a throng of ingrates or of traitors; and I am concerned to prove that truth, in every way permitted and supplied to me by the various episodes of my story.

Three full years passed in this way. One thing only came to disturb my peace of mind a little and rob me in part of those emoluments which by every right would seem to have belonged to the poet at the Opera. In spite of Taylor, Banti had her little Adonises in secret and changed them more often than most ladies change their hats. She had at that time given first place on her amatory list to that ape of a Federici. This everybody knew, except Taylor! Federici being desirous of cheating me out of the profits I derived from the sale of librettos in the theater, made the lady believe that if she could obtain that privilege from the manager "he, Federici, would oblige him, with a vengeance, to do her every last pleasure;" and for Taylor (which meant for Banti herself) he would guarantee to raise the huge sum of a thousand guineas, and perhaps more, on condition that he, Taylor, allow a certain Frenchman and the latter's niece to have a box free for two or three seasons. *Nota bene:* a box accommodated four, five, or six persons. There were from sixty to seventy performances a season. Each person paid, and still pays, I believe, half a guinea a performance. Anyone who has passed the first stage in arithmetic has no need of my further calculations!

It was decided, therefore, that Monsieur D.L. should have the box, and Mr. Taylor a thousand guineas, on loan without interest!

"But Da Ponte," Taylor remarked, "what will he say?"

"He will shout a little," they answered in chorus, "and that will be the end of it!"

It was not that way. I printed and sold all the operas written by me, *Evelina*,[19] namely, translated from the French, with music by Sacchini—a success: the *Armida*, a comic operetta in one act for Bianchi, one of the best things written in lighter vein by him, also a success; and a cantata which I wrote for the marriage of the Prince of Wales, and which was later on produced in celebration of an English victory. The profits from all the other operas for two whole years went to Federici; and I looked on and said nothing, waiting for the opportune moment to punish him. But what was my own punishment for such consideration? To have lent fresh fuel to his treachery and ingratitude!

Banti, meanwhile, either hankering for some new adorer (secret, needless to say) or because of some hurt, real or imaginary, she may have received from Federici, became an enemy of his and so violent that she could neither bear the sight of him, nor hear his name mentioned in her presence. Whereupon the favors of that capricious woman began raining all on me. She was satisfied only when I was with her; I was all she could see or hear of, with her friends and with the manager himself; she praised my kindness of heart, my hard work, my unselfishness, my talent, and sometimes even she eulogized my attractive eyes! I was then forty-nine years old. I had a wife whom I loved, much younger and more beautiful than she. It was not therefore to be wondered at, if I played deaf, and I do not claim any credit for having done so. But the more I seemed disposed not to catch her meaning, the more that wild cat seemed bent on making me understand. Came the time for

---

19. *Première* of *Evelina*, Jan. 10, 1797; of *Armida*, June 1, 1802; the cantata was *Le nozze del Tamigi e Bellona*, given for the victory of Jervis off Cape Saint Vincent, March 11, 1797. Sheppard, 235–6.

Taylor to go to his countryplace with his family, taking Banti along, of course. Once that was decided, Banti sent for me.

I had the bad luck to find her alone, and she came running to greet me.

"*Signor poeta*," she cried, "you must make ready to come to the country with us. I have something very important to tell you . . . Do come, dear . . . do that favor for your good friend Banti."

Speaking thus she took me by the hand, drew me close to her, an expression on her face that would have frightened the chaste Joseph . . . and Taylor came in!

I lingered a few moments with them, taking various orders from them both. The lady repeated her invitation, the manager seconded it, and I departed. But my embarrassment was acute. To save, as we Italians say, both the goat and the cabbages, I decided some days later to visit them, but in my wife's company. When the woman saw us, her face flared like a Fury; but soon laying hold on herself, she feigned cordial welcome. When we found ourselves alone together, she said to me brazenly:

"With your wife! Well . . . so much the worse for you!"

I pretended not to understand, and the matter was not broached again either by her, or by me.

I spent three days with Taylor there, and having had occasion to examine him at very close range, I felt so convinced that, left to himself and provided with plenty of money, he would have been one of the best men in the world, that I shed real tears of pity for him. At the Opera, Banti herself was, and made him, a viper. At Holywell, she was affable, gracious, and positively charming. Taylor's infinite considerateness for her, his undemonstrative generosity, his simple ways, his hospitality toward everyone who came, made even Banti a very different person from what she by nature was.

One day Taylor asked me if I would like to go to Italy. I was burning with eagerness to visit my old father and my family again, dear ones whom I had not seen for more than twenty years. I answered at once that I would make any sacrifice to go. He then went on that he had implicit confidence in my honesty and in my good taste, and would offer me a hundred guineas to pay part of my traveling expenses, if I would leave at once and secure for him one of the best comic actresses, and one of the best instrumentalists, in Italy. I accepted joyfully, left at once for New Yorck [London], bought a carriage, and scraped together, what with cash and gems, the not inconsiderable sum of a thousand pounds sterling. Then, when everything was ready, I embarked for Hamburg.

My passage was short and pleasant. Leaving London on the second of October, I was at Hamburg by the tenth, and continued without misadventure on my way, to reach Castelfranco on the second of November.

Keen to enjoy my journey in every possible detail, I left my wife at Castelfranco, and begged her to rejoin me at Treviso, twelve miles distant, on the morning of the fourth. It was early evening when I arrived at Conegliano, only eight miles from Ceneda; and in less than an hour I found myself at the door of my old home. As my feet touched the ground which had borne my cradle, and I breathed in the first emanations of that sky which had nourished me and given me life over so many years, a trembling laid hold on all my members, and such a thrill of gratitude and veneration coursed through my blood, that I stood transfixed and motionless for a long time; and I know not how long I might thus have remained, had I not heard through the windows a voice which I seemed to recognize and which went sweetly to my heart. I had left my hired wagon some distance off in order not to give warning of my approach by the creaking of the wheels. I had covered my head with a kerchief, that no one might recognize me from the windows in the light of the street lamps. Then I knocked on the door.

I heard someone cry from a window:

"*Chi è là!*—Who is there?"

I strove to disguise my voice as I answered with one word:
"Open!"

But that word was enough to enable one of my sisters to recognize my voice and cry with a shrill exclamation to the other girls:

"It's Lorenzo!"

They were down the stairs like lightning, flinging themselves at my neck and almost suffocating me in their caresses and kisses. Then they carried me to my father, who on hearing my name, but still more at sight of me, was too overcome to stir for several moments.

In addition to the surprise and the pleasure occasioned him by my unexpected arrival there was a preceding circumstance to render both his pleasure and surprise infinitely keener. It was the second day of November, in other words, All Souls' Day, a festival especially solemnized in Catholic countries, all relatives and friends coming together early in the evening and spending many hours of the night in feasting and in innocent amusements. It happened, therefore, that my father found himself surrounded by children, children-in-law, grandchildren, and had invited them to join in the following toast:

"Let us drink to the health of our Lorenzo, and pray God that He may give us the grace to see him, before I die."

They had not yet drained their glasses when I knocked at the door and "Lorenzo!" "Lorenzo!" began ringing through every nook and cranny of the house! One would have to have no heart at all to fail to conceive the emotion of my very aged father (he had passed eighty at the time)[20] at that extraordinary moment. I can imagine it myself, from my own feelings. We

20. Born in 1722, Gasparo Da P. (Geremia Congeliano) was 76. He was still living in 1800. Nic., 302.

stood clasped in each other's arms for many minutes; then, after a reciprocal round of kisses, caresses, embraces about all
the family, which lasted till nigh midnight, I heard a commo-
tion out of doors, cheery cries, voices calling loudly:

"Lorenzo! Lorenzo!"

Going to a window I could see a crowd of people in the
moonlight. They were asking to be let in. The door opened;
and, in a moment, the room where I was, was thronged by my
good friends in that town, who had all come, on news of my arrival, to see me. I was to learn that evening just how much joy
a human heart can hold and how truly the poet cried *Dulcis
amor patriæ, dulce videre suos!*

Though those friends and comrades of my youth were dear
to me one and all and their visit an infinite joy to me, I shall
nevertheless record only two names, as of persons whom I
loved and esteemed particularly, and who requited my affection with equal tenderness.

Antonio Michelini and Girolamo Perucchini were two angels
of friendship, and my heart wills that I speak of them in preference to all the others. The sweetness of their characters, their
good will toward me, the esteem in which they accordingly held
me and my verses, had rendered them so precious to me that in
those early days I was not happy without being with them, nor
they without me. I was treated by both of them as a brother, and
by their parents as a son. We counseled with one another, exchanged secrets, stood by one another in our boyish love affairs.

Michelini was not profoundly lettered, nor a poet; but he
loved literature, had good taste and excellent judgment, and
was, moreover, a boy of my age. I know not whether he be still
alive, but that is my ardent hope; and if these Memoirs ever
chance to fall into his hands, may he know what my sincerest
feelings are and be further assured that just as I have preserved
them to the eightieth year of my life, so shall I preserve them
in an unforgetting heart until the last moment thereof.

Perucchini, *diis faventibus*, still honors his country with his rare endowments—not long since I had most happy news of him. To the qualities of a noble and delicate spirit he adds an inexhaustible fund of learning and an exquisite taste in every manner of literature. He used to compose, and perhaps still composes, verses full of grace and spirit: he is a learned lawyer, a great statesman, and an eloquent orator.

What the feelings aroused in me by the visit of these two gentlemen, who, with others hardly less dear to me, came to celebrate my return after twenty years of absence, I leave to the imagination of those who have known the joys of true friendship!

After some hours of tender joviality, the party broke up. Then my father wished me to get some rest, and asked me to sleep with him. I lay down a little sooner than that good old man, since he knelt at the foot of a Crucifix which he kept near his bed to say his customary prayers. They lasted half an hour, and ended, in tone of half-weeping devoutness, with the words: *Nunc dimittis servum tuum in pace!*

The which finished, he came to the bed, clasped me in his arms and repeated, in Italian:

"My son, I have seen you again! I die content!"

He extinguished the lights and we lay silent, both, for some moments; then, hearing him sigh, I asked him to tell me what the matter was:

"Sleep, sleep, my child," he answered with another sigh. "We can talk tomorrow!"

After some time I judged that he was sleeping, and I too went to sleep.

When I awoke, in the morning, I found that he was no longer in bed. He had risen and stolen softly, softly, from the room, before sunrise, and gone to market to be in time for the best fruits of the season and the choicest viands for breakfast and for dinner. My little sisters, their husbands, the children of those who were mothers, and my two young brothers, Paolo and Enrico, were all waiting at the door of my bedroom to come rushing in at the first sounds they heard. I know not whether I had occasion to clear my throat, or cough, or turn over in bed: all I know is that in a second I could see a phalanx of men, women, and children, charging into my room, flinging the windows open wide, and then descending upon my bed to crush me and almost suffocate me in caresses and embraces. A little after my father came in. The good old man was laden with fruits and flowers, which latter were strewn by the family all over my bed till I was covered with them head to feet, to a din of cries of delight and enjoyment at all that festive uproar. A pretty servant girl entered, with coffee; and all that numerous assembly formed a circle about my bed, sat down, and made ready to take breakfast. In very truth I remember having seen neither before nor since that morning a happier or more adorable spectacle. It was as though I were the center of a circle of angels rather than of mortal folk.

My little sisters were all pretty girls; but Faustina, the youngest of the seven, was a veritable angel of beauty. I suggested taking her back to London with me and my father was willing: but she said neither yes, nor no. I suspected at once that, though she was not yet more than fifteen, she was no longer mistress of her own heart; and gradually our conversation turned on other matters. No one had spoken of my two dear brothers, Girolamo and Luigi, both snatched from us by death in the flower of their years. I, too, was careful not to speak of them, in order not to sadden the joyousness of the day with sorrowful memories. But another sigh on my father's part took me back to his sighs during the night. Again I asked him for an explanation. He did not answer, but observing that his eyes were filling with tears, I guessed the reason and changed the subject. So far I had spoken not a word of my wife. I thought that now it was a good moment to make mention of her; and to restore the mood of gaiety, which my father's tears had banished for a moment, I began:

"Mesdames my sisters, you could not have supposed that I came all the way from London alone! No indeed, I brought a beautiful young girl with me, one of the dancers at our Opera. I may let you see her tomorrow or day after tomorrow."

"Is she really pretty?" asked Faustina.

"Prettier than you!" I replied gaily.

"Prettier than I am? We must see about that! Wait till we have a look at this wonderful jewel!"

This interchange brought the good humor back again. The family sat about for a little while longer in my bedroom, then they all withdrew to give me time and liberty to dress. Only my father remained. The sorrows in his heart needed some outlet. I thought it might be better to allude to his two lost children.

"Oh! if those two boys were here!" he exclaimed in answer; "how happy they would be and how happy we!"

I wept, and so did he. But in the end I succeeded in cheering him, promising that before I left Ceneda, I would show him something to compensate him, at least in part, for his loss. . . .

Returning to these two brothers of mine, I think it my duty to correct an inaccuracy I left in the second part of these Memoirs when, in speaking of the death of one of them whereof I had news in Dresden, for some reason I confused their names. It was Luigi, and not Girolamo, who died at that time at the age of twenty-two or twenty-three years, a youth full of talent, urbanity, and charm, beloved of his people, respected and honored by the scholars of Padua (where he was near to obtaining his doctor's degree in medicine), and adored by the celebrated physician, Della Bona, whose favorite pupil he was. Girolamo died two years after that; and I remained "to mourn their death and my survival."

And now again to pleasanter things! I paid calls on all the friends who had visited me that evening, and on several of my old loves, who welcomed me with a joy and a courtesy equal to mine in seeing them again. Not until dinner time did I tell my family and a few friends that I would be obliged to depart the next day for Treviso, and perhaps for Venice. My leaving so soon was a great disappointment, but when I promised to come back with the beautiful girl, my sisters (and Faustina first among them) cried: "Good! Good!" and we spent the remainder of the day in perfect happiness.

Chancing to allude to Bonaparte, my father told me a little story, which really touched my heart, and constrained me to supreme veneration for the memory of that great man. Not very long before my return to Ceneda, the French army had gained a decisive victory over the Germans, I forget whether on the Tagliamento or on the Piave.[21] Bonaparte, general of that division, came to Ceneda, where, there being no barracks, he ordered his soldiers and officers to find lodging in the houses of the inhabitants. On first acquaintances, all those young Frenchmen, gay by national character and flushed through the victory they had won, fascinated the ladies of the town. When my old father heard of Bonaparte's order, he locked the doors of his house and stationed himself at a window to wait for the general to go by. Our house was situated in the center of the great *piazza* and exactly adjacent to the café most patronized by the townspeople. It was not long before Bonaparte appeared with his officers, and took seats in the café, to partake of some refreshment. My father lost no time. Taking advantage of a moment so opportune, he called from a window, asking permission to speak:

"Who is the general of the French?" he asked.

"I," shouted Bonaparte in answer.

"General," my father resumed, "the aged man who is now addressing you is the father of seven honorable girls, who lost

21. Tagliamento, March 16, 1797. Nic., 302.

their mother many years ago. Two only are married. The others are here with me. Their older brothers are not now with them to watch over them, and I, their father, am obliged daily to leave my house to earn their bread. I respectfully beg that your order that your brave warriors be quartered in our houses may not extend to me. I ask that these white hairs of mine, the innocence of these my daughters, and the honor of my sons, may be protected by you. If that much you grant me, I shall kneel before this Crucifix" (and he drew from his bosom a Crucifix he always carried) "and pray God to bless you and your arms with prosperity. If you do not heed my plea, I shall refuse to open the doors of my house. I have a barrel of powder ready here and at the first signal that your soldiers or your servants give to open them, I swear on this same Cross that I will save the honor of my daughters with that powder."

The eloquence with which he delivered this harangue, the courage of the good old man, and the applause that greeted him from the bystanders, so pleased Bonaparte, that he graciously granted the request. My father's house was the only one in Ceneda and the neighboring countryside, that was not debauched in those days by the victorious French! More than thirty women of Ceneda left the town with them on their departure and were sent back a few days later to their homes to implore pardon and pity of their fathers, husbands, and employers! The good *Cenedesi* were compassionate I was told! They were more forgiving than I would have been!

On the fourth day of November I left for Treviso. As my intention was to return to Ceneda with my wife at once, I proposed taking my youngest sister and her brother Paolo with me—Paolo had known my Nancy at Trieste.

When the news spread abroad that I was on the point of departure, all the young people of the town gathered about the door of our house waiting for me to come out. I thought it was to wish me a good journey and to urge me to return.

259

Nothing of the kind! It was to ask me with one voice not to take Faustina with me: and since the prayer had almost an element of threat, I was obliged to promise, nay to swear, that I would bring her back to Ceneda with me before three days should pass.

I reached Treviso late in the afternoon, but my Nancy did not arrive until eight or nine on the morning of the fifth. I was standing at a window of the inn waiting for her. When I saw the carriage coming, I ran downstairs to meet her. My brother had twitted me for the anxiety I had shown at her delay of several hours. He thought he was going to see some *ballerina*: "Now," he said to my sister, "we are going to see at last that rare jewel, more beautiful than you!"

We went up to the living room of the tavern, my wife wearing a veil over her face. My brother remembered the black veil of Trieste and did as I had done with it at that time. He had loved my Nancy with a passionate devotion, and had asked me a thousand things about her a thousand times; but I had always answered in general terms, without giving him reason either to suspect or hope to see her again as my wife. His surprise, accordingly, is not easy to imagine, and much less describe. Faustina was a beautiful girl and vain enough to believe herself such; yet she said aloud to my brother:

"It's true, it's true: she is prettier than I am."

That spontaneous compliment was the first pleasure I had in Treviso.

But I had others even greater, in that city. Once my arrival was known, my very sweet friend, Giulio Trento, came hurrying to my room and not twenty minutes had passed when a procession of people was arriving there. Most of them were now men of mature years, settled in various posts, professions, or offices of importance in that city, but who had once been my pupils in that respected seminary. Their age, only slightly younger than mine, their stations, and the many years that had passed since those days, did not prevent them from coming to me with transports of gladness and from honoring me with the glorious title of "our dear maestro." I learned from one of them that Bernardo Memmo was in that city. I ran to him at once, and the sight of that excellent, learned, and thoroughly noble gentleman was not the least of the pleasures I experienced in Treviso during all that happy visit. Teresa was still with him. A widow, ugly, fat, and much aged, she was still the idol of the man and absolute mistress of his will!

I was about to return to Ceneda, when I suddenly remembered that one of the prime purposes of my journey to Italy was Taylor! Hearing, accordingly, that two *prime donne* of great merit were singing in Venice, I resolved out of hand to go there, and sent my consort to Ceneda with Paolo and Faustina.

I arrived in Venice at a time when the Germans were in possession, and I was obliged to drain two goblets bitter to the heart of any good citizen. The first concerned my wretched country, the second myself.

I had heard much talk about pitiful conditions in the city, but what I had heard was child's play compared to what I saw in one night and one day. I thought I should like to see the *Piazza* of St. Mark, which I had not visited for more than twenty years. I entered from the direction of The Clock, from under which, when one is entirely through the opening, but not before, one has a view of the whole of the great *Piazza*. My reader may judge of my surprise and affliction. In the good old days one could see in that vast expanse only the contentment and the joy of an immense concourse of populace. Now as I turned my eyes in every direction, I could see only sadness, silence, solitude, desolation. There were just seven persons in the *Piazza* when I entered. *Quomodo sedet solo civitas plena populo!* were the only words I could proffer at that instant. I walked along the so-called *Procuratia* of St. Mark; and my surprise increased at seeing that even the coffee shops were empty. In eleven of them, I counted altogether twenty-two persons and no more. Reaching the last, a face decorated by a nose of extraordinary size struck my gaze some distance off—indeed, I saw the nose before the person. I drew nearer and recognized Gabriel Doria, son to a cook of the Barbarigos, of that Barbarigo, to be exact, who had perorated against me on account of the thesis I had published at Treviso. This Gabriel had been an *angelos* in his way, not indeed the one who

> giù i decreti del Ciel porta, ed al Cielo
> riporta de' mortali i preghi e'l zelo,

(bringeth down the decrees of Heaven and to Heaven rebeareth the prayers—and the deserts—of mortals,)

but just a spy of the Inquisitors of State! Before I left Venice, that last time, the fellow was married to a certain Bellaudi woman, in whose house I had rented a room. The brother of this lady had married the daughter of a Florentine who was living in the city, a young girl charming, pretty, and of very estimable character. But the graces of such a wife did not prevent him from admiring those of a not cruel *venezianella*, and in the end from falling enamored of the latter to the point of detesting his consort and desiring her death. But examining her husband's clothes one day, I know not whether through some suspicion she may have had, or for some other reason, she found sewed in the lining of his vest a packet of letters, one of which was of the following tenor:

My dearest darling:
     The time of our happiness is drawing nigh. The woman I abhor will soon be a mother. I myself will be her midwife, and our troubles will be at an end. If that is

not enough, we will put her to sleep. My sister shares our secret.

Your devoted one.

The other letters were, more or less, to the same purport. When I arrived home, I found her alone in her little sitting room. The moment she saw me, she hastened to give me the package of letters and begged me to leave the room and read them. I could not describe the horror that came over me as I examined them! The woman was of marvelous sweetness of disposition: she loved her husband, was faithful to him, and well behaved. I myself nourished sentiments of esteem and affection for her. Perhaps in others than in me, such an affection might have become a dangerous thing, but I had made myself a rule never to mingle love and crime.

I believed, nevertheless, that it would be a crime not to do something to save that innocent creature. I hurried to her father and gave him the papers to read; but that old man, a childish and spineless dotard, could do nothing but weep. Not only that, he could not offer her shelter in his house, which was scarcely large enough for him. Having a cousin in Venice, newly married, I appealed to him and he consented to give her a room. She reached his house at six in the evening and was a mother before nine. I then went to Zaguri, told him the story, and left the letters with him. Zaguri, that same evening, happened to be in private conference with one of the Three, whose voices alone made all Venice tremble at that time, when Gabriel Doria arrived. The man was admitted to secret audience, and delivered his message. The Inquisitor then returned to Zaguri and told him with horror in his voice that his, Zaguri's protégé, Lorenzo Da Ponte, had seduced the wife of an honorable citizen, induced her to flee her husband's house, and gone to live with her. Zaguri thereupon told him the facts as they were and gave him the letters of that "honorable citizen." That gentleman read them with shudders, and turned on the accuser the wrath he had conceived against me.

About ten o'clock that evening I started for my quarters, but found the door of the house locked, and heard a voice shouting from within:

"You don't get in here!"

I went to an inn for that night. The next morning I went back to Zaguri. The moment he saw me he cried:

"Lucky for you that you left me those letters!"

And he went on to relate the whole affair, telling me not to worry.

The husband, meanwhile, continued openly to frequent the house of the Venetian woman, and living with her there. His wife sent him his son,[22] and he dispatched the infant to an orphan asylum! And I? . . . For all the rule I had made for myself, for all of the principles of wisdom I had laid down for my conduct in the course of my life . . . must I speak on? Must I confess a weakness of which I have since felt ashamed and repentant a thousand times? Yes, I will confess; and I hope that my example will serve as a lesson to all those who trust themselves too far, and who refuse to admit the truth of the great maxim which warns us that "love is not conquered save by flight."

I did not flee. The sense of security which Zaguri had inspired in me, the close intimacy of the woman's husband with the Venetian girl, and above all else, my own inclination which I called pity, led me to frequent the lady's house most assiduously; and she, seeing in me rather a guardian angel than a friend, welcomed me always with so lively a gratitude and with such transports of joy that it was not long before all those noble sentiments . . .

---

22. Da P. does not mention a second child, not Bellaudi's, which also went with the Trovatelli. See above, 70, note 37.

(By a strange accident, a page will here be missing in my story. I had already written it; but then thinking to dry the ink, by mistake I took up the inkwell in place of the sand box and poured over it ink instead of sand. I have not time to recopy it. I shall therefore allow my reader to write it over as he may please.)[23]

The man Doria, accordingly, approached me with a greeting, which I returned. After a number of reciprocal iniquities, he alluded of his own accord to the lady in question, informed me that she had been reconciled with her husband, and told me where she was living. Not thinking I had any reason to fear the man, I said:

"I will go and call on her!"

And so I did. She received me as joyfully as a loving sister might welcome a brother. The rest of the family, and the husband himself, greeted me courteously and seemed delighted to see me; and we parted with evident manifestations not only of reconciliation, but of friendship.

Thence I went to pay calls on other friends, among them on my very dear Perucchini and on the excellent and humane Lucchesi, who had been my hospitable Philemon in Trieste. Zaguri was not in Venice, and Giorgio Pisani, who had meantime obtained his freedom, was then, I heard, in Ferrara.

The naming of that city reminded me of Madame Ferraresi, and I had the whim of going to see her. She received me with an "Oh!" of delight, and on hearing that I had authority to engage a singer for the London theater, she seemed disposed to lavish many attentions upon me. However much I may have longed to enjoy one of my usual vendettas by rendering her a favor in return for the harm she had done to me, I did not think it an honest or a fair thing to give her the least hope, without

---

23. It was first written by Professor G. dalla Santa in 1915, and thereafter by Nic., 273.

first hearing how her voice was. I furthermore knew that she had already appeared at the London Opera, without winning any great applause. I begged her, nevertheless, to sing a few arias, which she did without too much bashfulness. I could see that she was still a singer of great merit, yet I did not dare continue on that subject too long, for fear of arousing false hopes in her.

We began to jest on the matter of lovers. She imparted that she was without a "serving cavalier," and begged me to attend her that evening to the Opera. A little later, accordingly, I took a gondola, and there still lacking some time to the performance, bade the boatman stop at the *riva* of some café that we might have an ice. When he had left the boat, she reached for one of my hands, gazed at me intensely, and exclaimed in tone of theatrical levity:

"Do you know, Da Ponte, you are handsomer than ever?"

Delighted of a chance to have my little revenge for the wrongs she had done me, I replied:

"I'm sorry not to be able to say as much of you!"

She fell back silent, blushed, and I thought her eyes filled with tears. I was sorry then, pressed her hand tenderly, and told her I had been joking, but that, having consecrated the remainder of my life to another woman, I thought I had no right to speak of love, particularly with her. The "particularly" seemed to please her. The owner of the café was at hand with the ices. The gondolier resumed his post. We had no further talk of the past.

At the Opera, the *Re Teodoro* of Casti was being given that night. The *prima donna* was excellent, but I learned that she had been already engaged for the coming Carnival and I did not even try to bring up the question of London. After the performance, we went to supper with two other very pretty singers, but I was looking for voices and not for complexions. After escorting *la* Ferraresi home again, I went back to my hotel, satisfied with my calls and with the receptions my friends had given me.

The day following (the eighth of November) was replete with memorable events for me. I went out at a fairly early hour, desiring to see Venice again in all her aspects. Returning to the *Piazza* at St. Mark's, I found no greater press of people in the forenoon than I had found there the evening before. I entered the shop of a *caffettiere* who knew me, and asked for some coffee. There were six or seven persons present, taking the same drink and talking politics. I began to listen.

"We are done for, with these new masters of ours," one of them remarked (the Germans had entered Venice shortly before).[24] "A few days ago meat was selling at eight *soldi* the pound; now it's at eighteen. The tax on coffee has doubled; a bottle of wine one could buy for three *soldi* is now costing not less than six. On tobacco, salt, and sugar we are to have a municipal tax of sixty percent!"

"But that's nothing!" another interrupted, "I am counting up the two millions they are asking of us!"

"Two millions of what?" replied a third. "Two millions of oyster shells?"

"Two millions in silver piastres!" exclaimed the fourth.

The shopkeeper had been on pins and needles all this time. Finally he made his way into the midst of the group and cried in a hoarse trembling voice:

"Please, please, gentlemen! Not such talk here! I have no hankering, nor do I think any of you have, for testing the limberness of their military clubs."

He then led us into a smaller room, closed the windows and doors, and told us how the evening before a number of young Venetians had been talking and laughing together a short distance away from his shop. Some German soldiers who were

---

24. Jan. 28, 1798.

passing concluded that they were discussing politics. They took two of them, who had been talking louder than the others, and after two or three hundred *potztausendsakerments*, laid upon them, "'twixt neck and cropper," a number of solid blows with their sticks, and then led them to the police station where, there being no one who knew Italian, they were held prisoners until morning.[25]

I departed from that café more sorrowfully than a tender son leaving the sepulchre of the mother he has loved.

Going on into the *Piazzetta*, I approached the fish market, and inquired as to prices, in order to discover whether taxes had been laid on gifts of the sea as well. An old man, wasted, unkempt, sunburned, who had every appearance of being a beggar, overheard my query, and assuming that I intended to make some purchases, sidled up to me and asked whether I would allow him to carry the fish home. As I turned to him to answer, he stopped, drew suddenly back, and exclaimed in tone of amazement:

"*Santo Dio!* Whom do I see! Lorenzo Da Ponte!"

I had a hard time in recognizing him, but after studying him carefully, I thought I knew, and in an amazement equally great, uttered a name!

---

25. Abuses by subalterns rarely reach the Throne undisguised. May it please God that this little volume come into the hands of him who holds the reins

> delle belle contrade,
> e che qualche pietade alfin lo stringa.
>
> . . . .
>
> Udì miei voti il ciel!
>
> (Of my fair country, that some pity
> at least may stir his heart. . . .
> Heaven heard my prayer!)

May my reader remark this last verse! —L. Da P.

I was not mistaken. He was the brother of that lady whom for three whole years I had loved more dearly than life, and for whom I had renounced the beautiful Matilda and the amiable daughter of the "honorable beggar." To meet the miserable creature in that state aroused all the sentiments of charity and pity in my heart; and in a flash the crimes and ingratitudes of the sister vanished from my mind along with the caprices and follies of the brother. Finding him almost naked, without a hat on his head or boots on his feet, I threw my cloak over his shoulders, invited him into a gondola with me and took him to my inn, meantime sending the boatman to a second-hand dealer with orders for the latter to bring some clothes to that tavern. I then led the wretch to my room, bade him drink of some wine, to refresh him in spirit and strength, gave him socks, boots, a shirt, and trousers wherewith to cover himself; and leaving him alone in my bedroom until he should have washed and dressed, I went to see if the clothier had arrived. He was not long in coming. I bought from him everything that I believed would be necessary for the moment, and then re- turned to my room, where I found my unfortunate quite trans- formed in aspect. He had not only washed, but also shaved; and when I gave him the remainder of the clothes that the dealer had brought, I could not truly say whether his contentment were the greater, or mine. I ordered food and various liqueurs brought to my room and begged him to sit down to eat and drink with me. He proffered several times to speak, but he was so bewildered by his feelings of pleasure, amazement, and grat- itude, that he could not for some time complete the sentences he began. Finally, however, he took courage, and, seizing my hand, wished at all costs to imprint a kiss upon it. Then he cried, bitterly weeping:

"My sister is dead. Oh! that she were here, to see and un- derstand what she has lost!"

I adjured him to change the subject, and tell me through

what misfortunes or accidents he had been reduced to such deplorable misery. He then spoke as follows:

"You know, sir, of what family I come" (he was, beyond any doubt, from one of the noblest and most ancient of Venice), "a family whence issued Doges, Procurators of St. Mark, admirals and generals, prelates and magistrates of highest fame—my own uncle was an Inquisitor of State, and my grandfather, Ambassador to Constantinople. But none of my people were ever rich, and everything they had came of the offices they exercised under the Republic. When the Republic fell, more than three hundred families, who drew their principal sustenance from the same source, fell as mine fell into the indigence and humiliation you see. I am worse off than the others, because in my youth I was wild and vicious and failed to get an education. That is why I find myself with a beautiful and virtuous wife, four children, and a sister to support, without a profession, without talent, without resources; and were it not for the charity of kindly people and that little hamper with which I earn now two, now three *lire* a day, we should all be dying of hunger. For pity's sake, Signor Lorenzo, depart from the city quickly! An honest man such as you could not remain here very long without danger. This is no longer the Venice you knew. Once upon a time we trembled at the name of an Inquisitor of State; now we tremble at that of a soldier; and where once a Venetian had three masters on his back, he now has thirty thousand, and not with sequins on their brows and wands in their hands,[26] but with bayonet and musket. We are surrounded, moreover, by hordes of people who through fear and through hatred have destroyed all commerce and annihilated manufactures, redoubling needs without limit, cutting off all means of earning,

---

26. The agent of the Inquisitors wore *ex officio* a red cap with a sequin stamped with the image of Saint Mark; and when he donned that cap, it was the signal for everyone, great and lowly alike, to obey him. —L. Da P.

creating a thousand opinions, a thousand interests, a thousand bickering parties, bringing on rivalries between citizens, rancors, enmities, bad faith, and the miserable necessity of doing anything in order to live. To cap the climax of our ills, our young men, sane and robust, who might through their industry or their labor bring succor to their families, are forced, the moment they are able to bear arms, to spend their lives in the barracks, where they are taught to fight far from their beloved country. Those who are left with us are the women, the children, the infirm, and the aged. What can be done to support them? Just what I am doing, and sometimes worse! . . . There you have Venice!" His countenance as he spoke showed such fire of resentment, indignation, and truth withal, that I no longer saw in him the faro gambler of the "Yes, Excellency," and "No, Excellency," or the ragged beggar of the fish basket. I seemed rather to be hearkening to a David, or a Jeremiah, pouring tears or raising lamentations over the ruins of a Babel or a Jerusalem. Never had I imagined in the fellow such acuteness of mind, such discerning judgment, or sentiments so noble and delicate. Verily, *vexatio dat intellectum!*

He remained more than two hours with me. I gently forced upon him a gift of a few sequins (twelve, I think) and he departed, overwhelming me with thanks and benedictions; and I heard of him no more.

Whether the words of that unfortunate nobleman were so many rents in my heart, let him who reads imagine! What thoughts and considerations he had stirred in my soul, burning, as it always has burned, with an ardent love for a country which, despite the wrongs she did to me, I regarded ever as the most brilliant, illustrious, and glorious in the world; whether one go back to her origins, or examine her growth, her primal laws, her victories, her form and situation, her monuments, or consider, finally, the character of her inhabitants, known to the princes and nations of the world as the *boni veneti* from

271

the earliest days of her national existence,[27] *boni* not only, but courteous, hospitable, humane, and charitable; and such continuing to be in spite of the luxury and the vices introduced by commerce, by the accumulation of immense riches, and still more by Time, that all things human spoils and destroys! Her miseries at that moment tore my heart and filled me with despair; for I could foresee, besides, that her ills would be augmented in time beyond all measure.

While I sat ruminating these gloomy thoughts, I heard a knock at the door of my room. I opened, and there faced me a young man of handsome aspect, who inquired of me with impeccable urbanity whether it were my pleasure to be combed or shaved. His manner so pleased me, indeed, that though I needed neither the one service nor the other, I bade him enter and ordered a shave. While he was sharpening his razors, I asked him how things were going in Venice.

"*Come va le cosse, la me domanda!*" (How are things going, you ask?) And here he put down the razor. "*E come vorla che le vaga, cara Ela, con questa xente che no ne capisse, né nu capimo* (How do you expect them to be going, my dear man, with these people who do not understand us and whom we do not understand?), *che se tiol tuto quello che gavemo, che no ispende un soldo chi li pica*—who take all we have and never spend a cent even if you prod them to it—*a che se se lamentemo i ne bastona!*—and if we complain, they club us!"

"And the French?" I then ventured, "How did they treat you when they were in Venice?"

"The French? The French? God bless them where they are! God bring them back quickly to this city! At least we understood a few words of what they said. We saw them laughing, joking, having a good time, and if they sucked the purses of the rich, at least they spent generously with the poor—the shop-keepers and our working people; and our women—oh, take my word for it—*che voleva più ben ai francesi che a una gran parte dei venesiani!* (They liked the French better than most of our Venetians!)"

He took up his razor again, fitted the basin to my chin, handed me a towel, and began his work. After some moments of silence, he asked me whether I liked poetry.

"A little!" I replied.

"If I can remember it," he said, "I would like to recite a sonnet that will make you laugh."

And, truly, it made me laugh. They were verses such as a barber would write (but not so good as those of a Burchiello). Two of them, nevertheless, were in my opinion very worthy of being read. I retained them, and shall always retain them, in my memory:

> Napoleon nell'Adria entrò coi galli,
> ma prese al suo partir quattro cavalli.

> (Napoleon to Adria came with the cocks, but went away with four horses.)

This double allusion to the name of the French nation and to the four bronze horses which the French carried away from Venice, seemed to me very witty; and, in fact, everything he said amused me immensely, and in some measure helped to lighten my despondency.

When he had finished shaving me and combing my hair, I offered him a piastre; but he thought I was expecting him to change the money, to pay him the usual wage of a few *soldi*. Laughing he cried:

"By San Marco, where do you think I am going to find ten *lire* to give you in change? I do not earn ten *lire* in a fortnight."

"What?" I said. "Don't people shave in Venice anymore?"

"Yes, sir," he replied, "they shave—once a week; and they pay two *soldi*; or more often they say: 'I'll see you tomorrow,' and tomorrow never comes!"

I then told him that I gave him the coin to pay for the time he had lost with me and for the delicious verses he had recited. It would be difficult to imagine his surprise and his joy. I could hardly get him to leave my room. In the end, however, he departed, and I fell back again into my sorrowful meditations. Though the pleasure I took in performing acts of humanity and of charity somewhat tempered the bitterness that oppressed me at the sight of the extraordinary misery in which my country had been plunged, I nevertheless resolved, then and there, to remain no longer than that day in Venice.

I was on the point of going out, to pay some other calls, when to my greatest surprise, I saw the reconciled spouses entering my room. After a brief exchange of conventional ceremonies, I invited them to remain to dinner with me, and they accepted. Between wines and viands, they both told me stories which truly excited me. The man Doria, of whom I spoke a little back, was their principal subject. Neither public decency nor my own sense of delicacy would permit me to recount them as they were. I will say simply, that after a few words, I gathered that Doria was now "serving cavalier" of the lady in question; that the moment he saw me in Venice, he flew into a rage of jealousy, and vowed both to wife and husband that my stay would not be very long in that city. They repeating to me the things I had heard from the beggar-nobleman, I did not doubt that he would easily succeed in his despicable design; and had the hour not been already far advanced, I should straightway have departed from that wretched town where not the most honest and innocent of men could count himself for a moment safe.

They tarried with me some time, however, and would doubtless have remained until night; but observing that I sat thoughtful and uncommunicative, they finally begged liberty to depart. I accompanied them to the stairs. As the woman offered me her hand in farewell, she cautiously slipped a letter into mine. It read as follows:

> After twenty years of separation, I have seen you once again, O revered benefactor of mine, my savior and friend! Permit me to express to you my liveliest and most distinguished thanks for the favor you have done me: a favor that adds a thousand new sentiments of gratitude and affection to those I then felt. I have seen you! I judge that you are happy! What more could I ask than that? But flee, Signor Da Ponte, flee! Depart quickly from this city which never was, and now is much less, worthy of you! Aside from the peril that threatens you, should you prolong your stay, from the traps of a traitor who is jealous of you, you would be compelled to see things in my own house that would make you tremble and shudder with disgust, without your being able to help me. That cursed Doria is my tyrant! He has the votes of all the family, he has those of his wife, he has those of my husband, who, partly through need, partly through perverseness, has sold me to the most inhuman of all men on this earth, a man whom I hate more than death, yet whom I must pretend to love, in order not to be parted again from my children and not to die of hunger with them. In my house you must have seen . . . well—he is their father! . . . But flee, Signor Da Ponte, flee! And do not forget your poor . . . Angioletta.

One would have to have a heart of stone not to bathe such a letter with a few tears. But I could see very well that tears would be all I could give her.

I remained at the inn till after seven. Then I went out, first to a café, and thence to the Opera. But my mind was so cluttered with sad thoughts and dire forebodings that I did not hear a word that was spoken or a note that was sung. Along toward the last scene, a voice that I knew began calling from a box near mine:

"Da Ponte! Da Ponte!"

I turned and saw and recognized, to my infinite delight, the Abbé Artusi, my friend of those many years, a man of talent, wit, and learning, not the least among good poets, and first among excellent citizens. He had entered that box a moment earlier to greet a friend. Turning he chanced to see me, recognized me, ran to embrace me, and the opera finished, left the theater in my company and attended me to my inn.

We were approaching the tavern door, when we saw two persons standing on watch there, and one of them straightway drew off, but not so quickly that I did not recognize Gabriel Doria! The other, advancing to meet me, asked whether I were Signor Lorenzo Da Ponte. I replied that that was my name.

"Signor Da Ponte," he then said, "I have something to communicate to you."

I went, without remark, to my room. He followed, and the Abbé likewise. When we arrived there, he drew a paper from his pocket, and read:

"By order of His Imperial and Royal Majesty, Signor Lorenzo Da Ponte will be pleased to leave Venice tomorrow before evening."

I inquired whether I might ask his name, or his office, and he replied that he was an agent of His Imperial and Royal Majesty under the Magistrate of Police. Then he asked whether I desired to see his credentials; but my friend Artusi, who knew him, made me a sign of which I caught the meaning perfectly. I answered that that would not be necessary, but I begged him to assure His Imperial and Royal Majesty as well as the Magistrate of Police, that the rays of the new sun would not see me in Venice.

When he departed, I burst into a laugh so loud that the innkeeper entered my room to inform me very quietly that Signor
Gabriello Doria was in the adjoining room with the messenger
of H.I.R.M. under the Magistrate of Police, and that my laughter might be taken as an act of contempt. I thanked him for the
warning, begged him to serve me supper, and turned to talk
music with my good Artusi. After supper we went out and
when we were quite alone, he told me things about the country that whetted beyond measure my keenness to be off.[28]

I could not leave, however, without some little revenge.
The wife of Captain Williams,[29] a valorous Englishman beloved
of the Emperor, who had made him commander of a fleet, was
an intimate friend of my wife. The gentleman himself knew
me and had great friendship for me. He was not, unluckily, at
that time in Venice, though expected there from day to day. I
wrote him the following letter and left it with Artusi for him:

NOVEMBER 8.

Most honored Sir:

   With my Nancy I have come to Italy to see my father,
and to Venice to perform certain errands entrusted to me
by the manager of the London Opera. I spent two days
only in this city, saw a few friends, and hoped to linger a
few days longer, in order to see you. But at this moment
(twelve o'clock, midnight) an official of the Police brings

---

28. Signor Montani, my most courteous Florentine reviewer, found nothing beautiful or amusing in these stories. As for the amusement, he, alas, is right. As for
the beauty, it is a question of tears. The cause of the tears here, however, is
as beautiful in a self-respecting Venetian as the fall of Jerusalem is for an Israelite.
—L. Da P.

29. Identified by Sheppard (260) as James Ernest Williams (1761–1804), commander of an Austrian flotilla stationed at Venice in Jan. 1798.

me an order from His Imperial and Royal Majesty (who lives in Vienna) to depart from Venice before tomorrow evening. Will you be so kind, on your return, as to look into this matter somewhat carefully and thus give both to me and my wife a new sign of your patronage and friendship? Your most obedient servant,

L. Da Ponte.

We shall shortly see how roundly I was revenged by that honest Englishman!

The next day I left Venice before dawn, taking a gondola for Fusina *en route* to Padua, whither, barely arrived, I heard, not without great sorrow, that a break was hourly expected between the Imperial and the French armies in that neighborhood. The armies were separated only by Verona, and, in case of conflict, my passing would be rendered very difficult. I therefore decided at once not to return to Ceneda myself, for fear of being detained there by my people. Instead I sent a message by the post urgently summoning my lady. I then planned to set out with her along the road to Bologna.

We had scarcely taken seats in our carriage when we heard shouting in various directions:

"*Halt!*" "*Halt!*"

Our driver drew rein, and two German soldiers, with an officer also German, appeared at the windows of our carriage to reexamine our passports, which we had obtained shortly before. I handed them to the officer. He looked at them and then ordered the coachman to drive along after him. He stopped at the door of a public office and bade us enter there.

I was quite well known in that city. It was not on me, therefore, that their investigations turned. But having heard comment on my wife as a young girl of some amiability and a certain vivacity and wit, some suspected she might be a French spy, all the more since they had heard that she spoke several languages. In fact, they began to examine her, one addressing her in French, another in Italian; and she replied to each in the language used.

"The young lady," remarked one of them ironically, "is well versed in many tongues!"

"Oh sir!" she answered, "I speak other languages, and among them my own."

"What is your country, signora?"

"I am English, sir! I speak French because I was for a time in France; German because my father was born in Dresden; Dutch, because I lived in Holland for some time; Italian because it is the language of my husband."

They were on the point of pressing their inquiries when General Klebeck entered the room. He knew me very well, and the operas I had written in Vienna. He ran to greet me, gave me his hand, and asked me what it was all about. I explained briefly, and that good gentleman, on whose command that office depended, gave orders that we be allowed to proceed and added in his own handwriting a number of flattering titles and warm recommendations to our passports.

I drove on from Padua, accordingly, and started for Bologna, the city where, ordinarily, all the operas in Europe find their mart for singers, dancers, and musicians of every kind.

I stopped for several days at Ferrara to enjoy the companionship of my sometime patron and friend, Giorgio Pisani, who had then obtained his freedom. He welcomed me, truly, with transports of joy, but my pleasure at seeing him was not of the same enthusiasm as his. His misfortunes, his imprisonment for so many years, the fall of the Republic, the vicissitudes of his family, had wrought such change in him that he no longer seemed the wise, sapient citizen of the Republic, but a rabid, and desperate revolutionary. I saw him, however, often, and met through him all the leading gentlemen and French officials of that city by whom I was feasted and honored, partly by favor of

Pisani, and partly through the success there of my operas, which had been performed for many years in that magnificent theater as well. Pisani urged me to stay in Ferrara, and had a prospect of procuring my election as poet to the then Cisalpine Republic; but I thought myself comfortably fixed in England. I had not much faith, besides, in the permanence of that Republic, and still less in the wisdom of poor Pisani, whom I heard harangue the populace once, not daring to hear him the second time.

Quite different the case with Ugo Foscolo, a young man already of the greatest promise, whose public speeches in Bologna I attended a number of times with marvelous delight. His delivery was full of fire, energy, conviction, his style ornate and graceful, of the purest his language, his figures alive, noble, luminous. I was concerned to meet him and gain some intimacy with him. He courteously paid me several visits, and I boldly predicted the position he would one day make for himself among the first *literati* and poets of his age and of Italy. He must have remembered me for some years at least, after the last visit he paid me at Ferrara.[30] I certainly have always remembered him and will continue to do so every day as I turn to the incomparable "Letters of Jacopo Ortis," or perhaps more especially to his *Sepolcri* and other divine verses, which I alone had the glory of introducing to the admiration and enjoyment of the keenest minds in this illustrious and—if the boast may be permitted—by me alone Italianized, city.

I passed several delicious days with this noble man of letters and other cultivated and charming individuals in Bologna; so much so that I almost forgot my principal mission, *qual chi per buon soggiorno obblìa il viaggio*! But a letter came from London, announcing among other things, the reconciliation of

30. Ugo Foscolo was attracted to some shirts of very fine linen that he saw in my rooms—that is why I judge he must have remembered me for some years. —L. Da P.

Banti and Federici. That news roused me quickly from my pleasing torpor and set me to thinking seriously of Taylor's real interests. As there was no singer of special note in Bologna, I resolved forthwith to go on to Florence.

Aside from the pressure of musical matters that were drawing me thither, I was mightily impelled by my eagerness to see that famous city, which I had never visited before. The cold was excessive, and I did not venture to take my wife with me. I ran to the office of the post to see if there were an opportunity for Florence. I was told I could leave on the spot, if I did not object to a lady's riding with me. The owner of the post then pointed out to me a girl of prepossessing aspect, plainly but neatly gowned, and almost attractive. I thought it a little strange that such a lady should be traveling thus, but a little out of curiosity to know who she was, and partly not to lose time, I accepted her company.

We left Bologna about four in the afternoon, and for fully two hours she neither spoke to me, nor I to her. She was the first to break silence, her first words as follows:

"I am terribly sleepy!"

"So am I, to tell the truth!" I replied.

We were again silent for many minutes. It was she, again, who spoke first, to tell me that she could not sleep.

"Nor can I!" I answered.

"Would you mind my talking a little then?" she ventured.

"I should be delighted, madam."

A Dialogue Bizarre.

"Where do you come from, sir?"

"Venetian, at your service!"

"I am a Florentine."

"Two beautiful cities!"

"The most beautiful in all Italy! I have been in Venice many

281

times. It is beautiful! But Florence! . . . It takes more than that to equal Florence! Have you been in Florence?"

"No, signora, I was never there."

"You'll see! You'll see what a paradise it is! Then there are the women! . . . So many angels! You like pretty women?"

"As much as is proper in a man of my age, and married already."

"You have a wife?"

"Yes, the woman you saw at the door of my inn, where we took the carriage."

"That girl? She was your wife?"

"None other!"

"Pardon me, but I thought she was your daughter. *Bravo!* You have good taste! But—is she really your wife?"

"The idea, signora! Are there really wives and not really wives?"

"Oh—she might have been your lady, and you her serving cavalier!"

"Excuse me, madam; my wife is not an Italian. She was born in England!"

"English women do not have cavaliers?"

"No cavaliers, madam!"

"Poor things!"

"Why?"

"A serving cavalier is the gentlest beast in the world!"

"I should say that a husband who submits to one is a beast even more gentle.—Are you married, signora?"

"I was, but thank Heaven, that is over. Death freed me in six months!"

"A lady of your merit will soon find another husband."

"I, another husband? That, sir, is a pill that may be swallowed once, but not twice, by a woman who has an ounce of brains."

"Then you will have a serving cavalier, I suppose!"

"I have had one or two, and I hope to have others. Just now, to tell the truth, I am without one. Would you care to be my cavalier as far as Florence?"

"Signora! I would not be good at it."

"I will show you how, and, I assure you, once you begin, you will enjoy it."

"I have no desire, madam, to become the gentle beast ... that madam likes so well."

We were at this point in our conversation, when we heard shouting in the distance.

"Stop!" "Stop!"

Two young men were asking if there were not a place for them in the calèche, to go with us as far as Pietramala. I was very eager not to be alone with the woman any longer. I not only consented, but begged the coachman to take them, as there was room aplenty; which he did willingly for a certain price they gave him.

The scene changed at once. The little lady, not so concerned now to find a cavalier in a man past fifty, turned her charms and coquetries on the two young men, expert enough in that art, and before we reached Pietramala their intimacy had progressed so far that anyone would have taken them for old and familiar friends. We dined together that evening, and in the morning all three had the good favor to let me depart alone in a carriage with places for four, where I had ample room to draw my moral conclusions on that trifling episode.

One thought among others, occupied my mind.

"If one of those travelers," I said to myself, "who have such wonderful partiality and tenderness for the honor of Italy, had chanced to meet such a woman on his travels, what would he have written in his informing narrative of the women of Italy?" Anyone who has read Smollett,[31] Sass, or some other

31. Tobias Smollett (1721–1771), *Travels through France and Italy*, London, 1766; Henry Sass (1788–1844), *A Journey to Rome and Naples*, London, 1815. Nic., 304.

traveler of like stamp, may easily guess what would have been said. For myself, I shall say nothing, nor make any long comment on this little story, leaving that double burden to those who read these pages. I shall say merely that, for one silly girl who calls herself a Florentine, and whom I would sooner have taken for a woman of Porcile, Pietramala, or some other little hole in Tuscany, there are hundreds and hundreds of women in Florence who, in grace of mind and manner and all those merits and virtues which especially adorn their sex, can vie, without fear, with the most cultivated and amiable ladies of the world. I have found them hospitable without ostentation, educated without pedantry, affable without forwardness, interesting without pretense, courteous without immodesty, good-mannered without affectation. Add to such admirable qualities the sugar of a "speech that is felt in the soul" and try if you can to suppress a longing to live and die in Florence!

I was able to stay only a few days in that city, but what I saw as regards buildings, gardens, pictures, statues, and historic monuments, delighted me in the extreme, and left me sorrowful that I should have to leave so soon. What struck me above all was the manner of "conversation" practiced by many of the most illustrious ladies in Florence. I was invited one evening to the *conversazione* of one of the leading matrons. To nobility of birth this lady coupled all the graces of a cultivated and natively superior mind. She was a widow, rich, young, beautiful. Her house was always open to foreigners of distinction, but along with these, and with princes, dukes, and peers from all parts of the world, she received, feasted, and honored all people of talent, particularly poets, painters, sculptors, historians, physicians, lawyers, and so on. There was music only once a week, saving special occasion, such as the first reception to some eminent musician. Dancing was permitted only once a month. Politics were rarely discussed; and cards were entirely banished. The principal topic of that assembly was literature. Every evening there were readings of poetry, learned papers, essays in light vein, and, two or three times a week, comedies, or tragedies, the parts for men and women being assigned by lot. Not being able to upset established custom, I was obliged to allow my name to be placed with the others in the urn, and it fell to me to read the part of Aristodemus in Monti's beautiful tragedy of that name. The second evening, I was invited to read some poetry of my own, and I delivered my dithyramb "On Odors," which seemed to be applauded. The third evening I listened with infinite delight to a reading of Alfieri's *Saul.* I was amazed. Yet there was nothing to be wondered at. All those who took part had been pupils of that great poet in declamation.

I said to myself at that time: "If certain English ladies were here, who spend so much time in kicking their heels and legs to the ugly music of a bad violin, what idea would they get of the ladies of Italy, and what would they say of themselves?" What I said to myself of English women then, might I dare now, respectfully, reverently whisper in the ears of my still more beloved Americans? And, confining myself to a very small number, might I ask why those young ladies, so dear to me, whom I have had, and have, the sweet and honorable task of instructing in the beautiful language of the Arno, and who read the delicious works of our poets with such great delectation and grace, should not be allowed to give evidence of their talents and of the efforts of their instructor by occasionally reciting to a chosen number of friends those same works which they so highly esteem? Are they not allowed to play and sing in public? Are they not allowed to dance? Why not read then? I have asked the question. Without awaiting the reply, I return to Florence.

Discovering, to my great disappointment, that not even in that city were there individuals suitable for the London Opera, I decided to return to Bologna. I should call my journey rather ridiculous than unfortunate. The cold was excessive, and the snow deep all along the road. I set out at night with a driver who had a rickety carriage and two wretched horses; but he was the only one who was willing, at an exorbitant price, to take me to Bologna. There was continued talk of an imminent rupture between the armies. I hastily departed, therefore, at all risks.

Just before reaching Pietramala, my carriage turned over while I was sleeping most enjoyably. On awakening I found myself in a bed of snow, downy enough, but a little too cold, and the carriage on top of me in place of a coverlet, with no way of extricating myself. It was night; but, by good fortune, the sky was very clear and the moon bright. My charioteer seeing the danger I was in, *Non cadde no—precipitò di sella*; and with an *affé di due*, a favorite oath of the Florentines, which came from his heart, cut the traces of the carriage with marvelous dexterity, that I should not be suffocated by some movement of the horses. Exhorting me to patience, he then ran to a little house not far off for assistance; and returning shortly with two peasants, succeeded with their aid in dragging me, stiff with cold and with chattering teeth, from that snowy inferno. They carried me to Pietramala more dead than alive. There the courteous hostess of the inn, who remembered me, tucked me quickly into a bed and rubbed my legs and arms with snow for a good half hour. A drink of excellent *Chianti* and two or three glasses of *kermes* (an exquisite cochineal liqueur of prodigious strength made only in Florence), set me up so that in less than three hours I was in condition to proceed again. My driver, meantime, had gone to bed, leaving word with the host that his carriage and his horses would not be able to take me to Bologna without danger; that I should give him what I thought just and proper for the road covered, and provide myself with another carriage.

The host advised me to take two horses, one for myself and

the other for a guide to accompany me as far as Bologna, and at sunrise I was on the road again, the host himself having supplied the horses and the guide. The animal I rode was not larger than a little donkey but it was tractable and strong. I arrived at Bologna without further incident late that afternoon.

The following morning I went to a certain Tamburini, a famous theatrical broker of those days, who provided actors and singers for almost all the theaters in Europe. There I engaged Madame Allegranti[32] and Signor Damiani, two singers of the first class, and the only ones I succeeded in finding disengaged in Italy. The rumor of renewed war between the Imperials and the French was growing more persistent every day. I thought it better, therefore, to leave for London without any delay, and Allegranti was delighted to go with me, taking along her husband and a child. We left Bologna toward the end of December and reached Augusta (Augsburg) without incident on the first of January.

There we found Captain Williams, the gentleman of whom I made mention when I left Venice. We were received by him with greatest evidences of warm friendship, and after the first exchanges of greeting he cried:

"Da Ponte, I have avenged you. The official who expelled you from Venice without warrant was made to resign at my instance, and the spy Doria was also removed from his post."

He insisted at all costs on our lingering a few days at Augusta; but his hospitality was almost the cause of irreparable losses to me. While we were at table with Williams one night, the son of Banti, who had not reached his twelfth year, and a lad of the same age who was with me, ran away through some childish caprice from the inn where we had left them, taking many of our valuables. Only after diligent search, made by a

---

32. Maddalena Allegranti (Mrs. Harrison), a friend of Casanova's; and Vitale Damiani—both second- or third-rate artists. Nic., 304.

number of soldiers dispatched by Mr. Williams, did we at last find them in the house of a peasant who had given them shelter for the night, in virtue of stories they told him. So it turned out that their running away had no more consequence than of delaying our journey a little.

We thence continued on our way, not only without disaster, but in perfect harmony, until we reached a German village, not far from Brunswick, which had lately been burned by the French, being left with only a few houses and a single tavern. Night being near, we were obliged to stop there, though it was a very tumbledown affair and none of the rooms had as yet been reequipped with windowpanes. Only the room on the ground floor and the adjoining kitchen were habitable. We entered, with the other passengers, and shortly asked to be served supper. The landlady asked us what we wished, and I replied:

"Soup, if you have any!"

"Soup?" asked the woman.

"Yes, meat, or chicken, if you prefer!"

"Meat, on Friday!" screamed the woman, as though gone mad.

"Out of my house, cursed heretics!"

The woman's husband, considering the condition of the ladies and of my wife especially, tried to placate her, but in vain. She snatched up the keys to the rooms and left the house herself. By our good luck she overlooked the keys to the pantry, and the host, half-conscious of his duty at least, handed them to my wife and advised her to help herself. We dined; but when we asked for beds, he informed us that his wife, in leaving, had locked the rooms and carried the keys with her. We then decided to put the ladies and the children in the carriages, and I stretched out with Mr. Harrison (such the name of the prima donna's husband) on the hay near the horses in a sort of stable. But we could not protect ourselves from the cold even with double cloaks, and there were no end of rats, of an enormous size, which began nibbling at our boots. This obliged us to return to the inn, where the odor of thirty and more breaths, heated by a great rusty iron stove, all but suffocated us. All this respiration had for accompaniment the consoling music of a semi-chorus of snorts and snores from persons sleeping on a number of tables hung about on cords in all parts of that room. These tables, so laden, were suspended directly over our heads, at a continual and imminent risk of falling on top of us and crushing our bones.

We left at break of day, and arrived safely as far along as Harburg. The harmony and concord which we had mutually preserved intact up to that time, began thenceforward to be troubled. I had observed that, on reaching inns, for some seven or eight days past, Mr. Harrison, who had more smoke than sense under his eccentric dome, had occasionally been seeking pretexts for quarrels. I said nothing, in order to keep the peace, but what was to come of his strange caprice we shall soon see.

After stopping two days at Harburg, we asked for passage across the Elbe. We were told however that it was frozen, but that one could travel on the ice as far as Hamburg. Seeing that many other persons were doing that, we decided to try it too. A few days before, the ice had broken at a certain point along the river, swallowing up a carriage and drowning six horses and numerous passengers. When we passed that spot, we could see a part of the carriage sticking out of the ice. It is easy to imagine what horror such a spectacle occasioned us.

Nevertheless, we arrived safely at Hamburg. There the good hotels were crowded full of people, and we considered ourselves more than lucky to find two rooms in one of the less wretched places. We decided to stop there. As my carriage was the first to arrive, I was the first to enter the inn and see the rooms. I took care to choose the best, having observed that Harrison had chosen the best for himself all along the road.

When he learned of my choice, he asked me, with raging inso-lence, by what right the *signor poeta* had made bold to do such a thing.

"By the same right," I replied, "that you, *signor semi-virtuoso*, have made bold to do so hitherto!"

The fellow came of a noble family of Ireland and had once been an officer in the Imperial army, stooping only through spinelessness and financial need to marrying the actress who was traveling with me.

One word led to another, and after a very long argument, he challenged me to a duel with pistols. He had half made the same challenge three or four times during the preceding week. Partly not to worry my wife, and partly through a natural aver-sion to dueling, I had pretended, on those other occasions, not to catch his meaning. This time I lost all patience and snatch-ing up one of the two pistols which he had just laid out on a chest of drawers, I shouted:

"Show your courage, coward! Take your weapon!"

The ladies threw themselves, trembling and weeping, be-tween us; but he, with marvelous calm, remarked:

"Don't be afraid. I would not fight with a man who is not of my rank."

The two ladies burst out laughing, and I followed their ex-ample. With a coward of those proportions, I thought it better to end things that way. After two or three days of mutual re-serve, he was the first to offer me his hand, admitting that he had been in the wrong, and I, without hesitation, gave him mine.

We remained for a whole month in Hamburg where expenses were so great that my purse was almost entirely drained: of the thousand guineas I had with me on my departure, I reached the capital of England with less than fifty. That enormous expendi-ture, however, I did not regret then, nor will I ever regret it at any time in my life. The pleasures and joys I experienced on that journey were so great and so many that all the gold in the universe would not have sufficed to pay for them. I had here and there, it is true, a little unpleasantness; but that was, at the most, only like a little too much pepper on viands otherwise delicious.

Toward the end of February the ice broke and we left for London on the first of March, arriving at Dover after a good voyage. I had written to Taylor, some days earlier, to send us passports to that city. I therefore hurried to the Aliens' Office to see if they had arrived. Who would have believed it? There were passports for everybody except for me! I had already heard from London that Federici had become reconciled with Banti, and that was enough to convince me that my name had been deliberately omitted. How did I manage to continue my journey with the others? I had brought with me from Italy a child of that wretched woman, a boy eleven years of age. His name chanced to be badly written, and a director of the office, who knew me, read *Ponti* instead of *Banti*, adding that for a little lad of that age passports were not necessary. I believe, nevertheless, that I owed my passage to his honesty rather than to any oversight, inasmuch as on my leaving him, he pressed my hand and exclaimed with smiling face:

"Go right on, right on, Mr. *Da Ponte*."

This little incident was enough to give me a foretaste of what to expect from the impresario, and from his advisers at whose instance my name had been omitted from the passports. One may imagine how I was received! A cold bow, a few words, a blank face, and glances now of a fox now of a basilisk, were the sweet harbingers of my future agonies. Three days had not passed when Mr. Taylor sent for me. He asked for an account of what I had done, and found nothing to disapprove, though Federici told him that Allegranti was too old and Damiani a second-rate singer. After a dry "All well," came the "but": . . . "And now the accounting!"

The confidence he had reposed in me for more than three years, both in his own private business and in that of the Opera, had not encouraged me to take all the precautions that would usually be taken in such matters. I was nevertheless fortunate enough to find all papers and documents necessary to convince him that I had handled a sum of from six to seven thousand sterling with the greatest scrupulousness and that, aside from the legal interest, he had not lost more than a hundred pounds altogether; and that, everything considered, he was in my debt to an amount of two hundred and fifty pounds which I had advanced for him. Those people were in the habit of cheating him—on three notes discounted by Gallerino, Taylor lost two hundred and fifty sterling on an amount of seven hundred —and they had persuaded him that I was one of their band. Not trusting himself, therefore, he had one of his lawyers ex- amine my accounts. Though prepossessed against me, the man found my statements so clear, that he was obliged to tell Taylor in my presence:

"If all your agents were like Da Ponte, things would be go- ing much better."

Taylor began to whistle, took up his pen, and signed an or- der to me for two hundred and fifty pounds, payable at his bank (there, at the moment, fortunately, he had funds on hand); whereupon he wished a good day to me and to the lawyer and went away. He had not said a word as to my post as poet at the Opera, and I did not know what inference to draw from his silence. But let us stop right here—for something good is coming!

On the tenth day of March, at six or seven in the morning, I was lying tranquilly in my conjugal bed, receiving the congrat- ulations of my wife for my birthday, when suddenly I heard the door of my room open. A man entered without speaking. He threw open the window, and then stepped to my bedside, commanding me to rise, dress myself, and go with him. I kept a loaded pistol hanging within reach of my bed. I seized it with a loud cry, and ordered him to leave the room. Seeing me determined, he did so, but stationed himself outside the door to wait for me, and sent me word that he had a warrant for my arrest on a note for three hundred pounds endorsed by me for Mr. Taylor and not paid by the latter.

He took me to his house, and there for the first time in fifty-two years of my life I saw myself confined in a room with windows secured by heavy iron bars, in company of a number of other persons also confined. I wrote to Taylor, but saw neither him nor reply from him for all that day—I was obliged to spend the night there. In the morning, however, I was able to find two persons to go my bond[33] and toward twelve o'clock I was allowed to leave.

I had taken just a few steps when a second officer presented me with another warrant on another note of that gentleman. I gave bond for that too, but before I could reach home, I was presented with a third. Thus it came about that within less than twenty-four hours, I had the honor of being arrested three times on behalf of my worthy impresario, who, being a member of Parliament at that time, had the privilege of not being subject to imprisonment for debt![34] During those twenty-four hours, I was able to appreciate the full value of the third of Casanova's three precepts!

This however was only the prelude to a noisy symphony that was played for me for more than three months by Banti, Federici, Taylor, usurers, lawyers, and constables of all the courts of London, by whom I was arrested not less than thirty times in three months, always for debts of Taylor! I was

33. The bond is given not for the payment of the debt but for the debtor's appearance in court at a certain time. —L. Da P.

34. Taylor secured election as Member from Leominister, June, 1797. Sheppard, 16.

reduced in the end to not letting myself be seen in public except on Sundays.

What my life was like can be imagined! I could appeal to no one except Taylor, but with him neither appeals, nor prayers, nor tears availed. After using my last penny to pay the costs of judges, constables, confinements, lawyers *pro* and *contra*, carriages, messengers, and so on; after handing most of the furniture in my house over to creditors of that cruel man, I was constrained to declare myself bankrupt: and I believe I must have furnished the first example in England of a poor man going into bankruptcy without owing a penny to a person in the world!

That procedure freed me from the peril of arrest (the word "arrest" is the exact one, since the constable takes the debtor by force, wherever he finds him); but what was left me to live on? True it is that I succeeded in saving my printing press, of which, since it had also been mortgaged by Taylor, his creditors could not take possession: but the keys to the room where it lay were in the hands of the mortgagee; and it was not until some months later, and on paying a guinea a week, that I was allowed to make use of it. My hopes, therefore, were confined entirely to my salary as poet and to the sales of librettos written by me. But that very salary had been garnished by a merchant who had lent Taylor money; and at the Opera only old operas were being given in order that all the profits might fall to Federici—he was continuing in his post as prime minister to the Opera, and secret chamberlain to the Messalina of Harmony.

This was about the time, if I mistake not, when Federici and Gallerini as well were imprisoned for endorsements they had written on notes of the manager: and all three were cowardly enough to implore my assistance in getting out of jail. But however vile they may have been, I was just as stupid and just as much to be condemned for working in behalf of two infamous rascals (such in truth Gallerini also was, as we shall shortly see). I therefore fell into my favorite, though for me always fatal, maxim of doing good to my enemies in the hope of changing them. But I recognize at last that kindnesses which are done to rogues are naught else than fresh stimuli to unpunished iniquity and fresh encouragement to them to do one harm: and that it would be easier to extinguish a fire with oil or with spirits of wine, than to correct the evil in a rascal with charitableness.

In less than two months, they were out of prison through my efforts alone; and what was my reward? At the moment of his release, Federici swore eternal gratitude and obligation to me. But he ran that same day to the manager and asked and obtained, in compensation for the inconvenience he had suffered, along with a new contract, the sole right to sell librettos! And Gallerini, after having robbed me of a number of books and sold them to a bookseller (who revealed his name in selling them back to me), threw himself at my feet, implored and obtained my pity and his life; and a few months later gave false testimony in favor of an assassin who robbed me of a thousand guineas, and was the cause of my total ruin and of my departure from London!

And what was the reward I had from Taylor? For three entire weeks he ceased to see me! I sent him two letters; he burned them without reading them! Having vainly sought to obtain if not pity, justice, by all possible means, I wrote the story of the foregoing and sent him a printed copy of it. Though I used a studied moderation in my narrative, it was nevertheless sufficient to make him fly into a fury and mediate revenge. Hiding his evil intent in silence, he sent a person to me, who, partly by blandishments, partly by threats, obtained from me all my copies of that pamphlet, made me promise on my honor to burn the original, took my bills and my pecuniary claims on Taylor, gave me on account fifty guineas, which were perhaps the tenth part of what I had spent for the manager, and went away.

Reassured by that promise of mine, Taylor thought he was free to throw off his mask and revenge himself. Only three days later, he sent his lawyer to me and informed me bluntly that he had no further need of my services at the Opera[35]; and not satisfied with that, two days thereafter he had an order served on me from the Aliens' Office to leave London. Feeling no pinch of conscience for any political wrong-doing, and being very certain that my ideas and principles of conduct could not be displeasing to the Government, I had the courage to present myself to the director of that office, who was pleased to receive me with admirable courtesy and cause the quashing of that unworthy order, which minor employees had dared arbitrarily to issue at the instigation of that ferocious man.

It is easy to believe that my separation from the Opera pleased many people; but more than all others, it pleased the dear *Brigidina*, who aside from the hatred she then bore me at the instance of her secret lover and on account of the stinging memory *spretæ formæ*, had a special reason for estranging Taylor from me at just that moment. I must explain that the second or third passion predominant in the woman was, as I have said, the good liquor of Bacchus. Some time previous I had used one of Taylor's usual notes to buy three hogsheads of excellent wine, and the keys to the cellar where they were stored were in my possession. That Bacchante tried several times to get them from me, in order, as she said, "to draw a few bottles for Taylor"; but I knew the full depth of her insatiable thirst and always refused to give them to her. She had never been able to obtain more than five or six dozen bottles at divers times. She hoped therefore that if I were to

---

35. Summer or autumn of 1799. Sheppard, 17. Perhaps early in 1800. Nic., 305.

lose Taylor's confidence along with my post as poet, she would be able easily to possess herself both of the keys and of the wine.

And so it turned out. The day after my dismissal, a servant of the lady came to my house and asked me for the keys and several papers of the manager which were still in my hands. Since I was somewhat slow in obeying, he handed me an order in writing from Taylor himself. Then I obeyed. But I had foreseen that very thing. I had sold two of the hogsheads the day of my dismissal and paid two notes of five hundred pounds, which, to my good fortune, fell due on the day she asked me for the keys. On her finding in the cellar only the hogshead that had been already in part reduced, the hisses and cries of that Fury were loud enough to be heard in the street. A few minutes later, the same servant was at my house again, demanding to know what I had done with the other two hogsheads.

"The manager," I replied, "will find among the papers I sent him, the explanations that he asks of me."

In fact he found the two notes! He cursed and swore; Banti wept; I laughed. But let us finish the story. Eighty-eight gallons of wine had remained in the hogshead I had failed to sell, the keys whereof were given to Madame Trinkemdown. How long did they last? Twenty-eight days! On the twenty-ninth, they sent a servant to buy several dozen more of a certain Badioli in whose shop I chanced to be present at the moment. Thirty-six bottles of wine therefore were drunk each day by Madame Banti, Taylor, and their thirsty friends. At that rate, how many did they use in something over five years? Let us leave the reckoning to the creditors of that unhappy man! It is for their benefit that I publish this anecdote.

To return to my dismissal. Since I could expect anything from a man of Taylor's character, weak by nature and rendered more so by Amor and Bacchus, this blow from his rascality did not surprise me. I learned, nevertheless, that Taylor had long withstood the wiles of a most infamous cabal before condescending to the unworthy step which was later to cost him so much remorse and in the end destruction. Allegranti and Damiani[36] made their appearances at the Opera and, as the result of intrigues, either they failed to please, or were said not to have pleased. Thereupon the rascal Federici began to reinforce his maneuvering. He led Taylor to believe that I had been well aware of the scant merits of the two singers; had allowed myself to be influenced by a present of a hundred guineas, which each of them had paid me (the wretch was accustomed to accepting such commissions himself), and had therefore engaged them for his Opera against my own conscience. Taylor occasionally mentioned to Banti the losses I had suffered on his account, but she assured him that I was very rich, and urged him to go to my house and be convinced. He came in fact and asked to see my printing room. Divining his motives, I told him that the key to that room was in the hands of William Fox, who had advanced two hundred and fifty pounds sterling to me, some time before, that I might pay one of the usual notes not paid by him. That he might have no doubt as to the truth of that, I showed him the creditor's receipt and his note that I had paid with the mortgage! This device also failing, accordingly, they began saying that my salary as poet was altogether too high, and Lord Keinard [Kinnaird], one of the underwriters, favored making that saving. *Signor* Serafino Bonajuti was therefore suggested to Mr. Taylor. A salary of a hundred pounds sterling, without interest in the librettos, was suggested to *Signor* Serafino. *Signor* Serafino accepted; and *Signor* Lorenzo Da Ponte was dismissed!

---

36. Mrs. Harrison appeared on April 9, 1799, was "panned" by the critics, made a few more trials, and withdrew from the stage for good. Damiani became involved in a dispute over his contract and did not appear at all. Sheppard, 17.

I unexpectedly found myself therefore without property, without employment, without credit, and without friends other than Providence and my own courage. My wife, it is true, had some money which she had saved in connection with an enterprise which I had myself procured for her and her sister, but that was not in her hands and the person who had gotten possession of it, would not give it up . . . And here let us tear another page from these Memoirs in order not to renew an *infandum dolorem*, which could produce only fresh tears and fresh anguish—and to no purpose—both in my heart, and in the heart of——In a word, I found myself in a despondency which would be difficult to describe.

I reviewed in my memory all the acts of Providence I had experienced in my life; and it seemed to me that an inward presentiment kept whispering "There is no need to despair." I asked fifty guineas in loan—never mind of whom: they were refused me. *Santo Dio!* How I wish I could forget that! I do not think that death itself could be so bitter as that cruel refusal was, and as it is, whenever I remember it!

I went out of my house, and after two or three tears, began wandering about the streets of London, not knowing whither or why. Walking mechanically along and repeating frequently to myself: "There is no need to despair!" I found myself, without being aware of it, on the Strand, not far from Temple Bar. There I came to myself, as an ox, escaped from the slaughterhouse, came rushing along followed by barking dogs and an immense throng. A few yards more and it would be upon me! To save myself from the animal, I leapt aside into the shop of a bookseller, the door of which was open.

The tumult passed. My eyes chanced to fall on a well-bound volume, and curiosity impelled me to see what book it was.

It was a Virgil. The "Virgilian lots" coming to my mind, I opened and lo, the first verse that was offered to my gaze:

O passi graviora! dabit Deus his quoque finem!

The line accorded so well with the motto I had adopted: "There is no need to despair!"

I had several times had in mind to establish an Italian bookshop in that metropolis. The thought flitted through my head again, just then, and the execution of it seemed to me very possible. I asked the owner of the shop, if he had any Italian books.

"Too many!" he replied.

"I will come to see them," said I.

"You will do me a favor in taking them off my hands!"

In such discredit were Italian books in London, in the year 1800!

I went out of the shop filled with a strange courage, and as it were with a new spirit of hope, the source of which I could not understand. I said nevertheless to myself: "I am going to take Virgil at his word: *dabit Deus his quoque finem!* We must see about setting up a permanent shop for Italian books in this city. We must revive the taste for our beautiful literature." But as I thought of the condition I was in, I could only laugh at myself and my plan.

Just then I happened to meet a singer from the Opera— Benelli. He took me by the hand and said:

"Friend Da Ponte, I am very glad I met you. Tomorrow or day-after-tomorrow, I must get away for Naples. I shall have to sell a note that I got from Taylor in settlement of my pay at the Opera. I was going to my lawyer for that purpose: but if you could find someone to give me a hundred pounds sterling for a piece of paper worth one hundred and seventy-five, I'll be glad to take such a loss, in view of the need I have of that amount to get to Naples."

I took the check and promised to give him a reply within an hour.

I hurried to a certain usurer of my acquaintance and offered him a gratuity of fifteen guineas; and, on condition that I add my guarantee by endorsing the note, he gave me the money. Thus I suddenly found myself sixty pounds sterling in pocket, which in good conscience I thought I could retain in view of the danger I was running, through my endorsement, of being afterwards obliged to pay the whole. I thought it an honest thing, however, to inform Benelli of what I was doing. As I handed him the hundred pounds, he said:

"I am very glad the sixty pounds are going into your pocket. If by chance Taylor should not meet the note, I will gladly repay the money you are giving me."

Without losing an instant, I flew to the bookseller on the Strand. He received me with laughing face, led me into a little room on the first floor, and spoke as follows:

"Here you see nothing but Italian books. If you want to buy them in a lot, so that I can use this room which I greatly need, I will be glad to make you a very good price. Listen—give me thirty guineas cash, and the books are yours!"

Though the books were covered with dust and worm eaten, it was easy for me to read, as he stood speaking, the titles on several of the backs. The first that offered itself to my eye was a life of Michelangelo, in-folio; the second, a life of Tasso by Serassi; the third, the life of Cellini; a life of Petrarch, the fourth. I asked him to repeat his offer, and counted out thirty guineas on the spot. He ran into the shop, wrote a receipt, and brought it back to me smiling, begging me to remove my property quickly.

His smile, to tell the truth, worried me a little; but when I looked more carefully at the shelves, which did not contain less than six hundred or seven hundred volumes in various sizes; and when I discovered what treasures were there, I too smiled, but at the ignorance of that bookseller! On the other hand I was pained to see the low estate into which our literature had fallen in that country. Not to detain my reader on trivial things, I shall not enumerate the precious works the room contained. Suffice it to say that when I sold them in my shop they earned for me not a penny less than four hundred guineas!

This new act of Providence roused a thousand hopes in my spirit, and was to me a good augury for the success of my favorite plan of restoring to pristine luster the literature of Italy which was no longer held in the esteem it enjoyed in that noble city in the days of Gray, Spencer, Dryden, the great Milton, and of many others of the *bella scola dell'altissimo canto*.

I then went to all the bookshops in London, spending the other thirty pounds on excellent books, which were also sold to me at ridiculous prices. On the first of March in the year 1801, I had in my shop nine hundred volumes, all of excellent titles, which soon reached the number of one thousand six hundred through other acquisitions I made at public auctions and through a good shipment of modern books which came in from Italy for Signor Nardini and which he could not, or did not choose to keep on his own account. Among these were a Muratori, a Tiraboschi, a Fabroni, and a Signorelli, writers of the greatest merit, who helped me, once their incomparable works began to be read, to kindle the enthusiasm of the many wide-awake and erudite Englishmen, among others of the celebrated Roscoe and Walker, to whose achievements the literature of Italy owes so much glory, and whom I myself was able to supply with many works for the execution of their magnanimous enterprise, which was of such use to me in my effort to restore to their proper places the letters and the *literati* of my country. I immediately made and published a catalogue, and for several days I had the supreme delight of seeing the foremost scholars and the foremost gentlemen of London in my store, bestowing their approval on my new establishment and patronizing it with their purses. Among these I will cite with pride the venerable names of Lord Spencer, William Payne,

Lord Douglas and Lady Devonshire, who in less than a week despoiled my shop of four hundred volumes at least, and enriched my purse with as many guineas, of which two thirds and more were profit.

I wrote at once to Venice, Florence, Leghorn, Paris, and from all those parts I drew an immense number of classical works, both ancient and modern. I continued frequenting the auctions, and for many months had no competitors. But little by little, the bookmart of London began to scent the sweet, and the price of Italian books rose out of all proportion, particularly of old editions. I, meanwhile, proceeding at the same rate, and delighted to see things going so prosperously, succeeded in enriching my collection beyond belief. In less than a year, I had more than eight thousand selected volumes in my store, all works much sought after, and better paid. I then canceled the mortgage on my printing press, and issued a number of Italian booklets, among which a little sample of my own poems. These I had no better reason to publish than a desire to give work to two young printers whose abilities I was desirous of testing. To this publication, however, I owe the purest and greatest of the pleasures experienced by me in the whole course of my life: my friendship, that is, with my beloved and respected Thomas Mathias,[37] a man revered by me above all men on earth.

The story of this illustrious man of letters is too important in its bearing upon me for me not to feel obliged to speak of it at some little length. A perfect master of the Greek, Latin, English, French, and Italian languages, learned, erudite, full of genius and taste for beautiful poetry, he had a fairly poor opinion of all Italian writers of comic opera, and for those in

---

37. Thomas James Mathias (1776–1837), author of *The Pursuit of Literature* (1794), various editions of Italian works, among them an abridgement of Tiraboschi, and an anthology of Italian lyrics. Nic., 307–8.

particular who wrote for the London stage. He had expressed
that opinion and that disdain in divers works, especially in his
Demogorgon, a graceful satire, full of pleasing wit. It was Signor R. Zotti, a teacher of Italian in that city, and a man of great
merit in letters (at that time more a friend of truth and mine
than he afterwards became),[38] who spoke to him of me in such
a way as to make him desire to see me. He came to my shop,
without telling me who he was, and asked me for various books.
While I was looking for them, he saw a little volume of poems
on the counter, and picking it up, began reading the first *canzone*. At each verse he read, the gentleman's eyes and attitude
seemed to give signs not of satisfaction only, but of wonderment. I had found the books he asked me for, but he continued
reading. At the fourth strophe of the *canzone*, he stopped, and
turning to me, asked eagerly who the author of the poems was.
But he had opened already to the title page and read aloud:

"*Saggi Poetici di L. Da Ponte*—with whom I have the pleasure of speaking?"

"At your service!"

"And are you not the poet at our Opera?"

"I was."

"You, the poet at the Opera, and the author of this ode?"

(It was my ode on the death of Joseph II.)

"Will you do me the favor," he went on, "of coming to see
me tomorrow morning and of permitting me meantime to take
these poems with me?"

I replied that I would be proud of that honor. He took a pen,
wrote his name and the street and number of his house, and
went away.

---

38. I hear that Zotti is no more. Let me bury in his grave the memory of certain
things, of which, should I accuse him now, he would not be in a position to defend
himself. I will say simply, for the benefit of such as heard him speak of me, that he
became my enemy without cause. —L. Da P.

At the hour appointed, I went to his house. He received me with the courtesy and good manners native to a person of his kind, had breakfast served, and asked me how ever I had come to lower myself to the point of writing dramas for that stage where such utterly miserable things were for the most part produced. I asked him if he had read any of my dramas or seen them performed. I do not remember whether he said "no" or avoided a reply by saying that, supposing mine to be like all the others, he had paid no attention to the words, contenting himself with hearing the music. I then recounted briefly how I had begun my theatrical career; informed him that I had composed a number of books for the Opera at Vienna as well as for that in London, and begged him to read some of them, not because I thought them perfect—either that was impossible in the nature of the thing, which did not admit of perfection, or else was impossible for me through lack of time, lack of talent, or through some other particular circumstance; but because I hoped that here and there he might find some scene not altogether unworthy of being read, or at least worthy enough to induce him to make peace with the poets of the Opera at London, though they were not so many Zenos, nor so many Metastasios. He promised me to do so, but after an hour or so of conversation on such topics, he began to speak of my ode, desired to hear me read it, read it again himself, saying such things of it as really to give me reason to puff with pride. From that moment he began to love me, respect me, be my patron, and for three years continuous he did nothing but pour out upon me the graces and the favors of a friendship and a generosity without limit. We shall shortly see how far the kindness of a man so great and so respected went for me and my poetry.

But my prosperity and my favoring Fortune did not stop just there. Toward the beginning of the new season at the Opera, that cursed woman who terrified with her perverseness as much as she pleased with her voice, and who brought sorrow upon multitudes of good people for every rascal to whom she brought a laugh, came to the holy resolve of returning to Italy. Taylor elected to accompany her as far as Paris and stopped there for some time for reasons which are not at present our concern.[39] However, in place of that singer, they engaged for the opera the excellent Madame Billington and Madame Grassini, the latter of whom brought with her a composer of greatest fame and real merit—Winter.[40] Meantime, the creditors of the Italian Opera, dissatisfied with Taylor's management, succeeded in getting the Opera into other hands; and these new people who had no Federicis, or Bantis, or other Achitophels[41] of like nature at their heels, bade a hearty farewell to *Signor* Serafino and recalled me to my post. I did not hesitate to accept the offer, which was really made me in a most gracious manner; and it was not so much for the pecuniary advantage, of which at that moment I had no pressing need, as to mortify that seraphic *vespertilio* who, partly by the patronage of Lord Holland, and largely through the ignorance of Taylor and his henchmen, had been represented as a soaring eagle. They gave me an order forthwith to write two serious operas for the two singers in question; and it was on that occasion that I wrote the *Ratto di Proserpina*[42] for the former, and the *Trionfo dell'amor fraterno* for the latter, sources both of a real triumph for me because they induced Mr. Mathias, whom above all I was eager to please, to take a less disdainful view of the poets of the opera.

---

39. June 1802. His term in Parliament ending at that time, Taylor no longer enjoyed immunity from arrest. Sheppard, 18.

40. Peter von Winter (1755–1825), Court Conductor to the Elector of Bavaria. Sheppard, 288. Giuseppina Grassini. Nic., 308.

41. II *Samuel*, XVI, 23.

42. Madame Billington's *Proserpina* opened May 3, 1804; and Grassini's *Trionfo*, six weeks earlier, March 22. Sheppard, 289.

Affairs at my stores, meantime, were progressing with admirable prosperity. I must however do justice here to a great number of cultivated, learned, and honorable Italians, among whom I may be permitted to give first rank to Leonardo Nardini and to Pananti,[43] excellent philologists both, excellent grammarians, and good poets; placing next after them Polidori, Boschini, Damiani and Zotti, not to mention many others; who instead of slandering me or envying, *more latronum*, my zeal and my enterprise in propagating and dignifying our language, supported me with patriotic cordiality and not without advantage to themselves and others, and placed every instrument that would help at my disposal. Not content with instructing others most efficaciously in the beauties, graces, and essential qualities of the Italian tongue, they wrote some beautiful and useful things themselves, published many of our most celebrated authors, and imported from Italy the best that appeared there in all forms of our literature. But the man who contributed most of all to the happy outcome of my undertaking was the same Mr. Mathias, above mentioned with praise, who republished a considerable number of our classics with learned prefaces and annotations, and whose eloquent and cultured pen convinced his wise countrymen that it was a most useful thing for the practitioners of humane letters to add to the treasures of Greece and Rome the precious gems of the Arno. Among numerous works, both in prose and verse, of the most prominent geniuses of Italy, which his ardent zeal for the literary glory of my country brought forth in most delightful form in the noble type of Bulmer, his infinite kindness toward me did not shrink from including that same ode which had been the fortunate beginning of our acquaintance, and from equipping it with most beautiful notes and remarks,

---

43. Filippo Pananti (1766–1837), a political exile in Paris who moved to London in February 1803, and eventually succeeded Da. P. at the Opera. Nic., 309.

such, in truth, that they would doubtless have induced me to believe my poem a great thing, had I not known of experience that, just as the beautiful and the good are smirched by people inspired of envy, so are they aggrandized and exaggerated by souls who allow themselves to be deluded by excessive benevolence. I cannot, however, refrain from feeling the weightiness and the value of such kindness; and however much the precept *nosce te ipsum* may lessen me in my own eyes, praises falling from lips so venerable most often fill me with pride.

While everything was thus smiling upon my efforts and designs, I fell most unfortunately into two mistakes which in the end were to bring misery and desolation upon my family and lead me to the cruelest despair.

My first mistake was to become entangled with Domenico Corri,[44] a man of good talent in music, but frivolous, visionary, and sometimes a liar.

I needed a space big enough to accommodate my stock of books which at that time amounted to some twelve thousand volumes. But what especially influenced me was the excellent location of the building Corri occupied. That induced me to rent first a part of his shop, which was a very large one, and, in the end, the whole building.

Corri wrote good music himself. The famous Dussek was his associate and father-in-law, and sold his beautiful sonatas through Corri's store. Sales were easy and prices good. Nevertheless Corri and Dussek both were buried in debts, and it seemed that neither the one nor the other had sufficient sense to conduct their business at a profit. Misled by many

---

44. Domenico Corri (1744–1825) had been in London since 1774, where he had joined the German composer Johann Ludwig Dussek (1761–1812) as a musical publisher, marrying, meantime, Dussek's daughter. Dussek fled, on his failure, not to Paris, but to Hamburg. Nic., 306. In the Corri speculations Louisa Niccolini dabbled a little too.

fine appearances, and many finer words and promises, I entered into a sort of partnership with them, burdened myself with all their debts, which I punctually paid: only to find myself in less than six months engulfed in a dreadful abyss, from which I could not possibly find issue save at the price of most of my skin. I lost just a thousand guineas with those two wretches. Dussek, *insalutato hospite*, went to Paris. Corri went to Newgate whence he was released in a short time on a pardon. I was left with a bundle of notes in hand, which some day, when my tapers give out, I may use to light my fireplace.

Much more serious, however, was my second mistake. I must explain that that Gallerini, who had negotiated Taylor's notes for several years, had retained in his hands all those which he had renewed without canceling either dates or signatures. It was not apparent, on that account, that they had been paid. They could therefore be placed again in circulation and the person who accepted them was obliged to pay them over again—such, at least, was the opinion of Lord Kenion in a suit brought against Taylor, who proved that he had been defrauded. But the court ruled that the receiver of those checks should not be made to suffer because the agent of the manager was a thief.

The fellow was on the point of selling a very considerable number of such notes, when I had word of his frauds and hurried to Perry, the publisher of the *Morning Chronicle*, at that time Taylor's agent and friend. I informed him of what was going on. He entreated me to find some recourse and I, through a remnant of pity for that deluded soul, and even more through love of justice, maneuvered Gallerini so well that I got out of his hands some twenty-five thousand pounds sterling of such paper, in exchange for a gratuity of fifty guineas (which Mr. Perry later had the honesty to repay me). This service alone might have seemed enough to incline Taylor to regard me forever as his savior and obligate him for the rest of his life to give me proofs of affection and gratitude. But how much more than that did I not do for him, and how did he repay me?

Having held off for some months in Paris, in hopes that between Perry and Gould—the latter had become his partner—matters could be arranged, he made up his mind to return to London secretly. Being no longer a member of Parliament, this secrecy was very necessary; but it did him no good. Gallerini had already placed some notes in the hands of Hill, the most rascally lawyer in all the courts of London. Gallerini learned of his arrival, discovered his whereabouts, and gave him into the hands of the constables. I knew nothing, whether of his return, or of his incarceration; but a singer at the Opera heard of it, came to me, and gave me the whole story, adding to it these words:

"Here is the moment to confound Taylor and let the world know who Da Ponte is. You must go and get him out!"

Words that were an electric fire upon my heart! In an instant there came to my mind the state in which I had been in Holland, Cera's dream, the bread, the herring, the chess, the tears, the verses repeated by me at that happy moment when the invitation to be poet at the Opera came. And in spite of the cries of my wife, of all the family[45] and of many friends, forgetting losses, injuries, injustices, I flew with the same singer and with one of my brothers to the house of the constable where Taylor was under lock and key.

I asked to see him. The singer went to his room and delivered my message. When Taylor heard my name, he was struck

---

45. The family at this time (winter of 1803–4) consisted of the following persons: Ann, Da P.'s wife; Paolo, his brother, whom he had brought on in 1800 (?) to take a position in a piano factory (Nic., 306); Louisa Niccolini, his sister-in-law; and her husband Charles (lately returned, as I believe, from America); three children: Louisa, born in 1793; Frances (Fanny), born in 1799; and Joseph, born in 1800. Another child, Lorenzo L[uigi?], was scheduled to appear at any moment.

dumb, and would scarcely believe it. He had been taken to that place toward ten in the morning. It was already past seven in the evening when I went to him. He had written and written again to all those who boasted of being his friends. Not one had answered. The harshness of others must in consequence have rendered my voluntary appearance the sweeter and more unexpected to him. I entered the room, held out my hand, and he extended his. I know not which of us had the more palpitating heart; whether I from the pleasure I was enjoying in foretaste in my hope of freeing him; or he, in his surprise and admiration at so extraordinary and so unexpected a kindness. After a few moments of silence, he was the first to speak. Our short dialogue was as follows:

"Mr. Da Ponte, you here?"

"Yes, my dear sir, here to succor you and free you."

"Is it possible?"

"You see I am here—it must be possible."

"What can I say?"

"There is nothing to be said, but something to be done."

Again he took my hand, pressed it with much warmth, seated himself, and fell silent. After taking breath and courage he explained that Hill was the man who had put him in prison for one note of six hundred pounds and another for three hundred; that he could give security for the first, because it was a simple instrument; but that the second had to be paid at once or before he could be released, since it was garnished with a certain legal paper, which the English call a "warrant of attorney." He added that if his creditors should discover that he was in prison there would, by morning, be such a quantity of processes against him that he would spend the rest of his life in jail. I wasted not a moment in taking my leave, rushed Rovedino and my brother to hunt for Gould, while I closeted myself with the constable who held the warrant of arrest, and disposed him to accept a new note from Taylor endorsed by me for the simple instrument, and for the other, half in cash and the other half in thirty days on an obligation from Gould, who came in about ten and, after some objections, signed the note which I offered to the constable. I bribed the man with twenty guineas, and before eleven in the evening the manager was in Haymarket. He spent a few moments with me and left me with these words:

"Mr. Da Ponte, what you have done for me today, cannot be repaid in words; but the future will show you whether I know how to be grateful."

His gratitude was to extend no farther than to sucking the last drop of my blood, and in the end to drowning me in the most overwhelming misery!

Since the seductive siren had left London and Federici had been forced to flee, I thought indeed that this last favor of mine would not be forgotten for some time. Knowing his hiding place, accordingly, I continued from that moment serving him rather as father than as friend. For more than six months I alone supplied him with the necessaries of life: I alone exposed myself to every hazard and every trial, to settle his affairs: I alone bought up many of his debts for four, three, two, and finally one shilling the pound. I alone obtained large sums from Gould to quiet constables, conciliate lawyers, obtain postponements; I, finally, was the one who paid the note given to the constable that night to effect his release from the danger— by his own confession—of remaining in prison for the rest of his life.

How did I meet that note? Allow me, my most generous friend, to repay in words and sentiments of gratitude the magnanimous act of which you, and you alone in the world, as I believe, were capable.

I had received notice from the prothonotary that Taylor's note to Hill had not been paid. That amounted to six hundred pounds, which I did not have at my disposal at the moment;

and in order not to lose my credit, which was very good at that time, I resolved to sell at auction a part of my books, trying to procure the money I required from some auctioneer. The books were already packed, and Stuart, the bookseller, was to come to my store to get them toward noon that day. I remembered, meantime, that I had promised Mr. Mathias to go to breakfast with him. Toward nine I went to his house. The moment he saw me, he caught my perturbation from the expression on my face, and inquired the cause of it. I tried to evade, but he insisted, till in the end I had told him the whole story. He listened sympathetically, reproved me for my lack of wisdom, ordered breakfast served, and, that finished, invited me to read from Petrarch.

We chose the divine *canzone* which begins: *Quell'antico mio dolce empio signore* . . .

It produced marvelous effects on the spirit of that distinguished man of letters. When we came to the verse: . . . *tal merito ha chi ingrato serve,* he cried in a faltering voice that seemed to come from the heart:

"That is the case of my poor Da Ponte!"

He seemed to forget Petrarch after that, so full was he of feelings of pity and solicitude for me.

"And what do you think of doing now, my poor friend?"

I informed him of my decision, of which he seemed not to approve. After a brief silence he again took up the Petrarch, glanced at his watch again, and dismissed me with these words:

"Go to your store and stay there for half an hour!"

I did so. Stuart had not yet come. When he came, I had no further need of him! My second guardian angel, before the half hour had passed, sent his valet to me with all that I needed in that urgency, and a note in the following tenor:

My dear friend:

Here is what you need to meet Taylor's note. God

313

grant that it be the last money you have to pay for such a man. Come and see me tomorrow morning.

Your friend, T. M.

Such generosity stunned me. I knew only too well the precarious state in which I then found myself, and the immense embarrassments in which I had become involved for Taylor's sake. I could foresee the impossibility, or at least the supreme difficulty, of ever repaying him. I remained some time irresolute, uncertain as to whether I could accept the money. Some slight hope, however, I had in virtue of Taylor's rosy promises the evening of his liberation. That unfortunately influenced me, and made me decide to accept. Oh, how many times thereafter I cursed, as I still curse, that moment! I received from you, most generous friend, one of those kindnesses which a well-bred soul knows it can never repay! And to what end? To fatten the purses of two assassins, to make Taylor's ingratitude more shameful, and draw from your noble hands a considerable sum that you could have put to a better use, helping meantime only to postpone my ruin for a little, and make it more lamentable in the end, or rather, indeed, irreparable.

That storm passed, I continued devoting myself with closer attention than ever to enlarging my business. Dulau and Nardini had a printing press that had flourished for many years and issued a number of worthwhile editions. It was now on point of closing, through the failure of Dulau. Nardini suggested that I become his partner in Dulau's place, and I accepted.[46] We published a number of things, among them, at my

---

46. I was the partner, accordingly, of Signor Leonardo Nardini, not Dulau's, as the writer in the *Antologia* of Florence mistakenly asserts. The point is of some importance. —L. Da P.

own expense, the *Animali parlanti* of Casti, a poem that found many partisans even in the English capital.

While this book was in press, the Abbé Michele Colombo,[47] a meritorious man of letters, a great philologist, a cultured poet, and my very particular friend, arrived in London as tutor and custodian to two young Italians of aristocratic birth. The three of them came frequently to my store. It happened that one day when they were there, some proofs of Casti's poem were brought to me for correction, and the young men, looking them over, asked my opinion of the work. After answering their question I added:

"It seems to me that this poem would be much more popular if the allusions were made clearer, something that could, in my opinion, be very easily done. To admit of a more general reading of the poem, a number of lines," I continued, "might also be changed or omitted, as too dirty, or at least as too free." They seemed to agree with what I said. But when they called on Casti in Paris, they said such things to the good old man that he could not refrain from writing me a very sharp letter which will be read, as I would guess, with much interest.

PARIS, NOVEMBER 29, 1802

My dear friend:

It is more than a month since I received from a

---

47. This new Casti episode (really of 1802) is a little out of chronology in the *Mem.*, Casti having died early and not late in 1803. Colombo was in London in April, 1803, after Casti's death, accompanied by three, not two, young men: Giovanni Bonaventura Porta, a certain Galiani, and one Baldelli. Da P.'s intended edition of the *Animali parlanti* (not a "fake" to torment Casti, as Nicolini supposes—Sheppard, 296, has found the London edition of 1803) was betrayed to Casti, in 1802, by a Count Maniaco of Friuli. Nic., 307. Apparently Da P. remembered Maniaco as one of Colombo's boys. Casti caught his indigestion not at Bonaparte's, but at a dinner at the Spanish Ambassador's. Nic., 307.

certain Maniaco, if I mistake not, but in your name, three elegantly printed volumes containing a collection of poems by our best authors. I have delayed thanking you for them, because Maniaco allowed me to hope that within some days I would be receiving a letter from you. The letter has not appeared as yet; I think therefore that I should no longer defer expressing my thanks. The edition is neat and beautiful, a pleasure to look at and to read. I was not unaware of your fine taste, but to see such evidence of it prompts me to congratulate you.

I have known for some time that you have an edition of my *Animali parlanti* in preparation, and I am sure that you will make it equally beautiful. I have been told that you are thinking of making some changes in it, substituting new expressions for certain ones that you deem not likely to please in England, as contrary to the proprieties of the English tongue. In truth, one must approve and praise the restrained delicacy of that language; but when one writes in another tongue, it does not seem to me that if an author adheres to certain phrases employed by his classics, a foreigner should be scandalized thereat. Ariosto has been printed several times in England, notwithstanding the fact that he did not scruple openly to use the word *p——a*, something which I never ventured in my *Animali parlanti*. Not only was Ariosto printed there—he sold widely. The same may be said of Dante who writes *c——* in a manner much less decent than I do; for, after all, I use the word only in certain proverbial expressions which exclude all indecency whatsoever. England is full of Ariostos and Dantes and other authors much less well behaved. If English readers were to stand rigorously on this modesty of theirs, they would have to give up their Greek and Latin authors, because in those languages things were called by their names.

If one consider the greater facility of sales merely, you know how much greater value is attached to the original genuine readings of a work as compared with those published with alterations and corrections, no matter how much better these may be than the original. If, not withstanding this, it was believed indispensable to change some expressions which all our classics use, why not write so to me frankly? I would have had no difficulty at all in changing such words as you might have indicated to me, that the work might not be taxable as a fabrication in several hands. And if, especially, you think you could gain by such a thing, I have always been your good friend, and will gladly accommodate you.

Yet for some time also vague rumor has been reaching my ears that you are thinking of publishing such interpretations and personal allusions as you, or whoever it may be, have been imagining you find in my poem. I have been so far from thinking you capable of such an infamous idea that I have never thought of writing you a word about it, persuaded that I could rest assured so far as you were concerned in this regard. How could I possibly allow myself to think such a thing? I have always had such a consideration for you, have always wished you well, have always tried to be useful to you within my powers, have always considered you a friend of mine, and know you are such, in fact; and in consequence incapable of betraying me to such an extent, by publishing things that absolutely, never, on my honor, on my most sacrosanct word, entered my head, and which would occasion me very considerable difficulties (on the part of persons who might think themselves attacked and who never overlook, and never forget, such things) and even put my life in danger? So far am I, I repeat, from believing you capable of such a thing, that I have persistently maintained to those who talked to me in this manner, that the thing was absolutely false; nor would I ever have written to you, had the above-mentioned circumstance not afforded me occasion—that, in case of need, you may defend yourself from such slanders, if ever they are uttered against you; since they would tend maliciously to give you character as an infamous and execrable man. My dear Da Ponte, I am sure that you yourself will not be less shocked at such a charge than I was.

In truth, satirical allusions against persons bespeak a character low, malign, and libelous, the which I do not think myself possessed of. Aside from which, an author who, rightly or wrongly, adopts the hope that his works may survive to posterity, once he turns to personal allusion, seems to renounce that sweet dream, because personalities have only a passing and temporal interest, since temporal and passing are the objects on which they bear; for, sooner or later after those who are so aimed at have disappeared from the surface of the earth, according to their greater or lesser importance no one is further interested in them, no one thinks of them more; and there is left to the author nothing save his reputation as a mocker of others, which evil mockery may amuse some in the present, but can never be approved, above all by honest men. Therefore it is that I took every care in my *Animali parlanti* to give no occasion or motive to anyone whatsoever to make such malicious interpretations, and to deprive several of my enemies of the means of slandering, as is clearly apparent to anyone who will give himself the pains to examine any animal actor in my poem. I had in view ever the thing and never the person, the vices and defects of governments, never of governors. Certainly there are and will be always in the world characters more marked than others, and therefore more exposed to the critical eye of the public, as bodies that are raised above a plane surface are the first to strike the eye (thus I wrote in my preface). To such, after many, many centuries, applications may be made by those who desire to make them; but they must not be attributed to the author, who protests himself entirely unaware of them. To reveal great and interesting defects is an undertaking worthy of an upright and honorable author and may he put thereto all the frankness and courage that the truth and the defense of a good cause inspire in him! But personalities are unworthy, not only of an author, but of any honorable man. Such are my imperishable sentiments!

If in times past I have—ever with due precaution—made any such allusions, it has never been to produce them in public, but to keep them hidden, to read at the most in private circle to a few friends—a thing also very dangerous, because the bad faith and the imprudence of such friends may bring it about, as too often happens, that beyond the intention of the author, such things are published by printers who have more at heart any gain however vile and however slight, than any proper reserve whatsoever.

I have chosen to give you this long annoyance, because I have not only not the slightest distrust of you, but all confidence rather that, as occasion demand, you will fain be my advocate for the truth; and for that reason I have mentioned these things several as weapons of which you may avail yourself against my detractors, to spare me the unwelcome annoyance of purging myself of such impostures (should ever they be published), now through published pamphlets, now by employing every possible and efficacious access, through official and ministerial channels, to the respective governments, now on

my own behalf, and now through the support of powerful friends. How unpleasant and annoying such things
would be to me at my age I allow you to consider, who
know my character as a man unwilling to do harm or
hurt to anyone, even my slanderer; as a just complaint
on my part would not fail to do: for you know better
than I that in England constitutional liberty exists without doubt, but does not authorize calumny and falsehood, nor does it permit anyone whatsoever to attribute
to authors criminal and defaming intentions which they
never had . . .

Here is the reply I wrote to this letter:

Most revered Signor Abbé:
    The long and bitter war waged against me in Vienna I
have almost forgotten since I have been in London,
much as a man, who, his health recovered, forgets the
pains of an illness already cured. But the favors you did
me, not only have I not forgotten, but I remember well,
as I should, and am most grateful for them. It was only
on that account that I undertook to republish your *Animali parlanti*, a superb poem with which I hoped to
propagate ever more widely the literary glory and poetic
fame of the Abbé Casti and therewith to convince all
those who know little of Italy that the genius for beautiful poetry has not died and will never die in our country:
and that, until God *O la Natura, se non tocca a Lui*,
shall create another heaven and another sun for that first
"gem of the universe" (such it is my liking to call Italy)
the most marvelous poets will flower there. How then
could you now suppose, most venerated sir, that through
some hope of revenge or unthinking caprice, I could
disturb or try to disturb, the peace of your aged days, or

expose them to mortifications serious and perhaps fatal? No, no! Do not, my dear sir, believe me in any way capable of such baseness! I have respected, and respect, your rare talents too much: I have boasted and boast of having merited (at times) your esteem and your favor; and if I complained with my pen when I was hurt, that is the fate of human frailty: but hatred never, and much less revenge!

Live tranquil therefore in my regard; and may you be pleased to believe that Count Maniaco either ill understood my words or ill interpreted my intentions. I would send you a copy of the little edition I made of your *Animali parlanti*: but it did not turn out so beautiful nor so correct as I could have desired. If, however, it chance to fall into your hands and you read it, you will see indeed that I have made some changes in it, but few and of so little importance that I did not think it worth the trouble to annoy you with them. Why make them? you will say. Because among the many teachers of the Italian language we have in London, not one would have dared to read the poem without those changes, with the young men and the young women to whom they teach Italian: and it is for those young men and those young ladies that I undertook to make this edition, knowing well that for other lovers of poetry there were the genuine editions of Paris and Italy. To make these slight alterations I was not a little encouraged by an expurgated edition of the *Orlando Furioso*, which was printed some time ago on my presses by Signor Nardini, an edition which had a very large sale, and which caused that divine poem to be read by an infinitude of people who had not ventured to read it before: and if ever I should print the "Divine Comedy" of Dante, or Tasso's "Jerusalem" for the same purposes, I think that I would dare, with all the respect

due to those great men, to change three or four verses of
the one, and ten or twelve of the other: because neither
Dante, nor Torquato would become any less famous on
that account, nor would my verses, poor as they might
be, dim the light of so many others: but the teachers
of language and their pupils would not be embarrassed
and confused at the sound of a rather dirty trumpet of
Dante's demons, or at too vivid pictures of the beauties
of Armida. As for reprinting your most delightful and incomparable tales, I do not believe, to tell you the truth,
that that would be a good thing for me to undertake. I
thank you, nevertheless, for the offer you make me and
for your kindly thought.

And the famous "peddler of horns," what is he doing
at Vienna?[48] Have you news of him? Will you do me the
pleasure to tell me of him the first time you write? I am
most eager to hear from you whether it be true that that
"most horned beast" was the chief cause of your being
obliged to leave Vienna. I have the honor to be Your devoted servant and friend,

L. Da Ponte.

---

48. When I left Vienna, Leopold took Bertati as poet to his opera. A year later came
Casti: and that wretched dramatic cobbler was dismissed. But Casti was not fond
of hard work. He asked for an assistant and obtained one in person of Signor
Gamerra, a poet famous for his *Corneide*, a poem in seven or eight fat tomes
wherein he mentioned all the horns that had appeared in Heaven or on Earth from
the birth of Vulcan down to those of his own grandfather. This ungrateful *cornifex*
had not been a year in Vienna before he began butting with his benefactor, accusing him of Jacobinism; and poor Casti suddenly received a visit such as I had had
at Moedling. All his papers were seized and he was enjoined to depart from Vienna
at once. Casti lost much in losing Vienna; but the literary world gained his beautiful poem on *Gli animali parlanti*. Now that he is no more, it is permissible to say
that. —L. Da P.

I did not have—as I could not have had—the pleasure of receiving his reply to this letter. A few days later, a friend wrote to me from Paris that that extraordinary man had died of an indigestion, in the house, I believe, of Joseph Bonaparte, who was favoring and admirably providing for that rare poetic genius. He had passed eighty when he finished writing the poem in question. It made much uproar when it saw the light. Under veil of fiction, it contains very vivid pictures of leading personalities of Europe, and a critical history, so to speak, of the most important events of the Revolution. On the death of those characters and with the end of the Revolution, interest in the poem seemed to wane. It is not now read so universally as formerly: but anyone who knows real poetry, reads it and will always read it with amazement, and will find therein sketches full of a spirit, a vivacity, a robustness, a grace, most worthy of a Monti, of a Foscolo or of any other poet that Italy has ever produced.[49]

These things happened toward the end of the year 1803. At the time my bookstore had reached the apex of its prosperity. I could then count on my shelves some fifteen thousand volumes in choice works, both ancient and modern, among which a considerable number of rare books, classics in first editions, Aldines and Elzevirians. London had not seen, and I dare say, will never again see such a collection in the shop of a single bookseller.

But scarcely had my past wounds closed, scarcely was I beginning to take breath and again nourish hopes of a sweet and tranquil life, than so many misfortunes gathered above my head that after a long battle " 'twixt Fortune and my endurance," I was constrained to yield and depart from England. It will be seen, I hope, by all, that not through frivolousness

---

49. To see the fire an Italian poet of eighty or more can be capable of, one should read the Seventeenth Canto of that poem. —L. Da P.

of mind, not through evil principles or practices, not finally through lack of courage or persistence, did I lose London; but rather through a series of combinations and circumstances which neither human strength could resist, nor human counsel stave off. It was, nevertheless, the inscrutable Will of Him who "e'en from evil draweth good" that through those very combinations and circumstances, I should find myself almost forced to come to America, a most blessed part of the earth, whither I shall try to lead my reader along the paths that Providence pointed out to me.

The first blow struck at me by that so bitterly resisted Hand was a rain of new notes of Taylor, all endorsed by me, notes which his fierce creditors either sold or entrusted to the vilest, shrewdest, and most cruel barristers in London. It is difficult to picture or give even a faint idea of this to Americans, whose most holy laws entirely prohibit recourse to practices invented by human perfidy to the destruction of the poor.[50] Among the many infernal inventions of that ilk, I will mention one which, to my belief, is not known in America, and of which chiefly, in my latter days in London, it was my lot to fall victim. When a note comes due and is not paid by the buyer of it, all those who have endorsed it, are, after a brief notice served on them, subject by law to imprisonment; and the costs, which are not light, and which go in greatest part into the pocket of the prosecuting attorney, fall in the end on the buyer or on the one who is best able to pay. On notes of Taylor or others I found three, four, and even eight or ten names of

---

50. They were not so different in Da P.'s time, though American practice was limiting extreme imprisonment for debt to three months. Some of the old rigors still survive in actions against non-residents, and for bastardies and contempts. Certainly the revolution that has taken place in knowledge, conceptions, and practices of credit since 1830 must be accounted one of the greatest achievements of "the stupid Nineteenth Century."

endorsers, which were not worth a penny, but which had been procured by the lawyer, through that device, for the sole purpose of tripling and quadrupling the expenses of collection (a practice permitted by the Government since it also has its share). On a note of thirty pounds left unpaid for two days only by the parties, my dear brother Paolo was obliged to pay more than thirty in costs! And he went to the courts with the matter, believing he was being abused. The expenses then rose to more than a hundred, and the year of worry cost that excellent youth his life. The infamous lawyer who robbed me of a virtuous and adorable brother in the first flower of youth is living at present in a city in the State of Pennsylvania!

I was accordingly tormented anew by Taylor's creditors and he, to tell the truth, would have been glad to help me, though quite unable to do so. I therefore had recourse to my first project, being ashamed to give the least sign thereof to my protector and benefactor, Mathias. I placed more than two thousand volumes of chosen works in the hands of the Stuart earlier mentioned, who advanced me the money I needed in order to pay, not the debts, but the expenses of barristers, constables, and usurers; and a few days later he sold them at auction for less than half of what they cost me, and for less than a quarter part of what they were worth.[51] The money he derived from that sale was not enough to repay all that he had advanced to me. He then took another thousand volumes which had the same fate as the first, and thus plucked the flower of my stock to no other purpose than that of retarding my utter ruin for a time.

While I was still staggering under the dreadful shock of this blow, another followed which I would consider it a crime not to mention here. Signor Nardini, my partner and friend and

---

51. The catalog of the sale, which took place April 16–24, 1804, is still to be found at the British Museum. Sheppard, 299.

godfather to my children, had joined a certain Cuthbert in a number of transactions from which they hoped both to reap enormous profits. To that end they had an agent in Rome, in whose honesty and intelligence they had implicit faith. I know not what reasons they had for beginning to question the faithfulness of that agent. I know that suddenly they changed their tone, and Cuthbert, shrewder than Nardini, after much confusion, quarreling, and threatening, suggested selling his share to Nardini; and Nardini, as I believe, innocently and with the best intentions, suggested that I buy it. I may have allowed myself to be persuaded with too much ease. At any rate in a very short time I found myself in such embarrassments that I could extricate myself only with immense losses; and these, after my departure from London, were followed by losses on the part of my brother to whom that sly merchant with his fine words easily showed fireflies for lanterns. So many and so great were the losses of that dear and honest youth that after it all he died, only two years following my departure from London! Despite these multiple disasters my credit was still good. My notes circulated and found easy discount in the banks of London. Since my difficulties came from creditors of Taylor, I was blamed and pitied at the same time. The number of my books, however, was enormously diminished. I therefore resolved to rent other quarters which would cost me less, and see whether little by little it were not possible to set my business in order again. But scarcely was I beginning to take breath when the accursed bloodsuckers of the Forum, with their subalterns and deputies, were upon me throwing me back into my despair.

It was in those circumstances that my wife, having received an invitation from her mother, who was already living in America, obtained my consent to go there; and for the sole desire of making her happy, I permitted her to take with her her four children, one of whom was then not more than a year old. It is true that a natural yearning for peace, and the good things I had heard said of that country, had given me the thought of possibly rejoining her there one day. But that was only a passing flash, and the condition I was in, my post in London, my books, my connections, afterwards made our union in America seem an impossible thing; and when I spoke of it as something remote to my faithful counselor and friend, Thomas Mathias, he answered:

"What would you do in America, Lorenzo?"

You will see, in proper time, O generous soul, what I did in America, and what the sixteen lustra I have on my shoulders still do not prevent me from doing!

The day of my wife's departure was fixed, and on the twentieth of September, precisely, in the year 1804,[52] she set out with her four children from London. I accompanied her as far as Gravesend, where she embarked on a vessel which was to leave for Philadelphia with the excellent captain Collet.

From London to Gravesend our journey was nothing but tears: but at the moment when I left that vessel to which I had attended her, at the moment when I gave her a last embrace, a last farewell, and a glance at her and another at those four children, I seemed to feel a hand of ice plucking at my heart to tear it from my breast; and my repentance and my sorrow were

---

52. Da P. confuses the date of departure with the date of arrival in Philadelphia. Capt. John Collet, of John Collet & Sons, 152 Walnut St., Philadelphia (importers of hardware, tools, pipes, fertilizers), sailed in the good ship *Pigou* (362 tons burden) which reached Philadelphia on September 20, 1804, fifty days out from London (U.S. Gazette, *ip. die*). Ann Da P. with little Louisa, Fanny, Joseph, and baby Lorenzo, must have sailed, therefore, on Aug. 1, or 2. From the log of the *Pigou*: "Aug. 4, spoke brig *Bremen*, of Baltimore, in need of bread; Aug. 31, spoke schr. *Hope*, Capt. Salisbury, 78 days from Petersburg; Sept. 9, lat. 41.20, spoke brig, Capt. James, of Portsmouth, 4 days out for Surinam; Sept. 12, spoke brig, *Young Edward*, New York for Bordeaux; and *Venus*, Capt. Haynes, from Virginia Capes. The *Jupiter*, Capt. Law, passed Gravesend, July 24th."

such that for more than half an hour I was in doubt whether I should take my family back to London or go to America myself and leave the rest to Providence.

My mind was in that state when, among the things I should be leaving, I remembered Taylor and the singer Rovedini. The latter had had recourse to me in pecuniary matters some time before, and I had consented to assist him, discounting a certain number of his notes, with promise to renew them two or three times when they should fall due, to give him adequate leisure to pay them. I therefore said to myself:

"What will Taylor do without me? What will Rovedini do?"

That reflection was enough to drag me apart from five beings who were taking with them almost all my heart, and carry me back to London. I would have said "all my heart"; but my Paolo was with me there, mingling his tears with mine, first trying to console me, then breaking into tears himself, till, in the end, his need of consolation was as great as mine. The vessel departed! How describe the effect of its first motion upon an adoring father and husband, who had himself pronounced his own severest sentence, in permitting their departure on so long a voyage!

I returned to London, as may be believed, disconsolate and despondent. I had given my wife permission to remain a year in America; but no sooner did I find myself without her and without my dear children, than the house where I was living, the city in which I dwelt, in truth everything about me, became so odious and unendurable that I was at numberless times on the point of letting everything go and flying to America.

My brother and Mr. Mathias, whom I loved as much as myself, and whose affection for me and mine was deserving of everything, were the two objects that alone prevented me from carrying out that resolve and held me impaled for another six months in a kind of inferno. I cannot hope to give more than a slight idea of what I was forced to suffer in those few months;

but the little I shall say, will, I am certain, be enough for anyone who has a heart. My losses, my persecutions, my calamities were so many and at the same time so great that I do not know, in truth, with which one to begin my story.

The day my family left was a holiday. I returned to London toward two in the afternoon and the remainder of that day was left me entirely free for my tears and my sorrow.

Not so the following day. A little after sunrise, and even before I have risen from bed, I hear a knock at the door of my house. I run to the window and discover a man whom I seem to know. I dress in haste and go down to open. I find there the apprentice of a lawyer (a *batchellor* he was called) who serves me with notice on three notes endorsed by me and not honored the previous Saturday by the buyers.

One of these was from Rovedini, the man on whose account I had remained in London the day before. The other two were Taylor's. The sum amounted in all to four hundred pounds.

I ran to Rovedini's for a new note, but he had gone into hiding two days before in fear of imprisonment and no one knew, or chose to tell me, where he was.

As for Taylor, I had little hope left of compromises. I went therefore to that lawyer, who among the harder and crueler was the hardest and cruelest. By dint of promises and prayers I obtained a delay of four days (agreeing, among other things, that he should lay all possible costs on buyers). By auctioning off another thousand volumes, I raised enough to pay those sums, with fifteen pounds in costs in four days!

Scarcely had I saved myself from that lightning bolt, than another no less devastating fell upon my head. I had sold to a certain Gameau and partner, French booksellers in that city, a large assortment of books to be taken to America as an experiment, for which Gameau had given me a two months' note. It was to come due within a few days; but before then

Mr. Gameau took flight to America (he assumed the name of Devillaret in New York). I had already discounted the note, and was therefore obliged to sacrifice other books to get it back. A few weeks later, the bookseller Dulau followed the example of his countryman; and though some months later he paid me almost in full, his failure cost me no end of expenses and trouble for which I neither was, nor did I ask to be, compensated by him.

After all this, can anyone believe there were further pills to be swallowed? Indeed there were, many such, and not very pleasant to the taste! The infamous Federici found means to force them down my throat from as far away as Italy.[53] He wrote divers letters to Taylor and all his friends, and feigning to be in extremest poverty, persuaded them to order me to pay him five guineas a month, to be deducted from my salary, in compensation for librettos of which he could no longer fleece me. I thereupon wrote such a letter to Taylor that I know not whether through fear or through a sense of justice, he decided to see me. He named the hour and the place, and I went to him.

Comrie, that same lawyer of whom I spoke some time back, was in his company.[54] After excusing himself as best he could for the wrong so violently done me in favor of Federici, he asked me if I had my accounts with me. It seemed to me rather strange that he should have called the lawyer to examine them. After all, however, I was very glad of it because the lawyer found everything most exact. Taylor made some remarks on divers demands I put forward, and on my claims as

---

53. He was conducting an opera at La Scala, in Milan. Nic., 309.

54. This Mr. Comrie had every appearance of being an honest man. I trusted in him blindly and was, as usual, barbarously tricked by him. For twenty-four years I have not succeeded in hearing any news of him. I would like to know whether he be alive or dead, and ask the favor of as much from some honest soul. —L. Da P.

to compensation for damage. I canceled all such claims at once; but in the end it was found that he owed me six hundred pounds sterling, even calculating things in his fashion. Then he said:

"Six hundred I owe and five hundred I give to Mr. Da Ponte, as a slight compensation for the damages he has suffered and for the services he has rendered me; and in payment of the latter sum I assign him Box No ——— which is in the hands of Mr. Comrie and which he will be good enough to sell in order to pay Mr. Da Ponte."

Though the box was not worth the third part of the losses I had indirectly sustained for him, it would nevertheless have been sufficient to give me some relief and in time, perhaps, enabled me to recover the ground I had lost. But what did such a fine gesture amount to in the end? Between another great bundle of notes of Taylor, Corri, and Rovedini, which daily fell due and came to me alone for payment; and divers little delinquencies of booksellers and others, which taken together made up a huge amount, I soon found myself in such embarrassments that, no longer seeing any issue from them, I resolved to call all my creditors, expound my situation to them and place the whole matter in the hands of two reputable gentlemen, who, when accounts had been balanced, would have enough to pay everybody down to the last penny.

A day was fixed for the meeting. Meantime I was concerned to see Taylor, in order to have his opinion. After listening to my project, he found it ridiculous. Said he:

"In all these years, since you have been in London, you have not learned to know the sort of men you have dealt with more than with any others?"

In truth, all my creditors, or, more exactly, all of Taylor's, Corri's, and Rovedini's creditors, were either lawyers or usurers!

"Of course," he went on to say, "you might try it; then if it

331

does not succeed (as it will not succeed), you can get away to America, stay there until my affairs are settled—(as you know, when the boxes sold on term return to me, my affairs will be settled), and then come back to London without fear. I promise, meantime, to send you your full salary as poet, so long as you remain there, and you can send me a few books for my Opera."

These words delighted me. Nevertheless, I resolved to find out whether it were possible to make those hard heads listen to reason.

About six in the evening on the first day of March[55] in the year 1805, they all met together. My lawyer presented a statement of my accounts and offered to collect what was owing to me and to pay what I owed to others. They listened patiently; drank twelve bottles of wine (for which, to do me a favor, they allowed me to pay) and after many "We'll see's! We'll figure it up's! We'll talk it over's!" and like meaningless chatter, they bade me good night, about nine o'clock, and departed.

I had begun to suspect that what Taylor had told me was true. I went home and to bed, and after a few hours fell asleep. My slumber could not have been sounder, when a knock at the door awakened me. I hurried to see who was there and heard a familiar voice calling:

"Let me in, Mr. Da Ponte."

I knew it was a constable of the court; but since he was the only one among so many whom I believed to be honest, sincere, and capable of charity and friendship, I went at once to open to him. It was then that he told me, with tears in his eyes, that by ten o'clock on the following morning he would have eleven writs against me; that my creditors (twelve in all) had promised him a fine gratuity if he had me in his house of detention before noon; but that the cruelty of those treacher-

---

55. Read "April." See first note in Part Four. —A. L.

ous wretches had so moved his heart, that he had come to warn me and advise me to leave London.

I thanked him as he deserved, and offered him several guineas, which he refused disdainfully, even insisting that I accept a few of him! I need not describe the confused emotions that assailed me at that moment. He embraced me, and went away. It was not yet midnight. I dressed hurriedly and ran to see Gould, who was then managing the Opera. I informed him of what had taken place, and of Taylor's suggestion, and asked him for a hundred guineas in advance on my salary. He gave them to me without hesitation. I returned home, lay down for a few hours, and, toward dawn, dressed, and went at once to the City to look for passage. I did not have to hunt very long. In the very shop I entered to inquire whether any vessels were leaving for America, I found Captain Hyden who had stuck up a notice advising of his departure for Philadelphia, to take place on the fifth day of that same month.[56]

There was no time to lose. I went to the Aliens' Office, interviewed the director of that bureau himself, and told him all my troubles. With a grace and a courtesy worthy of such a man, he ordered that I be given a passport forthwith and that no one in that office should dare speak of my departure. Then I hired a carriage and drove to Gravesend with my brother.

When I told him that I was leaving for America, his sorrow was so great that I thought he would die. But by dint of entreaty and reasoning, he seemed to grow a little calm, above all when I gave him solemn promise to return to London within six months, or else find a way to have him come to America. But neither the one thing nor the other was to be. He died in London two years after my departure; and I am still in America.

---

56. Read April 5, 1805. See next note. —A. L.

PART FOUR

MY PASSAGE FROM London to Philadelphia was long, disastrous, and full of annoyances and strain. It lasted not less than eighty-six days,[1] over the entire course of which I was without all those comforts, which my age, my state of mind, and a tremendous voyage at sea, might seem to have required,

1. One has to visualize Da P. declaiming in Italian to his pupils on the terrors of the Atlantic. He told this story a thousand times, and the horrors grew more horrible and the voyage longer as the years went by. Starting let us say at 60 days in 1805, it had reached 70 by 1807, (*Comp.*, sailing from London, March 26), and 86 in 1823, when it was still bidding higher; for, between March 5 and June 4, the days are 90 or 92. The facts: Abishai Hayden (1758–1826), shipmaster of Nantucket, commanded the good ship *Columbia*, 205 tons, alternating voyages with his younger brother, Prince Hayden. The *Columbia*, Capt. Elder (*sic*) (*U.S. Gazette, Advertiser*, etc.), reached Philadelphia on June 4, 1805, 57 days out from London. Da P., therefore, sailed from Gravesend on April 7 (perhaps boarding the vessel two days earlier to hide). The curious error of the newspapers in naming the captain is easily explained: *Columbia*, (Hayden) Elder, London, 57—"Elder" being mistaken for a proper name. Prince Hayden was "Hayden Younger." Da P.'s

to make it endurable, if not a pleasure. I had heard tell that to
get to America, it was sufficient for me to pay a certain sum
to the captain of the vessel on which I embarked; and that he
would then provide me with the necessaries. That may have
been well enough for people who met honest captains, courteous and well bred and concerned to do everything possible to
make the voyage pleasant for the passengers. I fell into the
clutches of a rascal from Nantucket, whose accustomed business was whale-fishing and who treated his passengers like the
vilest sailors, whom, in turn, he treated exactly like those
monsters of the sea. He had with him only the coarsest provisions and of these he was a very sparing dispenser. My first
mistake was to pay him forty-four guineas before setting foot
on his ship, without contracts or papers, and without making
adequate investigation; asking nothing else of him than to be

---

voyage was long, yes, but not exceptionally so among trips that ranged as high as
70, 90, or 110 days. Its hardships, also, Da P. probably exaggerates. The *Columbia*
was not a whaler, but a packet regularly plying between Europe and American
ports, at times accommodating up to fifty passengers. That the voyage was "annoying" and "disastrous" there cannot be the slightest doubt. For a few days out,
the *nantuchino* began forgetting to cork and lock up his bottle (*Comp.*, 17), with
the result that Da P. lost some of that skill which had saved his life in Padua in
1777. He lost to Richard Edwards (Odoardo), a merchant on High Street, Philadelphia, steadily, day after day, and at the rate of six dollars a day; so that the
Columbia reached the Delaware and the bottom of his pocket, at the same moment. Wherefore was Mr. Richard Edwards obliged to pay $32.31 in duties for
"Mr. Da Ponte" on "one fiddle valued at $189.50," "one tea urn valued at $18.90,"
and a carpet valued at $50"; while "one trunk of books" and "one box of fiddle
strings and suspenders" were admitted free. Odoardo, of course, held the property
as guaranty for the loan, probably lending Da P. $4.00 more to take the stage,
which left "Mr. Anderson's at the Sign of the Sorrel Horse, 39 N. 2d St., at 1 P.M."
and "arrived in New York in 21 hours." There Mrs. Da Ponte, after the embraces,
dispatched the money to Edwards (*Comp.*, 15), recovered the property imported,
and saw her husband safely launched on the road to American citizenship, which
he was to attain in 1811 (Ward). —A. L.

taken to Philadelphia and fed. At the dinner hour, I began to foresee what my fate was to be. The meal was made ready on the deck aft. A rickety old table of worm-eaten pineboards, a tablecloth blacker than a charcoal-burner's shirt; three plates of nicked china, and three rusty iron knives and forks were the sweet preludes to the approaching feast. Messire the Nantucketer took a seat, invited me to sit down opposite him, and in a few minutes the African cook arrived with a great wooden bowl in one hand and a pewter platter in the other, which he silently deposited on the table, and, lowering his head, departed.

"Odoardo," cried my aquatic host in a loud voice, "Odoardo! Come to dinner!"

At the second call, "Mr. Odoardo" appeared, emerging from the vessel's cabin where he had been sleeping for some hours. He nodded his head a little and, without speaking to me or looking at me, sat down to the captain's right. His strange appearance did not leave me time to look at what that bowl contained. "Odoardo" was the image of a sleeping Bacchus, save that he was dressed like a miller in working garb, his *quondam* white linen according perfectly with the charcoal-burner's shirt and with the tablecloth of our Typhoïs. The latter, meantime, had set in front of me a little pewter plate with several spoonfuls of a broth he had scooped from the sailoresque bowl; a broth which I had at first sight taken for the water from boiled chestnuts. Observing that I sat gazing at it without eating, he said:

"What, Mr. Italiano, aren't you going to have some chicken soup?"

I was very hungry, and I am especially fond of chicken. I turned my eyes upon that dear bird! Let any hungry soul imagine my state of mind, when, staring at the object before me, I thought I saw not so much a boiled fowl as a crow that had lost its feathers in an argument with a cat. I allowed my two companions to riot at will among such appetizing tidbits. I swooped

339

down upon a huge piece of English cheese, which, to my good luck, lay at my right, and made a meal of it. Mr. Abissai Haydn, as the captain was named, looked at me a little sourly, gaped, and said nothing; but, noticing that a bottle of wine was also within my reach and fearing that I might treat it as I had treated the cheese, *la bocca sollevò dal fiero pasto,* got up from the place where he was sitting, gathered that bottle between his fins, drew out the cork, gave a little glass of it to me, and another to our friend the flour-grinder, recorked the bottle, put it under lock and key, and strode away whistling.

That, more or less, was the manner in which this harpooner of whales treated me during all that double Lent of mine; save that, instead of broth of chestnut water, or crow-chicken, every day there appeared either a bit of dried meat or a slice of salt pork, the mere sight of which would have been enough to banish the hunger of Count Ugolino. To cap the climax of my woe, I had not brought a bed with me. I was obliged, therefore, to make a kind of litter of the shirts and clothes I had with me in order not to ease my aged limbs on the hard wood of a very narrow niche on which one would have rested badly even with mattresses and pillows.

Despite all these hardships I arrived safe and sound in Philadelphia on the morning of the fourth of June. I hurried to the house of Captain Collet, who had brought my family to America. There I learned that they had settled in New York. I left about two o'clock in the afternoon, and reached that city on the following morning toward sunrise. I knew the name of the street, but not the number of the house, where my people were living. I went a short distance down the street and knocked at a door to ask for information. By a strange and delightful coincidence, it happened to be the very house in which they were staying. There is no need of telling how I was received. They had already begun to fear a shipwreck in view of the extraordinary length of my passage, and especially on account of the dangers of the Atlantic Ocean quite usual at a season when navigation is prodigiously impeded by floating masses of ice. In fact, not many days before my arrival, the *Jove* had gone down, with the loss of many lives.[2]

After some days of quiet amid the tender rejoicings of my family, I turned, without losing time, to business. Very little had I brought with me from London: a box of violin strings, a number of Italian classics of scant worth, several copies of a very fine Virgil, several of Davila's History, and from forty to fifty dollars in cash. Such the treasures which I had been able to rescue from the talons of usurers, constables, lawyers, enemies, and treacherous friends in London, where for eleven years I had followed the occupation of bookseller, printer, manager's agent, and opera poet! My wife, however, had brought with her from six to seven thousand dollars, not saved by me, however.

Fear of diminishing or consuming so tenuous a capital by sitting too long with folded hands, induced me to embrace the counsel of a man who, I supposed, was perfectly familiar with the line of business he was urging me to undertake.[3] I turned grocer accordingly; and let him who has a grain of sense imagine how I must have laughed at myself every time my poet's

---

2. On April 6, 1805, the *Jupiter*, Capt. Law, London to New York, struck an iceberg in lat. 44.20, long. 49, and sank after some hours. This episode—the *Titanic* disaster of its day—engaged public interest all through June. On the day of Da P.'s arrival came the stirring news of the rescue of the *Jupiter's* longboat by Capt. William Powers of Marblehead: "It blowing fresh and a heavy sea, skipper Wm. Powers, finding it impossible for the boat to board his schooner, flung himself with a rope over the lee quarter; and in that situation, seizing hold of each person separately, took them all on board, etc." How Da P.'s family could have worried over his fate is not so clear, unless they had had word of his intentions long in advance of his departure, and feared he might be on the *Jupiter*.

3. It was my wife's father who gave me the advice in question, thus becoming the innocent cause of my first misfortune in America. —L. Da P.

hand was called upon to weigh out two ounces of tea, or measure half a yard of "pigtail,"[4] now to a cobbler, now to a teamster, or pour out, in exchange for three cents, a morning dram, which was not, however, the *dramma* of the *Cosa rara* nor that of the *Nozze di Figarò*![5] So goes the world! Yet in spite of that, if the occupation I had assumed was not very dignified, my purse was not the loser by it.

My troubles began early in September. Yellow fever broke out at that time[6] and obliged me to depart from that city with my family. I withdrew to Elizabeth Town where I bought a little house and garden, and continued in trade. Unfortunately I took a licentious wastrel into business with me: and the consequence may be easily guessed. What with his exorbitant expenditure, and the calamity of having to deal with the foremost rascals in Jersey, in a short time everything had gone up in smoke. I then dissolved the partnership. It was found that he was in my debt to the amount of a thousand dollars, for which he gave me three notes payable in one, two, and three years. But on the maturity of the first, he fled to Jamaica.[7] I was about ready to abandon commerce when a little dinner of rather original device brought me to that decision very suddenly. It is an instructive little story, and quite novel. I will tell it briefly, without comment.

I owed a balance of one hundred and twenty dollars to an Irish grocer in New York. Chancing to be in that city, I called on him, and asked him to go over our accounts. There were

4. "Pigtail" was a kind of plug tobacco. —L. Da P.

5. "Dram," Italian *una dramma*, a sip of liquor. The difference from *un dramma* (an opera) is in the gender, not in the price. Some people will see my joke! —L. Da P.

6. A consideration rather than the cause. The plague had reached epidemic proportions, to the point of disorganizing public administration, in 1807, when Da P. returned. The move to Elizabeth was probably made to take advantage of Micheli's offer of partnership.

7. I must give the scoundrel's name: H. Micheli. —L. Da P.

some mistakes, and it would take some time to rectify them. Everything, however, was tranquilly attended to. After a time, his wife called him to dinner, and he insisted, almost using force, that I should dine with him. We talked little of business as we ate. I told him, merely, that I had left a variety of country produce in the hands of a merchant in New York and that I would instruct the merchant in question to sell them to him, paying him what I owed.

To that the Irishman made no reply, but called to his clerk to bring a bottle of wine and whispered a few words in the man's ear, beckoning to him, then, to withdraw. I drank a small glass of the wine with him, and we went back to our accounts. There was still a difference of thirty dollars in our calculations. I, in fact, did not owe him more than one hundred and twenty dollars. He was asking for a hundred and fifty. Night coming on, I told him that my presence was necessary in Elizabeth Town and that I had to be going, but would return to New York in a day or two and settle my bill with him. He made no reply to that either, but going, coming, talking of this and that, he seemed to be seeking pretexts to detain me. To succeed the better he went and got the bottle, drank "to my good health," insisted that I drink to his, and in some minutes the clerk was back, panting and dripping with sweat. The Irishman then told me that I could go or stay, just as I found convenient. He held out his hand. I shook it, and departed.

I had not gone forty paces when I felt a heavy hand clap down on my shoulder and a stentorian voice cry:

"You are my prisoner!"

I turned and could see that the constable who was arresting me was the clerk of my generous host of the sour dinner!

I asked him who he was and what he wanted of me.

"I am a deputy sheriff," he replied, "I ask you for the one hundred and fifty dollars you owe Mr. John Mackinley, or else bail from two owners of real property for your appearance at

343

the proper time. If you cannot do either the one thing or the other, you will be pleased to accompany me to prison!"

I said I would make no comment on this story. I shall do as I said, leaving the comment to my readers. I deposited several objects of value in the hands of Messrs. Bradhurst & Field, respectable grocers in New York. They went bail for me. A few days later I paid that man one hundred and twenty dollars which was all that I owed him. I did not see him or hear of him for more than four years. One day, however, I picked up a newspaper and read the following paragraph:

"John Mackinley was killed in Savannah yesterday morning, by a stroke of lightning!"

I will make no comment on that either!

On returning to Elizabeth Town, that dinner and that Irish bottle gave me such a terrible indigestion that I could not bear the mention of business. I sold as best I could such merchandise as was left me and set out to pay my debts. The income from the sale of my stock was not sufficient to pay all of them, so I sold my house and garden which I had hoped was to be the peaceful shelter of my declining years. I then disposed of several objects which had served to ornament the house or persons in the family,[8] and, between the first of December to the first of January, I had the satisfaction of paying three thousand four hundred dollars to my creditors. Thus, in the sixtieth year of my life, I did not hesitate a single moment to despoil myself of everything, in order to pay not my own debts, but those of an imprudent man whom I, more imprudent than he, had

---

8. Da P.'s family at Elizabeth in 1805 comprised: Mrs. Da Ponte, Louisa, Fanny, Joseph, Lorenzo; in 1806, Charles and Louisa Niccolini came on from England; and on Dec. 24, 1806, the stork brought a Christmas present in the person of Charles Grahl Da Ponte, so baptized (with names misspelled) on that same day by the Rev. John C. Rudd of St. John's (Anglican). For "60th" year, just below, read, of course, "58th"; for Da P. left Elizabeth early in 1807.

declared my partner in business, though he had cheated me in London a long time before. Those were mistakes for which I neither ask nor deserve pity!

Without help, money, friends, what could I do, what plans should I make in order to support a family that depended entirely on my labors? I returned to New York and I began to examine whether I could somehow make a living along the lines of Italian or Latin letters. In a few days I learned that as far as the Italian language and literature were concerned, they were about as well known in this city as Turkish or Chinese. As for Latin I found that it was cultivated generally and that "gentlemen in America thought they knew enough not to need the instruction of an Italian Latinist." Those were the very words that an American gentleman used in speaking to me a few days after my return from Jersey to New York. Of them I shall speak more at length at the opportune moment. Will my reader just bear them in mind!

I was almost hopeless of success, when the good genius of Italian literature willed that, as I was passing in front of the shop of the late M. Riley, bookseller on Broadway, it occurred to me to enter. I approached his counter and asked him if he had any Italian books in his store.

"I have a few," he replied, "but no one ever asks for them."

While we stood chatting, an American gentleman approached and joined our conversation. I was soon aware from his remarks that he was admirably read in a variety of literature. Coming by chance to allude to the language and literature of my country, I took occasion to ask him why they should be so little studied in a country as enlightened as I believed America to be.

"Oh sir," he replied, "modern Italy is not, unfortunately, the Italy of ancient times. She is not that sovereign queen which gave to the ages and to the world emulators, nay rivals, of the supreme Greeks."

He was then pleased to inform me that "five or at the most

six" were the writers of fame, of whom the country of those great men could boast over the past six centuries. I asked him, not without a sarcastic smile, to name those authors; and he: "Dante, Petrarch, Boccaccio, Ariosto, Tasso, . . ." And he stopped: "To tell the truth, I cannot recall the sixth."

He had been counting the names off on his fingers; he halted, accordingly, with his little finger held tightly between the forefinger and the thumb of his right hand, like a person thinking. I laid hold on those fingers and said, gaily:

"You will not let go of that finger for a whole month, if you allow me to hold your hand like this till I shall have finished naming one by one the great men of the last six centuries in Italy!"

"We do not know them," he said.

"So I observe!" I replied." "But do you suppose a teacher of Italian would find any favor and encouragement . . . ?"

The bookseller, who had been listening to our conversation, broke in vivaciously:

"There's not the slightest doubt of that!"

"If that be the case," said I quickly, "I shall be the fortunate Italian to make known to gentlemen in America the merits of his language, and the number and deserts of his greatest men of letters!"

Within three days, twelve of the most cultivated youths and maidens in New York were taking Italian lessons of me. The fifteenth day of December in the year 1807, I began my career as a teacher in New York, under the happiest auspices, in the house of the venerable Bishop Moore[9] ever of sweet, dear,

9. Benjamin Moore (1748–1816), who as rector of Trinity, and Bishop, was to perform little Louisa's marriage ceremony in 1809. Bishop Moore became president of Columbia. His son, Clement Clarke Moore (1779–1863), Da P.'s American Mathias, founder of the General Theological Seminary and later Trustee of Columbia. Clement Moore's residence was on the present site of the Seminary.

and honored memory to me. It was there that I laid the corner-stone of my fortunate edifice. The first to adorn it luminously were those incomparable young men, his son and his nephew; then Mr. John M. Vicker and Mr. E. Pendleton, four gentlemen whose knowledge, good manners, and Christian and social virtues are most justly appreciated by the noble and populous city of New York. The example of persons so illustrious could not but produce the most excellent impression upon the re-mainder of the citizens. In less than a month I had twenty-four young people to teach. Since, at the moment of my present writing,[10] I could count more than five hundred, it does not seem to me à propos to mention the names of them all

> benchè scritti nel cor tutti li porto,
> a mia gloria, a mia gioia, a mio conforto.

The kindness with which my lessons were listened to, the regularity with which they were attended, and the extraordi-nary favor accorded both to me and to the language of my country, in a short time created such an enthusiasm among the more studious young people of the town that, for my sec-ond trimester, I could only with the greatest difficulty provide for the number of my pupils. It seemed, however, that Provi-dence were giving me a strength, a steadfastness, a courage that my advanced years could not supply. It was not long before I

There many of Da P.'s "academies" were later held. It was an abiding friendship. Moore included a Da P. translation among his published poems, and submitted his verse to Da P. for criticism. The nephew: Nathaniel F. Moore (1782–1872), an ac-complished classicist, professor of Greek at Columbia, and a great friend, later, of Lorenzo L. Da P. John M. MacVickar (1787–1868) became professor of Philosophy at Columbia. E. Pendleton, unidentified, probably Edmund II, of Virginia.

10. The moment when I first printed these *Memoirs*. Later on, between the years 1826 and 1830, the number of pupils who learned Italian from me doubled. —L. Da P.

had the supreme pleasure of hearing the very learned gentleman who had not been able to remember the sixth of our classics, solemnly sing his recantation, and see him transformed into one of the most fiery and zealous promoters and patrons of the Italian language and of Italian authors, who, at his example and advice, were read, studied, and admired by the liveliest and keenest talents of both sexes.

Pray allow me, Mr. Clement Moore, to adorn this part of my Memoirs with your dear and respected name! Pray allow my grateful heart, mindful of the honor, the graciousness, the kindness, received of you, and of your never interrupted favor, and mindful no less, of the advantages and the glory shed by that same favor upon the sublimest geniuses of Italy, upon Italy herself and upon me—pray allow me, I say, to seize this occasion to make a public testimonial of my proper gratitude, and solemnly protest that if the language of Italy, if her noblest authors, are known and loved in New York not only, but in the most cultured cities of america, if, finally, I am enabled to make the glorious boast of having, I alone, introduced them, I alone, spread their fame, their practice, their light in America, the principal merit belongs to you. I should not easily be able to decide whether, in this fortunate event, I, my country, or your own, owe you the more. We have each enjoyed in our peculiar way the continued effects of your first favor, so admirably seconded by your most learned fellow citizens, and especially by the various members of your most honored family, who ever encouraged my effort, and with word and deed, lent ardor and strength to my zeal and my fondest desire to see permanently established in America the first born daughter of Greek and Latin letters; for the cultivation and diffusion of which, no less than of all the arts and sciences, both you and your learned, erudite, and scholarly cousin, Nathaniel Moore, are ever exerting yourselves with such happy success.

Back now to our sweet language!

Perceiving, to my unbounded joy, such general enthusiasm in the young people of those days, I neglected no means nor allurement to add fuel to the fire, and foment it. There were not in New York at that time any booksellers who had Italian books on their shelves. I erred, in the first edition of these Memoirs, in saying I imported a chosen number of classical works from various countries in Europe. It is true that I mentioned such hopes and desires to a certain bookseller in Genoa; but I had no other reply than that he would forward me the books on receipt of their cost—the sum amounted to a little more than ninety dollars (such the first encouragement the egregious booksellers of Italy gave me). It was my dear brother, Paolo, by no means rich, and harassed by terrible worries, who sent me the first series of our classics. I distributed them among my pupils, incited them to read and ponder them, and in less than three years I had the pure delight of seeing the libraries and the desks of studious Americans ornamented with the flower of our literature which was making its first appearance in this country.

I then proposed and succeeded in establishing day and evening assemblies in which no other language than Italian was spoken, where the most beautiful passages of our orators and poets were read aloud or recited from memory and where we performed little comedies or operas composed by me for the most dignified and respected young ladies in the city. the effect of such exercises was truly marvelous. They added the delight of amusement to the flame of general enthusiasm for the study of this beautiful language, and served at the same time to facilitate the acquisition and the practice of it. We once gave on a little stage I set up in my own house, the *Mirra* of the great Alfieri. Our audience was made up of one hundred and fifty persons who had all been introduced by me to the study of the Italian language within a space of three years. The delight occasioned by that divine production, and the general approbation of it is not to be described. I was obliged to repeat it the following evening to greater applause and before a greater number of spectators.

Despite all the advantages, and all the pleasure such noble and innocent exercises provide, I have not been able for eight years past to revive them in the city of New York, where—I wot not through what star malign—my absence of six or seven years allowed them to fall into disuse and forgetfulness.

Many were the causes which, from that time on, super-vened to check the development of our language, not in New York only, but in all America. Not least among them, in my judgment, was a prejudice. I call it frankly that because the most rigorous ascetics recommend theatricals even to the stu-dents of ecclesiastical seminaries, monasteries, and nunneries; and Maria Theresa, a princess who surely did not sin against the sanctities of religion or the obligations of modesty, did not blush to hear her own daughters repeat on the stage the moral precepts set forth in the impeccable verses of Metastasio, or depict with feminine charm the vicissitudes and caprices of Fortune, and sometimes even the philosophy and the delights of a virtuous love. The thing in itself, therefore, must be inno-cent and praiseworthy. But not infrequently do we criticize in others what we cannot do ourselves, seeking thus to cloak our disability under a mantle of virtue. A brilliant young lady who had astonished the whole city at a performance of one of my operas, was criticized in private gathering by the very ladies who crowded to her recitals.

But the prodigious numbers of my pupils would have pro-vided me with sufficient means to support my family in de-cency and educate my children, had I not had, as always, the bad fortune to encounter certain of those poisonous leeches who are ever in pursuit of honest people to suck their blood and repay them then with disdain, criticism, and often slander. Obliged by my duty as an historian to depict two or three of these, I shall call them "my friends;" because under cloak of friendship they came to me; under cloak of friendship they betrayed me; under a cloak of friendship they concealed the knife which afterwards they hurled at my back.

One such rascal was the primary, if not the sole cause for my exchanging New York for the most fatal village of Sunbury. The fellow was presented to me by a young Frenchman whom I loved and esteemed highly. He was an excellent distiller; but his great poverty deprived him of means for making his fortune. I entered into partnership with him and for some months everything went as favorably as could be desired. But the greed, the avarice, and the baseness of the wretch in a short time enriched him with my funds and my industry to such an extent, that my infinite patience wearied and I resolved to be rid of him. His revolting ingratitude so disgusted me that I was even tempted to leave New York to escape the sight of such a rogue. To deepen my misfortune it seemed to me that at just that period the ardor of the studious for Italian letters had somewhat cooled. My spirits were in that state of depression, when a letter came to me from a relative of mine[11] who had settled in Sunbury some time before. Therein she drew me such a wondrous picture of the place that I was seized forthwith with a desire to transport myself thither. On the tenth day of June in the year 1811 I took my family[12] with me and set out for Sunbury.

I arrived there and within three days I grew so enamored of the town, that I resolved to settle there. The welcome accorded me, to tell the truth, by the one who had written me the letter, was neither as tender nor as enthusiastic as I had a right to expect; but it was not any hope or any desire of aid

---

11. The Niccolinis appear in the Sunbury triennial tax list of Jan. 1811, not in that of 1808. They appear in the annual "cash box" of 1812, not in that of 1811 or 1810.

12. Increased now by Louisa's marriage, on Nov. 15, 1809 (Trinity), to Miles Franklin Clossey Jr., 2d son of M. F. C. Sr., originally of Bordentown, but since 1800 in business as storekeeper at 163 Broadway.

from others that determined that change in my mind. It was the amenity of the spot, a yearning for repose, and a deceitful appearance of needing naught save God and myself—just as I had in New York. In fact I had gathered together some three or four thousand dollars. I hoped, therefore, that one ounce of Fortune and two of brains should be enough to begin a business of some sort, on the profits of which I could support my little family not uncomfortably.

I communicated my project to Dr. G——, who I thought must be my friend. He greeted it with transports of joy and assured me of a happy outcome. As my little capital was almost wholly in cash, he advised me to turn it into a variety of merchandise, and above all medicinal drugs. I blindly followed his advice, but was soon to realize that it had been the advice of Achitophel. I returned to New York and set my affairs in order. Thence I proceeded to Philadelphia and exchanged several objects of value for others of lesser volume or in greater demand; and all would have gone well had I not had the misfortune to stumble on a hypocrite who cheated me cruelly: on Lorenzo Astolfi.

This fellow sold liqueurs and candies in the most frequented center of Philadelphia. Passing that way by chance, I stepped into his store, and hearing him speaking in Italian, entered into conversation with him. I had brought a quantity of *rosolio* and spices from New York with me. Thinking the goods fitted his purpose I offered him the sale of them. He came to my room the following day, took my samples, and invited me to come to his house. I went there, arriving just as he was sitting down to dinner—a fatal moment, it would seem, for me. He invited me to dine with him. Mindful of my famous Irish dinner, I tried to evade, but he shut the door and locked it and I was forced willy-nilly to break bread with him. The viands were excellent, the wine exquisite; and Signor Lorenzo treated me with such hospitality and courtesy, not that first day only, but on many others following, that I very soon regarded him as the best man in the world. The *vox populi* corresponded perfectly with this good opinion of mine. He was, people said, the most honest of men, generous, and a charitable Christian. That reputation he had acquired by going to mass once a day, confessing once a week, kneeling at the altars and smiting his breast, and each Saturday laying two wax candles and three cents' worth of oil on the altar of the Madonna of Good Counsel! In fact, he told me one day, his eyes moist with holy tears, that he was specially devoted to the Virgin, that she appeared to him in his dreams almost every night and was continually giving him helpful advice. Taking him all in all, I baptized him as a fool, but did not imagine him a cheat. Blindly therefore I placed everything in his hands, blindly I suggested that he sell everything as goods of his own, and then, the costs figured, divide profits with me. Seeing from my readiness to agree and from my demonstrations of affection, that he could do anything with me, he seized the opportune moment to offer me in part payment a chaise and a horse, which I took for four hundred and fifty dollars, though, as I afterwards found out, he had paid only three hundred for them.

Our bargain struck, I announced my departure. He threw his arms about me, promised to commend me to his beloved Protectress, and helped me into the chaise. I drove off, thanking Heaven for having found such a rare friend; but—in all things in this world *lauda finem*.

Half way along the road, a shaft of my chaise broke, though without anything serious happening to me. This breakdown, therefore, was only a beam of light from the thunderbolt that was later to crash upon my head in that same wagon!

I reached Sunbury safe and sound, and full of hopes and of daring. I rented a small house at once,[13] and began doing business. I had brought with me, along with medicinal drugs,

---

13. On Water St., along the river, which had become Broadway, officially, in 1808, and is now Front St.

a stock of general merchandise. Dr. G—— desired that the medicines be deposited in his house, where sales would be almost instantaneous; but the other things I took all to mine, where, in a very few days, they were sold for cash with moderate profits. Satisfied with this first operation, I returned to Philadelphia and laid in a new stock and paid a visit to my new friend—all was going well: more blandishments, more courtesies, new protestations of friendship!

I lingered there some days, because a second "friend" was calling me to Boundbrook![14]

At the time of my trading in Elizabeth Town I had sold goods on credit to many bad payers in New Jersey, and, among these, to a William Teller. When I returned to New York, he had still some hundred dollars owing to me and I had about abandoned hope of ever getting them. Though notorious as a poor payer, such nevertheless was his artfulness, that the most cautious and most conservative individuals had been fooled by him. For that reason he was in debt to merchants in New York where he did not dare to show his face, save on rare occasions, for fear of the constables.

One day, while I was going over some papers in my study, I saw him coming in upon me. I asked what he wanted:

"I have come," he replied, "to call on my good friend, Mr. Da Ponte."

Just then there was a knock at the door. I laid my papers down on my table and went out to see who it was. The son of Mr. G—— C—— and a constable were there in pursuit of him. They had come to arrest him! I thought it scarcely the generous thing to let him be taken from my house to jail. There being no other way to help him, I offered to go bail to the amount of the eighty dollars which he owed, and so managed to save

---

14. I have not yet studied the Boundbrook episode, with William, Peter William, or Samuel Teller.

him. Returning to my study I found my papers in some disorder; but since none of them could have been of any use to him, no particular suspicions were aroused in me at that time; but returning the papers to my diary in some irritation, I informed him of what I had done. He thanked me, promised to pay the eighty dollars, and went away.

Some months went by. As I already feared, it fell to me to pay. I wrote him. He did not answer. So now I went to see him.

After many lies, many inventions, much chatter, he offered me, in payment of the hundred and fifty dollars he owed me, a broken-down horse and an assortment of new harnesses for my chaise. Remembering the proverb "better a little than nothing," I accepted, in an evil hour, what he was offering. I gave him a receipt in full and departed. I had not had time to leave my tavern, than one of the sons of that scoundrel entered with a constable and declared me his prisoner. Surprise and bewilderment robbed me of the power of speech.

"I have bought of the English consul," he explained, "a check of one hundred pounds sterling payable by you to Mr. William Taylor, manager of the Italian Opera in London; you must either pay me, or be pleased to take a little walk with the constable here."

My reader has already divined the maneuver. At the very moment when I was exerting myself to free him from prison and incurring risk of paying, as I in fact paid, eighty dollars on his behalf, that traitor had fumbled among my papers and stolen that note which I had issued seven years before to William Taylor in London and paid to several money-lenders of that city, while the manager was in Paris. I shall not dwell longer on this horrible spectacle of iniquity. Mr. Pembel, the honorable proprietor of that inn, and my respected friend G. Scott, a lawyer in Brunswick, went bail for me and I returned to Sunbury. In due time I presented myself in court; but neither Teller, nor his son, nor their lawyer, had the audacity to appear. Seven full years

went by and I heard nothing more of them. That infamous old
man, however, came to the end he deserved. He stole a number
of documents from a public archive, was condemned to State's
Prison for life, and there finished both his days and his thiev-
ing. The prisons of New York never saw, and probably will never
again see, his like as a scoundrel. He came from Canada.

This business ended, I returned to Sunbury, and began again
to trade. I had had leisure, meantime, to examine things carefully and would to God I could now say of that town what I
might with justice have said in those first days. But the Sunbury of 1818 was not the Sunbury of 1811. I shall give, if I may,
some slight idea of it to my curious reader.

Sunbury is a little town of Pennsylvania, in the County of
Northumberland and about one hundred and twenty miles[15]
distant from Philadelphia. One arrives at the foot of a mountain thirty-six miles in length, which though steep and rocky
has been made by art of man of easy and not perilous ascent.
The roadsides are garlanded with bushes, shrubs, and trees of
every sort, splendid among which is an incredible quantity
of wild laurel, that in the springtime and during part of the
summer offers, with perhaps of all the flowers the most beautiful and graceful, the spectacle of one continuous garden. The
flanks of that mountain figure on both sides a theater of rustic
magnificence. Brooks, cascades of water, hillocks, precipices,
masses of white rock and multiform clumps of trees stretch
away in two broad and deep valleys, which end at other mountains of not dissimilar aspect. Here and there are little cot-
tages, shepherds' cabins, great quarries of coal and limestone,
tracts of well-cultivated land, very comfortable inns, and amid

---

15. The miles were giants in those days. Postal and stage coach rates were com-
puted at 122 miles between Phila. and Sunbury. The P.R.R. now calls it 165 miles
by way of Harrisburg. It is 155 *via* Reading-Shamokin, across the Ridge, and 185
via the Nescopeck Pass.

no end of deer, wild boars,[16] partridges, pheasants, and all other kinds of game, wolves, foxes, bears, and rattlesnakes, which last, though they rarely attack the wayfarer, add nevertheless a certain delightful terror, a certain touch of solemnity, to that majestic solitude. The waters are quite as "Clear, cool, and sweet," as those in which the deified Lauretta "bathed her fair limbs;" and at various seasons of the year there are trout so tasteful to the palate that the lakes of Como and Garda offer not better ones to the fastidious Lombard. Not till one reaches the last crest does Sunbury come into view. The entrance to the town promises little to the traveler's observing eye: no cleanliness of streets, no magnificence of structures, no thronging of inhabitants; but as one goes on a little more than half a mile to reach that part of the town which spreads along the bank of the Susquehanna, a noble and navigable stream, the view becomes truly marvelous in virtue of the various turns in the river, of the woods, the hills, and the villages which are sprinkled along the opposite shore.

In this delightful section of Sunbury was the house rented by me, surrounded by the most respectable families of the place, among whom the leaders at that time were the Grants, the Halls, the Bujers,[17] the Smiths. We soon became associated in the most cordial friendships and passed the first year and a great part of the second in perfect harmony, providing for each other those enjoyments and pastimes which good manners and the usages of respectable societies afford to people cultivated, prosperous, and honorable. Nightly gatherings, rural dances, jovial dinners, amusements of gentle company, were the delights of the saner part of that village. There was also at that time, as there is everywhere, the less attractive part of

---

16. Wild boars, no; wild turkeys, yes.

17. George and Thomas Grant; Charles Hall; John Buyers; Enoch Smith—all large landholders at the time, in that essentially rural community.

the town, but that was generally avoided by the better people, *cane pejus et angue*. The women, furthermore, were almost all amiable, virtuous, and, for the most part, pretty enough. I will name one, among the many, who, through her affability, her suavity of manner, her purity of character, and especially through her exemplary fulfillment of every domestic duty, may be put forward without fear as the perfect model of the housewife. Mrs. Elizabeth Hall[18] is the revered lady of whom I speak: daughter of one of the wealthiest citizens of the State of Pennsylvania, which gratefully and respectfully honors his memory; the wife and now unfortunately the widow of one of the most celebrated lawyers[19] of that county and happy mother to a family of handsome and most amiable children.

The first born of her sons studied languages with me.[20] A sharp memory, a quick mind, and great application to study were the fortunate presages of his excellent success in the profession of his father which he was expected to follow and followed. I loved him tenderly, nor do I think I ever neglected

---

18. Elizabeth Coleman Hall (1778–1858), of the Colemans of Maryland, one branch of whom had settled in Cornwall, owning land and developing the smelting industry in and about Lebanon and Lancaster. Da P. does not exaggerate the excellence and eminence of this American gentlewoman of the old school, fondled as a child by the First President of the United States, and courted as a young lady by the Fifteenth.

19. Charles Hall (1767–1821), wealthy "squire" and lawyer, prominent in Northumberland County especially after 1796, a man of almost forefatherly proportions, with important connections and correspondences with Philadelphia, New York, Boston, and London. He became the relentless executor of Louisa Niccolini's last willful testament; though he was Da P.'s protector and helper, and even served him as attorney in the direst straits, always without pay. He liked Da P., but preferred seeing him after five in the afternoon. —A. L.

20. Robert Coleman Hall (1792–1844), whom, in fact, Da P. prepared in the classics for Princeton. Da P.'s bitterness arises from the administration of the Niccolini inheritance, which young Hall took over on his father's death.

anything that might have or should have contributed to his welfare, in that portion of his education that was entrusted to me by his father then living. He is the only one, nevertheless, (nor could I say through what fault of mine) among almost twelve hundred young men and women who were instructed in languages by me in America, the only one, I repeat, who forgot my affection and efforts: the only one who has denied me any of those regards that well-born persons deem owing to those who contribute to the ornament of their minds; the only one who has denied himself the pleasures of consoling me in my afflictions, helping me in my misfortunes, coming to my succor in my need. He might without blame, risk, or damage to himself, have poured a balm of consolation on my unmerited wounds, helped an aged parent to apply a last hand to the education and settlement of a son; lent a weary octogenarian the means of offering some repose to his failing limbs; and he would have heard, even though far away, the benedictions of an entire family, grateful for a blessing which he might have bestowed without loss of his, and which, as it seemed to everyone, he should have bestowed, since, before him, his most honored father had bestowed it. I will explain more clearly in the course of these Memoirs some obscure portions of this paragraph, which has been violently torn from a pen dipped rather in tears than in ink. Let us go on with the story of Sunbury.

Once it became known abroad that I was versed in languages and letters, a number of young ladies of the village and of the neighboring town of Northumberland asked me to instruct them in these matters. I consented at once to their praiseworthy desire and among the emoluments deriving to me from this exercise and the profits earned by my little business, I was in a position to live comfortably without touching my capital. Things were at that pass when a very serious mistake of mine gave a wholly different turn to affairs. Everything or almost everything that I had sold up to that point had been for cash. The profit was slight, but I took no risk. My brother-in-law contended that selling on credit and in a public store would be of far greater advantage to me. To my misfortune I followed his advice. Not sufficiently acquainted as yet with the inhabitants of the place and of its environs, I allowed myself to be guided by him blindly. A "very good" from his lips or his pen had perforce to be for me my standard of guaranty. The moment my decision became known, customers came flocking to me from every direction. In a few weeks my not large storerooms were empty, but empty likewise was my till; that is to say, instead of being full of that beautiful metal which *lætificat cor* more than the wine that is red, it contained a fine bundle of bills, notes, and promises to pay, or like phantoms of money, most of which have, on balancing accounts, the same value that the leaves on the trees have toward the middle of November. My doctor brother-in-law, meanwhile, was congratulating me warmly on my great success. Going over the names which already filled a large book of which he had made me a courteous gift, he would repeat to encourage me: "Good, very good, all very good!" though at paying time, I found to my pain and surprise that all, or almost all, the "goods" of the doctor were "bads"; "bads," "very bads" for Mr. Da Ponte! The miserable consequences of this we shall soon see.

Things carefully considered, I thought it wiser to return to Philadelphia and to negotiate the notes that had been given me in Sunbury in exchange for my goods. I hoped, also, to find some hundreds of dollars in the hands of the good Astolfi. Then selling the horse of the Canadian for what he would bring, and perhaps my chaise and the other horse, I would have a new fund of from six to eight hundred dollars in cash, to buy a stock sufficient for opening a quite respectable store. But I lacked money to make the journey. I hurried straight to my advisor, therefore—according to what people said, he had the treasures of Crœsus—and asked him for a hundred dollars, offering him one of his "very goods," a note that would fall due within a few days. But from what I saw, his doctoral purse was no heavier than my mercantile one. He told me, however, that he would take me to his father, and that the latter would probably buy my medicines if I chose to sell them to him. I was delighted at that suggestion—I will not say why. I went; and the business was concluded in six words. For medicines that cost me more than six hundred dollars, I got: a repeater which I sold for one hundred and sixty; a note of one hundred thalers from W—— T—— which was made good five years later; and forty dollars in cash! What is somebody's loss is always somebody's gain!

With these treasures on my person, I clambered into my two-horse wagon and in less than three days was in Philadelphia. Astolfi's horse was not a bad animal; the other, though lame, seemed to have wings on his feet. On entering Philadelphia, I observed that he was limping more than usual. I had the sweet consolation of hearing that the beast had a sore on one foot, which the smith believed incurable, but that if I were bent on selling him anyway, he would buy him for six dollars! I thanked him for the offer and drove on.

Settled at a tavern, I hurried forthwith to my friend of the sweetmeats. The moment I was in his shop, I could see at a glance that something unpleasant had befallen that devoted worshiper of the Madonna. I approached and held out my hand. He then extended his, and began, rather constrained:

"And how is Mr. Da Ponte?"

He offered me a chair and sat down near me. We gossiped a little about the world in general; but not a word of the *rosolio* and the spices I had entrusted to him. My temper was beginning to roil, but I dissimulated, and asked placidly how things had been going.

"Badly, very badly!" he replied in a whimpering tone. "The

rosolio was worthless; the *maraschino* just as bad; the cinnamon had no smell. I do not believe I can get out of it the money I have already paid."

"If that's the case," I said, "I will give you back. . . ."

"Too late for that," he interrupted. "I have already sold a part of what you gave me. I will sell the remainder as best I can."

"And the profits?" I inquired.

"Profits? Profits? I'll thank the saints and the Madonna if I don't lose a hundred dollars!"

I looked him straight in the eye without speaking, and I left that shop of confectioned hypocrisy, beating my head with my two fists and crying:

"Cursed hypocrite, is this possible? Is this possible?"

I never saw him again; but I believe that he, too, came to a bad end.

Unable either to sell the horse, or discount the note, I bought some goods and started back along the road to Sunbury. Arriving at a certain height, where the village of Orvisbourg comes into view, the two shafts of my wagon broke; the horses took fright, and ran way. The bottom of the carriage, dragging along the ground, struck a stump that rose in the road, and in the terrible shock I was hurled upon a mound two yards away from the place of the collision, breaking a rib and my left collarbone and sustaining bruises and cuts in more than twelve places on my arms an legs. A pitying passerby carried me to a neighboring house, whence I was taken to a tavern in the village. From there, after twenty-two days of treatment, I was carried on a straw pallet to Sunbury. That bed was most appropriate in truth for a poet with his bones broken and his purse flatter than a beggar's; because the host, who was as devoted to the Madonna as my friend the confectioner, charged me fifty-six dollars for twenty-two days of his hospitality! May the Lord protect you, my dear readers, from such friends! Despite all the attentions and care lent me on that occasion by the various members of my family I felt the deadly effects of that accident for than three months.

Unable to move about and soon short of funds, I saw myself constrained to abandon trading and all I had been doing and dip into my little capital to meet the not inconsiderable expenses of my household. For an added misfortune, payment time had come, and no one was paying! I then began to open my eyes! But it was already too late. My poor brother-in-law was not at all, at Sunbury, the man I had known in Trieste. The unhealthy portion of the town had corrupted his good character and hardened his heart. The earnings of his profession, though very considerable, did not suffice for the passions and the vices which held him in sway. Examining his conduct more closely, I discovered that the advice he had given me to sell on credit, did not proceed from any sincere desire to promote my welfare but . . . let us stop here! May I not wound with a useless venting of my feelings, the tenderness of a sister who still loves his name and his memory, in spite of the losses, afflictions, and tears his waywardness and his weaknesses cost her and me! He is dead! Peace be unto him![21]

I was beginning, at last, to regain my bodily strength. But some trouble or other seemed to be bothering me internally so that it was found wiser to send me back to Philadelphia that I might consult a good physician. Before leaving Sunbury, I had talked with everybody who owed me money and finding it impossible to collect any from them, I agreed to wait until harvest time when they would pay me in rural produce. Almost all of them kept their word, and I soon found my house filled with meats, skins, butter, wax, hay, dried fruits, grain, and many other things of the sort. What I could not use for

21. Peter Grahl died between May 27 and 31, 1816; John Grahl around Dec. 18, 1814.

my own purposes, I sold for money, with the exception of the grain, which, in an evil hour, I thought of having distilled. In this latter operation I fell into the clutches of three rascals of Northumberland, who introduced themselves to me with the passport of a "very good" in their hands! I will not name them, because I should blush that the world should know I ever had dealings with such traitors. I shall print their infamous names in blank and speak of the affair itself. The thread of my story demands that I do so.

I deposited all the grain I had in their stores, and returned to Philadelphia, I sent at once for Doctor Physic,[22] and told him the story of my accident. He examined me in silence, ordered me twelve cuppings on my two sides, and turned toward the stairs to go away. Limping slowly after him, I asked what food I should take that day.

"None at all!" he replied, in a tone not at all mellifluous. but when he reached the door, he turned, with a less hypocritic face, told me to come to his house the following day, and gave me permission to eat two potatoes and four oysters. I sent for a surgeon. He applied the cupping glasses, and after sleeping for two hours I thought I felt better. I went out for a walk. I came by chance upon the fish market, where a beautiful—I know not whether carp or pike—struck my eye, I bought it, carried it home, ordered it boiled, and ate half of it with the best appetite in the world, taking instead of bread, two unusually fine potatoes, in partial obedience to the diet ordained by that eminent doctor. I went to see him the next day. He was delighted to hear that I was feeling better and had not transgressed his prescriptions, which he ordered me again to adhere to. I followed them rigorously, except that instead of two potatoes, I fasted on four, and instead of four oysters, on one little fish of about

---

22. Philip Syng Physick (1768–1853), 45 Arch St., Philadelphia, "father of American surgery," became professor at the University of Pennsylvania in 1805.

two pounds. In five or six days I was well. I then praised and thanked most cordially that so justly celebrated man, whom, in spite of everything, I would much rather have for my physician than for my blacksmith.

Feeling myself strong of body and in condition to move about, I began to think of business again. I sold the watch, the horses, my chaise, and a considerable quantity of spiritous liquors emanating from the grain that was being distilled for me. I found myself in possession of seven or eight hundred dollars, and with those funds I began trading again. Meanwhile the report spread about Philadelphia, I know not how, that I knew the art of treating distilled whiskey in such wise as to extract therefrom a quality of brandy not unlike that derived from wine by distillers in France. Two respectable merchants called on me and we drew up a contract of partnership for that purpose. Feeling quite prosperous, I decided to return to Sunbury to settle my affairs and to buy up as much grain as I could to distill it later into brandy.

Having sold my horses and carriage, I took a seat in the stage which runs first to Reading and thence to Sunbury. We left Philadelphia toward evening, planning to stop for the night at a village called La Trappe. When we reached a certain bridge, about two miles from that place, the night being very dark and the driver drunk, we were upset in a deep ditch, and of the ten of us who were in the stage not one came out of it without a fractured skull or a dislocated shoulder or some broken bone. I suffered a severe contusion on my left arm, splintered my right collarbone and so injured my back, the tip of my spine and my thighs that it was impossible for me to stir. They carried me to the inn, more dead than alive, and only after a cure of three weeks could they carry me to Philadelphia to have me attended by a better physician.

These two terrible accidents, befalling me in the same year, and at such an advanced age, were neither so fatal nor so

painful to me as was the visit of a traitor from Northumberland—his despicable name shall not befoul these pages—who
first robbed me of a property worth several hundred dollars,
then tried to smirch my name and reputation and sow the
seeds of discord among various members of my family. Your
pardon, kindly reader, if, after exciting your curiosity perhaps,
I suddenly halt my story at this point. There are crimes that
cannot be told without crime. Let us go back to my bed.

I was on the point of sending for Doctor Physic again, when
one of my friends who had heard of my misadventure, entered
my room in company with Doctor Barton.[23] My words could
not describe the devotion of that very learned doctor, nor his
many solicitous efforts to cure me quickly. Not satisfied with
that, he lent me divers books for my amusement, visited me
two or three times a day, sat sometimes for hours at my bedside that I should not be wearied at being so much alone. This
physician, as learned as he was humane, died a few years later;
but the memory of his kindness and courtesy remains and will
remain imperishably impressed on my mind as on the minds
of all good people. That peace be unto him which he brought
to me in his lifetime!

In three more weeks he had me cured, and I returned
straightway to Sunbury. I found affairs at Northumberland in
the greatest disorder. Everything had gone. I freed myself at once
of those two wretches; but the man I took in their places[24] was
not less ungrateful, nor less unfair in his dealings with me—of
this I may perhaps speak in due time. To save my reputation I
was obliged to hurry back to Philadelphia, where one of my distillers had passed a note of mine for some drygoods which I had

---

23. Benjamin Smith Barton (1766–1815), also a forefather of American medicine,
professor of botany and general medicine at Pennsylvania, and a stimulating force
in the intellectual life that centered about the American Philosophical Society.

24. William Taggart.

to pay for, and was then obliged to go into that line of trade.[25] Some time later I set out again along the road to Sunbury, arriving this time without any accident. It is certainly astonishing that at such an advanced age and after so many disasters I should have had the courage to undertake and successfully carry the burden of so many travels! The reader of these Memoirs will have reason to marvel all the more when I tell him that in the space of seven years only I crossed the Ridge seventy-two times, and not always in the season of the laurel blossoms.

After such evident proofs of human treachery, it would seem that a man not far from seventy might have begun to be diffident of men, or at least to study them carefully before trusting them. But it was as though Providence had willed that I should ever, all my life long, keep falling into the hands of knaves, and no matter how many wrongs I suffered, they were never enough to bring me wisdom; nay, to issue from one abyss was ever for me only the eve of plunging into a still deeper one.

I had brought from Philadelphia a large stock of general merchandise and not a little cash for trafficking in country produce, in grain especially. To my future misfortune, a certain Thomas Robins had at that time sold out his stock and was trying to rent his house and stores.[26] The occasion seemed to me propitious and I rented the building.

---

25. In 1814, in fact, Da P. at last opened a millinery store at 29 North 2nd Street, Philadelphia. The threat had been hanging over him since the days in Brussels, in view of Mrs. Da Ponte's proficiency in that line. The store, I suspect, was tended by Fanny, who seems to have lived preferably in the capital, probably at 135 Chestnut Street, with a close friend of Louisa Niccolini—one Frances Papegay. She was to marry in Philadelphia, three years later.

26. Lot 21, *i.e.*, So. East Corner of Market and Third Sts., just across Third from the future Brick House. Tom Robins lived on lot 23, directly across Market Street from Peter Grahl's. Robins' tannery was directly across Market Street from Da P.'s store, and when the east wind blew it must have smelled up the town. Robins *floruit* between 1783 and 1820.

The reputation of the man was what it had to be: drinker, gambler, sharper, sunk deep in filth, inured to vice, not above any breach of faith nor any fraud; with a hundred other blemishes on his character, any one of which is enough to blacken a man's name—such the general opinion of the sane part of Sunbury, as regarded the landlord of the house into which I moved with my already half-wasted capital. But my brother-in-law insisted that Thomas Robins was an honest man, and that was enough to make me his victim. After having fallen into the clutches of such a cherub, I stumbled, to cap the climax of my joys, upon a seraph of the same breed. This latter was a very shrewd Yankee who had come to Sunbury to seek his fortune. The Devil thrust him across my path, and, as usual, trusting a medical quack who praised him to the stars to me (I did not know they were cousins and from the same town) I engaged him as my clerk, bookkeeper, and agent, treating him more like a father than like an employee.

At first everything went well. I had changed my system. From seller, I turned buyer. The farmers brought me the produce of their lands, and I gave them goods or money according to their needs. No end of customers were flocking to my store; and I was not obliged to sell on credit, as I had been doing, in order to sell the more. Seeing my storerooms overcrowded and my stock almost gone, I bought a wagon and two horses, hired a teamster who was considered a sober and honest man,[27] and began trucking to Philadelphia, not only grain for the distilleries, but all sorts of rural produce, bringing back city goods in exchange.[28] This business seemed to prosper

---

27. Simon Perry.

28. "L. de Ponty's Wagon" was indeed famous all along the 'Pike, as one of a daily train of "Conestogas" that on some mornings passed the taverns in the wilderness a mile in length, pouring produce of the Susquehanna into the metropolitan markets. Da P. had 2 horses, 1813; 4, 1814; and 6, 1816, after his failure!

prodigiously, and I thought myself in a position to build a house of my own.

The house was eight months in the building, and then I could boast of having erected the finest edifice in all the town.[29] To be sure, I did not know at that time that a number of bore-worms of iniquity were gnawing at its foundations.

I went to Philadelphia very frequently to sell and buy, meanwhile leaving my affairs in the hands of my seraphic Yankee. The fellow was accustomed to calling on a certain woman,[30] who had a daughter married to a laborer in the employ of Big Tom. According to his story, these calls on the woman were for the purpose now of reading some chapter of the Holy Bible, now of having a little darning done on his socks, now of avoiding the temptations of dangerous company. The women, besides, were among our best customers; they washed and swept the store without pay; and he could trust them as he would himself! We shall shortly see the finish to such a pretty story.

Toward the end of November in the year 1814, he strides into my study *ex abrupto* and gives me his notice. Nothing could have astonished me more, but I asked no reasons, and raised no objections. Having settled his accounts with me, he bought a fine horse, and a set of splendid harness, and with his bag full of knives, forks, and spoons—some people

29. On lot 20, So. West Corner of Market and Third. At this moment, winter of 1814–15, Da P. was the "biggest taxpayer" in town, next to Charles Hall; and for the next thirty years, "L. de Ponty's three-story brick" was to be the only three-story structure in the county.

30. I identify her, giving the benefit of doubt, as Catherine Davis, wife of Daniel Davis, and mother of Elizabeth Davis, whose triple escapades with "Big Tom Hundred Legs" diverted the East End, and scandalized the West End of Sunbury Square nearly every Saturday night all through the years 1812–15. Whatever happened, Robins was always guilty and paid everybody's fines. O. P. unidentified.

said silverware—caracoling and complimenting, he went on his way. He had not been a year with me. The wages I paid him were very low, and before entering my employ, he had been so poor as not to be able to pay his board for more than two months in the place where he had been living—that board bill had been paid, and perhaps paid twice, by me. But all these observations entered my head only after his departure; and then I drove them out again as so many whisperings of the Devil. It was God's will however that I should soon be enlightened!

Toward evening that day the old woman—the mother—came to me. She usually swept out the store and washed the floor at that hour. I was standing on the threshold of the front door when she came up. I bade her enter with a motion of my hand and a few moments later, quite by chance and not in suspicion, I glanced inside the store. I could not see the woman, but a ribbon from her cap was showing from behind the counter. I could see that she was stooping over, rummaging through some merchandise. I drew to one side, saying nothing, to see what she would do. A few minutes later, doubtless not imagining that I had seen her, she stole very softly out. Very softly I followed, and discovered she had a large bundle under her cloak. I stopped her, snatched it from her, and ran back into the store. I found it full of articles she had stolen from my stock, I rushed to a justice of the peace and went to her house with a constable. The woman had fled. Her house was empty. I had her pursued in various directions, but whether they did not try, or were not able, or did not choose—no trace was found of her. I learned some time later that, laden with booty, she had walked all night and found shelter at last in a farmhouse. Two days later she returned to town.

I had her brought before a justice of the peace. She confessed that between the first of May and the twenty-sixth of November she had received from O—— P——, agent of

Lorenzo Da Ponte, for herself and family and her daughter and family, *"all the articles that was made use of in their families; that she had paid only for about five or six pounds of coffee and sugar, while she had received about thirty of each; that O. P. had taken out of Lorenzo Da Ponte's store two pieces of nankeen, one waistcoat, one hat, cloth for a coat and pantaloons, two or three pair of shoes, and often pieces of cloth or muslin, etc. for his own use."* There were other accusations but I will add just one of them, that the lawyer who defended such a rascal may blush at his own shame:

"She said also, that O. P. had told her that he had five hundred dollars in his trunk!"

The confession of the woman was further corroborated by that of her daughter!

I knew from that moment what my fate must be. My books balanced, I found that the fruit of all my labors for seven months past had gone down the throats and upon the backs of two Thaïses and into the traveling bag of that honest Yankee! The scoundrel had the impudence to write me a letter and threaten me with prosecution for slander!

On this terrible blow there followed another immediately which I think I shall recount here.

The unworthiness of the man in question made me re-solve not to trust people I did not know again. We had in our house a young American girl[31] of whose honorableness, good sense, and integrity we had had indubitable proofs over a period of twelve years. I put her in charge of tending store and took another woman for the housework. The first evening she prepared supper near the fireplace and then took a chair not very far from me. I had laid on the table an account book, in which I

31. Da P.'s aged mind more or less blended his two servant girls, the one an angel, the other a beast, till he could not tell which was which.

was keeping a number of bank notes, among them three bills of fifty dollars each. Supper finished, the girl quietly rises, takes the book, and lays it on a stand. But she had seen the money, and picked up the book in such a way as to let a part of the loose papers fall to the floor. Before going to my room, I picked up the book again and placed it at the head of my bed. Far from any suspicion, I went to sleep, and enjoyed a good night's rest. But what was my surprise and my distress when, on awakening in the morning, I chanced to open the book and find that just those three bills of all the others had disappeared! I ran at once to the spot where I had had supper, searched every corner of the house, and then called the girl—she was the only one on whom my suspicion could fall. I questioned, entreated, threatened, had her arrested. It was all in vain. One of my neighbors, a few days later, found one of the bills, hidden under a stone that had been moved from his doorstep. The girl had been seen fumbling about that very stone at sunrise the day before. Everyone told me nevertheless that all that would be very hard to prove at law, and I was obliged to swallow a pill of a hundred dollars.

I regret having to speak of such inconsequential things to readers who are doubtless expecting to find more important matter in this volume. It must be remembered however that the things of this world are all proportioned to the status of the persons to whom they happen and to times and circumstances. The story of a continued series of calamities, afflicting a man by now arrived at his very old age, unfavored of fortune, incapable of a base act, and sole supporter of a family of dependents, is not, in my opinion, any less interesting to a compassionate soul than the recital of a battle lost by a great general, or the shipwreck of a squadron by a commander of the seas. If anyone is without a soul responsive to that noble sentiment, if he believes that the vicissitudes of a man, neither famous nor great, are not adequate to serve as an example or to interest a reader, he is not required either for his own sake or for mine, to read on in these Memoirs.

It was in the midst of all these troubles that my sister-in-law ceased to live.[32] It would seem that her death might have been the source of some relief to my needs. The woman had been a widow for a few years and absolute mistress of a considerable wealth, acquired almost entirely through my charity and the industrious talents of her sister.[33] She had no children, and though I knew that she did not love me best of all in the world, I hoped nevertheless that, on coming to her deathbed she would not dare do me the injustice of depriving me entirely and forever even of the property which her sister had, in too great trustfulness and a misplaced sisterly confidence, deposited in her hands. Forgetful nevertheless of my kindnesses to her and of my rights as kin, she excluded me from an inheritance of fourteen or fifteen thousand dollars! May God not hold against her the harm and the discouragement which her testamentary provisions, dictated to her by an unjust hatred and by an ill-advised revenge, brought upon me and my whole family.

For the present—no more of that!

After so many rebuffs from Fortune and so many betrayals of traitors I saw myself constrained either to suspend business, or seek elsewhere the succor necessary for continuing. I mortgaged my house accordingly. Between goods and money I

---

32. The Niccolinis, on arriving in Sunbury, had moved into "The Stone House" of John Boyd, none other than the famous Wolverton Mansion (Maclay House) of today. Charles Niccolini died between Jan. 31 and Feb. 15, 1812, about six months after Da P.'s arrival in Sunbury. Louisa's will was proved Jan. 16, 1815. She must have died, therefore, not over a week earlier, and not more than three weeks after John Grahl.

33. The *buvette* at the London Opera, and some participation (more canny than his) in the London speculations.

received a certain sum that might perhaps have sufficed to set things in good order, had not the ignorance of the lawyer who drew the terms of the mortgage, and the leisurely rapacity of the lender,[34] brought it about that the succor arrived after the rout. Because of their dilly-dallying, the money which should have served to buy goods at a most advantageous moment, arrived out of season, and went for nothing save to pay debts. I found myself in consequence more embarrassed than before. Things were at this point, when news of the peace concluded between England and the United States of America arrived. This peace, which no one had been expecting, reduced prices by about fifty percent on all kinds of merchandise. A very strange misunderstanding had some time previous been the occasion of my replenishing my stock more lavishly than usual. I was passing through Reading one day when I stopped at an inn to rest my horses. In the room I entered, there was, among others, a Frenchman who knew me and who cried, the moment he saw me:

"Ah, Monsieur Du Pont, comment vous portez-vous?"

Thereupon, in low but still intelligible voice, I could hear the words running from mouth to mouth:

"Du Pont!" "Du Pont!" "Du Pont!"

I could not imagine what to think of this sort of echo aroused by my name. I asked for a glass of wine, and left the room. On my reentrance, numbers of persons[35] gathered in a

---

34. The ignorant lawyer was Dan Levy; the mortgagee was René Louis Gravelle (d. Oct. 1835 at Chauvigny, Haute Vienne, France).

35. I name four of them: John Riebsam and William Wiley, trading in Reading under the firm name of Riebsam & Wiley; and Hood Irvine and Charles Harper, trading as Hood Irvine and Co. They were, in fact, among the bitterest and most violent of Da P.'s persecutors, as they followed him to Sunbury—their virtue waxing all the hotter since they were imposing upon him by "unloading" in advance of a storm of which they had warning and he did not. Irvine was the man who forced Da P. into insolvency.

circle around me, and as though they had been friends of mine for thirty years, they told me that they had heard enough of me to be willing to offer me their stocks on Philadelphia terms and at Philadelphia prices. I went to their stores and made my selection. After I had paid in cash for the articles I chose, they all seemed desirous of opening more extensive dealings with me. The one offered me drugs, the other liquors; this one cloth; that one canvas—all of them agreeing to accept notes, cash, produce, anything, as and when it should be convenient for me to pay. I could not understand such anxiety to sell on credit to me, in persons who barely knew me, and whom I furthermore knew to be very cautious in trade. I could have carried all Reading away in my cart that day, had that vehicle been able to hold it. It was not till I was taking leave of them that the enigma became clear to me. Then one of those merchants begged me to pay his respects to "his good friend, Du Pont, a cousin of mine!" They had all taken me for one of the Du Ponts who make and sell gunpowder. They had been courting in the person of a humble storekeeper in Sunbury the rich manufacturer of the Brandywine! We shall soon see how dearly this misunderstanding was to cost me!

My perseverance, nevertheless, and the considerable earnings I made in that manner of traffic, might have long retarded my failure if not prevented altogether my ruin, had not a so-called attorney in Sunbury, I know not whether through downright malice of disposition or in hopes of finding clients for a law office or ill repute, given the *coup de grâce* to my credit. He went to Philadelphia, and both in that city and in the towns along the way, exaggerated my misfortunes, invented others I never had, and destroyed whatever confidence businessmen in those parts of Pennsylvania had in me. Frightened by his reports, all those who had had dealings with me, came down upon me like so many hungry dogs and made miserable slaughter of me and my business.

First to appear in this field of persecution was that merchant who had lent me the money on mortgage. It was Levy[36] who advised him; Levy who undertook to act for him on his return to Sunbury; Levy who tried three times to sell my house *sub hasta*, hoping to obtain it for himself or for one of his friends, "for little or nothing." To be sure, the law and my stubbornness disappointed that hope of his, but the comment that this effort aroused was as deadly to me as the sale itself would have been.

Two merchants in Philadelphia, who had been sending me goods in exchange for produce, kept what I sent, and returned my wagon empty. Two others in Reading hired a famous rascal to collect what I owed them and the first greeting he paid me was in company with the sheriff. Farmers, who previously had been trusting me, now wanted their money before delivering their produce. Just now it further happened that the two merchants in Philadelphia with whom I had been in partnership manufacturing brandy were unlucky enough to fail, and their collapse deprived me of a great help I had been receiving from their funds and their credit.

Yet despite this rain of fire upon my head, I would perhaps still be in that most accursed town, had not the Hand of Providence dragged me forth from it, as sometimes a drowning man is pulled from the water by the hair of his head. By dint of patience, sacrifice, hard work, I weathered this storm of calamity and persecution; got into my new house; stocked my store with goods; paid or assured payment to my more restless creditors; began supplying grain again to two different distillers —in short recovered my good credit.

I was inwardly rejoicing at having triumphed at last over so

---

36. Daniel Levy (1766–1844), son of Aaron Levy, founder of Aaronsberg. Dan Levy was a captain of militia in the War of 1812. A fiery, aggressive individual, he began using his fists and weapons at the point where his forensic eloquence failed.

many enemies: but little did I then know that, in escaping
from the water, I was only running toward the fire, and doing
my very best to plunge into it. But the Invisible Hand that had
come so many times to my rescue, freed me on this occasion,
too, from the jaws of lions and dragons, and rewarded my
courage and long suffering with one of the sweetest and most
desirable events in my life. It was those tribulations of
Sunbury that led me back over the paths miraculous, to my
dear and ever blessed city of New York; and what were, for others and for me, the happy effects of my return, will be seen
(with joy I declare it) in the remainder of this book.

Let us end the story of Sunbury.

My affairs were in this state of convalescence when that
same attorney advertised the sale of my house for a second
time. The news shook my merchants more than that first
time—one in particular to whom I stood owing six hundred
and eighty dollars.[37] I was very fond of the man. Hearing of his
uneasiness, I flew to Philadelphia and I tried to persuade him
that I had enough to pay everybody, but that he in any event
would be the last to lose a cent at my hands. He seemed satisfied, expressed his sympathy, praised my attitude, and promised to help me. I was so certain of his friendship and his
kindness of heart that I begged him to call on all those to
whom I owed any money and try to calm them.

He served me to the King's taste! On my taking leave of him,
he promised to come and see me the following day. Instead, he
went straight to a merchant[38] to whom I owed some one hundred pounds, advised him to arrest me, told him where I could
be found, and himself set out for Sunbury. There, he hoped
that while I should be in prison in Philadelphia and in virtue of

---

37. Hood Irvine, no less, who had a store also in Philadelphia. Comly, above, was
Charles Comly, and Allen, S. Richard Allen, 63 N. Front St.

38. A certain Jacob Carver.

a certain legal instrument I had executed to him, he would have leisure aplenty to possess himself of all I had in the world. The merchant in question followed his advice. About five o'clock in the afternoon, I was arrested in my house. I ran to various acquaintances and friends to get bail. One was not at home. One had sworn never to sign his name for any person on earth. One just laughed at me. Six in the evening was striking. I was already at the prison gate when the constable, a courteous gentleman, touched with pity at my situation and my years, cried:

"God forbid that I should lock in prison a gentleman of your age and your good presence. Go to your own house! I will see you tomorrow!"

For the second time in my life had I found in a person of that profession a pity I have not yet found in a thousand called great in the world!

He came in the morning. I had found two bondsmen, and before nine had struck I was on the road to Sunbury.

At Reading I learned that my assistant-protector had departed for that town four hours before. Arriving thither, he had an interview with two lawyers, who sent for the sheriff. Not finding him in, they sent messengers out to look for him on every hand, and in the confusion caused by this hurry to seize my house, his intention became known to many. Gossip spread the news throughout the village and soon reached the ears of Thomas "Hundred Legs." He ran full speed to my house, and by dint of much talking, shouting, cursing, succeeded in worming out of my servants, three stoves, a cart, six horses and their harnesses. Then he locked the doors, windows, and every entrance to my house, carried everything away to his own place, and aware that I was due to arrive that evening, sent a messenger to the tollgate on the Pike to inform me of what had happened. Eventually he came to meet me himself, and affecting the most cordial friendship, the traitor talked me into giving him also my horse and chaise to keep.

The lawyers on the other side came to see me a few days later, and we reached an agreement very easily. I reopened my store, and asked Robins to give me back my things.

He refused!

Do not, I beseech you, gentle reader, lose the curious thread of this story!

John and Thomas Robins were my bondsmen in two different actions: but Thomas owed me a hundred and ninety-seven dollars, on account of various purchases. In full agreement, we chose G. Grant, a respected citizen of our town, to go over our accounts and be our arbiter. Having examined the books, Mr. Grant ruled that I should pay the tax levied on the distilled liquors for which Thomas Robins, with the brother of the said Grant, was bondsman; and that, of the four hundred and eighty-eight dollars I owed the sheriff, for which John and Thomas Robins were my bondsmen, Thomas should pay one hundred and ninety-seven, the amount he owed to me, while the remainder I should pay; the which being done, my horses, cart, and harnesses, with the rest of my property, should be restored to me.

I paid the distilling tax on the whiskey at once, and offered to pay the sheriff my share if Thomas Robins would pay the one hundred and ninety-seven dollars he owed to me. But Thomas Robins had not such a sum at his command. Therefore both G. Grant and the other brother of Robins, as well, ordered that those effects should remain in his hands, until he should be able to do so! We shall shortly see the results of this unjust as well as absurd, sentence.

I asked permission to send my cart to Philadelphia with a load of produce. I obtained that permission as a supreme favor, but with the proviso that the cart and produce be delivered to one of the Robins' teamsters! I had had sufficient experience of the length of their claws! I insisted on sending my own. The man was not more than ten miles from Sunbury when that assassin overtook him, dumped the whole load on the road-side, so that half of it was spoiled, and returned triumphant and rejoicing with cart and horses to his tent of iniquity.

Who could deal with such a traitor in the town of Sunbury? Again I offered to pay my share due to the sheriff on account of the legal judgment of four hundred and eighty-eight dollars. Again Robins answered that he had not the money to pay his share; but he retained, nevertheless, by right of the stronger, all my property in his hands! My stoves went to pay some other debts of Mr. Tom Robins. My cart and my horses worked to carry wood, sand, stones, lime, coal, and so on, for the home of Mr. Tom Robins and for the friends, creditors, and satellites of Mr. Tom Robins; and on Saturday and Sunday nights they stood waiting at the door of various brothels of Mr. Tom Robins, all but dead of hunger and cold. I shouted, begged, threatened, appealed for help, appealed for justice! But nothing availed me. He had, one day, the impudence to send word to me that if I paid the four hundred and eighty-eight dollars to the sheriff he would give me back my cart and horses, and pay me the one hundred and ninety-seven he owed me, *when con-venient*; but that, in the opposite case, he would sell them at public auction!

He sold them at auction! But the buyers were all his dum-mies; so that everything, nothing excepted, was back a few moments later in the barn of this modern Cacus.

Since no other recourse was left to me, I saw myself forced to bring suit against him—a recourse *periculosæ plenum aleæ*, in the court of Sunbury, as we shall soon see. The arbitration day appointed, I named on my side two of the ablest and most respected citizens of the community—Mr. Lewis Duart, mem-ber of the legislature from that county, and Mr. J. Cawden, respected merchant of Northumberland. Robins chose two of his most intimate friends, and I made no objections, such con-fidence did the justice of my case inspire in me. Mr. O. Gobins, an honest, well-balanced person, experienced in arbitrations, was the fifth judge chosen by the other four. I plead my own case, with the assistance, however, of the attorney-general of that district, the eloquent Mr. Bradford. Thomas Robins spoke for himself. The witnesses were examined. Among these, too, appeared the confidants of that diabolical trinity: John, Gilbert, and Thomas Robins. The five withdrew; unanimously, Robins's friends included, they found against him in damages of five hundred dollars, which were, nevertheless, not more than half of my actual damage.

At the end of thirty days, he appealed! The appeal was not heard till almost two years afterwards! I was in New York! Two of the most prominent lawyers of those courts plead for me. Now give ear, most humane reader, to the monstrosity that was born on that occasion!

The very lawyer who had taken fees from me for his counsel; the very one who had assisted me at the trial of my action against Thomas Robins before the arbiters—bribed now by Robins and Robins's bondsmen—dared to appear before the district judge and a corps of jurors, the most intelligent of whom was a lame saloonkeeper, capable of everything except of reading and writing, and dared to argue that Robins had not stolen enough to be called upon to pay five hundred dollars to Da Ponte; and that honest gentlemen had other gentlemen as honest as he on hand to take oath to what he was saying and prove it. This testimony was heard—it had already been heard in the first instance—a horrible practice in the courts of Pennsylvania! And those honest and very enlightened jurors decided, *uno ore*, that *pro omni et toto eo* that most honest man, Thomas Robins, should pay, as an act of charity, two hundred and fifty dollars to Lorenzo Da Ponte! I drooped my ears like a poor tired donkey and in the secrecy of my heart paid worship to such an enlightened verdict. Minos, I do believe, never pronounced a juster one!

But let us drain the bitter cup!

The moment came for the payment to me of the two hundred and fifty dollars. But the property of Thomas Robins had become the property of his brother, Gilbert; of his brother John; and his brother-in-law P——. Mr. W. Brady, the sheriff of the county, had flown to the moon carrying with him all the papers, acts, and documents of that court.[39] The bondsmen of Mr. T——, bondsman of the sheriff, had also gone bankrupt! And thus went up in smoke six horses and a cart, that had cost me exactly six hundred and fifty dollars, and which the People's lawyer, his witnesses, and jurors, had revalued at two hundred and fifty!

Are there then no laws in most unhappy Sunbury? Yes, answers Dante, "Laws there are, but who lays hand to them?"

For if someone were to lay hand to them, not so many crimes, not so many abuses, not so many betrayals would go unpunished! A lawyer of that court would not have dared fraudulently to remit an instrument of sale signed by the grantors, to a wretch who, by that maneuver, cheated me out of three thousand *jugeri* of land for less than a quarter part of what they were worth. And another would not have had the boldness to extract three hundred and fifty dollars from me to escape paying himself, constraining me thereby to the harsh necessity of going to law with an assassin, with whom he thereupon joined to cheat me out of it, with the interest of eight years. And another, whom I got out of prison by lending him a note due to me on the part of the man who had imprisoned him, would not have refused, as he still refuses, to repay me the eighty-five dollars that freed him from prison and which he has had for almost nine years. Yet, these were among others just as many and just as bad, the extortions, abuses, betrayals that I suffered

---

39. Sheriff Walter Brady's term had merely expired in 1818. In all that quarter decade, no sheriff had had the courage to seek a reappointment.

at the hands of a Bojer, a so-called Sightzinger,[40] and a Good-
hart, in a town of this blessed America, so much admired for
her laws, her justice, and her hospitable brotherly love!

But these were not the greatest wrongs I suffered in that
place where they *bury* the *sun*. The one anecdote I am about to
relate will be the last touch of my brush to this portrait. Tired
of so many tribulations and lashings, I sold what little still
belonged to me, and divided the proceeds among my creditors.
I then moved into a small wooden house[41] I had built, and
opened a small store, the profits of which were barely sufficient to afford modest support to my family. Several slight sums
of money paid me by various persons who were in my debt; the
devotion of a most loyal American girl who had been with us
then for more than twelve years (and has now been with us for
twenty-four), and a most rigorous economy in domestic expenditure, would perhaps have brought me back little by little, if
not to a comfortable estate in life, to the state at least of a tranquil and peaceful poverty!

You who read my vicissitudes with heart capable of pity
and justice, shudder not, if you may, at my veracious recital of
this story!

I had gone out of my house on one of my ordinary domestic

---

40. Jake Sightzinger was a picturesque figure in the life at the East End of Sunbury
Square. One day, in a card game, he slipped a counterfeit $5 bill to Tom Robins,
and got away before the latter discovered it. Tom thereupon began circulating remarks derogatory to Jacob's character. In their first encounter next following,
Sightzinger must have had the better of it, for Tom sued him for assault and bat-
tery; in their second, Thomas would seem to have won, for Jake came back with a
similar action. Both dealt successfully, however, with the constables who came to
arrest them; whereupon Squire Chapman rose in his wrath and fined them both
two dollars. It may well be that Da P.'s aged memory is again failing him here. The
Sightzinger case sounds very like the Teller case.

41. Immediately adjoining the Brick House, on the West. It also was burned
in 1869.

errands when a messenger comes running to meet me, dusty, panting, and just in time to cry:

"For pity's sake, go home!"

I run home, trembling. Still some distance off I see a crowd gathered about the building in question. I draw nearer, and in my doorway I observe the sheriff (he had not yet absconded), Robins' brother, and some of their ruffians, who were busy stripping my house clean. In less than one hour there was not a thing left in it, not even a bed!

Not knowing the cause of such action, I hurried to the office of the prothonotary to inquire. I was told: that the person to whom I owed the four hundred and eighty-eight dollars, at whose instance my cart and horses had been seized, and for whom John and Thomas Robins were endorsers, had come down on the goods and chattels of Gilbert Robins, then deceased; and that John Robins, his executor and administrator, had therefore come down on me, and taken legal possession of my effects, in indemnification of that cart and of those horses, which, at the will and specific bidding of the said Gilbert, had been left in Thomas's hands, and which said Thomas had sold, over the objection and despite the offers of payment of Lorenzo Da Ponte, and calmly appropriated the proceeds to himself. I appealed to the proper tribunals and told the story of my persecutions. All that I was able to obtain were the beds, on which, after wetting them with my last tears for a few nights, I made salutary resolve to depart from Sunbury! On the fourteenth day of August in the year of 1818, at twelve o'clock in the morning, I bade my last farewell to that, for me, new Egypt and its most fatal inhabitants. I arrived at Philadelphia after a good journey and my intention was to settle there with my family, and spread the language and literature of my country, as I had done in New York. A young Italian[42] had arrived some time be-

---

42. Luigi Pittori. See Da P.–Colombo, Bern., 179.

fore in that city, bringing with him the principal treasures of Italian literature. The occasion seemed propitious for my plan. I began negotiations with the foremost men of letters of that capital and with the directors of the public library, proposing that they buy all or part of the books that young man had brought with him. I found with surprise and pain that Italian was no better known in Philadelphia than in New York on my arrival there. Yet I did not lose courage. I offered a few books to the public library through which sample might be had of such beautiful literature. Mr. Collins,[43] one of the most respected citizens of that city, and a director also of the civic library, exerted himself with much zeal in my behalf and seemed most anxious to see me succeed. I was told, however, that the library had no funds at that moment, but that probably within a short time some would come in and that then we could discuss the matter. This slight hope was enough to encourage me to seek every means of acquiring the books in question. I mortgaged, I sold, the little I still had, and offered to buy of that fine young man the *Storia letteraria* of Tiraboschi and two hundred and fifty volumes of the *Classici* of Milan, giving him one hundred dollars in cash, and for the balance my note in sixty days. He accepted my proposition; but at the end of sixty days I was dryly told by a certain not very courteous lawyer, that the library had no funds, and that I could keep my books. These were in the hands of a Frenchman, who had endorsed the note, and was holding them as security in his house. Having heard the lawyer's answer, he began to rave, overwhelming me with bitter abuse, and without giving me the slightest respite, sent the books to the French bookseller, ordering him to dispose of them at any price. That dear bookseller, of course, thought he

---

43. Zaccheus Collins (1764–1831), a merchant, patron of arts and sciences, *pars magna* of the American Philosophical Society, and, in fact, a trustee of the Old Library Company.

was getting those two hundred and fifty volumes for little more than one hundred and fifty dollars, though he knew they had cost me around four hundred! In order not to concede that victory, I went to the merchant who had mortgaged my house in Sunbury, and sold him for three thousand dollars a plant that had cost me five. Our accounts all settled, there remained to me just two hundred dollars! But that was enough to redeem those books wherein had been gathered the most beautiful flowers of our ancient literature.

This was my first glimpse of this noble, elect, and judicious collection, in which I know not whether I more admire the courage of the editors, the wealth of the annotation, or the vastness, sublimity, and beauty of the contents. I cannot express the joy that was mine at seeing myself owner absolute of such a treasure!

After considering for some time how to dispose of it, I concluded that Philadelphia either did not care, or else was not able, to appreciate it at its true worth. An inward voice seemed suddenly to be whispering in my ear: "Send it to New York!" I took the word as an inspiration from Heaven. Without delay I sent the half of those most precious jewels to this city, through that son who was too soon to be snatched from me.[44] He presented himself to my pupils and friends, and without the least difficulty, in only three days made profitable sale of them. He returned triumphant to Philadelphia, and along with the money brought a most gracious letter from my guardian angel, Mr. Clement Moore, urging me to return to New York, and devote myself again entirely to the cultivation and diffusion of our language and literature.

I should have left at once for New York, had not a matter of

---

44. Joseph stood very close to the family troubles and struggled to solve them like a little major. He began witnessing deeds and mortgages when he was twelve years old. Much of his mother's business correspondence is in Joseph's handwriting.

great importance detained me. A certain Giuseppe Mussi,[45] *notus in Judæa deus*, held various instruments of properties belonging to John Grahl, father to my wife. These had been deposited in his hands by the son of the said Grahl, at a time when both of them had failed, and were in prison. The lands had been occupied at a certain moment by an outsider, who had been cultivating them and enjoying them peacefully, without demand of possession whether on the part of Mussi, or of either of the Grahls. In the course of many years father and son both died and the only surviving daughter remaining heir, certain proofs of collusion between the two insolvents in prison came into my hands. I therefore demanded replevin of the lands by the occupant, in virtue of new instruments copied from public records, where those lands were registered as properties of John Grahl. Mussi objected, alleging that the lands belonged to him, and that, what with effects and cash, he had paid Peter Grahl two or three thousand dollars for them.

This dispute was enough to give Drummeller a good pretext for remaining in possession. I had a number of talks with Mussi, and, not sufficiently fathoming either his shrewdness, his rascality, or his rapacity, I thought I could arrange matters reasonably and pleasantly. I could not understand how a man arrived at the age of decrepitude, very well off, without family or needs, should attempt to cling, by trick or artifice, to property on which he could not have the slightest title in right. His assertion that he had given between two and three thousand dollars to Grahl's son on the point of bankruptcy and in prison,

---

45. That the Grahls were ever in prison for fraudulent bankruptcy I doubt. That they may have been victims of some *capias* proceeding, for which Mussi went their bail, is possible enough. But that could happen to anybody. I have even seen a *capias* issued against Charles Hall by some irate merchant in Reading. Mussi was a wealthy man long established in Philadelphia. I see no basis for questioning his honorableness. The Musgrave in question was Aaron Musgrave, a well-known merchant in Philadelphia.

seemed to me not only ridiculous and untenable, but impudent and shameful, because it implied guilt of fraud and perjury on his own part toward people whom he must have tricked with a fraudulent bankruptcy. I proposed nevertheless to pay him a certain sum of money, if he restored my papers to me; and I was glad to make such a sacrifice through a terror I had of reverting to the courts in Pennsylvania and especially in view of a well-founded suspicion, that grew stronger in me every day, that in the end I would be outdone by the wiles, rogueries, and malpractice of such a man.

One evening he told me, when more than usually *bene potus*, of a litigation he had had with a certain widow over a claim against her for six hundred dollars. There being no other way to obtain the money, he offered a bribe of two hundred dollars to the woman's lawyer in case the latter should allow him to win. He did win, in fact, by that device; whereupon the lawyer asked him for the two hundred dollars, and even brought suit against him. But he laughed at the lawyer, the suit, and the widow, did not pay a cent, and enjoyed his six hundred dollars in peace. When the holiness of the laws can be profaned with such impunity, what was to be the fate of a poor man? In fact, after vainly trying every avenue to an amicable settlement, I was forced willy-nilly to have recourse to lawyers.

I chose two of the best accredited in Philadelphia, and stated my case. They both opined that Mussi's claims were untenable at law. He suggested an arbitration, and I agreed. It seemed to me the wiser counsel to trust the judgment of three experienced men, than to that of a corps of jurors, chosen helter-skelter from the lowest elements of the people. I could not forget my jury at Sunbury! But show me the honest man, the man gifted with a sense of honor and rectitude, who can save himself from the artifices of rascals! While things were still unsettled, the man introduced me to a certain Musgrave, who to all appearances was a sensible person, honest, and of good manners. In a few days we became friends. Speaking of Mussi and my case, Musgrave told me one day these exact words:

"Mussi pretends to own no end of lands. But I know how he obtained the deeds and I wouldn't give him half a penny for the whole lot."

"I offered him a thousand dollars," I then replied, "to get back all the deeds. But he wants three thousand!"

"Not a penny, not a penny!" replied Mr. Musgrave vigorously. Let us hasten to the end. We chose the arbiters. The day for the argument was fixed. In virtue of some fine point which I did not grasp at that time, it was ruled that a single lawyer should speak for me, a single one for him! And in spite of the force of the arguments put forward by me; in spite of the fact that a certain note which Mussi produced with the signature of the father, Grahl, was in a handwriting entirely different from the one I produced and proved legitimate by comparison with numerous orders in Grahl's handwriting on banks in Philadelphia; in spite finally of an irreproachable witness who asserted the contrary of what Mussi said—and, note well, without corroboration; the three learned arbiters decided that Mr. Giuseppe Mussi should restore to Mr. Lorenzo Da Ponte the latter's lands, but, before that, that Mr. Lorenzo Da Ponte should pay to him not three thousand dollars, as he had asked, but three thousand and four hundred dollars as was just!

And who was the foreman of the arbiters? Mr. Musgrave!

And how did the business end? My poor family lost, through that decision, the only property it might have inherited on the mother's side. Mussi got nothing, even through the courts, from Drummeller, the man in possession; and I, more than five years later, found in the hands of a lawyer in New York a bill of costs, amounting to one hundred and sixty dollars, which the charity, humanity, and kindness of Signor Giuseppe reduced to one hundred and twenty!

That was the last calamity I suffered in Pennsylvania! *Claudite, jam rivos, pueri: sat prata libere.*

I settled my household affairs in Philadelphia, paid several small debts of the family, and with empty purse, but a heart overflowing with hope and joy, on the twenty-sixth day of April in the year 1819, I saluted from the opposite bank of its beautiful stream, the noble, populous, and to me beloved, city of New York.

My most courteous reader, I await you in the fifth part of these Memoirs, in which I promise you a wholly different scene.[46]

---

46. *Addendum*: Da P. has given only the gloomy side of the Sunbury picture. There was another, reflected in a glowing tribute that Sam Jackson was to pay him, years after his death, in 1862. Da P. left the town, as he says, in disgust, not in disgrace. More money was owing to him than he owed.

PART FIVE

ON THE SHORE of the Hudson, that lies like a mirror before the great city of New York, I hired a small boat for my luggage which consisted of a few clothes, a hundred and forty volumes of the *Classici* and a number of Bodonians; and, the river crossed, my feet were treading once more the stones of this blessed city to me so dear. The first breaths of air I drew were sufficient to freshen my spirits, recall a thousand tender memories, and create in me a consoling hope of better things. That is why I promised my friendly reader a different scene from those proffered in the earlier volumes of these Memoirs; and I shall be more grieved than he, if I should be disappointed in that hope, and not succeed in fulfilling my promise. True it is, that the good and evil that have come to me, since I left Pennsylvania, have been so intermingled, that it is no easy matter for me to decide on which side of the scales, as I weigh the one against the other, the balance would fall. Of this the judge must be my reader, whom, if Heaven vouchsafe me enough of life, I shall guide, step by step, now amidst roses and

violets, now amidst thorns and nettles, along all those paths
that have been traversed by me in the course of these varied
ten years.

Let us enjoy, for the moment, its auspicious beginning!

My limited means had not permitted me to bring my family
with me. One of my sons was my only companion—a youth of
rare talents, who from tenderest age gave promise of being in
time the pride of his family and the glory and support of my
old age. A desire to remove him from Philadelphia was not the
least of the incentives which determined my return to New
York. This son of mine was, even then, well advanced in the
study of the modern languages. Italian and French he wrote
and spoke correctly, and in his native language had few equals.
He had made a beginning also in Greek and Latin; but on turning to law he abandoned these entirely. Though his progress
under that eminent attorney[1] had been almost unbelievable,
dissipations among the young men of the city alarmed me to
such extent that I thought it dangerous to leave him longer
there without a father's guardianship. On arriving in New
York, therefore, I repaired at once to a tavern, and my first care
was to find him an able tutor in the ancient languages, which
he had neglected and in which he was obliged to be proficient
in order to be admitted to college—study in a college was a
necessary prerequisite to legal practice in the Forum. On the
18th of April, 1819, I entered my son in the academy of an experienced teacher; and the latter, enamored, as he said, of the
boy's rare talents, took such care of him that his progress in six

---

1. Da P., who was never a good proofreader, had probably mentioned and then canceled the lawyer's name in writing the story of Mussi. Charles Jared Ingersoll
(1782–1862), son of an even more famous jurist, Jared Ingersoll, was an outstanding figure in literary circles in Philadelphia, through his connections with Dennie,
and the "Portfolio." That magazine and its "cénacle" accepted Da P., though with
a certain wariness (see my monograph). Joseph studied with Ingersoll in 1818, and
returned to that law office again in the summer of 1820.

months only was unprecedented. I was more fortunate in my choice than my father had been with his rustic pedagogue, of whose callused knuckles I still bear vestiges imprinted on my snowy brow.

Having attended to that, I went to pay my first call on Mr. Charles Clement Moore, as the person who held (and he will always hold) the first place among my pupils and benefactors; and thence, my second, on his revered cousin, Nathaniel Moore, and on all the different members of their worthy families.

Their gracious welcomes responded fully to well-founded expectations on my part; but their activities in my behalf far surpassed anything I could have hoped for. In less than a week I had twelve of the most alert young men and ladies of the city to instruct in the "sweet tongue," among them, two very talented sisters from the family of my patrons,[2] who are and always will be among the most graceful flowers of my Tuscan garden. In response to their solicitations and even more to their example, many other persons in the city came to augment the number of learners from day to day, so that, in less than a month, I had twelve young ladies and as many young men under my instruction. It was not now difficult for me to dispose of the volumes I had brought from Philadelphia, eighty of which I had the joy of distributing among the more advanced of my pupils, who, with praiseworthy emulation and equal delight, read and studied them; and the sixty that still remained, they donated as gifts, at my suggestion, to the public library of the city, which, rich in Greek and Latin treasures, had not yet given place on its shelves to those of the glorious first-born of those ancients. As a sign of my gratitude, and in

---

2. One of these sisters is now the wife of Mr. L. de Rham. On the publication of this volume they will both be in Italy. I beseech all those who have the good fortune to meet them, not to neglect to honor and fête them as two luminous pillars of the Italian language in America. —L. Da P.

order not to be inferior to the others, I, too, deposited at the same time, fourteen little Bodonian editions of our most celebrated living poets, among which the immortal poems of Parini, Mazza, Cesarotti, Foscolo, Monti, and Pindemonte, besides a life of that illustrious typographer who, *te iudice Bonaparte,*[3] brought the palm in printing to Italy.

This was the first time that the city of New York had seen in one of its public libraries sixty volumes of our ancient classics and fourteen of our moderns; and this was the first stone laid by me in the foundations of that literary edifice, which, from the beginning of my career, I had had the lively desire and even some hope (perhaps vain, alas) of erecting.

In virtue of all this prosperity I soon found myself in a position to rent a little house,[4] furnish it with simple but decent furniture, call the rest of my family to New York and bear the considerable expense of their respectable maintenance and the

3. Read the history of the *Pater Noster*, printed by Didot and Bodoni in more than sixty languages, in the "Vita" of the former, volume two. —L. Da P.

4. Da P.'s numerous residences in New York were studied by Krehbiel, but without due caution, K. taking Da P.'s frequent movings as a sign of the instability of his fortunes. As a matter of fact, many of Da P.'s New York addresses were those of his classroom, which he moved about to accommodate his pupils. He would sometimes move, also, to the site most convenient for boarders at home, especially for a new boarder—thus he lured Gulian Verplanck. Krehbiel also included addresses of Lorenzo L. Da Ponte. During his first residence in New York, Da P. lived at 29 Partition St. (1807); then somewhere on the Bowery (1808–9), and finally at 247 Duane St. (1810–11). His first "little house," on returning, was at 54 Chapel St. (1819–20) with a classroom, probably, at 17 Jay St. The boarding house was probably at 343 Greenwich. The residence at 342 Broadway was quite pretentious as well as permanent (1829–36). In 1836 Da P. was living with Lorenzo L. and Cornelia at 35 Dey St., removing with them to 91 Spring St. (cor. of Broadway) just before his death. Da P.'s "poverty" has always to be understood in a relative sense. He kept a horse always, and two servants. At Sunbury his employees numbered at least four. In the days of his more strident complaint he was spending close to $3000 a year.

education of my two other sons. Both of these I at once entrusted to one of the most able tutors, and on the first day of October in that same year I entered my eldest son in the college in the city, which was on the point of reopening.[5] In the customary tests of the students this son of mine gave such proofs of admirable memory and intelligence that the examiners assigned him third place in his numerous class. Most encouraging, therefore, in this respect as well, was the beginning of my new course in life; and I blessed the moment when I had left Pennsylvania to return to New York.

Amid all these good prospects there still remained one obstacle to the rapid propagation of our language and literature which was the primary concern of my thoughts. For all of the eagerness, and, I might almost say, enthusiasm, which I had created six years before for our language in New York, it had never entered the heads of any of our fellow Italians to bring or send a collection of selected Italian works to their antipodes. At all times there had been, as there still are, enterprising spirits in Italy who sent, or still send, to the principal cities of America (as well as to other parts of the world) produce, manufactures, and goods of every sort. In almost every city one finds the wines and the grapes of Sicily, the oil, the olives, and the silks of Florence, the marble of Carrara, the gold chains of Venice, the cheese of Parma, the straw hats of Leghorn, the ropes of Rome and Padua, the *rosolio* of Trieste, the sausages of Bologna, and even the *maccheroni* of Naples and the plaster figurettes of Lucca. Yet, to the shame of our country, there is not, in the whole of America, a bookstore kept by an Italian! All the books in this city, aside from the volumes I introduced myself, have either been brought casually by travelers, or been sold at auction with other books on the death of some foreign inhabitant.

---

5. Joseph entered Columbia in the fall of 1819 with the Class of 1823, withdrawing at the end of his Freshman year to go to Philadelphia.

In such a dearth of elementary, as well as of classical works, how could I hope to teach my language to the country, and to undeceive those Americans who (stuffed with the oracles of Boileau, La Harpe, Bouhours, Johnson, Chesterfield, and those other tender friends of ours in Germany, England, and France) were either counting our writers on their fingers, or positively believing that the whole of Italian literature embraced a few spicy tales or a few light poems? On my return to New York, there was, to be sure, a store for French and Spanish books to which the proprietor had added a number of Italian volumes; but whether because he was the only dealer in the city, or had to get his books from France, his prices were so high at that time that the student frequently abandoned study in fright at the excessive expense.

I thought, therefore, that I would try to find a remedy for the difficulty, and without longer delay, wrote to a number of publishers and booksellers in Genoa, Venice, Florence, Leghorn, and other cities of Italy, informing them of my success, my plans, and future hopes; urging them to supply me with the books I needed, and making solemn promise of scrupulous payment. My first order amounted to only a hundred dollars; nevertheless—*piangendo scrivo, e tu piangendo leggi, nel bel paese là dove il sì suona*—I did not find a single bookseller with enough trustfulness not to answer with a most solemn "no." Those generous countrymen of mine were delighted to hear that "the excellent Signor Da Ponte was making such zealous efforts to introduce and spread Italian language and literature in America. A grateful posterity could be relied on to record his deserving name in the literary annals of the beautiful fatherland; but, as for sending him books without payment in advance, in truth such a thing was not to be thought of, as contrary to sound business practice, and the customs of exchange, and the cause most often of disagreements and disputes. Let the excellent Signor Da Ponte send his money to some banker, and he would immediately receive whatever he should be pleased to order."

In my scrapbook of curiosities, I have not less than ten letters to this purport.

At this juncture, I happened one day to be passing the door of a bookstore belonging to an American. He was just opening a large case on his doorstep. He spied me, and called:

"Look, Mr. Da Ponte! Here is something that will interest you!"

He opened the case and I could see that it was full of beautiful Greek, Latin, and German books, along with a small number in Italian. I did not have a very high regard for the purse of that bookseller (it will be seen why) and remarked:

"How do you manage to buy so many books, seeing that in a year's time, you have not been able to pay me the five dollars you owe me?"

"My dear Mr. Da Ponte," he replied, "I do not need money, nor do any of my competitors need money, to get books for a store."

"That," I said, "is a secret I should be delighted to learn."

"Secret? Secret?" he cried laughing. "There's not a merchant, big or little, male or female who doesn't know that secret! Not only our bookstores! Almost all the trading done in this town rests on credit from foreign merchants. What would become of business if there were no reciprocal confidence and one had to buy everything for cash? Counting duties and transportation, this case of books is worth not less than six hundred dollars, and not less than six thousand the stock you see in my shop. How could I do business without the proper breathing spaces in payments? And how could they keep on, with books or other goods in stock amounting to thirty, forty, fifty thousand, in value?"

"And how did you start in the first place?"

"I published a general advertisement in a number of European newspapers. It said just this: 'X.Y., bookseller and stationer in New York, books in all languages ancient and modern on his own behalf and on commission.' In less than six months I received from Leipzig, Hamburg, Paris, London, and many other places not only stationery and books, but prints, paintings, marbles, bronzes, not to speak of swords, guns, pistols, and the hundred other things I keep in this store."

"And when do you pay for those you sell?"

"When those who buy pay me."

"Why then," I asked, "do you not have books come from places in Italy?"

"*Pardon, Mr. Da Ponte! The Italian booksellers are not very liberal.*"

That shot was like a blow from Bronte's hammer on the nape of my bald neck, and I departed, like a whipped dog, my tail between my legs.

As I walked along, I could feel all the things that he had said fermenting in my brain. Eager as I was to find some way of furthering acquaintances with our writers, I determined to test my credit in foreign countries since I was held in so little esteem in my own. A friend of mine was leaving for Paris in just those days. I gave him a letter for Messrs. Bossange, publishers and booksellers renowned in that metropolis. In that letter I asked them bluntly for a certain number of classics, which I found listed in their catalogues. We shall see in due time what their answer was.

In this manner I passed my first year and almost half of my second, without anything supervening either to disturb my tranquillity or to alter the prosperity of my family. Passing clouds drifted over my head from time to time, impelled by blasts of malice, envy, and ingratitude from countrymen of mine, who, strange as it may seem, hated me with a deadly hatred.

To understand this situation, it must be explained that in the course of the seven years I had been living in Sunbury, Philadelphia, and other parts of Pennsylvania, a swarm of exiles had appeared in New York, who, without profession or means and, to their misfortune, without talents, exchanged their bayonets and muskets for dictionaries and grammars and turned to teaching languages. Hunger, verily, as the poet said is a *monstrum horrendum, informe, ingens,* driving the starving pauper to do or say everything. All those who made pretense of teaching Italian, viewing themselves and me in the mirror of vanity, thought it very strange that I should be having large numbers of pupils, while they were having very few and often none. They therefore became relentless enemies of mine, and endeavored in every way to do me harm. For some time their gossip and chatter worried me; but then, shortly perceiving that they had no teeth to bite with, I paid no more attention to their noise than does a rolling coach to barking dogs, not slackening its speed because they come running after it in the dust and mud.

Let us not allow their yelping to interrupt the thread of my story, and go back to the month of July in the year 1820.

At that time my eldest son was to give evidence in a public exercise of the progress he had made in the college session in ten months. His rare talents, attended by an excellent memory and an unparalleled love for study, left me no room for doubting that he would issue from that test with great glory. In the warmth of that hope, I entered his room one morning to encourage him. The boy was sitting near the door, plunged, it seemed, in deepest despondency. He leapt to his feet when I entered and without speaking handed me a letter he had folded. Terrified at the expression on his face, I hurriedly unfolded the letter and read these words:

> My dearest father:
>
> Since we returned to New York, I have been wasting my time as you must have seen. I have studied unceasingly day and night, and I believe I have profited as much

> as any other student in everything I have studied in that
> college in which I myself asked you to place me. I fore-
> see, however, that all my efforts will be vain and that I
> should never reach that grade of honor which is always
> the strongest stimulus to incite young men to study.
> Permit me to return to Mr. Ingersoll. I shall not obtain
> my degree in New York under two years. One year will
> be enough in Philadelphia.

The sound of the last word made me tremble. Joseph (that
was my son's name) read my thought in my eyes and begged
me to finish reading his letter. It ended thus:

> The reasons why you brought me away from Phila-
> delphia are not unknown to me. Have no fears on that
> account, my dear father. I know what I owe to you, to
> my family, to myself. If I desire to return to that city, it
> is in order to save you and give you joy, not to cause you
> despair and in the end kill you.

These words were so potent upon me that I did not find
courage to refuse him the favor he was asking, and which was
afterwards to cost me so many tears and so much pain.

"Well," I said, "if that is your wish, and if Mr. Ingersoll con-
sents to take you back . . ."

He did not let me finish, but handed me a letter from Mr.
Ingersoll, to whom the boy had already written. I found that
that eminent lawyer was delighted to have him back as an apprentice in his office; and, as evidence of his pleasure, was entrusting to him the tutoring of his own sons. Joseph then
confided the true causes of his sudden resolve. It would serve
no purpose to repeat them here. I will say simply that they
seemed to me very natural in a boy so avid of glory.

Toward the end of July, he left for Philadelphia, and I went to Staatsbourg, where I passed two blissful months at the homes of the Livingstons in company with the Muses, the Graces, and the delights of hospitality and friendship. I returned to New York early in September and that month, too, was full of happiness for me.

Among a chosen number of the new pupils who vied with each other in asking for my lessons, Fortune brought me a lady who was and is without doubt the brightest jewel in my Tuscan crown—so I call, as I shall always call, my New York pupils. Aside from the great delight I experienced in instructing her, in view of the smoothness of her pronunciation, the rapidity of her progress, and her ardent love for our writers, I had, in addition, the joy of occupying a distinguished place among her dearer friends, a place from which neither my misfortunes nor the slanders, hypocrisy, and envy, of a hundred enemies have ever been, or will ever be, able to dislodge me. A loving daughter of adorable parents, a tender sister, a solicitous wife, a fond mother, she found a way, in all those positions, to hold some portion of her affection for the one who taught her the language which was, and is, her sweetest pleasure. Ten years have passed since the fortunate moment of our first acquaintance; and whereas, generally, affections are wont to grow cold with the passing years, in this rare matron they seem to have warmed from day to day. Unimaginable the number and variety of ways in which she exerts herself to give me ever new proofs of her courteous regard. She consoles me in my afflictions, rejoices in my joys, visits me in my infirmities, defends me from my traducers, exalts me before her friends, and whatever issues from my pen or from my lips, is to her the sweetest of nectars, the most fragrant of flowers. She has, moreover, an art, a delicacy, in making her dear gifts (and she delights in making them often) that renders it difficult to say whether more precious be the gift, or the graciousness with which she proffers it. Such the portrait of that most beautiful, amiable, and virtuous lady, Mistress Frances Leight, now Cottenet! New York did not need to hear the title to recognize the portrait; yet I could not but adorn these pages with her to me most dear of names; for, if ever it come to pass (and my hope is that it will come to pass) that she should travel one day in Italy, may all good people find ways to do her the honor she deserves, and recognize in her one of our staunchest pillars of literature in the most illustrious city of America. And may they know that her example has more availed me in spreading our language in this city than all my arguments and all my efforts and those of hundreds and hundreds of other students. In those days she was the true model of a well-bred lady. It was a most natural thing that all others should wish to do what she was doing. It was through this, as it were, prestige of hers that, between the beginning of October and the beginning of December, not less than fifteen young ladies chose to learn Italian of Signor Da Ponte, because it was of Signor Da Ponte that Mistress Leight was learning it.[6]

This general partiality inordinately increased the numbers of my persecutors and one among these essayed the most infamous of means to ruin me. I told the story of that episode in the first volume of the first edition of these Memoirs, and I shall recount it again here in a note, should anyone care to go to the trouble of reading it.[7] There is really nothing beautiful or entertaining about it. I imagine nevertheless that it might serve for instruction, if not for pleasure. However, all the intrigues of that cannibal, as well as of my many other adver-

---

6. Mrs. Frances Leight-Cottenet's album of poems written by Da P. was discovered by Carlo Leonardo Speranza and published by March., 412–460. —A. L.

7. In the first ed. of the *Mem.*, Da P. devoted some ten thousand words to a polemic with an Italian teacher, named Marc Antonio Casati. In the "History of Ital. Lit. in N. Y." he attacks Ferrari, Aloisi, and others; in the "Story Incredible but True," Strozzi and Sega. —A. L.

saries of the same kind, redounded in the end to my advantage or honor.

In those days the whole political world, along with the English capital, was in excitement anent the famous controversy then existing between Caroline of Brunswick and her royal consort; and on that occasion an Irish lawyer of notorious reputation[8] was minded to publish a certain letter addressed to that king, the principal purpose of which was to blacken, calumniate, and debase the name and character of the Italian nation. His diatribe appeared in the public prints with all the usual sarcastic remarks of newspaper editors in Ireland, England, and America. As the oldest Italian resident in this city, I thought myself called upon to take up arms in defense of the country whose language I had disseminated with happy success, and whose literature I had exalted. My patriotic zeal, my love of truth, found their contentment in my writing and delivering before a numerous gathering of intelligent auditors, an oration which repelled the man's slanders and lies, but I also published it that same day in the press, and, to make it available to everyone, had it translated into English. The effects of this discourse were as satisfactory to me as possible. I shall speak here of one of them only, since it gave birth to a new institute of mine and opened to me a wide portal for providing the city of New York at last with Italian books.[9]

---

8. Charles Philipps, 1783–1839, member of the City Council. Da P. published P.'s article with his reply: "Apologetical Discourse on Italy" in answer to a letter by C. P., N. Y., 1821. Da P. delivered his oration in the "Lecture Room" on Barclay St. before "one of the most numerous assemblages of wit and fashion which ever graced an apartment in this city." Odell, *Annals of N. Y. Stage*, II, 602–3, quoting the *Columbian.* —A. L.

9. This new "institute" was "Ann Da Ponte's Boarding House." After Mrs. Da Ponte's death, it seems to have been conducted by Cornelia Durant–Da Ponte, wife of Lorenzo L. It was still flourishing at 208 Greenwich St. in 1840.

Just one day after the delivery and publication of my speech, a young American[10] came to my house and asked for instruction in our language. In the course of three lessons only I had leisure to note his marvelous keenness of wit, his vast learning, and the soundness of his judgment. He had completed the usual college studies and was a good Greek and Latin scholar. But his favorite pursuit was mathematics, wherein he was very well versed even then, though to please his people, perhaps, he was still studying medicine. The young man's family living several miles from New York, he said to me one day in conversation that he was eager to find lodgings in the city, nearer the medical college and its professors. Prompted as it were by an inspiration from Above, I straightway offered him my house; and on the first of May in the year 1821 he came to stay with me, bringing with him his two most amiable brothers, the which was the occasion of the coming of three other cultivated young men who showed themselves desirous of following the example of the others.

In this manner was my home boarding school founded. In it now five, now six, intelligent young men lived with me, more as my sons and friends than as my pupils, to be instructed in our language and letters. They would leave my

---

10. Henry James Anderson (1799–1875), professor of mathematics at Columbia, and a distinguished astronomer. He married Fanny on Aug. 3, 1831, thus associating Da P. posthumously, in his descendants in this line, with the distinction and the wealth he aspired to so arduously himself. Fanny's children by this marriage: Henry C. Anderson, July 11, 1832–Aug. 12, 1839; Elbert Ellery, Oct. 31, 1833–Feb. 24, 1903; Fannie, Jan. 5, 1836–Aug. 31, 1842; Arthur E., Oct. 5, 1838–Dec. 18, 1838; Edward H., April 5, 1840–1886; Walden A., 1842–Aug., 1843. Walden died at sea and Fanny herself was not to return from that voyage. She died in Paris, Jan. 1, 1844. The Da Ponte line descends from this marriage in two branches, that of the celebrated Elbert Ellery Anderson, and the hardly less distinguished, Edward H. Anderson.

house after one, two, or several years, to devote themselves to the activities or professions which they had chosen to embrace. The one who never changed houses was that splendid youth, who was the first to come, and whom I will now name to his, but even more to my own, glory, though everyone knows him to be Mr. Henry Anderson, a man of letters of greatest promise to his enlightened country. He dwelt two years with me as a medical student, one year, or a little more, as a physician. He has now been with me for six months past as professor of mathematics in the noble college of Columbia, to which post "in callow youth wisdom mature" advanced him with the universal approbation and applause of the city and of the nation. I believe he will leave my house only to pay a visit to my country; and may it please Heaven that this may take place before I leave this Earth; because I yearn to hear from his lips what I have heard from so many others of my dear pupils: that "the most beautiful country in the world is Italy."

I was, as may be believed, at the peak of happiness when the bitterest of human disasters plunged my family into despair and tears. Six months had passed since my son's return to Philadelphia. I had had none but good news of him, and no reason to suspect that those who wrote of him to me were all in league to deceive me. Imagine then my stupefaction and my affliction, when toward the end of the month of December I suddenly saw him appear at home, so emaciated, so pallid, so wasted, that to see him and judge him lost were matters of the same instant! To spare mortal anguish to a father's heart I shall not recount the causes and the beginning of this terrible event. I shall say simply that, after another six months of a strange and painful illness, which the most experienced physicians either could not identify, or found greater than their skill, this dear son of mine was taken from me before he had completed

407

his twenty-first year.[11] Aside from the heart-rending grief this incomparable loss brought upon me, so bitter, strange, and overpowering were the consequences of his death for me, that I saw myself hurled in one moment from the apices of happiness into the depths of most desperate misery. A thousand thousand cruel circumstances united to torment me and make me loathe my very existence; and, as a culmination of evils, these were of a nature so delicate and at the same time so extraordinary, that they deprived, and still deprive, me of that inadequate solace of the sympathy of others which I should surely wring from pitiful hearts, were I permitted to speak of them. Perhaps from my tomb one day may rise the cries of that anguish which certain social obligations permit me in my lifetime to utter only in silence.

To so many calamities was added an extreme and almost irremediable scarcity of funds; for, in addition to the great expenses incident to the sustenance of a numerous family with doubled servants, doubled physicians, costly medicines and a funeral, this son of mine had left quantities of debts unknown to me, the greater part of which honor compelled me to pay, though the testamentary dispositions of a vindictive woman cut me off from the boy's inheritance of several hundreds of dollars ... But let me entrust this new demonstration of human perfidy to the faithful words of the sepulcher. They may then serve as a lesson to others, though they could not serve as a comfort to me now.

In such a state of things my despair may be more easily conceived than described. While I was in my greatest affliction of spirit, one of my tender pupils, who were all seeking every

---

11. Joseph was buried in St. Paul's Churchyard, June 19, 1821, aged 20 years, 8 months ("consumption"). By Louisa Niccolini's testament, Joseph's little inheritance of $600 went in lots of $150 to the principals of Louisa, Fanny, Lorenzo, and Charles. The story of Joseph's debts was probably written for the benefit of Robert Coleman Hall, after letters in the same sense had failed of effect.

means to console me, gave me the *Prophecy of Dante* written by Byron, hoping to distract me from my sorrow through a reading of that sublime poem. He was not mistaken. The sweet melancholy—I am repeating here the words I wrote to that supreme poet,[12]—which pervades that poem from its first pages, did not, to be sure, alleviate my sadness, nay it seemed rather to nourish and augment it; but such nourishment had within itself, "I know not what of gentle tenderness," so that I not so much read, as devoured, all four cantos, without once putting aside the book from my hands. A certain analogy, making the due allowances, which I seemed to find between Dante's experiences and mine, inspired me with a will to translate that work into Italian verse, and I straightway applied myself to the task. But to escape a spot that reminded me at every instant of the causes of my grief, I suggested to my student-guests withdrawing with them to some country place, and they willingly consented. The constant companionship of those kindly young men was of the greatest solace to me. In their love and attentions I seemed to get back again a little of the much whereof Death had robbed me. The place, furthermore, chosen by me on that occasion as a refuge of peace, contributed greatly both to the alleviation of my broken heart and to the rousing of a sorrowful inspiration in harmony with my present state and the character of the poetry I was covering with Italian vestments of sorrowful hue.

This retreat of ours was situated on a country estate belonging to the illustrious and honorable family of the Livingstons. The town so delightful in itself, with its richly cultivated fields and environs and the noble stream that girt it, seemed to receive added beauty, new light, and new qualities from the sister Graces who adorned it.

---

12. See letter written by me to Lord Byron published in front of that translation. —L. Da P.

My life in that, as it were, miniature Eden was as follows. I rose from bed in the morning at sunrise and spent an hour reading some Italian prose writer or poet, now with my pupils and now with my children. I made my rural breakfast in their company, and a half hour afterwards, I would find some spot, now under a peach, now under an apple tree, and still weeping, translate a portion of that poem which would ever add a touch of sweetness to my tears. When my inspiration would seem to weary, I would hurry to the dwelling of those three incomparable damsels to have it brought to life again; and they, with grateful welcome written on their angelic faces, and with their divine enthusiasm for our authors, would cause me to forget my anguish and pass blissful moments in the bosom of their hospitality, and in the ineffable pleasure of instructing them. A little less than two months I passed in this sort of life: and though my painful wounds were not healed thereby, I nevertheless obtained the strength and the courage to endure them. Returning to New York, I applied myself without further delay to the problem of educating my two other sons. They had now finished their preparatory studies in the usual schools for boys, and were come of age to choose professions for themselves. The elder seemed inclined toward that of Justinian; the other, to that of Hippocrates.[13] I had the good fortune to obtain

---

13. Lorenzo L. Da Ponte (1804?–1840) did open a law office at 7 Pine St., in 1823. However, he followed in his father's footsteps as a teacher of Italian and of the classics, becoming professor of Italian first at Maryland University (obituary notice) and later at New York University (1832–1836). In the intervals of these appointments he was a private teacher of Italian. He left voluminous writings: a constitution of the text of Æschylus; a revision of Lamprière's Antiquities; a history of Florence under the Medicis; and the American translations of his father's librettos (often attributed to Da P. himself). That genius which his father had in Latin, Lorenzo L. had in Greek. He was a slow-moving, absent-minded fellow, greatly beloved for his droll ways and words by Dr. Anderson, and, strangely enough, by General Daniel Sickles, afterwards a lifelong friend of Durant Da

for them the patrons most eminent in those two professions; and, since my means in those days were very much reduced, I arranged an exchange of lessons with incredible ease. I accordingly began lessons in Italian with the children of those professors, and they instructed mine in their respective pursuits.

By that time I received a letter from Florence, informing me that my *Orazione apologetica*, as well as my translation of the *Prophecy of Dante*, had reached that city, and that both of them had been graciously admired and praised by cultured Tuscans, not only for the things I said, but for the utter purity of my style. It was Signor Giacomo Ombrosi, who knowing me only by name, wrote that letter to me. As a man of great culture, and vice-consul, at that time, of this Republic, he was probably delighted to see that there lived in America an Italian ready to defend his beautiful country; and though I might have assumed that the greater part of his praises arose from that consideration alone, his words nevertheless gave me courage to beg a favor of him. I straightway

---

Ponte. Lorenzo L. married Cornelia Durant of Philadelphia, at Christ Church in that city, June 12, 1826. The Durants were Presbyterians. Cornelia was a niece of President Monroe's wife. Cornelia removed to New Orleans after her husband's death in 1840. Their children: Lorenzo Da P. III, Oct. 1827–Oct. 9, 1836; John Durant V. (Victor? Vincent?), Feb. 10, 1829–1894 (this is the celebrated Durant Da P.); Angelo Grahl, April, 1836–Nov. 1, 1837; Algernon Sydney, 1839–July 6, 1840. The Da Pontes of New Orleans descend from Lorenzo L. through Durant.

Charles Grahl Da Ponte (1806?) opened a physician's office at 108 Lawrence St. in 1828. Later he was his father's partner in the book store at 342 Broadway. He was in New Orleans (with Cornelia's father) in 1831. I find him at Easton, Pa. in the fall of that year, whence he sent his father the translation of the preface to the "Sonnets to Ann." He was again with, or in touch with, his father in 1833, when he translated the "Story Incredible but True." He is mentioned in his father's administration papers as living in 1838. But he had already vanished completely from the Da P. circle, in consequence of what differences one cannot even conjecture. A letter to Fanny on Lorenzo's death in 1840 describes Lorenzo as "your almost only brother." There is no trace of Charles in New Orleans. He may have gone West.

411

urged him to have a bookseller in that city send me a certain number of Italian books which I needed at that time; and since I was certain I could not obtain them without paying for them in cash, I did not hesitate to deprive myself of many objects necessary to the decorum of my family to assemble the hundred dollars more or less which would nearly cover the costs of those books. It was Mr. G. F. Darby,[14] a rare and true credit to the Italian name in America, by virtue of a universal esteem and of his well-known traits of a kindly heart and a courteous manner, who took it upon himself to have the sum delivered for me through his respected house in Leghorn. And, for almost ten years thereafter, without the slightest interest and for the sole delight of helping me, Mr. Darby continued, as he still continues, to support me admirably in all my activities. The books were sent back to me by the very vessel which had carried my letter and the money, and almost at the same time came the other books which I had ordered from Messrs. Bossange in Paris—they, to my great delight, showed themselves most courteous and trusting. Mallet, their agent in this city, received an order to deliver the books to me "to be paid for at my convenience," with a most gracious letter, in which they offered me on very favorable terms everything that was at that time listed in their catalogues. But neither the reduction of the Florentine bookseller, nor those of Messrs. Bossange, were adequate for my plans, which, to tell the truth, I would have renounced entirely, had not Messrs. Fusi and Stella, publishers and booksellers in Milan, of their own accord made certain very fair offers and proposals to me, which I was most happy to accept, and which they maintained with the greatest exactitude over a period of more than eight years.

---

14. A splendid young man, who unfortunately fell from a horse, and was killed. —L. Da P.

Now when I could see in my house a thousand volumes of selected classics, I decided, in order to give Americans some idea of our treasures, to publish a *Catalogo ragionato*, which I had made up several years before for the use of my children. At that time I had not had available either Tiraboschi, or Andrés, or any other historian of our literature; and the village in which I wrote that survey had never had the honor of seeing even the binding of an Italian book. I could not hope, therefore, let alone expect, not to fall into an error here and there, both in matters of judgment and in dates, which I drew entirely from memory, according as my opinions and preferences dictated. I dare believe, nevertheless, that despite such mistakes, both my *Catalogo* and my remarks contributed much to a knowledge of our authors and the diffusion of their works in this part of the world; and I had the joy some time since to learn that several booksellers and collectors of public libraries had used it in importing from Italy gems of our literature which had previously been altogether unknown in this vast America. Nor do I choose to overlook another great good that I learned had derived from that *Catalogo*. It chanced, through an Italian, to reach the City of Mexico, and was the cause, I dare say for the first time, of transporting into those regions a few beams of our literary splendor. The Italian in question was Signor Rivafinoli[15] of Milan, a man widely known for his great enterprises and for his travels. Passing through New York in the year 1824, and happening to see my *Catalogo*, he came at once to my house, bought many fine books, and took them with him to Mexico. He afterwards persuaded others to bring books with them, and they inspired many Mexicans to learn our language and study our writers. I myself had the pleasure of giving lessons to many Mexicans and of sending many Italian books

15. After the period of the *Mem.*, Rivafinoli was associated with Da P. in launching the latter's Italian Opera House in New York (1834). Russo, 132.

to that city, among others the works of Machiavelli, Beccaria, Filangieri, and Gioia.

During a full half of the year 1823, nothing happened to me deserving of record in these Memoirs. Fortune seemed to have struck a truce with me, and my displeasures all arose either from remembrance of ills past or from seeing myself hated without reason by my unjust compatriots. For that matter my affairs in every respect were improving from day to day. The numbers of my pupils both at home and in the city were continually increasing; my health was excellent and so was that of all my family. The bookcases of my pupils were being gloriously filled with our most celebrated classics.

But I must here narrate a trifling incident that happened to me at this time, which, insignificant though it be, will amuse my reader and show more clearly how strangely bitter was the war which my troublesome persecutors were waging against me at all hazards.

One day, toward the end of December, I drove up to my house in my usual wagon. It was a very cold day. I leapt out in great haste and ran inside to get warm. Coming out again shortly to finish my rounds, I found that horse and carriage had disappeared, nor, for all my inquiries and offered rewards, did I get any trace of them for some two weeks. Then a French gentleman (the late M. Bancel of fond remembrance) had the kindness to send me an advertisement he had seen in the newspapers, through which I found my horse and carriage and recovered them on payment of twelve dollars to a stableman, with whom a suspicious looking individual had left them after using them for his own amusement for half a day.

What embroidery would you suppose, kind reader, that one of my cowardly enemies stitched to this innocent little plot? "Da Ponte," said he, "was short of money. He pretended he had been robbed of that outfit to excite the compassion of his pupils with that pathetic recital, and they rewarded the fine impostor with the magnificent gift of six hundred dollars: which pocketed, the stolen carriage reappeared. That was the way that shrewd old rascal cheated Americans worth the fleecing over a long period of years."

An epiphonema most worthy of the lips of a man I will not identify here, that my pages be not soiled with his detestable name! To hear the story of the things I had to put up with here in America on the part of a band of rascally exiles would make one's hair stand on end—men who made their way into my compassionate heart with the usual weapons of the hypocrite and the fawner and then ended their jest in the cry: "Death to him! Death to him!" spitting in my face the blood they had sucked with cunning from my veins!

The recital of such things, however, containing nothing "gay or beautiful" as was wisely remarked, I shall not, in order not to weary my reader, speak of them at all in these Memoirs; or, at least, I shall speak of them only when ignorance of the facts and the power of calumny strengthened by my silence might cast equivocal shadow upon the light of truth or the purity of my honor, *quem nemini dabo.*

I shall speak, instead, as much for my own satisfaction as for that of my readers, of the few good, faithful, and honest friends, who with their constant benevolence and cordiality are consoling my advancing years, repaying me abundantly for all the hurts and wrongs inflicted on me by my unjust persecutors, and restoring my love for mankind. A prominent place among these, next after my older friends, I would bestow on a young Florentine who was introduced to me by merest chance by one of my neighbors. I liked his pleasing address, his agreeable manners, the unequivocal signs he gave of a cultivated and polished mind, and especially with the sweetness of the speech on his Florentine lips. I ventured to ask him to stay with me for a few days, hoping to banish, or at least to soften, in his sweet companionship the anguish into which my family had been plunged in those days through the untimely death of her who was its most graceful ornament, and whom I abstain from naming in order not to renew the unspeakable grief of her people.[16] I shall name, instead, for my own solace and the comfort of others, the gentle spirit whose name I have so far withheld and whom my curious reader already desires to know.

He was Doctor Giuseppe Gherardi, brother to that excellent Signor Donato, who for a number of years taught his beautiful Tuscan accent and the purity of his native speech at Cambridge and at Boston, just as he is now teaching it at Northampton; and the honor of whose friendship increased my desire to offer hospitality to his brother on the latter's travels. After several refusals, natural, in truth, to the delicacy of a well-bred spirit, he gracefully yielded to my insistent prayers. He lived with me for the short time he was able to linger in this city, and our lively and learned converse not only shed a consoling balm upon us all, but caused us fresh, though sweet, tears at the moment of his departure. Neither time nor distance, nor the irresponsible chatter of a person it would pain me to name, have served to diminish, and still less extinguish, his esteem for me, his sincere good will, and his continual desire to make me happy, which he has shown me for many years and still continues to show me, now with most charming letters and ready help, and now with his very dear gifts. Any who know the temper of my heart will easily understand to what extent, from my very experience of the bites of ingratitude and envy, I must flush with gratitude and affection at the evidences and services of a friendship so rare. Yet, among those services there

16. Antoinette Louisa Caroline Da Ponte Clossey, born in London, 1793-4, married Miles Franklin Clossey, Nov. 15, 1809, buried, New York, St. John's Churchyard, July 26, 1823 ("consumption"). Mother of Matilda Ann, of whom, below; and of Franklin Clossey, born Sept. 14, 1821; died, Feb. 19, 1822 ("anemia"). Louisa's line became extinct in Matilda.

was one so remarkable that I cannot be satisfied with mere reference to it, but must relate it in detail with the liveliest sentiments of joy and thankfulness.

I have never considered (and of this be God my witness) that whether for my talents, or much less for any writings of mine, I was entitled to any distinguished place among the brilliant geniuses of my country; and if at times my overarrogant vanity seemed disposed to murmur or feel resentment at never seeing the name of Lorenzo Da Ponte mentioned in the European press among the writers of our time, I would drag it straightway to my bookstore, and read to it now a scene from Alfieri, Manzoni, or Niccolini, now fifteen or twenty lines of the great Parini's *Giorno*, Cesarotti's *Ossian*, Foscolo's *Sepolcri*, Monti's *Bassvilliana*, or the *Canzone* of Pindemonte; and the conceited rogue would droop in shame, and for six months at least, "stow his pipes in his bag," as we say. But at one thing, nevertheless, I marveled long. "There is," I would say to myself, "not a gazetteer, journalist, or news writer, who does not too often fill his columns with trifles. 'Count So and So arrived yesterday from London bringing six horses of the King's stud.' 'So and So, a locksmith, has invented a key that will open any door in the city.' There is a three-page article in praise of the wrinkled throat of a eunuch; and another announcing the arrival of an elephant and two monkeys in such and such a place—and a hundred other things of no account. And yet for more than twenty years there never appeared a writer charitable enough to deign to color a scrap of paper black to let the literary world, and Italians especially, know the work I was doing in America! Is it possible," I said, "that no one of them in all these years has heard from the many travelers who go from America to visit Italy, or read in the many periodicals that are sent thither, of the sacrifices I have been making, the losses I have sustained, the obstacles I have overcome, the intrigues, rivalries, and vexations I have disregarded, and the fatigues to which I have exposed myself in my declining age, in the miraculous enterprise of introducing the Italian language into the vastest and most remote portion of the globe, and of making known, diffusing and establishing there our divine literature, which before my arrival was either unknown to all or despised of all—to such an extent had those who had learned everything they know from Italians, slandered and degraded us?"

Whose the courteous hand, at last, to break that ice and free my patriotic zeal from such an annoying thought? It was the same Dr. Giuseppe Gherardi, who conjointly with my old and incomparable friend Pananti, managed so to rouse in my favor the celebrated compiler of the Florentine *Antologia* (celebrated, Signor Montani undoubtedly must be called), that not only did he condescend to make honorable mention of my name in two very fine articles in his excellent journal, but said of me, of my writings, and of my glorious enterprise in America, things that I never dared hope for, and that I was, as I still am, far from believing that I deserve. After illustrating and noting with great courtesy and liberality what seemed to him worthy of some praise, he also turned, as befitted a wise and discreet critic, but with all possible urbanity and reserve, to point out my defects and my errors. Nor could I truly say whether I am more grateful to him for the praises he lavished on me or for the slight censure that accompanied them; for, if the praises filled many people with a desire to read me, the censure served to instruct me in my errors and inspire me to correct them; the which, with very good grace and taking advantage of his advice, I have tried to do, as I hope he will see if he has the gracious patience to reread these Memoirs in their second edition.

In two points, nevertheless, with all the respect due to a man of letters of such discerning judgment, I shall try, if not to justify myself, at least to attenuate my fault. "The style of the Memoirs," says my learned censor in one place, "will not perhaps altogether satisfy Colombo." I have read, reread, and studied, all the writings of my dear and precious friend Colombo; and though I consider him, along with Monti, perhaps the most charming and the most polished of all the Italian writers of our time, and the worthiest of imitation not excluding Cesari, I do not, however, think that the style of his *Cadmiti*, of his lectures, or of his pamphlets, would have rendered my Memoirs any more precious or more popular than the style I actually adopted for them. And here is my reason. I had already placed in the hands of my pupils for their apprenticeship all those celebrated works that are read by most people; but neither the selected stories of Boccaccio, nor the letters of Bentivoglio, nor *Le notti romane* of Verri, nor the *Lettere* of Foscolo, nor the *Lezioni* of Cesari, nor the *Cadmiti* of Colombo himself, were grasped by them with the facility that I should have desired, if they were to make rarer use of dictionaries, and enjoy the most rapid progress possible in the study of our language. It was then that I resolved to write these Memoirs, and deliberately chose a style that was simple, easy, natural, without affectation or flourishes, without transpositions and long sentences with the verb at the end, quite frequently preferring words in common usage and not of the Crusca to words antiquated or rarely used, even though they had passed through "the great sieve." And my decision was most fortunate. Of the seventy-five young ladies who read those little volumes, in 1825, in my three sections, few were those who could not translate them splendidly in a month's time, and there were many who, through a reading of these Memoirs alone, arrived at writing correctly and with some grace in three, or as little as two, months. In proof whereof I have republished letters of these talented young ladies, and have at least another hundred among my papers, which to my glory and theirs I intend one day to publish, may it so please Heaven! A second defect he notes in these Memoirs, justly perhaps, and that is a certain lack of connection in the narrative: "a most signal merit," says my censor, "so much admired in the Memoirs of Casanova." I must observe, however, that, though everything I have written in these volumes is the purest truth, I thought it the wise and honorable thing to say nothing of certain matters, as I protested in the epigraph appended to my first edition.[17] These omissions may have broken the thread of my story at times, and made it appear somewhat disconnected. Casanova did the opposite. He frequently omitted what he might have, and should have, said out of duty as an historian; and to fill in badly or well those lacunæ, and consolidate, so to speak, his plot, he allowed his prolific pen to invent things out of whole cloth. I do not say this to detract an iota from the merit of Giacomo Casanova or of his Memoirs, which are written with much charm and are generally read with delight. But I knew that extraordinary man as well as body ever did, and I can assure my reader that love of truth was not the principal excellence of his writings. I am glad to seize this opportunity to show this, not in hopes of excusing myself, but of undeceiving such as may think everything he wrote to be of finest gold.

Many the anecdotes that he relates which I may be permitted at least to doubt; but of one of these I must speak, since it fails to pay due honor to the memory, so revered by me, of the immortal Joseph.

Casanova boasts of having made a certain bold retort to that prince, which the latter, though a most forgiving sovereign, would most infallibly not have suffered from him.[18] The truth, therefore, of the matter is as follows.

Giacomo Casanova had a head as full of projects as his

---

17. "*Omnia non dicam, sed quae dicam omnia vera*," which Da P. turns at the end of the *Mem.*: *omnia nunc dicam*, etc.

18. The Emperor was blaming those who purchased their nobility. Casanova remarked: "How about those who sell it?"

purse was, often unfortunately, empty. He spent some time in Vienna, living in any way he could, but more particularly by means of gambling: the Abbé Della Lena and Giacometto Foscarini were, for the most part, the *lapis* philosophic, or rather the mint, that produced that fine gentleman's sequins. Finding himself at the green of his candle one day he took it into his head to suggest to the sovereign a certain Chinese *fiesta* which would provide no end of amusement for the capital and no end of money for its organizer and master of ceremonies. He wrote such a long prospectus, however, that it was enough to terrify the Emperor when he presented it to him. *Cur, quia, quomodo, quando*, was the Imperial comment thereon. This done, Casanova came to me, wished me a good day, made me sit down, shoved a pen between my fingers, and spoke as follows—a neat little dialogue:

"Da Ponte, we are friends."

"No doubt of it."

"I know your honesty! You know mine!"

(Silence.)

"I have done everything in the world, but I never cheated a friend."

(I smiled: the Abbé Della Lena and young Foscarini were great friends of Casanova's! Nevertheless . . .)

"In order to carry out my project, I need not more than a thousand piastres. Give me your note for that amount, payable in two months. I will be sure to honor it at the time due."

I laid down the pen, evaded as best I could, and rose from my chair. He flew into a rage, and, frowning, departed. I did not see him again for several days, but I learned that Foscarini had lost a large sum to him and given him a note on which he hoped to raise the funds for his Chinese *fiesta*.

One morning I was in audience with that sovereign on matters pertaining to his Opera. Our Giacomo begs admittance. He enters, bows, and presents his prospectus. The Emperor glances at it, but observing the length of it, folds it up again, and asks him what he wishes. . . . Casanova, having expounded the project, illustrating with annotations appended to the *Cur, quia, quomodo, quando* (the half line he quotes in his Memoirs), Joseph desired to know what his name was.

"Giacomo Casanova," he replied, "is the person who humbly supplicates this grace of Your Majesty."

Joseph sat silent a few seconds. Then with his usual affability he remarked that Vienna did not like such spectacles, turned away, and began writing. The petitioner did not say a word and departed in great humiliation. I started to follow him; but Joseph called me back. "Giacomo Casanova!" he exclaimed, three times. Then he resumed his talk with me about the Opera. A few days later I saw that irascible man. He was in a positive fury. Unimaginable the things he said of that sovereign; nor was I, whatever I did or said, ever able to make him change his opinion. I decided finally that it was better to let him bark, since the yelpings of a Casanova could only increase the splendor of that adorable sovereign in the eyes of those who knew them both. I thought, nevertheless, that it was my duty to speak of it here, in order to give this additional proof of my grateful veneration of the memory of my adorable lord and benefactor.

Of another crime, a very serious one, I am solemnly accused by Signor Montani. The subject is of the greatest delicacy, and I should not care, in looking for excuses, to make, as we say, the patch worse than the rent. But unable to resist a natural desire that all people have to justify themselves, I shall speak, though "with pebbles in mouth" as Byron says, that nothing but the truth may issue from my lips.

The different languages I used when I had occasion to speak of Joseph, and when of Leopold, reveal, says my critic, as great an ardor of partiality for the former as of bitterness and gall toward the latter. May those who venerate the memory of that sovereign in Tuscany, where he more especially spread the emanations of his beneficence and of his royal virtues, hear me tranquilly, and then be my judges.

I had been living ten years in Vienna, when the Emperor Leopold ascended his hereditary throne. Over all that not negligible space of time I had, as everyone knows, enjoyed the good grace of the excellent Joseph, as much in the matter of my private conduct as a citizen, as in the filling of my post. The constant favor of such a sovereign should at least have proved that I had committed no crimes, and of that I was assured both by the most vigilant of magistrates and by my own conscience. For his wisdom and clemency and for the justice of his laws, Leopold had deserved the adoration of Tuscany and that fame of his which had resounded gloriously throughout the world. In me also, as may be believed, he aroused, therefore, the tenderest and sweetest hopes, and it was with an equal liveliness of affection that I expressed both my feelings of sorrow for the death of the former and those hopes that everyone shared in the ascension of the latter to the throne. Let anyone who reproaches me examine with some care the lines I wrote on that occasion, and see whether anyone could have said anything greater or more honorable than I said at that time of that sovereign. I shall repeat here only a few of those verses. To them I hope no discerning reader will deny the excellence of a most obvious sincerity and of a boundless devotion. "To thee alone," I wrote, "to thee alone, mirror of kings, belongs the glory of rescuing the world from its darkness. . . ."

If those two lines be not sufficient, let friends of justice read the remainder of the ode. I neither desired nor hoped for recompense for what I wrote. But I could not imagine either that after so manifest a demonstration of my innocence, on the one hand, and, on the other, of my obsequious fidelity and devotion, the most formidable of punishments should fall upon my head—a punishment which for more than a year kept me in an agony of despair and misery, thrust upon my innocent back the uniform of the vilest convict, and exposed me to the derision and the insults of a herd of rogues who hated me only because I was not a rogue of their ilk. On the death of the father, my innocence, it is true, was recognized, and my long weeping solaced by the pity and justice of the son; but, obliged as I was, to write the story of the whole affair, in order to dissipate every shadow of blame by which my good name was threatened, what could I do, what should I have done? What would any honorable man have done in my situation? Did my pen perchance at times forget, in the throes of my agony, the great distance that separates one of the greatest monarchs and a poor maker of verse? But why should anyone disdain to hear in my writings things that Leopold himself heard from my lips without anger and in the end not without compassion? I call before the tribunal of that monarch all those who thus condemn me. These few words of our dialogue are sufficient to convince them that they are wrong. "He stood thoughtful a moment, took two or three turns up and down the room in silence, then turning suddenly upon me as I still knelt there, and his face brightening, he said, 'Rise,' and he held out his hand to help me, 'I believe that you have been persecuted and I promise you compensation—is that enough?'"

I was once on another occasion describing the effect which this act of heroic moderation had upon me, when a talented young lady, hearing that these Memoirs had been suppressed by the government censors in the States of the Emperor, made this comment:

"Instead of prohibiting them, he would have done well to scatter them through the whole world. A volume of praises would not have said of Leopold what that fine gesture said." I subscribe to this high-minded judgment, and go back to happenings in America and to Dr. Giuseppe Gherardi.

After spending some days with me, he left New York to go to Boston for a visit to his brother. On his return to my house, he spoke joyfully of a certain article that had appeared in the month of October of that year (1824) in the *North American Review*, a journal of wide renown in America, wherein, according to things he had heard from many people, Italian literature and the Italian language were spoken of with high esteem. My jubilation at such news may easily be imagined. I hurried without delay to the bookstore where that paper was sold. I bought a copy and without taking time to go home, began to read it. Great was my delight when, at the beginning of the article, I seemed to gather that the primary purpose of the writer was to promote the study of our literature particularly—*that an acquaintance with Italian literature should be widely diffused.*

"So," I said to myself on reading that, "we are going to have in America, too, a Roscoe, a Ginguené, a Mathias! Now things will go better!"

But, reading on, I was soon aware that our apparent Pliny was unexpectedly assuming all the severity of an Aristarch, and my joy turned to grief—it was like the monster in Horace, who first shows a fine face on a human head, but gradually reveals a horse's neck and a fish's tail.

I then concluded it was my duty to refute the erroneous opinions of that censor.[19] I published some "Remarks" on his article. They seemed very sound to all cultivated and open-minded readers, but, instead of convincing the still "young *athleta*" of his errors, encouraged him to publish a second article—sharper, bitterer, and more full of errors and of prejudice. I had determined to give him a second lesson of a different sort than my first, which, for that matter, was adjudged "balsamic" by one of my most talented pupils, who thus expresses himself in a witty letter:

---

19. The author was Prescott, no less. *North. Am. Rev.*, Oct. 1824.

"I knew no more about the sound scientific work of Italy than that critic in Boston, to whom you administered such a salutary balsam." ("Irritating" he should have said.)

But then, thinking the matter over, I could see that what that critic was saying was only an exaggerated repetition of what so many other copiers of Boileau, Johnson, Chesterfield, and their followers had been saying, and that anything I might write would be only playing a pipe to a man without ears. So, instead of getting angry, I began to laugh, as all educated Italians do at the absurd opinions of those judges of them. In fact, if the things so many great men had written did not avail to change such opinions, how could I change them even in many volumes? How could I convince our critic, so certain of his own views, that the images and metaphors employed by Petrarch in the three *Canzoni* on Laura's eyes are things of inimitable beauty and exquisiteness and not mere affectations and conceits, as he, and so far, he alone, was pleased to call them. That admission had not been wrung from him by the eulogies of Gravina, Bettinelli, Casaregi, and a hundred other Italian and French writers (to say nothing of our great trumpeter, Ginguené), who united in calling those three *Canzoni*, "Three sisters divine." Could I convince him—if not even a French writer of note[20] could do as much—that Boileau changed his views in later life respecting the "Jerusalem" of Tasso? And what shall I say of poor Metastasio, whom the esteemed contributors to the *North American Review* rate so low, despite the thousand beautiful things that Rousseau, Arteaga, and Andrés wrote of him, not to mention Italians? One thing only I tied to my finger at that time, with a view to vindicating the good taste of our Italians on some occasion when leisure from my occupations would permit—occupations highly agree-

20. *L'Abate Olivet, Storia dell'accademia di Francia, carta 18; Serassi, Vita di Torquato Tasso.* —L. Da P.

able to me by their very nature, but greatly increased in number by the happy event of which I shall now speak.

Though, to my joy, I could see the interest in Italian letters increasing daily both in New York and other cities of the Union, I still thought there was another way of making them both more widely spread and more highly esteemed; but, to tell the truth, I did not dare to hope for such a thing. What, therefore, was my delight, when a number of persons assured me that the famous Garcia, with his incomparable daughter[21] and several other Italian singers, was coming from London to America, and in fact to New York, to establish the Italian opera there—the *desideratum* of my greatest zeal?

He came, in truth, and the effect was prodigious. Unimaginable the enthusiasm in the cultivated portions of the public aroused by our music when executed by singers of most perfect taste and highest merit. The *Barbiere di Siviglia* of the universally admired and praised Rossini, was the opera fortunate enough to plant the first root of the great tree of Italian music in New York.[22]

A short time before our singers were to arrive, a young American, a youth of much talent, and a great lover of the noble art of music, was talking of it with friends of his one day in my presence, and as it were *ex cathedra*. Finding his notions erroneous, I remarked in jest:

"Silence, King Solomon! You know nothing of music yet!"

That excellent young man felt a flash of anger, but I begged him to be calm and promised soon to convince him. Sometime later Garcia arrived. The "Barber of Seville" of the Rossini mentioned was announced for the opening night. I took him to the fifth performance, with others of my pupils, and that admirable music caught them up, along with the rest of the

---

21. Manuel Vincente Garcia (1775–1832). Mme. Malibran (1808–1836).

22. New York *première*, Nov. 29, 1825, at the Park Row Theater. Russo, 126.

audience, into a sort of ecstatic spell. Having observed from their perfect silence, the expressions on their faces and in their eyes, and their constant clapping of hands, the marvelous effect that music had had on them, I approached my sceptic, when the performance was over, and asked him what he thought of it: "Mr. Da Ponte," he said generously, "you are right. I confess with real pleasure that I did not know an iota about music." Not far different the impressions of the first performance on all those who did not have their ears lined with that sheepskin of which drums are made, or some particular interest in speaking ill of it—(a newspaper critic of the dishonest tribe honored Italian music with the name of "monstrous")—whether to give the palm to the music of other countries, or to praise to the stars the clucking of some amorous hen. But despite such prattling, the delight in our music in New York was so constant, that few were the evenings when the theater was not filled with a large and select audience; and that happened, when it happened, I believe, through lack of poise in the Spanish conductor.

How great an interest I took in the continuance and success of such an enterprise is too easy to imagine to require words of mine. I clearly foresaw the many enormous advantages our literature would derive from it and how it would tend to propagate our language through the attractiveness of the Italian Opera which, in the eyes of every cultivated nation of the world, is the noblest and most pleasurable of all the many spectacles the human intelligence ever invented, and to the perfecting of which the noblest arts have vied with one another in contributing.

But however beautiful, however esteemed, the operas set to music by Rossini might be, it seemed to me that to give fewer performances of them and alternate them with those of other composers would be a most profitable thing, both for the reputation of the excellent Rossini and for the treasury of the producers. A good fowl is certainly an appetizing dish; but it was served often enough by the Marchioness of Montferrat at the dinners which she gave the King of France, to prompt that Majesty to inquire whether hens were all one could find in that country. I mentioned the point to Garcia; he liked it; and at my suggesting to him my *Don Giovanni* set to music by the immortal Mozart, he uttered another cry of joy and said nothing but this:

"If we have enough actors to give *Don Giovanni*, let us give it soon. It's the best opera in the world!"

I was as happy as could be at such an answer, both because I hoped for an excellent success, and from a keen desire, natural enough in me, to see some drama of mine presented on the stage in America. But looking over the field, we discovered that the company lacked a singer capable of playing the part of Don Ottavio. I undertook to find him myself, and I did find him; and then when the manager of the Opera refused to incur additional expense, between me, my pupils, and my friends, we provided the money to pay him; and *Don Giovanni* appeared on the stage.[23]

I was not disappointed in my hopes. Everything pleased, everything was admired and praised—words, music, actors, performance; and the beautiful, brilliant, and amiable daughter was as distinguished, and shone as brilliantly, in the part of Zerlinetta as her father seemed incomparable in the part of Don Giovanni. Varying, in truth, were opinions in the audience as to the transcendent merit of those two rare portents in the realm of harmony. Some preferred Rossini, some the German, nor could I say with assurance which had the more partisans, *Il Barbiere di Siviglia* or *Don Giovanni*. It should be observed, however, that Mozart, either because he is no more or because he was not an Italian, not only has no enemies, but is exalted

---

23. New York *première*, May 23, 1826. Russo, 128.

to the heights for his supreme merit by impartial judges and connoisseurs; whereas Rossini has a very goodly party of enemies, some because they are envious of his renown, others through malice inborn and an accursed instinct to criticize and to depreciate anything remarkable that Italy produces.

I am going to tell, at this point, a little story that will make my good-natured reader laugh a little. I happened, one day, to be at good cheer and letters in company with four wizards from as many different countries—one of them a Spaniard, the second a Frenchman, the third, a German, and the fourth, an American. Each of them, as was natural, was praising the language and literature of his own country to some point beyond the planet Saturn. Don Quixote, said the Spaniard, was worth the whole library of the King of France, which, so people said, was the richest and most beautiful in the world. The Frenchman gave the same boast to Voltaire, supreme in the epic, supreme in the lyric, supreme in the tragic. The German was satisfied with Klopstock and Goethe; and the novels of Cooper, and the *Columbiad*, were good enough for the American! I was anxious to put in a word for our writers, but "scarce my lips to speak did part" when those four wiseacres arose and with sarcastic smiles began to put on their coats and hats. At the door, one of them spoke as follows (I am sorry to be obliged to say that he was the American—he came from Boston!):

"Mr. Da Ponte, I have lived in Italy many years, and visited and studied all the principal cities, but, to speak quite frankly, the only good things I found there were your macaroni with Parmesan or Lodi, and your beef *à la mode*."

"With a touch of garlic!" added the Frenchman.

A peal of laughter in four voices was the fine signal of unanimous approbation. Then, laughing too, not with them, but at them, I said:

"Very well, if you gentlemen will do me the honor to dine

with me tomorrow, you will find Neapolitan macaroni with Parmesan cheese, and beef *à la mode* with a touch of garlic."

They accepted all four in one voice, with gurgles of joy; and I heard one of them whisper to his companions:

"Let's go, and we'll have a laugh."

What laughing there was, was done by me. All four came punctually and after a brief apology for the savage compliment they had paid me the preceding day, they began again for my benefit to intone the usual antiphony of the anti-Italian psalm —the extravagances of Dante, the word play of Petrarch, the plagiarisms of Boccaccio, the absurdities of Ariosto, the counterfeit gold of Tasso, and the sickening sweetness of Metastasio —such the fragrant appetizer those wizard guests of mine fed for an hour to my most patient ears. At last dinner was served, and the moment we were in our places, one of the servants uncovered a dish of macaroni richly sprinkled with cheese, and another a beef stew with the touch of garlic, the aroma fragrant enough to awaken appetite in the dead.

At this toothsome display the same American cried:

"Good for you, Mr. Da Ponte! There's the one good thing they have in Italy!"

I was waiting for that remark, and had instructed one of my servants exactly as to what he should do. Quick as lighting, he removed the platter of spaghetti and the stew, and instead of them, brought two huge platters of boiled corn on the cob. "And here." I cried, "is the one good thing in America. Sail in, gentlemen!"

Some of them twisted their noses; the others protested; but neither the stew nor the macaroni reappeared on my board for that meal.

After this macaronic but instructive episode, I must return to Rossini, who supplies me with part of my matter for another episode, no less amusing than the last. As the works of Rossini were performed one after the other, the applause of connoisseurs and friends of truth seemed to increase. A certain Mr. So and So, I know not whether out of professional jealousy or for some other motive, boldly raised an anti-Rossinian standard and said and wrote of that great genius things that an envious lunatic or an ignorant boor might say. Zealous friend of my illustrious nation and of all the talents that distinguish themselves therein, it was really impossible for me to call quits with such a man and at once I took pen in hand to defend the fame of an illustrious individual Italian, just as I had at first defended the entire nation and then its literature and language. And, trusting that I shall be pleasing Signor Rossini, as well as all those who have passed so many delicious hours under the spell of his music, I will transcribe here a part of what I wrote, in refutation of the ill-founded accusations which that malevolent critic laid to his charge. Perhaps that English sheet in which I published my article, may not have reached Italy.

> Anonymous Sir:
> I have read, partly with disgust and partly with laughter . . . etc., etc.!

Such the reply I made to that critic at that time; and I was glad I did in view of an odd event that is *à propos* at this point.

An American gentleman, a great lover of music and well-versed in our language, since he had lived many years in Italy and visited all its foremost cities, sat near me in the theater at the performance of a popular opera. Toward the middle of the first act he turned toward me and said, smiling:

"Mr. Da Ponte, when this aria is over, I shall make myself comfortable for a little nap; when such and such a piece comes please awaken me if I am still asleep; and I think that I may well be, because this wretched opera is the best sedative in the world. That unfortunately is the case with all the operas that come from Italy."

432

I did not know what answer to make, and in a few moments I could hear him snoring. I awakened him at the piece indicated, after which he either went to sleep again or pretended to do so, and thus for all the rest of the opera. Then we separated.

Two or three days later, my *Don Giovanni* was to be performed. I went to the theater in the forenoon and found his name written in the usual list of allocations, and, there being room for me also in the same box, I had my name registered there at once. He was already in his chair when I arrived. I seated myself at his side. Toward the end of the first act I decided to speak a word to him; but he, with a gesture almost of annoyance, motioned me to be silent. As the curtain fell after the *finale*, he said:

"Now, Mr. Da Ponte . . . what did you wish to say to me?"

"I wanted to ask you just when you intended going to sleep."

"Tomorrow night! With performances like this not only is there no sleeping during the music, but there is no sleeping afterwards, all night long."

The compliment tickled my vanity a little, all the more since I thought I saw him paying as much attention to the so-called "recitatives" as to the sublimer flights of music. The performance over, he constrained me with gentle insistence to go to supper with him. The feast lasted not less than two hours and we talked of nothing but theater. All his remarks seemed to me most sound. He was an enthusiastic admirer of Goldoni and Alfieri.

"Immense," he said, "the merit of these two great geniuses. They are the two strongest pillars of your theater, and any fair-minded critic must regard them as the restorers, nay the creators, of a true Italian comedy and tragedy; and not the least, perhaps, of their merit is to have given new Roscuses to Italy; for it is not possible for a man who knows barely how to read, to perform the beautiful scenes of such writers without being an excellent declaimer, and if he is not one, becoming one."

I hung on the words of that excellent reasoner as devotees of old listened to their oracles; and my joy at hearing him, anyone with a grain of good sense may imagine. But his final remark was this:

"France, as everyone knows, has not such good singers as Italy, but the operas given in Paris are, in general, good plays, charming, and full of wit; and the acting, whether by native talent or superior training, is excellent. That is why it rarely happens that a French opera makes, to use a technical expression, a fiasco."

Now will my patient reader listen to me for a few moments. In the first three parts of my Memoirs, the cities in which I lived, the character of the posts I held, the distinguished individuals with whom I had to deal, and a certain play of Fortune that seemed bent on subjecting me to the extremest test of her capricious power, supplied me with ample and excellent material wherewith to interest and entertain my reader. The country I have been inhabiting for more than five *lustra* past, yields me no such adventures. I am therefore in the situation of a preceptor of botany traveling about with his pupils to instruct them in that science; and who, after showing them the attributes and the virtues of trees, plants, and flowers, must now pass through desert lands or cross barren mountains, and in order not to waste time, discusses the properties of the shrubs and brambles he has at hand. Living as I am here in America, I can write only of my domestic affairs, and of those events and cares of civic life in which I have been and still am, if not the protagonist of the tragicomedy, at least one of the leading actors. From all such, nevertheless, a wise reader may learn something useful; the person with the eye to see *la dottrina che s'asconde sotto il velame delli versi strani*, may learn the rules of good living both from the precepts of Socrates or Plato, and from the child's tales of Æsop. Many writers (among them the brilliant Baretti) main-tain that more may be learned from the reading of some private "Life" than from that of many histories of peoples and nations. Indeed, if, in my own youth, I had read the story of a man who had had the same experiences that I was to have, and whose conduct had been more or less the same as mine was, how many, many errors might I not have avoided, the consequences of which cost me so many tears at the time and are still bitterly afflicting the years of my decrepitude! Now I, too, can say, indeed must say, with Petrarch: "I know my error and excuse it not."

But the harm, at my age, is beyond remedy; nothing else is left me but repentance. May others at least learn from my example what I did not have the opportunity to learn from the experience of others. Let them learn not to trust, as I have trusted, a few honeyed words; let them not open their hearts to people whose characters and habits they have not tested for years and years; let them turn hearts of stone and ears of bronze upon those who ask for pity in the language of adulation; let them not measure the rectitude of others by their own; let them not say: "That man has no reason to cheat us, hate us, betray us; therefore he will not hate us, cheat us, betray us." Let them say rather the exact contrary, because the exact contrary is what has happened to me. If they have some talent of nature or some favor of Fortune, let each try to hide it from others with the greatest care, and not hope to change the intent of evil doers with sufferance and kindnesses.

After this little outburst, necessary to a spirit depressed at the period when I am writing by a most grievous and unforeseen event, I must go back to the reflections on the theater delivered by that very discerning American; and I allow myself to hope that if this volume reaches Italy, some shrewd impresario will read it, and follow my advice; whereby Italy will be seen again taking first rank in the field of the Opera, just as, all critics to the contrary notwithstanding, she holds first rank in the field of comedy by virtue of an ill-censored Goldoni and in the tragic, by virtue of an Alfieri. And since I am back on the Opera again, I will stop there for a moment to relate an amusing little incident, which delighted me when it happened and will now be pleasing to anyone who reads of it.

I had had my *Don Giovanni* translated literally into English[24] and the manager of the Opera had courteously granted me the privilege of printing the librettos of it on my own account. I sold a prodigious number at the theater and the profits of the sale repaid me abundantly for my expenses and work. But good luck did even more to my advantage. For the convenience of spectators not well acquainted with our language, it is the custom in America to place the libretto of the opera that is to be produced in the evening in a number of stores and shops. I had left several of mine at a certain store where lottery tickets also were for sale. As I entered there one morning the shopkeeper said to me:

"Mr. Da Ponte, send me some more books at once. We had sixteen left and we sold them last evening. I will pay you the six dollars I owe you now. Sit down!"

While he was counting out the money, my eyes fell on an advertisement:

"Lottery drawing tomorrow; tickets, six dollars."

"Give me a lottery ticket," I called, "and keep the money."

He did so. I put the ticket into my pocket and went home.

That was the first time I had opened the door to Fortune by spending any money at that game, and so little did I hope that she would take advantage of it, that the sleep of a single night allowed the experiment to pass entirely from my mind. Toward evening the next day, however, as I sat at my desk writing, I heard a repeated knocking with gay calls at my door.

24. By Lorenzo L. Da P.

I opened, and I saw a clerk from that shop coming in to announce that I had won five hundred dollars. Accustomed most often to rebuffs, and very rarely to favors, of Chance, I had difficulty in believing him; but finding that it was true, I gave a few dollars to that messenger of good tidings, and my blessings to Mozart, *Don Giovanni*, the Opera, and lottery shops. Three days later I went and collected the money, at sight of which a single thought filled all my mind: to make use of it entirely in purchasing new books wherewith to set up a select, if not a rich, public library in the city.

It was then that I brought on from cities in Italy a goodly number of beautiful and costly works, among them the *Rerum Italicarum scriptores* of Lodovico Muratori, that glorious monument to Italian scholarship, the extremely rare *Giornale* of Apostolo Zeno, the works of Visconti and Winckelmann, and the *Memorie della società italiana* and a similar book on Turin, not to mention magnificent editions of Dante, Petrarch, Ariosto, and Tasso. I thought that the College might prove to be a point of support for my establishment. In a little book which I entitled *Storia della letteratura italiana in New York* and published in the year 1827, I narrated in detail the paths I followed and the means I adopted to erect and perpetuate within its sacred walls a glorious monument to our letters. I recounted how, in furthering the project, I myself deposited there a certain number of volumes, employing in their purchase all the tuition that twenty-eight pupils of that College paid me for ten months of lessons and how I was afterward able, through the influence of my two most noble pupils, Charles Clement Moore and Henry Anderson, to add to the volumes I had given, many other beautiful works acquired at the expense of the College itself; so that now more than seven hundred selected volumes are to be found there, whereas on my arrival, there was naught but an old, worm-eaten Boccaccio with a broken binding. But to my greatest disappointment this was only a fire of straw, and the slight results of my efforts induced me to renounce the decorative title of professor, which they had accorded me, together with all hope I had of seeing my plan succeed in that institute.[25] However there is a proverb that says: *Semel abbas semper abbas*. Everyone continued honoring me with the title of "professor," and the pupils of that college invited me also to a certain annual banquet at which both pupils and professors met together. Being in good humor that day, instead of going myself, I sent this Latin quip to the individuals who had invited me, and it made a laugh:

> Sum pastor sine ovibus,
> arator sine bovibus,
> hortulus sine flore,
> lychnus sine splendore,
> campus sine frumento,
> crumena sine argento,
> navita sine navibus,
> ianua sine clavibus,
> arbustus sine foliis,

25. Da P. was appointed Professor of Italian in Columbia on Sept. 5, 1825—he had applied for the post in person on May 2nd. Since these were the days of the old "classical curriculum," where all subjects were specified and required, he had no chair in the Faculty, and no salary. He seems to have resigned in June, 1826; but as he says, his resignation was never accepted. He tried to revive the work as a proposition in book-selling during the year 1829–30, but found no students. Though he was accounted a Columbia professor from 1825 to the time of his death in 1838, his attendance was confined to the two academic years mentioned and his actual work to the first of them. Da P. was succeeded in these empty honors by Felice Foresti, one of the exiles he detested. The situation was not far different with professors of the other modern languages, French, German, and Spanish, which did not obtain real citizenship in the curriculum till the days of Charles Sprague Smith, 1880, and following.

> taberna sine doliis,
> Olympus sine stellis,
> chorea sine puellis,
> artifex sine manibus,
> venator sine canibus,
> fons sine potatoribus,
> pons sine viatoribus,
> sacerdos sine templo,
> professor sine exemplo.

I had neither pupils nor salary!

If, however, so little attention was paid to the study of Italian in the College of the city, the general delight which our music occasioned on the stage, did not permit me to lose all hope of attaining my goal in the end.

"Your music," some young ladies said to me one day, "is beyond dispute very beautiful; but our not understanding Italian makes the plays less interesting."

"Why then," I replied, "do you not study that beautiful language, too?"

"Because as you well know," they answered, "it is the fashion now to learn Spanish."

It seemed quite natural that after the revolution in Mexico and in a country so especially devoted to commerce, men should learn that language; but I found it just as strange, for reasons which everybody knows but which I dare not repeat, that ladies should give their time to it. Convinced that such a predilection in people arose from their not being aware of the difference between those languages as regarded the number and merit of their writers, I kept studying and studying to think of some suitable way to undeceive them. One day I had stepped by chance into a wine shop to procure some wine for my family. When I told the merchant the kind I wanted, he presented me with three bottles and said:

439

"Here are three different grades of the wine you are asking for. Sample a glass of each, and take the one you like best." I did so, and I bought the wine I liked best, but that good acolyte of Bacchus had given me an idea. Acting on it at once, I ran home and drew up a paragraph which I sent the same day to the newspapers. In it I proposed establishing a triple class, in which, at the moderate tuition of ten dollars, Spanish, Italian, and French would be taught. "There," said I to myself, "you have your three bottles of different grades. Let's see which of the three will get the most drinkers."

I chose as my colleagues the two best teachers in the city—Pillet, of honored and venerable memory, for the French, and Vigliarino, a native Castilian, for the Spanish. We had seventy-five pupils for the first term of three months and exactly one hundred for the second term. And which was the favorite bottle? Neither one of my associates had more than twenty-two or twenty-four pupils. I had as many as seventy, most of them drinking exclusively of the bottle from the Arno; and the enthusiasm with which they read our authors, and the progress made by a great part of them, and particularly by the young ladies, astounded not only New York and America, but the most cultivated critics in Italy. The praises I accorded, the prizes I distributed, and the other artifices I used to excite emulation, produced the most wonderful effect, making our pupils capable not only of writing and speaking Italian with grace, but of enjoying with astonishing keenness the most recondite beauties of our sublime writers.

And truly I know not whether through error of judgment, or because they are entirely ignorant of our classics, certain teachers of Italian are wont to place in the hands of their pupils nothing but those puerile stories and ridiculous anecdotes of which the grammars are full—at the most, the *Novelle* of Soave and the *Lettere d'una Peruviana*, or even, sometimes, the wretched productions of their own ridiculous heads—two great abuses, against the practice of which I should consider it a crime not to throw myself. The first is harmful to the pupil, who, as a result of such negligence, barely glimpses the threshold of our literary edifice. The other is insulting to our letters, with which the foreigner is but little acquainted, and not distinguishing the offal from gold, easily comes to believe that those insipidities, fit for stoning, represent the highest beauties of our literature. The verses which Aloisi wrote for the "Gallic Hero," translating "riotous mirth" as "the riotous myrtle," and the dedicatory letter of the suicide Fiorilli to his *Bettina grammaticale*, are quintessences of wit in comparison with the ridiculous twaddle which a young lady from Philadelphia, who had studied our language for three years, handed me with these sweet words:

"Here, Mr. Da Ponte, is a little book of delightful verse, recently published in this city by a brilliant countryman of yours. If you care to read it, I can lend it to you."

I identified both the book and the author by the size of the volume and its binding, and thanked her for her kind thought, but without succeeding in hiding a little smile. The young lady seemed to disapprove.

"Envy! Envy!" she cried and turned her back on me and went away.

This dorsal salute did not leave me very well satisfied. I ran home, shut myself up in my room, and having already had the book as a gift from a good friend of mine—he had sent it to me to give me a laugh—set myself to making notes to it, which I sent as a present to that young lady, and which I will offer to my patient reader among the notes to this volume. As a sample, meanwhile, of the song of this swan I envied, I will quote for anyone who cares to laugh, this proemial sonnet "To the Reader" (with the author's punctuation).

> Se mai fia che tu creda ch'io credessi
> che piacer ne trarresti, queste rime di
>   Jacopo leggendo
>
>   .   .   .   .
>   Qui venne per raccor e vele e sarte!

Sarte means ropes, and I should advise this supreme poet to use one at once.

These, my dear fellow Italians, the coadjutors Fortune bestowed on me for the raising of a palace in America to the Tuscan muses! What better could they have given me for the tower of Babel? Would you hear how this fellow spoke of me? One of my pupils asked him one day if he knew Da Ponte.

"Yes," he replied, decorating his dried-up face with a cur-like sneer. "Mr. Da Ponte thinks he is a poet!"

I sent word to him that he was mistaken; that I did not pretend to be a poet myself, but that I only thought I could recognize those who were not, and that I would seek every possible means and paths to identify them to others.

Someone reported my retort to the young lady of the dorsal salute. She came sometime later to New York, and chance brought her to the house of one of my pupils where I had occasion of seeing her. She was no longer angry, and seemed, in fact, now disposed to atone with courtesy for her un-ladylike rebuke. Loyally seconded by the young lady she was visiting and without a word anent her poetaster and his doggerel, I begged her to come to my house the following day to see and hear the progress my class had been making. Forgive me, most amiable daughters of my intellect and of my heart, if my aged vanity cannot refrain from adorning these pages, no longer with your initials only, but with your revered and beloved names. My class was not, in truth, very large that day, but the twelve who had come together there were the fairest flowers of my garden—Miss Bradford, the two little Duer sisters, Miss

Glover, Mademoiselle Dubois, a little Robinson tot, the two Weiman sisters, a Johnson, a Kennedy, and a granddaughter of mine, fourteen years old.[26] After the daily lesson in writing we were in the habit of reading two of our classics one day and two more the next. Tasso and Alfieri were to be explained that morning; but I had some Dantes and Petrarchs brought from my store, and after having each of the young ladies read and translate a few stanzas or scenes from the first two, I begged to have recited from memory by one some sonnet, by another some stanza, of our great lyricist. At all this my visitor was greatly surprised; but what seemed most to impress her was the frankness with which I invited her to open the first volume of the *Divina Commedia* and ask my girls to interpret any passage she preferred. On the successful outcome of that experiment, I asked her which of the first six cantos she would like to hear declaimed. She asked for the third. It was the young girl of fourteen who had the honor of the floor.

The test lasted more than three hours, whereupon the room rang with applause. I then approached the young woman and asked her modestly whether I had any reason to be envious.

"No, indeed," she answered, "to be envied rather!"

She spoke as a prophet. That was precisely my fate, in America especially; and the envy of which I was the mark was not that desire natural to everyone to possess some good that another has, and which Petrarch depicts so admirably in his two verses:

> Quanta invidia ti porto, avara terra,
> che abbracci quello cui veder m'è tolto;

---

26. Louisa's daughter, Matilda Ann Clossey, born at Sunbury in 1815, died in New York, the day before her announced marriage to a young man of the Starr family, on Oct. 3, 1832. Some of the letters which this delightful and intelligent child wrote to her aunt, Fanny, survive.

but rather that feeling of cruelty which spurs a person to say and do everything he can to harm the object of his envy; which cares neither for charity nor justice, but like the fiercest tiger, after having torn and dismembered its prey, delights in soiling its tusks and fangs in blood. And of that, too, the Poet gives a picture in the sonnet which reads:

> O invidia nemica di virtute . . .
> da radice m'hai svelta mia salute!

That, truly, has so far been and still is my destiny. Neither by kindnesses nor by patience have I ever succeeded in placating that ferocious hydra which chose to spread her poison among my own fellow countrymen and among those especially who were, after a fashion, following my profession as teachers.

And it will seem a strange thing to my reader that in the twenty-five years since I have been in America, I have not been able to keep the friendship, let alone win the esteem, of a single language teacher; though I was the first to introduce Italian into this country, spread it about, enhance its dignity, sparing myself no trouble, effort, or expense to establish it on firm foundations.

Leaving a hundred others covered under a veil of "native charity," I will say a word here of just one, a man separated from me by an immense expanse of land and sea, enjoying a real glory for his labors and his learning. I hoped I would find him on my side, if not for my talents and writings, for my noble enthusiasm at least in promulgating, defending and exalting the studies which he loves and honors, nay rather in creating them here in this part of the world opposite to his; and out of that love of the same illustrious poet which spurred me to ask advice of him.

In reading our classics with my pupils I did not fail, as may well be believed, to place in their hands those authors which I judged most suitable to their respective ages, stations and talents. After the most noble Tuscan prose writers, I introduced them to the poets. Metastasio was always the first among these; after that the others of highest renown, but always leaving the *Divina Commedia* and the *Rime* of Petrarch for the last. Though all these authors were generally loved, nevertheless, in spite of everything, who was the most admired and studied? The Ghibelline!

This very proper admiration accorded to the Father and the Prince of our literature obliged me to very serious study of that divine poem, that its obscurities might be clarified and the difficult passages explained. I had already studied and pondered the more celebrated commentators; but it still seeming to me that room remained for annotations, I myself ventured to make a few to different cantos, which one of my most learned pupils published in a journal he was then compiling.[27] Though my observations were generally liked, I nevertheless thought, to make sure of their soundness, that I would send a copy of them to Biagioli, a commentator truly of great merit, and of whose annotations I had sold no less than ten copies in America. In the preface to the first edition he invites the scholars of "the beautiful country" to inform him wherever he may have erred through ignorance or too great eagerness, and promises "to welcome their luminous observations and corrections with open arms and reprint them with the names of their authors in a new edition, should ever there be one." But Signor Biagioli did not receive me with open arms, nor did he think me worthy of a reply. I knew, therefore, to my shame, that he neither placed me among the scholars of Italy (on that point I

---

27. Dr. Anderson, who, with William Cullen Bryant and Robert Sands, edited the *New York Review and Athenaeum* in 1825 (it survived less than a year). Da P.'s notes on Dante were unearthed by Koch.

agree with him); nor did he think my observations worthy of being printed.

The silent judgment of such a learned scholar so crushed me that I no longer dared continue the work I had begun. I will confess, nevertheless, that the suspicion sometimes flitted through my mind that I had highly offended that great critic, whom those who agree with Lombardi do not consider the kindest soul in the world, though he avows himself most teachable and ready to change his mind, withdraw his views, and confess his mistakes, the moment they are pointed out to him. He may have thought it strange that an obscure language master, who had lived for more than five *lustra* in America, should venture to hold opinions contrary to his in the interpretation of Dante. But you well know, my dear Signor Biagioli, that even the good Homer sometimes nodded, and that a blind man found a horseshoe that others with eyes had not seen. It may very easily be that your perspicacious intellect sees the beauties of Dante much better than I. But it would be impossible, in my opinion, that you should love the glory of that poet more. So I shall turn, with your permission, to those same scholars in Italy, humbly begging them to judge between us in several places of that poem, which, according to your explanations, do not seem to me worthy of Dante. But to prevent this fifth part of my Memoirs from being but a thread of episodes, I shall append in a note the more considerable differences in our explanations, begging some friend of Dante, and more than anyone else my revered Colombo, to let me know his opinion whether through publication or through private letters; and I shall not be slow in sharing them with my pupils, and especially with the masters and students of this College, in which I first introduced my native language in that same year, interpreting that supreme author according to my lights, hoping to establish in that College and through those pupils a firm and abiding retreat for our letters.

I found with time however, that a hidden borer, a sort of subtle corruption, kept undoing everything that I did out of plain enthusiasm; and that, even had I succeeded in placing the magnificent library of Apostolo Zeno in that institute, I should after all have been able to say with Dante: "*Books* there are, but who puts hand to them?"

For, beyond any doubt, I would not have had a single student in that language after the first year, since a certain one of the professors was convinced, and tried to persuade the others, that our literature had little that was great in it (though he was not very familiar with it), and that the Germans were superior to us in all the sciences and arts. This is not the place to say more on that subject. His opinion will, however, merit some reflection at the proper time.

Things being at that pass, and desirous at all costs of bringing my plan into effect, it occurred to me that I might obtain from my other friends and pupils what I no longer hoped to receive from the College. I accordingly deposited eight hundred volumes of classics in the public library and published the following poem addressed: "To my Dear Pupils, to Encourage them to Found a Public Italian Library!"

> Sulla prora del ricco naviglio . . . etc., etc.

The moment my plan and my activities became known in Italy, all good people there made haste to praise and second my patriotic efforts; and in addition to many letters of congratulation and applause which I received from a number of learned, zealous, and brilliant Italians, there were not a few who sent me beautiful books as gifts, that I might enrich my library with them.

The first to set this noble example to the others was my revered and adorable patron and friend, Thomas Mathias, who, with admirable courtesy and grace, presented me with his own most beautiful works, and furnished me with a means to make Americans see with their own eyes how a learned and open-minded English writer, who had studied and pondered our Italian authors to such extent as to make himself the most respected and the greatest of all foreigners who have written in our language—how, I repeat, such a scholar too spoke and judged of those sublime geniuses which other nations (not excluding the American), whether through lack of study or strength of prejudice (with a few exceptions), either despise entirely or are pleased to depreciate. The example of this herculean champion was imitated by many Italians, from whom, in the brief space of a year, I had more than sixty volumes in offering to my library.

But the one who stood distinguished among all others, after my British donor, both in the value of his gifts and in the gracious manner of making them, was that cultivated, erudite, and excellent man of letters from Trieste who, though last in time among my rarest and most illustrious friends, nevertheless occupies one of the first places among them, through numberless proofs of pure benevolence, singular gentleness, and unequaled liberality, which, without any merit of mine and through the sole kindness of his heart, he gave me, and which he continues to give me not only with rare persistence, but with ever growing ardor. The generous gift of all his works both in prose and in verse, works which declare him one of the most zealous citizens, profound scholars, and elegant writers of our times—that gift, in itself very precious, is nothing in comparison with his other kindnesses toward me; kindnesses which I can indeed prize and appreciate keenly as of duty a grateful soul should appreciate, but which I shall never, no matter how much I try, be able to find words and figures adequate to depict. Permit me, therefore, my dear and incomparable friend, after this ingenuous declaration of my inability, to leave in respectful silence sentiments and things which neither my tongue nor my pen would be capable of expressing, and be pleased to rest assured that neither time nor distance will be able to cancel from my mind the slightest part of that esteem, gratitude, and benevolence which I owe you; that it is, and will always be for me, a sweet thing to bless you and love you; that I will forgive, or rather do forgive, all the wrongs and hurts done me by Fortune, for the blessing She has bestowed on me of knowing you and being loved by you; and that, at the moment of the great passing, the last word to issue from my lips will be the adorable name of Rossetti.

Now back to my bookstore.

In it, as I said, I had deposited eight hundred volumes of our classics, costing, bound, not more than twelve hundred dollars, and which were soon to increase in number through the gifts promised me—volumes which each subscriber with his heirs would have the right to read for years and centuries for the very moderate price of five dollars. Yet, who would believe it? Neither through my persuasion, nor through my prayers, and in this rich, cultivated, and thickly populated city of New York, where I had fifteen hundred pupils and even more friends, have I been able, in three years of effort, to obtain more than seventy persons willing to disburse five or ten dollars for a foundation so useful and so ornamental; and among those only two Italians: Signor F. Mossa, of Palermo, and my patron in Trieste, Signor Rossetti. And it is to be wondered at that whereas my *Catalogo ragionato* was enough to rouse the curiosity of scholars in other cities of the Union to the point of establishing noble libraries in their universities and colleges, New York alone has so far failed to enrich herself, save partially, with such a treasure! Let no one suppose that being a commercial city of the first order, and without commerce of consequence, whether active or passive, with Italy, New York would find the Italian language of scant usefulness and an Italian library a superfluous expense; for in that case, I would ask of what utility to commerce Latin and Greek can be, which are cultivated with such enthusiasm and partiality by these same business-men, and for which the most sumptuous libraries have been erected, and not with the moderate expense of five or ten dollars, but with a profusion of money? What shall I say, fur-thermore, of the immense sums that are squandered on learn-ing them? And were it at least true, to speak only of Latin, that the proficiency of those who study corresponded to some extent with the expense! As a matter of fact, be it through in-adequacy of method or of competence on the part of the in-structors, or of diligence on the part of the students, very few are they who ever master the real savor, the "urbanity," of that language, and fewer still, those who, passing from school to office, remember what they have read and studied after one or two years.

There was a young American who had learned Italian from me in only six months. He said to me one day:

"I wish I could learn Latin from you, too. I have studied it, to tell the truth, for a number of terms, but I have been travel-ing steadily now for three years and I have all but forgotten it."

"Only three years?" I asked.

"I think so, Mr. Da Ponte."

I then showed him certain Latin verses that I had composed the day I entered upon the eighty-first year of my life and ex-actly fifty years since leaving the schools. After he had read and reread them to get their meaning clearly (and this he could not do without my aid), this is what he said to me:

"Sir, to be quite frank, if I did not know you to be a man of truth, what you say would seem impossible to me."

"Your wonder will cease," I replied, "when I describe to you the method we use generally in the study of that language. In the first place you must remember that of people who are des-tined to business, very few have any interest in Latin. On the other hand doctors, lawyers, and, particularly, ministers of the

Altar, and those who intend to dedicate themselves to the no-ble art of literature, all, without exception, do study it. And to cure your surprise I have only to tell you how they study. After passing from elementary grammar to the higher (for these our schools have each two excellent professors), the students ad-vance to the school of the humanities; and thence, in the meas-ure of their progress, some in two years, some in a longer time, to the school of rhetoric, where Latin is studied for two years more. Students of the humanities as well as students of rheto-ric are obliged at certain hours of the day to speak nothing but the language of Cæsar, Sallust, and Cicero; and a big heavy iron chain is put around the neck of the one who makes a mis-take or speaks in any other tongue; and he wears it until an-other delinquent is found. Three evenings a week the more expert meet together in a room and criticize the classic poets and defend them in turn. Through such exercise, *vertunt in succum et sanguinem*, and have them, so to speak, as much at their fingertips as their daily prayers. The better scholars among these latter are free to study Greek or Hebrew after their third year; but, as to their native language, and especially the Italian poets, these were very little studied in the school where I was educated, and those who felt inclined to study them, were obliged to do so in private and hide from the vigilance of the supervisors as best they could. Doctor Modolini, general super-visor of studies in the school in question, a good Greek scholar and an excellent Latinist, surprised me one day while I was composing a sonnet.

" '*Sonetti non dàn panetti*' (Sonnets earn no breadlets), he said to me with scowling face, and snatched what I had written from my hands.

"After that," I continued, "you must not find my octoge-narian verses so miraculous. I can assure you that all my schoolmates who were with me in that College could do just as well, if they are still living."

451

And I pledged myself to furnish him with actual proofs.

He listened to me with close attention. Then he broke out with these words:

"Now I understand why so little Latin is known in America. But if so much study is required to learn it well, I shall content myself with the languages I understand, and leave Latin to the Italians."

Saying which he left me, and came back the day following, bringing me all the Latin books he had (with the exception of Ovid's *De arte amandi*), to exchange them for the same number of Italian books.

I could say something more on this point; but some would consider me presumptuous, others prejudiced, and I have already written elsewhere that, having offered twenty-four years ago to teach that language in New York in our fashion, I was bluntly told that Americans did not need the help of foreign Latinists to learn all of that language that they required. There were even some who maintained that the American, or rather the English, pronunciation, was better than ours; and it is not so very long ago that a few alert minds became convinced of the contrary, and had recourse to me to learn a better pronunciation. The which, undoubtedly, must be found in Italy, since Italy was the first creator of it, and conserves the most probable sounds of its early origins, which sounds (though vitiated and corrupted by time) have come down to us from father to son and are retained in a new language with new beauties. And I would not fear falling into error, should I venture to assert that the lack of a real taste for classical Latin is one of the principal causes why Italian is esteemed so little and by so few in the United States; because in Ireland, Great Britain, and Germany, where the contrary is the case, they not only engage the very best minds in Italy to teach it, but they establish distinguished chairs for public teachers of it; and our works are studied, translated, and admired by real scholars. The slight success

I had obtained in America as compared with my desires and my hopes, would certainly have discouraged anyone but me; but I decided to make one final effort, and it is not yet decided whether or not it is to have some success.

I had heard from many travelers, and my brother and friends of mine in Italy had written, that Giulietta Da Ponte, one of my nieces, had, in addition to an excellent voice and many charming personal qualities, the unusual gift of a very moving style of singing that was full of expression and sincerity. Signor Baglioni had been her teacher. He was a man of perfect taste and great knowledge in music and had trained the most celebrated singers in Italy. I had known him as a man of great worth at Prague, at the time my *Don Giovanni* was performed there. A little through a hankering to see some of my own people after thirty years of separation, but also in hopes of attracting students to Italian, and of helping my library through the interest a music of such charm would arouse, I was almost tempted to invite this brother of mine to America, and advise him to bring his daughter with him. I was not, however, unaware of certain Italian prejudices, notably of the reluctance some families have to allow their children to appear on the stage. I hesitated, therefore, unable quite to make up my mind to write. While I was wavering in this uncertainty, lo, a letter from my brother, in which he himself put forward the proposal that he come to America, and bring Giulietta! My delight may easily be imagined. I did not delay a moment in answering, and sought every means to smooth out such difficulties as seemed to hinder the execution of his plan.

One of the most serious of these, and one which I adjudged at first insuperable, was the difficulty of obtaining passports for New York. Still mindful of things past, and especially of the clemency with which the now reigning Emperor had consoled and alleviated my distress in Vienna, I made up my mind to appeal directly to him; and I composed an ode of which the censors in a number of cities would not permit publication, but which, when handed to the Sovereign himself by my brother, obtained the favor requested out of hand. I was at the height of joy. So many difficulties arose, however, that after a long correspondence and endless preparations, both they and I began to lose hope of our seeing each other again.

"I foresee," Giulietta wrote toward the end of the year 1827, "that in spite of all your efforts, we shall never get to New York."

As this hope languished in me, another arose in connection with the library, and encouraged me to a new experiment. One day I was reading the preface to one of the volumes in the works of which Mr. Mathias had made such precious gift to me. The eloquence and the force with which that judicious writer spoke of the merits of the Italian language and of Italian literature, wrought such effect in me that I said to myself:

"Can a man with two ounces of brains in his head read the pages I have just read without feeling a conviction of truth, and desiring to possess a blessing and enjoy a delight such as he enjoys and possesses to whom the treasures of the Italian Parnassus are opened?"

Following the lead of that noble preface, it at once occurred to me to write an oration and deliver it on the occasion of my seventy-ninth birthday, to a select audience of pupils and friends, who were generally accustomed to honor my house with their courteous presence on such anniversaries.

While I was assembling materials for that discourse, a cruel accident, which people generally thought would cost me my life, changed the aspect of everything. The house where I lived was not in the center of the city. In order to accommodate my triple group of young ladies, I had been obliged, therefore, to rent a room more conveniently located to which I would go at a certain hour agreed upon, to conduct the larger of my Italian classes. It was the seventeenth of December. The night,

after a few hours of rain, had turned very cold. A light and almost invisible crust of ice had therefore paved the streets
and the steps that led down into my yard. Scarcely had I set
foot on the first ice-covered step on my way down, which
chanced also to slope a little, when I slipped and fell prone,
striking the other three steps one by one with my back, till
my body was one bruise from the tip of my spine to my waist.
I was in the hands of physicians for more than a month and
though tormented with hot lotions, punctures, cuts, removals
of skin, and despite a thousand gruesome prophecies, I had the
satisfaction of being able on Christmas Day to receive my angelic pupils and give thanks to the Most High for my recovered
health and for the opportunity He proffered me on that bed
(which, it was believed, and perhaps hoped, would be my
deathbed) of seeing in very clear fashion to what lengths human duplicity and the baseness of adulators can go.

Returning therefore to my customary and beloved work as a
teacher, I was not long in remembering the plan I had made
before my fall; and reading and pondering that preface anew,
I wrote a lecture, which I here present to my reader in this last
Part, and which I delivered on my birthday to a beautiful circle
of pupils and friends. Those, who prefer not to interrupt the
thread of my Memoirs, may omit reading this oration. I, however, have impelling reasons for publishing it.

Oration of Lorenzo Da Ponte Delivered before his Pupils
and Friends on the Evening of the Tenth of March in the
Year 1828, the Seventy-ninth Anniversary of his Life.
"Desiring to give you . . ." etc., etc.

Everyone applauded the things I said, but my triumph ended
in fine words. An oration that long served to win me only one
subscriber!

What then was left for me? My house was filled with books

455

but my purse was beginning to feel its empty spaces. Then living with me to my good fortune was Mr. Julian Verplanck, a most cultivated person, a patron of letters and enjoying great prestige in Congress, of which he was himself a member. One day I gave him a catalogue of my books and begged him to present it to the directors of the Government library, and to secure me if possible the honor of supplying their excellent collection with some works in Italian. Mr. Verplanck left for Washington a few days later and, to my good fortune, remembered my prayers to good effect. With the cooperation of one of the most illustrious members of that very noble assembly, Mr. Everett, he was able to procure me an order for a considerable number of selected and costly works, among them magnificent editions of Dante's *Divina Commedia*, of Ariosto and Alfieri, the *Rerum Italicarum scriptores* of Muratori (which for the first time had seen the banks of the Hudson), and the works of Tiraboschi and Visconti. This pecuniary replenishment, in excess of four hundred dollars, came to me like manna from Heaven at a time when I knew I would be receiving a large shipment of books on science and mathematics; among these the works of Manfredi, Riccati, Cagnoli, Brunacci, Cardinali, Guglielmini, Vallisnieri, Lami, Gori, Morelli, Lanzi, Venturoli, and Micali; authors imported by me from Italy to confound a certain and otherwise very learned friend of mine, along with others of his stamp, who stubbornly maintained that, in the more serious and austere branches, Italy was not to be compared with Germany, forgetting or pretending to forget that *c'est de l'Italie que nous tenons les sciences* (as an ingenuous French writer admits in the preface to the *Encyclopédie*).

In fact, all these works reached me in great part a few days later; but with them came others which I had not ordered, and which were not adapted to American needs. Among these were a magnificent edition of Dante and another of Tasso's *Jerusalem*, beautiful things in truth, but much too costly to find easy sale in this country. In sending them to me, however, the bookseller thought he was giving me a demonstration of true friendship. He had, moreover, certain connections with a person whom I revered and loved beyond all belief. Desirous of showing my consideration for both, I resolved to accept the books on certain conditions. After making vain effort to sell the more splendid of them, I thought of a new device for getting them off my hands—and it partially succeeded.

I drew from my catalogue a series of selected volumes to the value of some four hundred dollars. Then I invited forty persons to inspect them, and suggested forming two classes of students, in the one of which I would make a fresh start with Italian, teaching it as far as could be done in forty lessons; while in the other I would read and expound Dante's *Commedia*, with some other classics the students had not yet read, to be chosen by themselves. Each one in attendance was to pay ten dollars, the total tuition covering the full cost of the books. These were to be divided into eight sets, or, in other words, into eight prizes, and drawn by lot from an urn.

As a matter of fact when twenty had subscribed, they grew impatient of delay, and asked permission to draw half the prizes, and this was done. If this device, which was something entirely new to other teachers of language, did not add an obol to my purse, it surely won me the incomparable delight of introducing the sublimity and the divine beauties of our Dante to twenty more among the noblest and most cultivated minds in the city. For all twenty elected to read him in the second course, among them six young ladies and a young bride whose enthusiasm and admiration for our unique poet surpassed that of the men!

But neither readings in Dante nor in any of our poets could make people forget the charms of our music. In this connection I am going to relate an incident as pleasing as it was extraordinary.

I must explain that I had been telling about for a long time that my niece was coming to New York and would probably bring some other good singers with her. But her arrival was so long delayed that people in musical circles were all making fun of me and let not an occasion pass to twit me and make game of me. One morning we were reading the twenty-eighth canto of the *Purgatorio* and the young lady, whose turn it was to read, came to the beautiful terzina which runs:

> Una Donna soletta, che si gìa
> cantando, ed iscegliendo fior da fiore

> (a lady walking alone, singing, and flower from flower dissevering).

She stopped, and queried in jest:

"Mr. Da Ponte, this singer who is picking the flowers— couldn't she be your niece?"

I was expecting Giulietta's arrival at that time about as much as finding a pearl in the dark. But I came back:

"No joking! No joking! My niece is coming!"

"But when, when?" they asked in chorus.

"When is she coming? She is coming today!"

I spoke truly in spirit of prophecy. Hardly had I finished the sentence than a loud knocking at the house door caused me to run to the window. Thence I could see Mr. A—— who was calling, his face wreathed in smiles:

"They have sailed!"

I dashed down the stairs as fast as I could; and there at the bottom, the gentleman met me and handed me a letter from my angel in Trieste, definitely announcing the arrival of my brother in that city with his daughter Giulietta, and their imminent departure for New York. The lesson of that morning turned into a general riot of gaiety, and my joy and that of my family no one could imagine, much less describe. There I was, a man already past the eightieth year of a much troubled life; a man with a tender, affectionate, sincere heart, who for more than thirty years had not had the comfort of seeing any of his people, and had almost lost hope of such a blessing! What sort, what excess, of consolation must I not have felt at the sudden news of the near arrival of a brother who alone was still left to me,[28] whom I had loved above everything else from his tenderest years and whose constant letters, breathing love, respect, esteem, gratitude, nourished my fondest hopes of perfect reciprocation of affection! To this sweet prospect was added the ineffable delight of seeing for the first time and pressing to my heart a niece of whose beautiful personal traits of sweet character and gentle manner I had received most gratifying reports from hosts of friends, and who was already shining through a distinguished and admired talent in the most musical city of Italy (such Venice is) and in an art that I had hoped should contribute to a greater diffusion of Italian—which has been and will always be the first and the last of my prayers—and to perpetuating in a noble library its incomparable literature still so inadequately known!

But in the garden of human delights there is no rose without some thorn. The no little expense which I was obliged to meet on account of the departure of my brother from Venice, the voyage with his daughter, and other domestic fortuities, dismayed and discouraged me, through the natural fear a man of limited means must have of not being able to come off with honor. In the transports of my enthusiasm I had written to the most precious and liberal of my friends, Doctor Domenico Rossetti of Trieste, not to look too closely at expenses; and

---

28. Another brother of mine was supposed to be living in America: but if he still lived he would have replied to the letters I wrote him. Not having done so he either no longer is alive or cannot be my brother. —L. Da P.

had pledged my honor and my sacred word to him to pay promptly, that he might make the same pledge to others. That angelic soul did not hesitate, did not delay, in aiding me; but when he wrote: "I am well aware that four hundred and twenty dollars will make a great hole in a poet's purse," I trembled, I confess, from head to foot, not seeing the fount from which such a sum must gush; and, to add to my misfortunes, it had to be paid on sight. This fear did not afford me leisure to enjoy the full sweetness of their imminent coming, which my heart would have speedy, and my slender moneybox, postponed. But on the eighteenth day of February I learned that the vessel on which they had embarked had reached port, and a few hours later a carriage stopped at the door of my house, and they got out of it.[29]

Then my boundless delight left no more room for fears and we passed all the remainder of the day and a great part of the night in the privacy of our family in caresses, embraces, and reciprocal questions, attended now by laughter and now by tears.

Vanquished, or to be more exact, exhausted by that fury of tender affections, we finally embraced again and went to our rooms to rest. I did not go to sleep until after many hours; but when my eyes closed, everything we had talked of in the course of that day became a whirling confusion in my imagination and the remainder of that night I spent with our good father, my brothers, my sisters, and my friends, in Venice, Treviso, Ceneda, and other cities in Italy. I doubt whether I ever have had dreams more delicious in all the course of my life. It seemed to me that we were all gathered together at a great table, eating, drinking, and talking of gay things; and there with us was my beloved Colombo, inviting us all to drink, and

29. Giulia Da P. was a daughter of Agostino Da P., Lorenzo's brother, who, as a "political broker," so to speak, had presented Da P.'s appeal in 1791. Giulia arrived with Agostino, Feb. 18, 1830.

intoning, before touching his glass, the following line: *Quam dulce et quam iucundum habitare fratres in unum!* the which we all repeated in chorus, raising such a din that my dream was broken. I could see that the sun was already high. I rose in haste and asked whether breakfast were ready. I found one of my pupils in his usual room, and told him the fine dream I had had:

"Mr. Da Ponte," he remarked, "the dream is beautiful indeed; but you would do well to remember the other adage: *rara est concordia fratrum.*"

The cruel warning fell like a lash upon my spirit. I replied simply:

"*Dii omen abvertant.*"

Meanwhile the rest of the family came into the room and renewed caresses, embraces, questions, made me almost forget that remark of evil augury. After a gay breakfast I went out with my brother to set things in order. Several hundred dollars had still to be paid for obligations contracted in connection with the voyage, in addition to the three hundred I had already spent before their arrival. Though the drafts were at sight, I managed to meet them with some pecuniary sacrifice. The news was spreading meanwhile about town that the long-awaited Giulietta had arrived. The most prominent gentlemen and ladies of New York, and above all my pupils and their families, were eager to see her and hear her. They saw her, heard her, liked her, everyone, both for her demeanor and her talents. Even my brother's frank, offhand manner pleased and was applauded as well by my friends as by various members of my family. My happiness was such as I had pictured in three lines of my ode to the Emperor[30]:

---

30. That is, to the Emperor Francis I, in requesting Agostino's passports. The lines are in the 9th stanza of the poem which begins: *Dal duol, dagli anni e dalle noie oppresso. . . .*

> Tal nell'anima mia
> creerà pace e gioia,
> e caccerà martir, pianto e cordoglio.

And what did I not do, what did my family not do, to make that peace and that joy abiding?

After spending a few days in family gaieties we turned all our thoughts and all our efforts to the business in hand, to ways and means, in a word, for showing our Giulietta off, on her first appearance, to the best advantage. Others wished her to begin her career with a private concert; I alone was of different opinion: and while they were arranging matters in their way, I made such a contract with the manager of our largest theater that they changed their views and applauded my dexterity and good judgment. I obtained for her the fine sum of twelve hundred dollars for her two first appearances, and half the box-office receipts for the third, as a "benefit." The money was paid into my hands; and may those fine gentlemen and ladies who dubbed my story a "puff" be pleased to read these verses, which my extemporaneous Muse dedicates to them: *Signori increduli—fremer non giova* etc., etc.

But leaving our verses, let us return to Giulia, to whom my stubbornness proved advantageous not only in terms of money, but even more so in reputation. After having agreed to her appearance that first evening simply as a singer, that she might grow a little accustomed to a public new to her, I thought it well to see, and let others see, how good she was at acting. I therefore wrote[31] a sort of opera of which the following little preface will give an adequate idea:

---

31. Not only did Da P. not write it; he even used the occasion to get rid of old librettos left over from editions he had used in England. He may have added some new selections to the medley, here and there.

TO THE INHABITANTS OF NEW YORK

Neither the conditions at present prevailing in our
Opera, nor the scant number and quality of our singers,
nor, finally, the time allotted me for writing these verses,
could afford me sufficient means for writing anything to
deserve the name of an opera, nor as such do I present
this to an enlightened audience. Lacking time, actors,
and a score, I have composed this poetic trifle for no
other purpose than to amuse to some extent a respected
audience, and offer opportunity therewith for a new
singer, to give some demonstration of her abilities as an
actress (whatever they may be)—something she could
not do in a so-called "concert." After puzzling long over
the title I might give to such a work, I settled on that of
Ape musicale. I do not offer, therefore, in guise of gardener to Apollo, an operatic lily, rose, or narcissus,
reared by me on the summits of his mountain; but like a
bee, which, sucking the essence of divers flowers min-
gles them, to store in its cells the sweetest and most
pleasing of honies, thus, uniting as it were in one center
the most beautiful harmonies of our favorite composers,
I have hoped to give one of the most agreeable pastimes
to the courteous and discreet reader.

I was mistaken. The *Ape musicale* did not please[32] and I realized at rehearsals that it could not please: but the new singer,
who had overcome her natural timidity, shone in all her luster; and so it was in the third performance and still more in the
fourth—and that was the most important thing for everyone!

---

32. The first to criticize were two of the worst singers. The poorest wheel on
the cart is always the one that creaks. F[erri] and R[osich]—do they know how to
read? —L. Da P.

However, the good effect of her beautiful voice and of her exquisite method reached only real practitioners of music and the most cultivated connoisseurs: and I must state the reasons for that. The music she selected for her performances was unquestionably very beautiful. Still it must be confessed that music of that kind was not made for every taste and every ear. People who are accustomed to the songs of the streets, to ballads, waltzes, and the like popular nonsense, find themselves in a world utterly strange when certain pieces are sung; and sometimes, to tell the truth, even the more intelligent in the musical art find themselves in the same world. Desire to appear original, pedantic imitation of some favorite composer without possessing his genius, and sometimes lack of real knowledge of music, make a great number of modern masters strive for the difficult, the extravagant, the noisy, hoping to hide their defects in such ways.

But such music fails to satisfy (as many people assure me) even our Italians today; and if indeed they like it, it is only after hearing it sung at least half a dozen times by the singers for whom it was written. One of the most judicious and subtle connoisseurs of that fine art lately wrote me from Venice as follows:

> The music which is now being sung here, is, alas, something too far removed from the natural; and American ears, which are not so much crude as virgin, will not be able to enjoy the affected style that is the fashion among us. If people over there find the little things my son writes too studied—little gems of this music that they are—what headaches would they get from our really pretentious things, which are often unintelligible even to me? I perceive that to get an opera capable of appealing to the general, when sung in a language different from the common one, will not be such an easy matter: and I

464

am convinced that Cimarosa, Paisiello, and others of that time, would have better success than our moderns.

I had already written in the same tenor before this letter came, and I was pleased and proud to find myself in agreement with a man so learned and so qualified to pass judgment on an art of which he himself was one of the brightest ornaments as a simple connoisseur, just as his *filius sapiens et gloria patris* at present is. All Venice will know that I am speaking of my most esteemed and accomplished friend, Girolamo Perucchini. In view of this, what marvel that certain arias of Vaccai, Generali, and of others of their order, beautiful as they were, were not generally admired in America, and by people especially who had been accustomed previously to hearing only the songs and ballads of Kelly, or Polish, Scottish, or Irish airs, with, of course, the most favorite national anthem, *Yankee Doodle*?

To auditors of this school who did not, and could not, reasonably praise a song they did not understand, we must add a horde of biased judges—partisans, patrons, aspirants, professional rivals, people driven to teaching music in order not to starve. Such folk, with their vulgar *puffs* and the reviews of certain reporters, critics, and paid writers of the press, who talk in tone of authority on whatever they know least about, fill the minds of the less intelligent with a thousand prejudices, a thousand errors, and of those above all who never dare proffer a judgment till they have read all the newspapers in town.

An event too near at hand will prove that it is not to the glory or advantage of any of my people that I argue thus. My great love for our language and our writers, and an honorable desire to spread and to establish more widely and more solidly our sciences and our letters in this country, were the principle spur that impelled me to encourage my brother to bring his daughter with him to America. She was not made for the stage nor the stage for her. It was her destiny to come just here to America, and depart again almost immediately, and assume on the great stage of the world a place worthy of her education, her parentage, and her birth.

For whom then am I writing these remarks? I write them for the benefit of those good singers who may someday decide to come to America, and for that singer in particular who was invited to come at my suggestion to be a worthy companion to our Giulietta. Let such not trust to the sole merits of a beautiful voice. *Vox cantat*, we are wont to say; and there is no denying that voice is one of the chief requisites in a singer. But unless the voice be coupled with good music, it will have the effect of a coat of very fine cloth which, if poorly cut by the tailor, will make you laugh. It will be sage counsel therefore, to provide the singer with a good dowry of arias and of so-called "concert pieces," with melodies, obvious, natural, and sweet to the ear, without being trivial and vulgar. Such melodies linger on the ear and in the hearts of those who hear them; lovers of music hum them over as they leave the theater; the music dealers rush to reprint them; and when they are published, people who know how to sing as well as people who do not, buy them and sing them over and over again, returning to the theater many times to hear them. Two or three pieces of this sort are sometimes enough to make an opera succeed, with honor to the singer, glory to the composer, and what is more important, profit to the producer. Let us leave, therefore, to those who enjoy it, that pretentious music which forces the singer to wriggle his body, twist his mouth, choke and gasp to reach such and such a note, deliver such and such a trill, and get his voice heard now in the blur of an accompaniment, now in the din of a tempest of flutes, drums, horns, bassoons, and trombones, which needs only a bell and a cannon or two to be perfect.

Before long Signor Dorigo (to him I have been alluding)

will be coming to New York, and perhaps not alone; because, if what my friends in Italy write me be true, such has been the excitement produced in the philharmonic world by my niece's success that many, and even the incomparable Velluti, seem eager to pay a visit to their antipodes. I have not failed of my constant encouragement and incitement, and my beloved Italian friends have been using every means to second this honorable desire of mine. I have already had a number of propositions from two of the foremost operatic producers in Italy; but foreseeing that they would not be compatible with the character and customs of this city, I have replied with proposals of my own. Of these I am daily awaiting either refusal or acceptance. Some such thing only could revive my hopes of seeing my prayers fulfilled, of seeing, that is, after so much effort, sacrifice, and opposition, a select Italian library in the illustrious city of New York. All other means I have tried. I have advised, I have implored. I have convinced a goodly number of the truly learned of the usefulness of the project; but nothing so far has availed. On the contrary it would seem that things are going from bad to worse. Listen to this, good reader mine!

Toward the end of November, in the year 1829, the president of Columbia College ceased to live.[33] A man of much learning and of generous inclinations was chosen in his place. Nevertheless, through differences of interest, religion, faction, there arose a sort of rivalry, or rather of opposition, among our citizens, whereby a great number of them suggested, and boldly sustained, that the foundation of another university would be of public benefit, in which the citizens of the town could be instructed on different principles and along new lines. The controversy was long, clamorous, and obstinate, *et lis*

---

33. William Harris, president from 1811 to 1829, succeeding Benjamin Moore, was succeeded by William Alexander Duer, 1829–40.

adhuc sub iudice pendet. Meanwhile, hoping to put an end to divisions and bring people into accord again, the trustees of the old College decided to reorganize their institute as a university and put forward such a reform as to meet general demands and remove the need and the call for a second institution. New curricula and new subjects were introduced; among these the study of the three modern languages: Spanish, French, and Italian. They did me the honor to recall me to the professorship in this last; and I accepted the offer joyfully, though with eighty years on my shoulders.

I really believed that I would again become a *professor sine exemplo*: without scholars, that is, and without stipend. For I reasoned thus: "The program adopted by the director of this 'reformed university' is certainly not favorable to our language. It is planned that, whereas professors of Greek and Latin (and for the latter, two are being paid) receive an assigned honorarium of two thousand two hundred dollars, with a certain number of pupils, the professors of the three modern languages must depend entirely on the will of the student, as regards the choice of the subject, and on the will of the parents, as regards stipend. But parents are paying the not insignificant sum of ninety dollars for ten months in the other subjects. It is not likely that they will burden themselves with further expenses for other languages; and those who do so (they will be few) will not be thinking of the language of Dante, but rather of the languages of Voltaire and Don Quixote, which are considered useful in commerce, whereas Italian is held to be a language of ornament and luxury. I shall not have a pupil therefore. If, however, through a spirit of ill-calculated economy[34] there be

---

34. Ill-calculated because the businessman, finding that neither Greek nor Latin is of any use to him in his stores, is forced to learn one or more of the three languages in question at double expense, and often from wretched masters; and that, too, at a time when press of business distracts him from study. —L. Da P.

a scarcity of scholars for those two languages also, perhaps, removing such an obstacle of my own accord, I may obtain for our language what the other two professors do not obtain for theirs."

I decided, therefore, to await the outcome of the first year and I saw very clearly that I was not mistaken in my forecast. Few the pupils of my very able colleagues: I believe that, between the two of them, they taught some fourteen boys. And I? *Piangete, O toschi, e con voi l'Hudson pianga!* NOT ONE!

My tears did not prevent me, however, from making a last effort, as follows. I suggested giving two lessons for forty weeks to one hundred pupils in that institution, each one of whom was to pay not more than fifteen dollars for eighty lessons; and presenting either to the students or to the university a thousand volumes of selected works, equal in value to the entire sum they would be paying.

I sent the proposal to an important person, whose voice and whose counsel is of great weight and authority for everyone.

I received the following reply[35]:

> Dear sir:
>
> I advise you not to insist too much on this point; because, to be frank with you, I do not believe that there is the slightest possibility that the Trustees will care to undertake altering the present system in the College, and obliging students to learn Italian. You are now a professor in the College and have the opportunity to teach it to as many pupils as shall choose to study with you. The Trustees can do nothing without changing their actual statutes, and this I know well that, whatever the

---

35. Part of a letter written me by Mr. Clement Moore. —L. Da P.

offers that may be made to them by admirers of the Italian language, they can never consent to do.

It seems to me that you are a little overanxious respecting the memory that you long to leave behind you. For what you have already done for love of the Italian language and literature, the name of Da Ponte, *clarum et venerabile nomen*, will always be held in grateful remembrance; and our young people of both sexes will look back in their declining age upon the hours passed in pleasant and instructive conversation with their illumined and elegant teacher, as on the most brilliant moments of their lives. Let that be enough for you, and do not try, like Bonaparte, to acquire all the glory in the universe for yourself.

Your true friend, C. M.[36]

However much the courteous, affectionate, and consoling phrases of the last paragraph of this most noble letter[37] may have pleased me, the pain caused me by the first sentences was just as great. My precious patron and friend does not realize, however, that everything I may have done seems to me, and will ever seem to me, little, if before returning to Earth I do not bequeath to this illustrious city the full treasure of Italian letters. In view of that noble aim, if ever I succeed in damming the torrent of woe that is now most unexpectedly pouring upon my suffering decrepitude from ungrateful hands, I still hope to show that, more than any wealth or comfort of mine, I have at heart the glory of my ill-known country.

---

36. Samuel Ward quotes a somewhat different text of this letter. See Russo, 123.

37. It is not through vanity but in defense of my honor unjustly wounded by one who had least occasion to hurt, that I published the last part of this letter also. Reader, forget not this note! —L. Da P.

For that reason I have opened a bookstore, where I take my chair at the cock's crow and stay till late into the night, leaving never, save for a few moments. Five months have already passed since I took up the trade of bookseller. I have no great occasion, in truth, to rise from my chair in the course of a day. My customers are few and far between, but I have, instead, the joy of seeing coaches and carriages drive up at every moment before my door and sometimes the most beautiful faces in the world emerge from them, mistaking my book store for the shop next door, where sweets and cakes are for sale. To make people imagine I have many customers, I am thinking of placing a placard in my window with the words: "Italian sweets and pastry for sale." Then if that jest chance to bring someone to my shop, I will show him a Petrarch or some other of our poets, and hold that ours are the sweetest of sweets for such as have teeth to chew them.

The month of October is at hand. My pupils and my friends will soon be leaving the pleasures of the country, recalled by the cold and the frost to business and study. I hope that my classes will flourish, and that, my desire being known, even the customers in my store will grow in number. For that I trust to the well-known benevolence and liberality of the individuals of whom I speak. In that sweet hope I close this volume.

I truly believed it was to be the last. Imperious circumstances, however, and episodes of greatest importance, though not yet sufficiently evolved, constrain me to postpone their recounting to another time.[38] This I shall do in a little volume which will serve as an appendix to the three already published by me. The story of the last will begin from the fourteenth day of September in the year 1830, at which time this one ends. Be not displeased, courteous reader, at this deferment. It

---

38. The Montresor venture.

arises from my honorable desire to inform you of everything
with the same ingenuousness and truthfulness which you
have found and approved in my first volumes; and I would
have you know that if, in accord with the epigraph to my first
edition, I was silent of certain things which charity and wisdom obliged me to overpass, *omnia nunc dicam, sed quæ
dicam omnia vera.*[39]

---

39. Da P. was to live eight years longer. His wife was buried in St. John's Ceme-
tery (Clarkson and Leroy Sts.) on Dec. 12, 1831, dying after six days of illness of
pneumonia.

A B O U T   T H E   T Y P E

The text of this book has been set in Trump Mediaeval. Designed by Georg Trump for the Weber foundry in the late 1950s, this typeface is a modern rethinking of the Garalde Oldstyle types (often associated with Claude Garamond) that have long been popular with printers and book designers.

Trump Mediaeval is a trademark of
Linotype-Hell AG and/or its subsidiaries

Printed and bound by R. R. Donnelley & Sons,
Harrisonburg, Virginia

Book design by Red Canoe, Deer Lodge, Tennessee
Caroline Kavanagh
Deb Koch

TITLES IN SERIES